CW01465089

# Baby Names
# And Their Meanings

PATIENCE WHEELER

Copyright © 2022 Patience Wheeler

All rights reserved

No part of this book may be reproduced, or stored in a retrieval system, or transmitted in any form or by any means, electronic, mechanical, photocopying, recording, or otherwise, without express written permission of the publisher.

# INTRODUCTION

Thank you so much for choosing Baby Names And Their Meanings on your journey to finding the perfect name(s). Here is a little introduction to help you better understand how this book is laid out. The first half of the book is made up of names for boys. They are listed in alphabetical order. The second half of the book is made up of names for girls. Again, in alphabetical order.

There are thousands of names to choose from. Each name has options next to it (divided with a | symbol), these options indicate alternate spellings or endings that I did not think warranted their own entry. For example, the difference between Annabelle and Anabelle. Some names have a further set of names below them indicated with "also", these names share the same meaning and origin and are directly next to each other in the alphabetical ordering, therefore, to save page space they have been added together into one entry. After the names you will find the meaning and the origin language. Many names will seem very similar in meaning in origin, this occurs as many names are simply variants of another. Sometimes the meaning changes slightly as elements are dropped from or added to the original name.

Names that are too obscure or unpronounceable to most readers have not been included, but that does not mean that there are no rare names, this book is filled with both rare and common names, it just means that you will not find anything completely and utterly unusable. Names with letters that do not appear in the English alphabet have also not been added, apart from some exceptions, where the name is considered well known, such as the names Esmé and Beyoncé. Well, that is it for the introduction. On with the names!

# Chapter 1 - Names For Boys Beginning With A

**Aarav | Aarov**
**Meaning:** Peaceful Sound
**Origin Language:** Sanskrit

**Aaron | Aaran, Aaren, Aaroni, Aarran, Aarron, Aaryn, Ahran, Ahren, Ahron, Aron, Aronn, Aronne, Arron, Arryn**
**Meaning:** Exalted / Enlightened
**Origin Language:** Hebrew

**Abbert | Abbertus**
**Meaning:** Bright Noble
**Origin Language:** Ancient Germanic And Old English (Cognates)

**Abbott | Abbot**
**Meaning:** Abbot
**Origin Language:** English

**Abden | Abdon**
**Meaning:** From A Farm With An Abbey
**Origin Language:** Old English

**Abdiel | Abdeel**
**Meaning:** Servant Of God
**Origin Language:** Hebrew

**Abdon | Abdown**
**Meaning:** Servant
**Origin Language:** Hebrew

**Abel | Abe, Abelio, Abellio**
**Meaning:** Breath
**Origin Language:** Hebrew

**Abenner**
**Meaning:** My Father Is The Light
**Origin Language:** Hebrew

**Abercrombie | Abercromby**
**Meaning:** From A Crooked Marsh /

From Near A River Bend
**Origin Language:** Pictish

**Abern | Abernus**
**Meaning:** Bear Of Dread
**Origin Language:** Old Norse

**Abert**
**Meaning:** Bright Noble
**Origin Language:** Ancient Germanic And Old English (Cognates)

**Abidan | Abiydan**
**Meaning:** My Father Is The Judge
**Origin Language:** Hebrew

**Abiel | Abeel**
**Meaning:** My Father Is God
**Origin Language:** Hebrew

**Abley | Ablee**
**Meaning:** Son Of The Littlest One
**Origin Language:** Old Welsh

**Abner | Abnar, Abnor, Abnur**
**Meaning:** My Father Is The Light
**Origin Language:** Hebrew

**Abraham | Abraam, Abrahaam, Abrahim, Abrahm, Abram, Abramo**
**Meaning:** High Father Of A Multitude
**Origin Language:** Hebrew

**Acacio | Acacius, Acatius, Akacio, Akacius, Akakios, Akatius**
**Meaning:** Innocent (Ancient Greek) / Acacia (English)
**Origin Language:** Ancient Greek And English

**Ace | Acer, Acey**
**Meaning:** One / Unity
**Origin Language:** Latin

**Ackerley | Ackerleigh, Ackerly,**

Acleigh, Acley, Akeleigh, Akeley
**Meaning:** From An Oak Tree Meadow
**Origin Language:** Old English

Acton | Actun
**Meaning:** From A Town With Many Oak Trees
**Origin Language:** Old English

Adair
**Meaning:** Spear Of Wealth
**Origin Language:** Old English

Adam | Aadam, Adamo, Adamos, Adamus, Adan, Addam, Addan, Adem
**Meaning:** Of The Humankind
**Origin Language:** Hebrew

Adard | Addard
**Meaning:** Noble Warden
**Origin Language:** Ancient Germanic

Adarian | Adarien, Adarion, Addarian, Addarien, Addarion
**Meaning:** From Hadria (The Name Of Two Ancient Roman Settlements Which Were Located In What Are Now Northern Italy And Central Italy) / From The Water
**Origin Language:** Latin

Addeney
**Meaning:** From Eadwynn's Island / From A Rich And Friendly Island
**Origin Language:** Old English

Adderley | Adderlee, Adderleigh, Adderlie
**Meaning:** From Ealdred's Meadow / From A Meadow Of Noble Strength
**Origin Language:** Old English

Addison | Adison
**Meaning:** Of The Humankind
**Origin Language:** Hebrew

Adeel | Adeil, Adil
**Meaning:** Unbiased
**Origin Language:** Arabic

Adelm | Adelmin, Adelmio, Adelmo, Adhelm
**Meaning:** Protects His Father
**Origin Language:** Ancient Germanic

Ademar | Ademaro, Ademir, Ademiro
**Meaning:** Famous Father
**Origin Language:** Ancient Germanic

Aden
**Meaning:** Fire
**Origin Language:** Old Irish

Adeo | Adio
**Meaning:** Given By God
**Origin Language:** Latin

Aderick | Aderic, Aderik
**Meaning:** Wealthy Noble
**Origin Language:** Ancient Germanic And Old English (Cognates)

Adi | Addi, Addie, Addy, Adie
**Meaning:** First
**Origin Language:** Indonesian

Adiel | Adiyel
**Meaning:** Ornament Of God
**Origin Language:** Hebrew

Adir | Addir
**Meaning:** Strong
**Origin Language:** Hebrew

Adiran | Addiran, Addiren, Addiron, Adiren, Adiron
**Meaning:** From Hadria (The Name Of Two Ancient Roman Settlements Which Were Located In What Are Now Northern Italy And Central Italy) / From

The Water
**Origin Language:** Latin

Adlai
**Meaning:** I Shall Be Drawn Up Of God
**Origin Language:** Hebrew

Adlay
**Meaning:** Justice Of God
**Origin Language:** Hebrew

Adler | Addler, Adlar
**Also:** Adley | Adlie
**Meaning:** Eagle
**Origin Language:** German

Adney | Adnie
**Meaning:** From Eadwynn's Island / From A Rich And Friendly Island
**Origin Language:** Old English

Adoard | Adouard, Adoward
**Meaning:** Noble Warden
**Origin Language:** Ancient Germanic

Adonai | Adonay, Adoni
**Also:** Adonis
**Meaning:** My Lord
**Origin Language:** Hebrew

Adoran | Adoram
**Meaning:** My Lord Is Exalted
**Origin Language:** Hebrew

Adrian | Addrian, Addriano, Addrianus, Addrien, Addrion, Adriano, Adrianus, Aidrian, Aidriano, Aidrianus, Aidrien, Aidrion, Aydrian, Aydriano, Aydrianus, Aydrien, Aydrion
**Meaning:** From Hadria (The Name Of Two Ancient Roman Settlements Which Were Located In What Are Now Northern Italy And Central Italy) / From The Water
**Origin Language:** Latin

Adrick | Adric, Adrik
**Meaning:** Rich Noble
**Origin Language:** Ancient Germanic And Old English (Cognates)

Adriel
**Meaning:** Flock Of God
**Origin Language:** Hebrew

Adrun
**Meaning:** Noble Rune / Noble Secret
**Origin Language:** Ancient Germanic

Adrwin | Ardouin, Arduin, Arduino, Arduinus, Ardwin, Artwin
**Meaning:** Friendly and Hardy
**Origin Language:** Ancient Germanic

Aduard | Adoard, Adoardo, Adoart, Aduardo, Aduart, Adward, Adwart
**Meaning:** Guardian Of Riches
**Origin Language:** Old English

Aedon
**Meaning:** Shining One
**Origin Language:** Ancient Greek

Aemon | Aymon
**Meaning:** Wealthy Protector
**Origin Language:** Old English

Aeron
**Meaning:** From Near The River Aeron (Wales)
**Origin Language:** Welsh

Aeson | Aison, Aisonios
**Meaning:** From Aeson/Aison (An Ancient Greek Town)
**Origin Language:** Ancient Greek

Aethon
**Meaning:** Fiery

**Origin Language:** Ancient Greek

Aetius
**Meaning:** Eagle
**Origin Language:** Latin

Aewell | Aewill
**Meaning:** Well / Spring (Of Water)
**Origin Language:** Old English

Afon
**Meaning:** River
**Origin Language:** Welsh

Afonso | Affonso, Affonzo, Afonzo
**Meaning:** Ready For Nobility
**Origin Language:** Ancient Germanic

Afton | Aften
**Meaning:** River
**Origin Language:** Welsh

Aharon | Aharown
**Meaning:** Exalted / Enlightened
**Origin Language:** Hebrew

Ahaziah
**Meaning:** Held By God
**Origin Language:** Hebrew

Aiden | Aedan, Aeddan, Aediyn, Aidan, Aidin, Aidon, Aidyn, Aydan, Ayden, Aydin
**Meaning:** Fire
**Origin Language:** Old Irish

Aighton
**Meaning:** From A Town With Many Oak Trees
**Origin Language:** Old English

Aiken | Aicken, Aikin, Ayken, Aykin
**Meaning:** Made Of Oak
**Origin Language:** Old English

Aikton
**Meaning:** From A Town With Many Oak Trees
**Origin Language:** Old English

Aillard | Aylard
**Meaning:** Noble Guard
**Origin Language:** Ancient Germanic

Aiman
**Meaning:** Lucky
**Origin Language:** Arabic

Aimon
**Meaning:** Homely
**Origin Language:** Ancient Germanic

Aindreas | Aindrias
**Meaning:** Manly / Brave Warrior
**Origin Language:** Ancient Greek

Ainsley | Ainslee, Ainsleigh, Ainslie, Ainsly
**Meaning:** From A Lonely Meadow
**Origin Language:** Old English

Airton | Aireton, Ayreton, Ayrton
**Meaning:** From A Town With A Gravel Bank
**Origin Language:** Old Norse And Old English (A Mix Of Both)

Aithan | Aitan, Aytan, Aythan
**Meaning:** Enduring
**Origin Language:** Hebrew

Aivar | Aive, Aiver, Aivis, Aivor
**Meaning:** From An Army That Dwells Within The Yew Trees
**Origin Language:** Old Norse

Ajax
**Meaning:** The Earth
**Origin Language:** Ancient Greek

Akeem | Akim

**Meaning:** Intelligent
**Origin Language:** Arabic

Akeley | Akelee, Akeleigh, Akelie
**Meaning:** From An Oak Tree Meadow
**Origin Language:** Old English

Akendin | Acendino, Acindin, Acindino, Akendie, Akendy, Akendyn, Akindie, Akindin, Akindy, Akindyn, Akindynos, Akyndin, Akyndyn
**Meaning:** Without Danger
**Origin Language:** Ancient Greek

Al | Ali, Ally
**Meaning:** A Short Form Of Any Of The Numerous Names Beginning With Al
**Origin Language:** Various

Alan | Ailin, Alain, Alann, Alano, Alanus, Alen, Allan, Allen, Allin, Allon, Allun, Allyn, Alun
**Meaning:** Little Rock
**Origin Language:** Old Breton

Alaric | Alareik, Alareiks, Alarico, Alaricus, Alarik, Alariko, Alarix
**Meaning:** All Ruling
**Origin Language:** Ancient Germanic

Alasan | Alassan, Alhassan
**Meaning:** Handsome / Virtuous And Devoted To God
**Origin Language:** Arabic

Alaun | Alaunius, Alaunos, Alaunus
**Meaning:** Healer
**Origin Language:** Gaulish

Alban | Albain, Albano, Albanus, Alben, Albon
**Meaning:** From Alba (Ancient Rome) (Latin) / White (Latin) / From Scotland (Alba Is The Scottish Gaelic Name For Scotland) (Scottish Gaelic)
**Origin Language:** Latin And Scottish Gaelic

Alber | Albor
**Meaning:** Albanian
**Origin Language:** Ancient Greek

Alberic | Alberich, Alberico, Albericus, Alberigo, Alberik, Albiric, Albirich, Albirico, Albirik
**Meaning:** Elven Ruler
**Origin Language:** Ancient Germanic

Albert | Aalbert, Albart, Albertas, Alberte, Alberti, Albertino, Albertinus, Albertito, Alberto, Alberts, Albertus, Alberz
**Meaning:** Bright Noble
**Origin Language:** Ancient Germanic And Old English (Cognates)

Albie | Ailbe, Ailbhe, Albey, Albi, Alby
**Meaning:** Rock
**Origin Language:** Old Irish

Albin | Albinius, Albins, Albinus, Albio, Albuis, Albus
**Meaning:** White
**Origin Language:** Latin

Albion
**Meaning:** From A White Island
**Origin Language:** Old English And Latin (a mix of both)

Albrett | Albrecht, Albreckt, Albrect, Albrekt, Albret, Albreyt, Albricht, Albrict, Albrikt, Albrit, Albrykt, Albryt, Allbrecht, Allebrecht
**Meaning:** Bright Noble
**Origin Language:** Ancient Germanic And Old English (Cognates)

Albry | Alberi, Alberie, Albery, Albri, Albrie
**Meaning:** Elven Ruler
**Origin Language:** Ancient Germanic

Albuin | Albewin, Alboin, Albuwin
**Meaning:** Friendly Elven One
**Origin Language:** Ancient Germanic

Alby | Albie
**Meaning:** Bright Noble
**Origin Language:** Ancient Germanic And Old English (Cognates)

Aldar | Aldarr
**Meaning:** From An Old Army
**Origin Language:** Old Norse

Aldemar | Aldemario, Aldemiro
**Meaning:** Old Noble
**Origin Language:** Ancient Germanic

Alden | Aldin, Aldon
**Meaning:** Friendly Old One
**Origin Language:** Ancient Germanic And Old English (Cognates)

Alderic | Alderico, Alderik
**Meaning:** Old And Rich / Noble And Rich
**Origin Language:** Ancient Germanic

Aldero | Alderio
**Meaning:** Old And Friendly
**Origin Language:** Ancient Germanic And Old English (Cognates)

Aldert
**Meaning:** Old And Hardy
**Origin Language:** Ancient Germanic

Aldery | Alderi, Alderio, Aldero, Aldheri
**Meaning:** Old Warrior
**Origin Language:** Ancient Germanic

Aldo
**Meaning:** Old
**Origin Language:** Ancient Germanic

Aldreth
**Meaning:** From A Port With Alder Trees
**Origin Language:** Old English

Aldric | Aldrich, Aldrico, Aldrik
**Also:** Aldridge
**Meaning:** Old And Rich / Noble And Rich
**Origin Language:** Ancient Germanic

Alduin | Aldewin, Aldoin, Aldoino, Aldovino, Aldowin, Alduino, Aldwen, Aldwin
**Meaning:** Old And Friendly
**Origin Language:** Ancient Germanic And Old English (Cognates)

Aldus | Aldous
**Meaning:** Old
**Origin Language:** Old English

Aleandro | Aleander, Aleandrie, Aleandry, Aliander, Aliandrie, Aliandro, Aliandry
**Meaning:** Mankind's Defender
**Origin Language:** Ancient Greek

Alec | Alek, Alic, Alick
**Meaning:** Defender
**Origin Language:** Ancient Greek

Aled
**Meaning:** From Near The River Aled (Wales)
**Origin Language:** Welsh

Alejandro
**Meaning:** Defender Of Mankind
**Origin Language:** Ancient Greek

Alem | Alim
**Meaning:** Learned

**Origin Language:** Arabic

Aleph
**Meaning:** Most Important
**Origin Language:** Phoenician

Aleri | Alari
**Meaning:** All Ruling
**Origin Language:** Ancient Germanic

Alerio
**Meaning:** Light-Hearted
**Origin Language:** Ancient Greek

Alesantar | Alesant
**Also:** Alessandro | Alesander,
Alesando, Alesandri, Alesandro,
Alessander, Alessandre, Alessandri
**Meaning:** Mankind's Defender
**Origin Language:** Ancient Greek

Aletto | Alletto
**Meaning:** Of The Noble Sort
**Origin Language:** Ancient Germanic

Alex | Alecks, Aleix, Aleks, Alix
**Meaning:** Defender
**Origin Language:** Ancient Greek

Alexander | Aleksandar,
Aleksande, Aleksander, Aleksandre,
Aleksandreus, Aleksandro,
Aleksandros, Aleksandru,
Aleksandrus, Aleksandur,
Alexandar, Alexande, Alexandre,
Alexandreus, Alexandro,
Alexandros, Alexandru,
Alexandrus, Alexandur
**Meaning:** Defender Of Mankind
**Origin Language:** Ancient Greek

Alexis | Aleksei, Aleksey, Aleksi,
Aleksie, Aleksio, Aleksis, Aleksy,
Alexe, Alexei, Alexey, Alexi, Alexie,
Alexio, Alexios, Alexius

**Meaning:** Defender
**Origin Language:** Ancient Greek

Alfarr | Alfher, Alfihar, Allfarr
**Meaning:** Elven Army
**Origin Language:** Ancient Germanic
And Old English And Old Norse
(Cognates)

Alfeo | Alfio, Alpheo, Alphio
**Meaning:** Resourceful / Pure
**Origin Language:** Ancient Greek

Alfie | Alf, Alfr, Alfree, Alfy,
Alphie, Alphy
**Meaning:** Elven
**Origin Language:** Ancient Germanic
And Old English And Old Norse
(Cognates)

Alfonso | Alfon, Alfons, Alfonse,
Alfonsus, Alfonz, Alfonzo,
Alphons, Alphonse, Alphonso,
Alphonsus, Alphonzo, Alphonzus
**Meaning:** Ready For Nobility
**Origin Language:** Ancient Germanic

Alford
**Meaning:** From Near A Ford With Alder
Trees
**Origin Language:** Old English

Alfred | Alfredo, Alfredus, Alfrid,
Alfryd
**Meaning:** Elven Counsel
**Origin Language:** Old English

Alham | Alhom, Allam, Allom
**Meaning:** From A Homestead Near A
Temple
**Origin Language:** Old English

Ali
**Meaning:** Exalted
**Origin Language:** Arabic

Alidor | Aliodor, Aliodoro
**Also:** Aliod | Aliodo
**Meaning:** Gift Of The Sun
**Origin Language:** Ancient Greek

Alior
**Meaning:** God Is My Light
**Origin Language:** Hebrew

Alisdair | Alaisdair, Alaisdar, Alaisdeir, Alaisder, Alaisdiar, Alaisdor, Alasdair, Alasdar, Alasdeir, Alasder, Alasdiar, Alasdor, Alesdair, Alesdar, Alesdeir, Alesder, Alesdiar, Alesdor, Alisdar, Alisdeir, Alisder, Alisdiar, Alisdor
**Meaning:** Mankind's Defender
**Origin Language:** Ancient Greek

Alisher
**Meaning:** Ali's Lion (A Combination Of Ali And Sher, The Persian Word For Lion)
**Origin Language:** Uzbek And Tajik And Arabic (In Combination)

Alistair | Alaistair, Alaistar, Alaisteir, Alaister, Alaistiar, Alaistor, Alastair, Alastar, Alasteir, Alaster, Alastiar, Alastor, Alestair, Alestar, Alesteir, Alester, Alestiar, Alestor, Alistar, Alisteir, Alister, Alistiar, Alistor
**Meaning:** Mankind's Defender
**Origin Language:** Ancient Greek

Alkest | Alcest, Alcesto, Alkesto
**Meaning:** Valiant
**Origin Language:** Ancient Greek

Alland | Aland, Alant, Allant
**Meaning:** From An Island
**Origin Language:** Old English

Allander | Alander
**Meaning:** From A Forested Land
**Origin Language:** Old Dutch

Allard | Alard, Alardus, Alerd
**Meaning:** Hardy Noble
**Origin Language:** Ancient Germanic

Allegro
**Meaning:** Cheerful
**Origin Language:** Latin

Allexton | Alexton
**Meaning:** From Eadlac's Town / From A Town Of Happy Playing
**Origin Language:** Old English

Allger | Algar, Algario, Algaro, Alger, Allgar
**Meaning:** Noble Spear
**Origin Language:** Ancient Germanic

Allown | Alon, Alown
**Meaning:** Oak Tree
**Origin Language:** Hebrew

Allvard | Allvar, Allvor, Alvar, Alvard, Alvor
**Meaning:** Guardian Of The Boulder
**Origin Language:** Old Norse

Allyre | Allar, Allerie, Allery
**Meaning:** Light-Hearted
**Origin Language:** Ancient Greek

Almarin | Almarindo, Almarino, Almerin, Almerindo, Almerino
**Meaning:** Famous Noble
**Origin Language:** Ancient Germanic And Old English (Cognates)

Almas
**Meaning:** Diamond
**Origin Language:** Arabic

Almer | Almar, Almaro, Almero,

Almir, Almiro
**Meaning:** Famous Noble
**Origin Language:** Ancient Germanic
And Old English (Cognates)

Almere | Aelmere
**Meaning:** From Near A Lake With Eels
**Origin Language:** Old English

Alonzo | Alonso
**Meaning:** Ready For Nobility
**Origin Language:** Ancient Germanic

Aloysius | Alaois, Alois, Alois,
Aloise, Aloisio, Aloisius, Aloys
**Meaning:** Famous Battler
**Origin Language:** Ancient Germanic

Alpha
**Meaning:** The First Letter Of The Greek
Alphabet
**Origin Language:** Ancient Greek

Alpheus | Alphaeus, Alphaios,
Alphius
**Meaning:** Resourceful / Pure
**Origin Language:** Ancient Greek

Alred
**Meaning:** Noble Counsel
**Origin Language:** Old English

Alrick | Alric, Alrich, Alrik
**Meaning:** Rich Noble
**Origin Language:** Ancient Germanic
And Old English (Cognates)

Alrix | Alreiks, Alrics, Alriks
**Meaning:** All Ruling
**Origin Language:** Ancient Germanic

Alrun
**Meaning:** Noble Rune / Noble Secret
**Origin Language:** Ancient Germanic

Alsandare | Alsandair

**Meaning:** Defender Of Mankind
**Origin Language:** Ancient Greek

Alstan
**Meaning:** Stone Of Nobility
**Origin Language:** Old English

Altan
**Meaning:** Red Dawn
**Origin Language:** Turkish

Altiery | Alterio, Altero, Altieri
**Meaning:** Old Warrior
**Origin Language:** Ancient Germanic

Altin | Altino, Altun
**Meaning:** Pure Gold
**Origin Language:** Ottoman Turkish

Alton
**Meaning:** From Near A River Source
**Origin Language:** Old English

Aluar | Aluarus
**Meaning:** Elven Army
**Origin Language:** Ancient Germanic
And Old English And Old Norse
(Cognates)

Aluin | Aluino, Aluwin
**Meaning:** Noble Friend
**Origin Language:** Ancient Germanic
And Old English (Cognates)

Alvan | Alven
**Meaning:** Albanian
**Origin Language:** Ancient Greek

Alvar | Allvar, Alvero
**Meaning:** Elven Army
**Origin Language:** Ancient Germanic
And Old English And Old Norse
(Cognates)

Alven | Alv, Alvi, Alvie, Alvy
**Also:** Alver | Alv, Alvi, Alvie, Alvy
**Meaning:** Elven

**Origin Language:** Ancient Germanic
And Old English And Old Norse
(Cognates)

Alverto
**Meaning:** Bright Noble
**Origin Language:** Ancient Germanic
And Old English (Cognates)

Alvin | Alvyn
**Meaning:** Noble Friend
**Origin Language:** Ancient Germanic
And Old English (Cognates)

Alvis | Alvise, Alviss, Alvys
**Meaning:** All Wise
**Origin Language:** Old Norse

Alvor
**Meaning:** Albanian
**Origin Language:** Ancient Greek

Alvred | Alvredus
**Meaning:** Elven Counsel
**Origin Language:** Old English

Alwin | Alwyn
**Meaning:** Noble Friend
**Origin Language:** Ancient Germanic
And Old English (Cognates)

Alwyn
**Meaning:** From Near The River Alwen
(Wales)
**Origin Language:** Welsh

Amadi
**Meaning:** Free Man
**Origin Language:** Igbo

Amador | Amadour
**Meaning:** Loves God
**Origin Language:** Latin

Amal | Amel
**Meaning:** Hope
**Origin Language:** Arabic

Amand | Amando, Amandus
**Meaning:** Worthy Of Love
**Origin Language:** Latin

Amani
**Meaning:** Wish / Desire
**Origin Language:** Arabic

Amarand | Amarando,
Amarandos, Amarandus
**Meaning:** Amaranth Flower / Unfading
**Origin Language:** Ancient Greek

Amari | Amar, Amare, Ammar
**Meaning:** Lives Long
**Origin Language:** Arabic

Amariah | Amaryah
**Meaning:** God Has Said
**Origin Language:** Hebrew

Amaro
**Meaning:** Famous Noble
**Origin Language:** Ancient Germanic
And Old English (Cognates)

Amatus
**Meaning:** Beloved
**Origin Language:** Latin

Amaury | Amauri, Amaurie
**Meaning:** Rich Worker
**Origin Language:** Ancient Germanic

Amaziah | Amasias, Amazias
**Meaning:** Lord's Strength
**Origin Language:** Hebrew

Ambrose | Ambroise, Ambros,
Ambrosi, Ambrosino, Ambrosio,
Ambrosios, Ambrosius,
Ambrosone, Ambrus
**Meaning:** Immortal
**Origin Language:** Ancient Greek

**Amdi | Amdy**
**Meaning:** Protects With The Edge Of His Sword / Protects From Terror
**Origin Language:** Old Norse

**Amelio**
**Meaning:** Worker
**Origin Language:** Ancient Germanic

**Americo | Americus, Amerigo, Amerika, Ameriko, Amerikus**
**Also:** Amery
**Meaning:** Rich Worker
**Origin Language:** Ancient Germanic

**Amias | Amyas**
**Meaning:** Friend
**Origin Language:** Old French

**Amico | Amicus**
**Meaning:** Friendly
**Origin Language:** Latin

**Amiel | Ammiel**
**Meaning:** God Is My Kinsman
**Origin Language:** Hebrew

**Amilcar**
**Meaning:** Brother Of Melqart (Melqart Is The Name Of A Semitic God Known As The King Of The Underworld, And Protector Of The Universe)
**Origin Language:** Phoenician

**Amin | Ameen**
**Meaning:** Trustworthy
**Origin Language:** Arabic

**Amintor | Amintas, Amyntas, Amyntor**
**Meaning:** Defender
**Origin Language:** Ancient Greek

**Amir | Ameer, Amiri**
**Meaning:** Commander / Prince
**Origin Language:** Arabic

**Amit**
**Meaning:** Infinite
**Origin Language:** Sanskrit

**Amitai | Amitay, Amittai, Amittay**
**Meaning:** My Truth
**Origin Language:** Hebrew

**Amleth | Amlet, Amlethus**
**Also:** Amlodi | Amlodhi, Amloth, Amlothi
**Meaning:** Annoyer Of Odin (Odin Is The Name Of A Norse God)
**Origin Language:** Old Norse

**Amnon | Amno**
**Meaning:** Faithful
**Origin Language:** Hebrew

**Amon | Amen, Ammen, Ammon, Ammoun, Ammun, Amoun, Amun**
**Meaning:** The Hidden One
**Origin Language:** Ancient Egyptian

**Amor**
**Meaning:** Love
**Origin Language:** Latin

**Amory**
**Meaning:** Ruler Of The Homeland
**Origin Language:** Ancient Germanic

**Amos**
**Meaning:** Burdened
**Origin Language:** Hebrew

**Amosis | Ahmose, Amasis**
**Meaning:** Born Of Iah (Iah Is The Name Of An Egyptian Lunar God) / Born Of The Moon
**Origin Language:** Ancient Egyptian

**Amund | Amundi**
**Meaning:** Protects With The Edge Of His Sword / Protects From Terror

**Origin Language:** Old Norse

Anael
**Meaning:** God Is Gracious
**Origin Language:** Hebrew

Anakin | Annakin
**Meaning:** Gracious
**Origin Language:** Hebrew

Anand
**Meaning:** Bliss
**Origin Language:** Sanskrit

Ananiah | Ananias
**Meaning:** God Is Gracious
**Origin Language:** Hebrew

Anders
**Also:** Anderson
**Meaning:** Manly / Brave Warrior
**Origin Language:** Ancient Greek

Andor
**Meaning:** Thor's Eagle (Thor Is The Name Of The Norse God Of Thunder And Lightning)
**Origin Language:** Old Norse

Andreas | Andras, Andrass, Andre, Andres, Andries, Andris, Andrius, Andrus
**Also:** Andrew | Andreu
**Also:** Andrien | Andrian, Andrin, Andriy, Andriyan
**Also:** Andy | Andee, Andey, Andie, Andre, Andrei, Andreo, Andrey, Andri, Andrii, Andrio, Andro, Androe
**Meaning:** Manly / Brave Warrior
**Origin Language:** Ancient Greek

Anfred
**Meaning:** Eagle Of Peace
**Origin Language:** Ancient Germanic

Angel | Aingeal, Ainjel
**Also:** Angelo | Angel, Angelico, Angelino, Angell, Angelos, Angelus, Anghel, Angioletto, Angiolo, Anjelo, Anjelus
**Meaning:** Angel/Messenger
**Origin Language:** Latin

Angus | Aenghus, Aengus, Anghus, Angos, Aongas, Aonghas, Aonghus, Aongus
**Meaning:** One Strength
**Origin Language:** Old Irish

Aniello
**Meaning:** Angel/Messenger
**Origin Language:** Latin

Anis | Anes
**Meaning:** Friendly
**Origin Language:** Arabic

Ankarl | Anckarl, Anckerl, Ankerl
**Meaning:** Harvester
**Origin Language:** Old Danish

Anrico | Anric, Anrik
**Meaning:** Home Ruler
**Origin Language:** Ancient Germanic

Ansano | Ansanus
**Meaning:** Heathen / God
**Origin Language:** Ancient Germanic

Ansbert | Ansberht, Ansoberht, Ansobert
**Meaning:** Divine And Bright
**Origin Language:** Ancient Germanic And Old English (Cognates)

Anscomb | Anscom
**Meaning:** From A Stony Valley
**Origin Language:** Old English

Ansel | Ancel, Ancell, Ansell
**Also:** Anselm | Ansehelm,

## Anselme, Anselmi, Anselmo
**Meaning:** Divine Protector
**Origin Language:** Ancient Germanic

## Ansgar | Ansgard, Ansgario, Ansgarius, Anskar
**Meaning:** Divine Spear
**Origin Language:** Ancient Germanic And Old English And Old Norse (Cognates)

## Anshel | Anshelm, Anshelmus
**Meaning:** Divine Protector
**Origin Language:** Ancient Germanic

## Anslow | Anslo, Anslowe
**Meaning:** From Near The Burial Mound Of A Man Called Andhere / From Near A Brave Warriors Burial Mound
**Origin Language:** Old English

## Anson
**Meaning:** Chaste
**Origin Language:** Ancient Greek

## Answin | Ansoin, Anssuin, Ansuin, Ansuino
**Meaning:** Divine And Friendly / God's Friend
**Origin Language:** Ancient Germanic And Old English (Cognates)

## Antec | Ante, Antek
**Meaning:** Of Ani (Ani Is The Name Of An Etruscan God, Thought To Be Equivalent To The Roman God Janus, The God Of Beginnings, Gates, Transitions, Time, Duality, Doorways, Passages, And Endings)
**Origin Language:** Latin

## Anthelm | Antelm, Antelmo, Anthelmo
**Meaning:** Protected By Zeal
**Origin Language:** Ancient Germanic

## Anthony | Anthonie, Antoni,

## Antoniy, Antony
**Meaning:** Of Ani (Ani Is The Name Of An Etruscan God, Thought To Be Equivalent To The Roman God Janus, The God Of Beginnings, Gates, Transitions, Time, Duality, Doorways, Passages, And Endings)
**Origin Language:** Latin

## Anthor
**Meaning:** Thor's Eagle (Thor Is The Name Of The Norse God Of Thunder And Lightning)
**Origin Language:** Old Norse

## Anton | Antun
**Also:** Antonello
**Also:** Antonio | Antonin, Antonino, Antoninus, Antonios, Antonius
**Also:** Antonis
**Meaning:** Of Ani (Ani Is The Name Of An Etruscan God, Thought To Be Equivalent To The Roman God Janus, The God Of Beginnings, Gates, Transitions, Time, Duality, Doorways, Passages, And Endings)
**Origin Language:** Latin

## Antor
**Meaning:** Thor's Eagle (Thor Is The Name Of The Norse God Of Thunder And Lightning)
**Origin Language:** Old Norse

## Antwan | Antawn, Antoin, Antoine
**Meaning:** Of Ani (Ani Is The Name Of An Etruscan God, Thought To Be Equivalent To The Roman God Janus, The God Of Beginnings, Gates, Transitions, Time, Duality, Doorways, Passages, And Endings)
**Origin Language:** Latin

## Apollo | Apollon, Apolo
**Meaning:** Drives Away Evil

**Origin Language:** Ancient Greek

Aqeel | Aaqil, Akeel, Akil, Akila, Aqil
**Meaning:** Wise
**Origin Language:** Arabic

Araldo | Arald
**Meaning:** Of The Ruling Army
**Origin Language:** Old English

Aram
**Meaning:** Highlands
**Origin Language:** Hebrew

Aramis
**Meaning:** Valley
**Origin Language:** Basque

Aran
**Meaning:** Wild Goat
**Origin Language:** Hebrew

Aranth | Arnth, Aronth, Arunth
**Meaning:** Prince
**Origin Language:** Etruscan

Araton | Aratonio
**Meaning:** Prayed For
**Origin Language:** Ancient Greek

Arawn
**Meaning:** Exalted / Enlightened
**Origin Language:** Hebrew

Arber | Arbor
**Meaning:** Albanian
**Origin Language:** Ancient Greek

Arbert | Arberto, Aribert, Ariberto
**Also:** Arbie | Arb, Arby
**Meaning:** Bright Warrior
**Origin Language:** Ancient Germanic

Arbon | Arben
**Meaning:** Albanian

**Origin Language:** Ancient Greek

Arbrit
**Meaning:** Bright Noble
**Origin Language:** Ancient Germanic And Old English (Cognates)

Arbury | Arburi
**Meaning:** From A Fortified Piece Of Earth
**Origin Language:** Old English

Arcas | Arkas, Arkas
**Meaning:** From Arkadia / Arcadia (Greece)
**Origin Language:** Ancient Greek

Archan
**Meaning:** Dedication
**Origin Language:** Sanskrit

Archer
**Meaning:** Archer
**Origin Language:** English

Archibald | Archembald, Archenbaud, Archibaldo, Archimbald, Archimbaud
**Also:** Archie | Archy
**Meaning:** Bold And Genuine
**Origin Language:** Ancient Germanic

Ardal | Ardhal
**Meaning:** Of High Gallantry
**Origin Language:** Old Irish

Ardath
**Meaning:** Flowering Field
**Origin Language:** Hebrew

Arden | Ardin
**Meaning:** Valley Of The Eagle
**Origin Language:** Old English

Ardit
**Meaning:** Golden Day

**Origin Language:** Albanian

Ardon | Ardown
**Meaning:** Fugitive
**Origin Language:** Hebrew

Areald | Arealdo, Ariald, Arialdo
**Meaning:** Of The Ruling Army
**Origin Language:** Old English

Areli
**Meaning:** Lion Of God
**Origin Language:** Hebrew

Aren
**Also:** Arend | Arends
**Also:** Arent | Arendt
**Meaning:** Ruler Of The Eagles
**Origin Language:** Ancient Germanic

Areo | Ario
**Also:** Ares | Areso, Arez, Arezo, Aris, Ariso, Ariz, Arizo
**Meaning:** Ruin
**Origin Language:** Ancient Greek

Areto | Aretas
**Meaning:** Virtue
**Origin Language:** Ancient Greek

Argie | Arg, Argeo, Argeu, Argi, Argio, Argo, Argy
**Meaning:** Glistening
**Origin Language:** Ancient Greek

Ari
**Meaning:** Lion
**Origin Language:** Hebrew And Old Norse (Cognates)

Aric | Arik
**Meaning:** Ruler Of Forever
**Origin Language:** Old Norse

Aridai | Ariday, Ariyday
**Meaning:** The Lion Is Enough

**Origin Language:** Hebrew

Arien
**Meaning:** Of The Star Sign Aries
**Origin Language:** English

Aries
**Meaning:** Ram
**Origin Language:** Latin

Arik
**Meaning:** Lion Of God
**Origin Language:** Hebrew

Arild | Arald, Areld, Arold
**Meaning:** Of The Powerful Army
**Origin Language:** Old Norse

Arion
**Meaning:** Spiritual / Noble
**Origin Language:** Sanskrit

Ariston
**Meaning:** The Best (First) Meal / Breakfast
**Origin Language:** Ancient Greek

Aristus | Arist, Aristaeus, Aristaios, Aristeo, Aristio, Aristos
**Meaning:** The Best
**Origin Language:** Ancient Greek

Arjan
**Meaning:** Golden Life
**Origin Language:** Albanian

Arkell | Arkill
**Meaning:** Stirrer Of The Divine Cauldron
**Origin Language:** Old Norse

Arlen
**Meaning:** Friendly Warrior
**Origin Language:** Ancient Germanic

Arley | Arlee, Arleigh, Arlie,

Arrlee, Arrleigh, Arrley, Arrlie
**Meaning:** From A Meadow Of Hares
**Origin Language:** Old English

Arlin | Arling, Arlwin
**Meaning:** Friendly Warrior
**Origin Language:** Ancient Germanic

Arlind | Arlindi
**Meaning:** Born Of Gold
**Origin Language:** Albanian

Arlo | Arly
**Meaning:** Friendly Warrior
**Origin Language:** Ancient Germanic

Arlott | Arlotto
**Meaning:** Rascal
**Origin Language:** Old French

Arlotto | Arlotus
**Meaning:** Vagabond
**Origin Language:** Old French

Arluin | Arlewin, Arlo, Arlwin, Arly
**Meaning:** Friendly Warrior
**Origin Language:** Ancient Germanic

Armael | Armaelo, Armel
**Meaning:** Prince Of Bears
**Origin Language:** Old Welsh

Arman | Armano, Armanus
**Meaning:** Hope
**Origin Language:** Persian

Armand
**Also:** Armani
**Meaning:** Army Man
**Origin Language:** Ancient Germanic

Armello
**Meaning:** Prince Of Bears
**Origin Language:** Old Welsh

Armen
**Meaning:** From Armenia
**Origin Language:** Old Persian

Armend
**Meaning:** Golden Mind
**Origin Language:** Albanian

Armin | Arminius
**Meaning:** Whole
**Origin Language:** Ancient Germanic

Armon
**Meaning:** Army Man
**Origin Language:** Ancient Germanic

Arndor
**Meaning:** Thor's Eagle (Thor Is The Name Of The Norse God Of Thunder And Lightning)
**Origin Language:** Old Norse

Arnell | Arnel, Arnelio, Arnello
**Meaning:** Ruler Of The Eagles
**Origin Language:** Ancient Germanic

Arnie | Aarne, Aarni, Arn, Arne, Arno, Arny
**Meaning:** Eagle
**Origin Language:** Ancient Germanic And Old Norse (Cognates)

Arnkell
**Meaning:** Cauldron Of The Eagle
**Origin Language:** Old Norse

Arnold | Arnald, Arnaldo, Arnhold, Arnoldo, Arnoldus
**Also:** Arnolt
**Meaning:** Ruler Of The Eagles
**Origin Language:** Ancient Germanic

Arnor
**Meaning:** Thor's Eagle (Thor Is The Name Of The Norse God Of Thunder And Lightning)

**Origin Language:** Old Norse

## Arnost
**Meaning:** Earnest
**Origin Language:** Ancient Germanic

## Arnoud | Arnau, Arnaud
**Meaning:** Ruler Of The Eagles
**Origin Language:** Ancient Germanic

## Arodion | Arod
**Meaning:** Ode To A Hero
**Origin Language:** Ancient Greek

## Arran
**Meaning:** From The Island Of Arran
(Scotland)
**Origin Language:** Scottish Gaelic

## Arremon
**Meaning:** Without Speech
**Origin Language:** Ancient Greek

## Arsenio | Arsenios, Arsenius
**Meaning:** Strong
**Origin Language:** Ancient Greek

## Artem | Artemes
**Meaning:** Safe
**Origin Language:** Ancient Greek

## Artemon
**Meaning:** Of Artemis (Artemis Is The
Name Of The Greek Goddess Of
Nature, Childbirth, Wildlife, The Moon,
The Hunt, Sudden Death, Animals,
Virginity, Young Women, And Archery)
**Origin Language:** Ancient Greek

## Arthur | Artair, Artur, Arturo
**Meaning:** Bear King
**Origin Language:** Old Welsh

## Artie | Art, Artio, Arto, Arty
**Meaning:** Bear
**Origin Language:** Old Welsh

## Artor | Artorius
**Also:** Artur | Arturus
**Meaning:** Prince Of Bears
**Origin Language:** Old Welsh

## Arun
**Meaning:** Dawn
**Origin Language:** Sanskrit

## Arvan | Arvon
**Meaning:** Albanian
**Origin Language:** Ancient Greek

## Arved | Arvedus, Arvid, Arvidus
**Meaning:** Tree Of The Eagle
**Origin Language:** Old Norse

## Arvel | Arwel
**Meaning:** Unknown Meaning
**Origin Language:** Welsh

## Arvie | Arve, Arvee, Arvy
**Meaning:** Tree Of The Eagle
**Origin Language:** Old Norse

## Arvin
**Meaning:** Friendly Soldier
**Origin Language:** Ancient Germanic

## Arvis | Arnvis
**Meaning:** Tree Of The Eagle
**Origin Language:** Old Norse

## Arvor
**Meaning:** Albanian
**Origin Language:** Ancient Greek

## Arwin | Arwyn
**Meaning:** Friendly Soldier (Ancient
Germanic) / Very Blessed / Very White
(Welsh)
**Origin Language:** Ancient Germanic
And Welsh

## Asber
**Meaning:** Bear Deity
**Origin Language:** Old Norse

Ascelin | Acelin, Acilin, Acilino, Acillino, Asce, Azselin
**Meaning:** Gentle Noble
**Origin Language:** Ancient Germanic

Ascolt | Askolt
**Meaning:** Ruler Of The Ash Trees
**Origin Language:** Ancient Germanic

Aseem | Asim
**Meaning:** Boundless
**Origin Language:** Sanskrit

Asger | Asgar, Asgeir, Asgier
**Meaning:** Divine Spear
**Origin Language:** Ancient Germanic And Old English And Old Norse (Cognates)

Asher
**Meaning:** Happy
**Origin Language:** Hebrew

Ashkii
**Meaning:** Boy
**Origin Language:** Navajo

Ashley | Ash, Ashlee, Ashleigh, Ashlie, Ashly
**Meaning:** From An Ash Tree Meadow
**Origin Language:** Old English

Ashton | Ashten, Ashtyn
**Meaning:** From A Town Of Ash Trees
**Origin Language:** Old English

Ashur
**Meaning:** From Ashur (The Capital City Of The Assyrian Empire)
**Origin Language:** Akkadian

Ashwin | Ashwyn
**Meaning:** Horse Possessor
**Origin Language:** Sanskrit

Aslan | Arslan
**Meaning:** Lion
**Origin Language:** Ottoman Turkish

Asmond | Asmund
**Meaning:** Divine Protector
**Origin Language:** Old Norse

Asriel | Ashriel
**Meaning:** I Shall Be Prince Of God
**Origin Language:** Hebrew

Aster | Aszter
**Also:** Asterion | Asterio, Asterios
**Meaning:** Star
**Origin Language:** Ancient Greek

Aston
**Meaning:** From An Eastern Town
**Origin Language:** Old English

Astor
**Meaning:** Hawk
**Origin Language:** Occitan

Aswin | Aswyn
**Meaning:** Divine And Friendly / God's Friend
**Origin Language:** Ancient Germanic And Old English (Cognates)

Atanas | Atanasio
**Also:** Athanos | Athanas, Athanase, Athanasi, Athanasios, Athanasius, Athos
**Meaning:** Immortal
**Origin Language:** Ancient Greek

Athenai | Athenaion, Atheneas
**Meaning:** Very Divine
**Origin Language:** Ancient Greek

Athol
**Meaning:** From Atholl (Scotland)
**Origin Language:** Scottish Gaelic

Atila | Atilla, Attila
**Meaning:** Big River
**Origin Language:** Ottoman Turkish

Atis
**Meaning:** Wealthy
**Origin Language:** Ancient Germanic And Old English And Old Norse (Cognates)

Atlas | Atles, Atlis
**Meaning:** Unenduring
**Origin Language:** Ancient Greek

Atley | Atlee, Atleigh, Atlie, Attlee, Attleigh, Attley, Attlie
**Meaning:** At A Meadow
**Origin Language:** Old English

Aton | Aten
**Meaning:** Solar Disk
**Origin Language:** Ancient Egyptian

Atreus | Atreo, Atreu, Atrio
**Meaning:** Fearless
**Origin Language:** Ancient Greek

Atsel
**Meaning:** Noble
**Origin Language:** Hebrew

Attavian | Attavante, Attaviano, Attavo
**Meaning:** Eighth
**Origin Language:** Latin

Attica | Attico, Atticus, Attika, Attiko, Attikos, Attikus, Attique
**Meaning:** From Athens (Greece)
**Origin Language:** Ancient Greek

Atze
**Meaning:** Behind
**Origin Language:** Basque

Auberic | Auberich, Auberico,

Aubericus, Auberigo, Auberik, Aubiric, Aubirich, Aubirico, Aubirik
**Also:** Auberon | Aubiron
**Meaning:** Elven Ruler
**Origin Language:** Ancient Germanic

Aubert | Auberto
**Meaning:** Bright Noble
**Origin Language:** Ancient Germanic And Old English (Cognates)

Aubin | Aubyn
**Meaning:** White
**Origin Language:** Old French

Audace
**Meaning:** Audacious
**Origin Language:** Latin

Audard | Audoard, Audoart, Audoir, Audoire, Audouard, Audouart, Audoward, Audward
**Meaning:** Wealthy Warden
**Origin Language:** Old Norse

Audax
**Meaning:** Audacious
**Origin Language:** Latin

Auden | Audenus, Audhen, Audhon, Audhun, Audin, Audon, Audunus, Audvin, Awden, Awdhen, Awdhin, Awdhon, Awdhun, Awdin
**Meaning:** Wealthy And Friendly
**Origin Language:** Old English And Old Norse (Cognates)

Audenzo | Audence, Audenci, Audencio, Audentius, Audenzio
**Meaning:** Audacious
**Origin Language:** Latin

Audley

**Meaning:** From Ealdgyð's Meadow / From The Meadow Of An Old Battler
**Origin Language:** Old English

Audmar | Audamar, Audmaro
**Meaning:** Wealthy And Famous
**Origin Language:** Ancient Germanic And Old Norse (Cognates)

Audric | Audricus, Audrik
**Meaning:** Wealth And Riches
**Origin Language:** Ancient Germanic And Old English And Old Norse (Cognates)

Audrien | Auddrian, Auddriano, Auddrianus, Auddrien, Auddrion, Audrian, Audriano, Audriano, Audrianus, Audrianus
**Meaning:** From Hadria (The Name Of Two Ancient Roman Settlements Which Were Located In What Are Now Northern Italy And Central Italy) / From The Water
**Origin Language:** Latin

August | Augustas, Augusto, Augustus
**Also:** Augustine | Augustin, Augustinas, Augustinus, Augustyn
**Meaning:** Exalted
**Origin Language:** Latin

Aulay
**Meaning:** Olive Tree
**Origin Language:** Latin

Aulbry | Aulberi, Aulberie, Aulbery, Aulbri, Aulbrie
**Meaning:** Elven Ruler
**Origin Language:** Ancient Germanic

Aulis
**Meaning:** Helpful
**Origin Language:** Finnish

Auncar | Anacario, Aunacario, Auncario
**Meaning:** With Grace
**Origin Language:** Ancient Greek

Aurelian | Aureliano, Aurelianus, Aurelien, Aurelio, Aurelius
**Meaning:** Golden
**Origin Language:** Latin

Ausen | Ausencio
**Meaning:** Increases / Grows
**Origin Language:** Ancient Greek

Ausil | Ausilio
**Meaning:** Protects / Supports
**Origin Language:** Latin

Auster
**Meaning:** South Wind
**Origin Language:** Latin

Austin | Aousten, Austen, Auston, Austyn, Awsten, Awstin, Awston, Awstyn
**Meaning:** Exalted
**Origin Language:** Latin

Auxen | Auxenci, Auxencio
**Meaning:** Increases / Grows
**Origin Language:** Ancient Greek

Avdiel | Avdeel
**Meaning:** Servant Of God
**Origin Language:** Hebrew

Avdon
**Meaning:** Servant / Worshipper
**Origin Language:** Hebrew

Avedis
**Meaning:** Good News
**Origin Language:** Armenian

Avel
**Meaning:** Breath

**Origin Language:** Hebrew

Aventin | Aventius
**Meaning:** Bird / Omen
**Origin Language:** Latin

Averard | Averardo
**Meaning:** Hardy As A Boar
**Origin Language:** Ancient Germanic

Averil | Averel, Averill
**Meaning:** Boar Battler
**Origin Language:** Old English

Avery | Averi, Averie
**Meaning:** Elven Ruler
**Origin Language:** Ancient Germanic

Avidan
**Meaning:** My Father Is The Judge
**Origin Language:** Hebrew

Aviel
**Meaning:** My Father Is God
**Origin Language:** Hebrew

Avlon | Avloni
**Meaning:** Channel / Glen
**Origin Language:** Ancient Greek

Avner | Avenir, Aveniru, Avnar, Avnor, Avnur
**Meaning:** My Father Is The Light
**Origin Language:** Hebrew

Awell | Awel, Awil, Awill
**Meaning:** Well / Spring (Of Water)
**Origin Language:** Old English

Axel | Acke, Aksal, Aksel, Axl
**Also:** Axlan | Axelan, Axelen
**Meaning:** My Father Is Peace
**Origin Language:** Hebrew

Axton | Acston, Akston, Axston, Axten

**Meaning:** From A Town Near Water
**Origin Language:** Old English

Ayalon | Ayal
**Meaning:** Gazelle
**Origin Language:** Hebrew

Ayan
**Meaning:** The Path
**Origin Language:** Bengali

Aylan
**Meaning:** Openness
**Origin Language:** Kurdish

Aylmer | Aylmar
**Meaning:** Famous Noble
**Origin Language:** Ancient Germanic And Old English (Cognates)

Aylward | Ailward
**Meaning:** Noble Warden
**Origin Language:** Ancient Germanic

Aymard | Aimard
**Meaning:** From A Hardy Home
**Origin Language:** Ancient Germanic

Aymeric | Aymerik
**Meaning:** Rich Worker
**Origin Language:** Ancient Germanic

Aymon
**Meaning:** Homely
**Origin Language:** Ancient Germanic

Azael | Azail
**Meaning:** God Sees
**Origin Language:** Hebrew

Azan | Azaan
**Meaning:** The Call To Prayer
**Origin Language:** Arabic

Azaniah | Azanyah
**Meaning:** God Hears
**Origin Language:** Hebrew

Azar
**Meaning:** Fire
**Origin Language:** Persian

Azarael | Azareel, Azarel
**Meaning:** My God Is Help
**Origin Language:** Hebrew

Azariah | Azarias, Azaryah
**Meaning:** Helped By God
**Origin Language:** Hebrew

Azaziah | Azazias, Ozazias
**Meaning:** God Is Strong
**Origin Language:** Hebrew

Azel
**Meaning:** Reserved
**Origin Language:** Hebrew

Azelio | Azellio, Azello, Azzello, Azzelo
**Meaning:** Small Land
**Origin Language:** Latin

Aziel
**Meaning:** God Is My Strength
**Origin Language:** Hebrew

Azrael | Azriel
**Meaning:** My God Is Help
**Origin Language:** Hebrew

# Chapter 2 - Names For Boys Beginning With B

Bailey | Bailie, Baily, Bayley
**Meaning:** Bailiff
**Origin Language:** Old English

Bakari
**Meaning:** Boötes (A Star Constellation)

**Origin Language:** Swahili

Baldric | Baldrik
**Meaning:** Bold And Rich
**Origin Language:** Ancient Germanic

Baldwin | Baldewin, Baldoin, Balduino
**Meaning:** Bold And Friendly
**Origin Language:** Ancient Germanic

Ballard
**Meaning:** Bald Headed
**Origin Language:** Old English

Balor
**Meaning:** The Flashing One
**Origin Language:** Ancient Celtic

Banks
**Meaning:** Dwells Near A Bank
**Origin Language:** Old English

Baptista | Baptist, Baptiste
**Meaning:** Baptist
**Origin Language:** Latin

Barack | Barac, Barak, Baraq
**Meaning:** A Blessing
**Origin Language:** Arabic

Baran
**Meaning:** Rain
**Origin Language:** Persian

Barclay
**Meaning:** From A Birch Tree Meadow
**Origin Language:** Old English

Barend
**Meaning:** Hardy As A Bear
**Origin Language:** Ancient Germanic

Barnabas | Barnaba
**Also:** Barnaby | Barnabe, Barnabie
**Also:** Barney | Barnie, Barny

**Meaning:** Prophet's Son
**Origin Language:** Old Aramaic

Barrett | Barret
**Meaning:** Strife
**Origin Language:** Old English

Barry | Bairre, Barra, Barrie
**Meaning:** Bright-Headed
**Origin Language:** Old Irish

Bart
**Also:** Bartholomew | Barthelemy, Bartholomaios, Bartholomei, Bartholomeus
**Meaning:** Son Of Talmai (Talmai Is The Name Of Numerous People In The Bible. It Is Unclear Which The Name Refers To)
**Origin Language:** Old Aramaic

Bartley
**Meaning:** From A Meadow With Birch Trees
**Origin Language:** Old English

Bartol | Bartolmai, Bartolo, Bartolomeo
**Meaning:** Son Of Talmai (Talmai Is The Name Of Numerous People In The Bible. It Is Unclear Which The Name Refers To)
**Origin Language:** Old Aramaic

Barys | Baris
**Meaning:** Snow Leopard / Wolf
**Origin Language:** Bulgar

Basil | Basile, Basileios, Basilio, Basilius
**Meaning:** King
**Origin Language:** Ancient Greek

Bastian | Bastien
**Meaning:** From Sebaste (An Ancient City In Asia Minor) / Venerable

**Origin Language:** Latin

Battista
**Also:** Bautista
**Meaning:** Baptist
**Origin Language:** Latin

Baxter
**Meaning:** Baker
**Origin Language:** Old English

Bayard | Baiard, Baiardo, Bayardo
**Meaning:** The Shade Of A Bay
**Origin Language:** Old French

Baylor
**Meaning:** Measuring Stick
**Origin Language:** Ancient Germanic

Bear
**Meaning:** Bear
**Origin Language:** English

Beau
**Also:** Beauden
**Meaning:** Beautiful
**Origin Language:** French

Beaumont
**Meaning:** Beautiful Mountain
**Origin Language:** French

Beavis | Bevis
**Meaning:** From Beauvais (France)
**Origin Language:** Old French

Beckett
**Meaning:** Stream
**Origin Language:** Old Norse

Beckham
**Meaning:** From Becca's Homestead / From The Homestead Of A Pickaxe Maker
**Origin Language:** Old English

Belen
**Meaning:** Rock
**Origin Language:** Turkish

Belenos | Belenus, Beli
**Meaning:** Strong
**Origin Language:** Gaulish

Bellamy | Bellamie
**Meaning:** Beautiful Friend
**Origin Language:** French

Bello
**Meaning:** Helper
**Origin Language:** Fula

Ben | Bennie, Benny
**Meaning:** A Short Form Of Any Of The Numerous Names Beginning With Ben
**Origin Language:** Various

Benaiah | Benayah
**Meaning:** God Has Built
**Origin Language:** Hebrew

Benedict | Benedetto, Benedictus, Benedikt, Benedito, Benedykt
**Meaning:** Blessed
**Origin Language:** Latin

Benjamin
**Also:** Benjy | Benji, Benjie
**Meaning:** Southern Son
**Origin Language:** Hebrew

Bennett | Benett
**Meaning:** Blessed
**Origin Language:** Latin

Benoni
**Meaning:** Son Of My Sorrow
**Origin Language:** Hebrew

Benson
**Meaning:** Blessed
**Origin Language:** Latin

Bentley
**Meaning:** From A Meadow Of Bent Grass
**Origin Language:** Old English

Benton
**Meaning:** From A Town Of Bent Grass
**Origin Language:** Old English

Berach | Bearach
**Meaning:** Sharp
**Origin Language:** Old Irish

Berard | Berardo
**Meaning:** Hardy As A Bear
**Origin Language:** Ancient Germanic

Beren
**Meaning:** Strong / Smart
**Origin Language:** Turkish

Berend
**Also:** Berin
**Also:** Berinard | Berinhard
**Meaning:** Hardy As A Bear
**Origin Language:** Ancient Germanic

Berkley | Berkelee, Berkeley, Berkelie, Berklee, Berklie
**Meaning:** From A Wood Of Birch Trees
**Origin Language:** Old English

Berlin
**Meaning:** From Berlin (Germany)
**Origin Language:** German

Bernard | Bearnard, Bernardino, Bernardo, Bernardus, Bernhard, Bernhardt
**Also:** Berny | Bernie
**Meaning:** Hardy As A Bear
**Origin Language:** Ancient Germanic

Bert | Bertie, Berto, Berty
**Meaning:** Bright

**Origin Language:** Ancient Germanic

Berthold | Berhtoald, Berhtold, Bertold, Bertoldo
**Also:** Bertil | Bertilo, Bertyl
**Meaning:** Bright Ruler
**Origin Language:** Ancient Germanic

Bertolf | Bertulf
**Meaning:** Bright Wolf
**Origin Language:** Ancient Germanic

Bertram
**Meaning:** Bright Raven
**Origin Language:** Ancient Germanic

Bertrand | Bertrando
**Meaning:** The Rim Of His Shield Is Shining
**Origin Language:** Ancient Germanic

Berwyn
**Meaning:** Fair-Haired
**Origin Language:** Welsh

Besarion | Bessarion
**Meaning:** Wooded Combe/Valley
**Origin Language:** Ancient Greek

Besart
**Meaning:** Golden Oath
**Origin Language:** Albanian

Bevan
**Meaning:** Graced By God
**Origin Language:** Hebrew

Bhaltair
**Meaning:** Ruler Of The Army
**Origin Language:** Ancient Germanic

Bharat | Bharath
**Meaning:** Cherished
**Origin Language:** Sanskrit

Biel

**Meaning:** My Strength Is God
**Origin Language:** Hebrew

Billy | Bill, Billie
**Meaning:** Desires Protection
**Origin Language:** Ancient Germanic

Bion
**Meaning:** The Good Life
**Origin Language:** Ancient Greek

Blaine | Blain, Blaina
**Meaning:** Little Yellow One
**Origin Language:** Old Irish

Blair
**Meaning:** Battlefield
**Origin Language:** Scottish Gaelic

Blake
**Meaning:** Black
**Origin Language:** Old English

Bo
**Meaning:** Wave
**Origin Language:** Chinese

Bobby | Bob, Bobbie
**Meaning:** Famous And Bright
**Origin Language:** Ancient Germanic

Bode | Boda
**Meaning:** Commander
**Origin Language:** Ancient Germanic

Boden
**Meaning:** Herald / Messenger
**Origin Language:** Middle English

Bodhi
**Meaning:** Enlightened
**Origin Language:** Sanskrit

Bodie | Body
**Meaning:** Herald / Messenger
**Origin Language:** Middle English

## Bohdan
**Meaning:** Given By God
**Origin Language:** Common Slavic

## Booker
**Meaning:** Bookmaker
**Origin Language:** Old English

## Boone
**Meaning:** Good
**Origin Language:** Old French

## Boran
**Meaning:** Thunderstorm
**Origin Language:** Turkish

## Boreas
**Meaning:** North Wind
**Origin Language:** Ancient Greek

## Boris | Borys
**Meaning:** Snow Leopard / Wolf
**Origin Language:** Bulgar

## Bosse
**Meaning:** Lives
**Origin Language:** Old Norse

## Boston | Bosten, Bostyn
**Meaning:** From Botolph's Town / From The Town Of The Messenger Wolf
**Origin Language:** Old English

## Bourkan
**Meaning:** Volcano
**Origin Language:** Arabic

## Bowen
**Meaning:** Well-Born
**Origin Language:** Ancient Greek

## Bowie | Bowy
**Meaning:** Victorious
**Origin Language:** Old Irish

## Boyan | Boian
**Meaning:** Warrior
**Origin Language:** Common Slavic

## Boyce
**Meaning:** Wood
**Origin Language:** Old French

## Boyd
**Meaning:** From The Isle Of Bód/Bute (Scotland)
**Origin Language:** Scottish Gaelic

## Bradley | Brad
**Meaning:** From A Broad Meadow
**Origin Language:** Old English

## Brady | Bradie, Braidie, Braidy
**Meaning:** Spirited
**Origin Language:** Old Irish

## Braith
**Meaning:** Broad
**Origin Language:** Old Norse

## Bram
**Meaning:** High Father Of A Multitude
**Origin Language:** Hebrew

## Bran | Brann
**Meaning:** Raven
**Origin Language:** Old Irish And Old Welsh (Cognates)

## Branco | Branko, Branko
**Meaning:** Glorious Protection
**Origin Language:** Common Slavic

## Brand | Brando, Brandr
**Meaning:** Sword / Fire
**Origin Language:** Ancient Germanic And Old Norse (Cognates)

## Brandon | Branden
**Meaning:** From A Broom Covered Hill
**Origin Language:** Old English

## Brannon
**Meaning:** Little Raindrop

**Origin Language:** Old Irish

## Branson | Bransen
**Also:** Brant | Brandt
**Meaning:** Sword / Fire
**Origin Language:** Ancient Germanic And Old Norse (Cognates)

## Brantley | Brantlie
**Meaning:** Sword / Fire
**Origin Language:** Ancient Germanic And Old Norse (Cognates)

## Braxton
**Meaning:** From Branoc's Town / From An Enclosed Town
**Origin Language:** Old English

## Brayden | Braden, Braeden, Braiden
**Meaning:** Thief / Salmon
**Origin Language:** Old Irish

## Braylen | Braylon
**Meaning:** Briar
**Origin Language:** English

## Brecken | Brackan, Bracken, Brackin, Breacan, Breacen, Breckan, Breckin
**Meaning:** Speckled
**Origin Language:** Old Irish

## Brendan | Brendanus, Brenden, Brendon
**Meaning:** Prince
**Origin Language:** Old Irish

## Brennan
**Meaning:** Little Raindrop
**Origin Language:** Old Irish

## Brent
**Meaning:** From A Hill
**Origin Language:** Ancient Celtic

## Brenton
**Meaning:** From Bryni's Town / From A Flaming Town
**Origin Language:** Old English

## Brett | Bret
**Meaning:** From The British Islands
**Origin Language:** Latin

## Briar | Brier
**Meaning:** Briar
**Origin Language:** English

## Bridger
**Meaning:** Bridge Maker
**Origin Language:** Old English

## Briggs
**Meaning:** From Near Some Bridges
**Origin Language:** Old English

## Brigham
**Meaning:** From A Homestead Near A Bridge
**Origin Language:** Old English

## Briscoe
**Meaning:** From A Birch Tree Woods
**Origin Language:** Old Norse

## Britton
**Meaning:** From The British Islands
**Origin Language:** Latin

## Brixton | Brixtan, Brixten
**Meaning:** From Near Brixi's Stone (It Is Unknown What The Meaning Of The Old English Personal Name Brixi Is)
**Origin Language:** Old English

## Brock
**Meaning:** Badger
**Origin Language:** Old English

## Broderick
**Meaning:** Reddish Brown
**Origin Language:** Old Welsh

Brody | Brodie
**Meaning:** From Near A Mire
**Origin Language:** Scottish Gaelic

Brogan
**Meaning:** Little Shoe
**Origin Language:** Old Irish

Bron | Bronn
**Also:** Bronson
**Meaning:** Brown / Brunette
**Origin Language:** Old English

Bronte | Brontë, Bruntie, Brunty
**Meaning:** Meal House
**Origin Language:** Old Irish

Brontes
**Meaning:** Thunderer
**Origin Language:** Ancient Greek

Brooklyn | Brooklin
**Meaning:** From Brooklyn (New York City)
**Origin Language:** Dutch

Brooks | Brook
**Meaning:** Brook
**Origin Language:** Old English

Bruce
**Meaning:** From Brix (A Commune In France)
**Origin Language:** Old French

Bruin
**Also:** Bruno
**Also:** Brunello
**Meaning:** Protected / Brunette
**Origin Language:** Ancient Germanic

Bryan | Brian, Brien, Brion, Bryen, Bryon
**Also:** Bryant
**Meaning:** Power / Hill

**Origin Language:** Old Irish

Bryce | Brice
**Also:** Bryson | Brycen, Brysen
**Meaning:** Freckled
**Origin Language:** Gaulish

Brynden | Brinden
**Meaning:** Prince
**Origin Language:** Old Irish

Buddy | Bud, Buddie
**Meaning:** Buddy
**Origin Language:** English

Burke
**Meaning:** From A Fortress
**Origin Language:** Old English

Burton | Burt
**Meaning:** From A Fortified Town
**Origin Language:** Old English

Bylun
**Meaning:** White God
**Origin Language:** Common Slavic

Byrne
**Meaning:** Raven
**Origin Language:** Old Irish And Old Welsh (Cognates)

Byron
**Meaning:** From Near Some Cow Sheds
**Origin Language:** Old English

# Chapter 3 - Names For Boys Beginning With C

Cade | Caed, Caid, Cayde
**Meaning:** Round
**Origin Language:** Old English

Cadell
**Meaning:** Battler
**Origin Language:** Old Welsh

Caden | Cadan, Caedan, Caeden,
Caidan, Caiden, Caydan, Cayden
**Meaning:** Place Of Battle
**Origin Language:** Welsh

Cadmus | Cadmos
**Meaning:** Man From The East
**Origin Language:** Ancient Greek

Cadoc
**Meaning:** Battler
**Origin Language:** Old Welsh

Cael
**Meaning:** Slender
**Origin Language:** Old Irish

Caelan | Calen, Caylen
**Meaning:** Little Slender One
**Origin Language:** Old Irish

Caelin | Caelinus
**Meaning:** Heaven
**Origin Language:** Latin

Caeson | Caeso, Caesonius
**Meaning:** Bluish-Grey/Bluish-Gray
**Origin Language:** Latin

Cahal
**Meaning:** Chief Of Battle
**Origin Language:** Old Irish

Cahir
**Meaning:** Man Of Battle
**Origin Language:** Old Irish

Cai | Caio, Kai, Kaio
**Meaning:** Rejoice
**Origin Language:** Latin

Cain | Caen, Caeno, Caino, Cayn,

Cayno
**Meaning:** Acquired
**Origin Language:** Hebrew

Cainan | Caenan, Caenen, Cainam,
Cainen, Ceinan, Ceinen, Cenan,
Cenen, Ceynan
**Meaning:** Possession
**Origin Language:** Hebrew

Cairo | Cyro
**Meaning:** From Cairo (Egypt) (English)
/ The Strong (Arabic)
**Origin Language:** English And Arabic

Caiside
**Meaning:** Curly Haired
**Origin Language:** Old Irish

Caius | Caios
**Meaning:** Rejoice
**Origin Language:** Latin

Calder
**Meaning:** Violent Water
**Origin Language:** Old Welsh

Caleb | Chaleb
**Meaning:** Wholehearted / Dog
**Origin Language:** Hebrew

Calisto | Callisto, Callistus
**Meaning:** Beautiful
**Origin Language:** Ancient Greek

Callahan
**Meaning:** Strife / Sociable / Church
**Origin Language:** Old Irish

Callan | Callen
**Meaning:** Chief Of Battle
**Origin Language:** Old Irish

Callias
**Meaning:** Beauty
**Origin Language:** Ancient Greek

Callum | Calum, Calumb
**Meaning:** Dove
**Origin Language:** Latin

Calvagh
**Meaning:** Bald Headed
**Origin Language:** Old Irish

Calvin | Cal, Calvino, Calvinus
**Meaning:** Bald
**Origin Language:** Latin

Calvus
**Meaning:** Bald Headed
**Origin Language:** Latin

Calydon
**Meaning:** From Kalydon/Calydon (A Greek City In Ancient Aetolia)
**Origin Language:** Ancient Greek

Camden | Camdin, Camdon, Camdyn
**Meaning:** From An Enclosed Valley
**Origin Language:** Old English

Cameron | Cam, Camren, Camrin, Camron, Camryn
**Meaning:** Crooked Nose
**Origin Language:** Scottish Gaelic

Camilo | Camillo, Camillus
**Meaning:** Disciple
**Origin Language:** Latin

Campbell
**Meaning:** Crooked Mouthed
**Origin Language:** Scottish Gaelic

Canaan | Canan
**Meaning:** Humble
**Origin Language:** Semitic

Cannon
**Meaning:** Clergy

**Origin Language:** Old English

Canyon
**Meaning:** Canyon
**Origin Language:** English

Caolin
**Meaning:** Little Slender One
**Origin Language:** Old Irish

Carbrey | Cairbre, Carbrie, Carbry
**Meaning:** Charioteer
**Origin Language:** Irish

Carl | Carlo
**Meaning:** A Free Man
**Origin Language:** Ancient Germanic

Carlisle | Carlyle
**Meaning:** Stronghold Of Lugus (Lugus Is The Name Of A Celtic God)
**Origin Language:** Gaulish

Carlman | Carlmann
**Meaning:** Manly And Free
**Origin Language:** Ancient Germanic

Carlos | Carlito, Carlitos, Carlo, Carolus
**Meaning:** Has Freedom
**Origin Language:** Ancient Germanic

Carlton | Carleton
**Meaning:** From A Town Of Freedom
**Origin Language:** Old English

Carmelo | Carmo
**Meaning:** Garden
**Origin Language:** Hebrew

Carmi
**Meaning:** Vine
**Origin Language:** Hebrew

Carmine
**Meaning:** Song
**Origin Language:** Latin

Carroll
**Meaning:** Carver
**Origin Language:** Old Irish

Carson | Carsen, Carsin, Carsyn
**Meaning:** Rock
**Origin Language:** Scottish Gaelic

Carsten
**Meaning:** Christ / The Anointed One / Messiah
**Origin Language:** Ancient Greek

Carter | Cartier
**Meaning:** Carter
**Origin Language:** Norman French

Carus
**Meaning:** Dear
**Origin Language:** Latin

Carver
**Meaning:** Carver
**Origin Language:** English

Carwyn
**Meaning:** Blessed Love
**Origin Language:** Welsh

Cary | Carey, Carie
**Meaning:** Dark
**Origin Language:** Old Irish

Casey | Case
**Meaning:** Vigilant
**Origin Language:** Old Irish

Cash | Cashton
**Meaning:** Case Maker
**Origin Language:** Old French

Casimir | Casim, Casimiro, Cazim, Cazimir
**Meaning:** Destroyer Of Peace
**Origin Language:** Slavic

Casper | Caspar
**Meaning:** Treasurer
**Origin Language:** Hebrew

Caspian
**Meaning:** From Kaspiane/Caspiane (An Ancient Land Near The Caspian Sea)
**Origin Language:** Ancient Greek

Cassander | Cassandro, Cassandros
**Meaning:** Surpasses Other Men
**Origin Language:** Ancient Greek

Cassian | Cassianus
**Meaning:** Empty/Hollow
**Origin Language:** Latin

Cassiel
**Meaning:** The Cover Of God
**Origin Language:** Hebrew

Cassius
**Meaning:** Empty/Hollow
**Origin Language:** Latin

Castiel
**Meaning:** The Cover Of God
**Origin Language:** Hebrew

Castor | Kastor
**Meaning:** Shining
**Origin Language:** Ancient Greek

Catello | Catellus
**Meaning:** Small
**Origin Language:** Latin

Cathal
**Meaning:** Chief Of Battle
**Origin Language:** Old Irish

Cavan
**Meaning:** Little Beloved One
**Origin Language:** Old Irish

Cayson | Caesen, Caeson, Caisen,

Caison, Casen, Cason, Caysen
**Meaning:** From Kálfr's Town / From A Town Where Calves Reside
**Origin Language:** Old English And Old Norse (A Mix Of Both)

Caytan | Caetan, Caetano, Caietanus, Caiton, Cayetano, Cayton
**Meaning:** From Caieta (An Ancient Town On The Coast Of Latium, A District Located In West Central Italy)
**Origin Language:** Latin

Cecil
**Meaning:** Aimless / Without Sight
**Origin Language:** Latin

Cedar
**Meaning:** Cedar Tree
**Origin Language:** English

Cedric
**Meaning:** Loving
**Origin Language:** Brythonic

Ceelan
**Meaning:** Little Slender One
**Origin Language:** Old Irish

Ceferino
**Meaning:** West Wind
**Origin Language:** Ancient Greek

Cefin
**Meaning:** Homely Birth
**Origin Language:** Old Irish

Celemen
**Meaning:** Clemency
**Origin Language:** Latin

Celestino | Caelestinus, Celestin, Celestyn
**Meaning:** Of The Sky / Celestial
**Origin Language:** Latin

Celino
**Meaning:** The Moon
**Origin Language:** Ancient Greek

Celyn | Celin
**Meaning:** Holly
**Origin Language:** Welsh

Cemal
**Meaning:** Beauty
**Origin Language:** Arabic

Cemil
**Meaning:** Beautiful
**Origin Language:** Arabic

Cena
**Meaning:** Keen
**Origin Language:** Old English

Cesar | Caesar, Caesarius, Cesaire, Cesare, Cesarino, Cezar, Cezarie, Cezary
**Meaning:** Has Long Flowing Hair / Has Beautiful Hair
**Origin Language:** Latin

Cester
**Meaning:** Christ / The Anointed One / Messiah
**Origin Language:** Ancient Greek

Chadwick | Chad
**Meaning:** From Ceadda's Village / From A Battler's Village
**Origin Language:** Old English

Chan
**Meaning:** Moon
**Origin Language:** Khmer

Chandler
**Meaning:** Candle Seller
**Origin Language:** Old English

**Channing**
**Meaning:** Wolf Cub
**Origin Language:** Old Irish

**Charles | Charls**
**Also:** Charlie | Charlee, Charly
**Meaning:** Has Freedom
**Origin Language:** Ancient Germanic

**Charlton**
**Meaning:** From A Town Of Freedom
**Origin Language:** Old English

**Charon**
**Meaning:** Fierce-Eyed
**Origin Language:** Ancient Greek

**Chase | Chace**
**Meaning:** Hunter
**Origin Language:** Old English

**Chauncey | Chauncy**
**Meaning:** Luck / Good Fortune
**Origin Language:** Old French

**Chayton**
**Meaning:** Falcon
**Origin Language:** Sioux

**Chaz | Chas**
**Meaning:** Has Freedom
**Origin Language:** Ancient Germanic

**Chen**
**Meaning:** Charm
**Origin Language:** Hebrew

**Chenaniah**
**Meaning:** God Establishes
**Origin Language:** Hebrew

**Chesed**
**Meaning:** Increase
**Origin Language:** Hebrew

**Chesley | Cheslea, Chesleigh,**

**Cheslie, Chesly**
**Meaning:** From A Meadow Where Soldiers Camp
**Origin Language:** Old English

**Chester**
**Also:** Chet
**Meaning:** From Near A Camp
**Origin Language:** Old English

**Chris | Cris**
**Also:** Christer | Crister
**Meaning:** Christ / The Anointed One / Messiah
**Origin Language:** Ancient Greek

**Christian | Christianos, Christianus, Cristian, Cristiano, Crystian**
**Meaning:** A Christian
**Origin Language:** Latin

**Christoph | Christoff, Christoff, Christophe, Cristoff, Cristoph, Crystoff, Crystoph**
**Also:** Christopher | Christoffer, Christoforos, Christophoros, Christophorus, Cristoffer, Cristopher, Crystoffer, Crystopher
**Meaning:** Bearer Of Christ
**Origin Language:** Late Greek

**Christos | Cristos**
**Meaning:** Christ / The Anointed One / Messiah
**Origin Language:** Ancient Greek

**Chuck | Chuckie, Chucky**
**Meaning:** Has Freedom
**Origin Language:** Ancient Germanic

**Cian**
**Meaning:** Long-Lasting
**Origin Language:** Old Irish

Ciar
**Also:** Ciaran | Ceiran, Ceiren, Ceiron, Ciaren, Ciaron, Cieran, Cieren, Cieron
**Meaning:** Dark
**Origin Language:** Old Irish

Cicero
**Meaning:** Chickpea
**Origin Language:** Latin

Ciel
**Meaning:** Sky
**Origin Language:** French

Cillian
**Meaning:** Little Church
**Origin Language:** Irish

Cimon
**Meaning:** Sleepy
**Origin Language:** Ancient Greek

Cirino | Ciro
**Meaning:** Shepherd / Protector
**Origin Language:** Old Persian

Clancey | Clancie, Clancy
**Meaning:** Red Warrior / Bloody Warrior
**Origin Language:** Old Irish

Clarence | Clarenzo
**Meaning:** Clarence (A British Ducal Title)
**Origin Language:** Latin

Clark
**Meaning:** Cleric / Scribe
**Origin Language:** Old English

Clarus
**Meaning:** Illustrious
**Origin Language:** Latin

Claud | Claude
**Also:** Claudius | Claudio

**Meaning:** Limps / Stumbles / Wavers / Hesitates
**Origin Language:** Latin

Claus
**Meaning:** Victory Of The People
**Origin Language:** Ancient Greek

Clay
**Meaning:** Clay
**Origin Language:** English

Clayton
**Meaning:** From A Clay Town
**Origin Language:** Old English

Clemens
**Meaning:** Merciful And Loving
**Origin Language:** Latin

Clement | Clem, Clem, Clemen, Clemente, Clementius, Clements, Clim, Climen, Climent
**Meaning:** Clemency
**Origin Language:** Latin

Cleon | Clion
**Meaning:** Glory
**Origin Language:** Ancient Greek

Cletus | Cleitis, Cleitos, Cleitus, Cleitus, Cletis
**Meaning:** Famous
**Origin Language:** Ancient Greek

Cleveland | Cleve
**Meaning:** From A Land With Many Cliffs
**Origin Language:** Old English

Cliamain
**Meaning:** Clemency
**Origin Language:** Latin

Clifford | Cliff, Cliford
**Meaning:** From A Cliff With A Ford

**Origin Language:** Old English

Cliffton | Cliff, Clifton
**Meaning:** From A Town Near A Cliff
**Origin Language:** Old English

Clinton | Clint
**Meaning:** From A Town Near The River Glyme (England)
**Origin Language:** Old English

Clive
**Meaning:** From Near A Cliff
**Origin Language:** Old English

Clyde
**Meaning:** The Cleansing One
**Origin Language:** Scottish Gaelic

Coby | Cobe, Cobi, Cobie, Cobus
**Meaning:** Supplanter (Wrongfully Seizes And Holds The Place Of Another)
**Origin Language:** Hebrew

Cody | Codey, Codie
**Meaning:** Rich
**Origin Language:** Ancient Germanic And Old English And Old Norse (Cognates)

Coen
**Meaning:** Brave Counsellor
**Origin Language:** Ancient Germanic

Cohen
**Meaning:** Priest
**Origin Language:** Hebrew

Colbert | Colobert
**Meaning:** Calm And Bright
**Origin Language:** Ancient Germanic

Colby | Colbie
**Meaning:** From Koli's Town / From A Coal Town
**Origin Language:** Old Norse

Cole
**Meaning:** Charcoal
**Origin Language:** Old English

Coleman | Colman, Coloman
**Meaning:** Dove
**Origin Language:** Latin

Coleson | Colson
**Meaning:** The People's Victory
**Origin Language:** Ancient Greek

Colin | Colinn, Collin, Collyn, Colyn
**Meaning:** Puppy
**Origin Language:** Scottish Gaelic

Colt
**Meaning:** Colt (Young Male Horse)
**Origin Language:** English

Colter
**Meaning:** One Who Looks After Horses
**Origin Language:** Old English

Colton | Coltan, Colten, Coltin, Coltyn
**Meaning:** From Cola's Town / From A Coal Town
**Origin Language:** Old English

Columbo | Colm, Colombano, Colombo, Columbanus
**Meaning:** Dove
**Origin Language:** Latin

Colwyn
**Meaning:** From Colwyn (Wales)
**Origin Language:** Welsh

Conan
**Meaning:** Little Hound
**Origin Language:** Old Irish

Conleth
**Also:** Conley

**Meaning:** Steady Flame
**Origin Language:** Old Irish

Conn
**Meaning:** The Head (The Most Important Person)
**Origin Language:** Old Irish

Connell | Conall, Conell, Connall
**Meaning:** Chief Of The Hounds
**Origin Language:** Old Irish

Connor | Conner, Conor
**Meaning:** Dog Lover
**Origin Language:** Old Irish

Conrad | Conrado
**Meaning:** Brave Counsellor
**Origin Language:** Ancient Germanic

Constantine | Constans, Constant, Constantin, Constantino, Constantinus, Constantius
**Meaning:** Constant (Unchanging)
**Origin Language:** Latin

Conway
**Meaning:** From Near The River Conwy
**Origin Language:** Welsh

Cooper
**Meaning:** Barrel Maker
**Origin Language:** Old English

Corbin | Corbinian, Corbinus
**Also:** Corbus
**Meaning:** Raven
**Origin Language:** Latin

Cordell
**Meaning:** Cord Seller
**Origin Language:** Old English

Corentin
**Meaning:** Hurricane
**Origin Language:** Old Breton

Corey | Corie, Cory
**Meaning:** Trooper
**Origin Language:** Old Norse

Corin | Coryn
**Meaning:** Armed With A Spear
**Origin Language:** Latin

Cormac | Cormacc
**Meaning:** Son Of The Chariot
**Origin Language:** Old Irish

Cornel | Cornell
**Also:** Cornelius | Corneille, Cornelio, Cornelios, Cornelis, Cornello
**Meaning:** Horned
**Origin Language:** Latin

Corrad | Cord, Corradino, Corrado
**Meaning:** Brave Counsellor
**Origin Language:** Ancient Germanic

Corvin | Corvinus
**Also:** Corvus
**Meaning:** Raven
**Origin Language:** Latin

Corwin | Corwyn
**Meaning:** Maker Of Shoes From Cordovan Leather (The Name Of The Leather Was Named From The City Of Cordova In Spain)
**Origin Language:** Old English

Cosmas | Cosimo, Cosme, Cosmo, Cosmos
**Also:** Cosmin
**Meaning:** The Universe / The Cosmos
**Origin Language:** Ancient Greek

Costantino | Costanzo, Costas
**Also:** Costin
**Meaning:** Constant (Unchanging)
**Origin Language:** Latin

Coty | Cotey, Cotie
**Meaning:** Rich
**Origin Language:** Ancient Germanic And Old English And Old Norse (Cognates)

Cowal | Cowall, Cowel, Cowell
**Meaning:** One Half Of A Joint Pledge (Together With Another Human Pledge / Hostage)
**Origin Language:** Old Irish

Craig
**Meaning:** Lives Near A Crag
**Origin Language:** Scottish Gaelic

Credence
**Meaning:** Credence / Believing
**Origin Language:** English

Creed
**Meaning:** Creed / A Confession Of Faith
**Origin Language:** English

Creighton
**Meaning:** From A Border Town
**Origin Language:** Old English

Crevan
**Meaning:** Fox
**Origin Language:** Old Irish

Crew | Crewe, Criu, Cru, Crue
**Meaning:** A Weir (An Enclosure Set For Catching Fish)
**Origin Language:** Old Welsh

Crispian | Crispin, Crispino, Crispinus, Crispus, Cryspin
**Meaning:** Curly-Haired
**Origin Language:** Latin

Crius | Crios, Kreios
**Meaning:** Ram
**Origin Language:** Ancient Greek

Crosby | Crosbie, Crossbie, Crossby, Crozbie, Crozby
**Meaning:** From A Village With A Cross
**Origin Language:** Old Norse

Cruz
**Meaning:** Cross (Of Crucifixion)
**Origin Language:** Spanish And Portuguese (Cognates)

Culann | Culan
**Meaning:** Dwells In A Secluded Spot
**Origin Language:** Old Irish

Cullen
**Meaning:** Puppy
**Origin Language:** Old Irish

Curran
**Meaning:** Little Spear
**Origin Language:** Old Irish

Curt | Coert
**Meaning:** Brave Counsellor
**Origin Language:** Ancient Germanic

Curtis | Curt
**Meaning:** Courteous
**Origin Language:** Old French

Cyan
**Meaning:** Cyan
**Origin Language:** English

Cyprien | Ciprian, Cipriano, Ciprianus, Ciprien, Cyprian, Cypriano, Cyprianus
**Meaning:** From Cyprus / From A Place Where Henna Grows
**Origin Language:** Latin

Cyren | Cyran, Cyrano
**Meaning:** From Cyrene (An Ancient Greek City) / Sovereign
**Origin Language:** Ancient Greek

Cyril | Ciril, Cirillo, Cirilo, Cyrille,
Cyrillus, Cyryl
**Meaning:** Lord
**Origin Language:** Ancient Greek

Cyrus
**Meaning:** Shepherd / Protector
**Origin Language:** Old Persian

# Chapter 4 - Names For Boys Beginning With D

Dachs
**Meaning:** Badger
**Origin Language:** German

Dacian
**Meaning:** From Dacia (An Old Name
For The Region That Is Now Romania
And Moldova)
**Origin Language:** Romanian

Dacre
**Meaning:** From Near A Trickling Stream
**Origin Language:** Brythonic

Dadrian | Daddrian, Daddriano,
Daddrianus, Daddrien, Daddrion,
Dadriano, Dadriano, Dadrianus,
Dadrianus, Daidrian, Daidriano,
Daidrianus, Daidrien, Daidrion,
Daydrian, Daydriano, Daydrianus,
Daydrien, Daydrion
**Meaning:** From Hadria (The Name Of
Two Ancient Roman Settlements Which
Were Located In What Are Now
Northern Italy And Central Italy) / From
The Water
**Origin Language:** Latin

Daedalus | Daed, Daedalos,

Daedalos, Daede, Daid, Daidalos,
Daidalus, Daide, Dayd, Daydalos,
Daydalus, Dayde
**Meaning:** Works Cunningly
**Origin Language:** Ancient Greek

Daemond | Daemund, Daimund,
Daymond, Daymund
**Meaning:** Day Warden
**Origin Language:** Old English

Daichi
**Meaning:** Great Earth / Great Land /
Great Wisdom
**Origin Language:** Japanese

Dakari | Dakarai
**Meaning:** Rejoice
**Origin Language:** Shona

Dakota
**Meaning:** Allies
**Origin Language:** Dakota

Dalciso | Dalcisio
**Meaning:** Pledge Of Nobility
**Origin Language:** Ancient Germanic

Dale
**Meaning:** From A Valley
**Origin Language:** Old English

Daley | Dalie, Daly
**Meaning:** Of The Assembly
**Origin Language:** Old Irish

Dallas
**Meaning:** From A Homestead In A
Meadow
**Origin Language:** Scottish Gaelic

Dalmin
**Meaning:** Protects His Father
**Origin Language:** Ancient Germanic

Dalton

**Meaning:** From A Town In A Valley
**Origin Language:** Old English

## Damari
**Meaning:** Calf
**Origin Language:** Ancient Greek

## Damarion
**Meaning:** Rebellious
**Origin Language:** Hebrew

## Damien | Damian, Damiano, Damianos, Damianus, Damion
**Meaning:** Tamer
**Origin Language:** Ancient Greek

## Damir
**Meaning:** Given The World
**Origin Language:** Slavic

## Damon | Daman, Damen
**Meaning:** Tamer
**Origin Language:** Ancient Greek

## Dana
**Meaning:** Wise
**Origin Language:** Persian

## Dancho
**Meaning:** God Is My Judge
**Origin Language:** Hebrew

## Dane | Dain, Daine, Dayn, Dayne
**Meaning:** Of The Danes (The Name Of A Germanic Tribe)
**Origin Language:** Old Norse

## Dangelo
**Meaning:** Angel/Messenger
**Origin Language:** Latin

## Daniel | Danail, Danial, Danihel, Daniil, Danilo, Daniyal, Daniyel, Daniyyel, Danyal, Danyil, Danylo
**Meaning:** God Is My Judge
**Origin Language:** Hebrew

## Danis
**Meaning:** Knowledge
**Origin Language:** Persian

## Danny | Dani, Danie, Danni, Dannie, Dany
**Meaning:** God Is My Judge
**Origin Language:** Hebrew

## Dante
**Meaning:** Enduring
**Origin Language:** Latin

## Daquan
**Meaning:** Spring (Of Water) (Chinese) / Sea Spirit (Old Irish)
**Origin Language:** Chinese And Old Irish

## Daragh | Dara, Darragh
**Meaning:** Oak Tree Grove / Fruitful
**Origin Language:** Old Irish

## Darby | Darbie, Derbie, Derby
**Meaning:** From A Deer Farm
**Origin Language:** Old Norse

## Darcy | Darcey, Darcie
**Meaning:** Of Arcy (A Town In France)
**Origin Language:** Old French

## Dardan
**Meaning:** Of The Dardani People (An Illyrian Tribe That Lived On The Balkan Peninsula)
**Origin Language:** Albanian

## Darell | Darrel, Darrell, Darryl, Daryl
**Also:** Darian | Darien, Darion
**Also:** Dariel | Dariol
**Meaning:** Of Airel (A Town In Normandy)
**Origin Language:** Old French

Daris
**Meaning:** Learning
**Origin Language:** Arabic

Darius | Daario, Daarius, Dareios, Dario, Darios, Dariush, Dariy, Daryush
**Meaning:** Possesses Goodness
**Origin Language:** Old Persian

Darnell
**Meaning:** From A Hidden Nook
**Origin Language:** Old English

Darren | Daren, Darin, Darrin
**Meaning:** Of Airel (A Town In Normandy)
**Origin Language:** Old French

Darwin | Deorwin, Derwin, Diorwin
**Meaning:** Dear Friend
**Origin Language:** Old English

Dash
**Also:** Dashiell
**Meaning:** Of Chiell (A Place Of Unknown Location, Most Likely Used To Exist In France)
**Origin Language:** French

Dathan
**Meaning:** Belongs To A Fountain
**Origin Language:** Hebrew

Daven | Davan, Davin, Davon, Davyn
**Meaning:** Little Dark/Black One
**Origin Language:** Old Irish

Daveth | Davit, Davith
**Also:** David | Dave, Davey, Davi, Davide, Davie, Davud, Davy, Davyd
**Meaning:** Beloved
**Origin Language:** Hebrew

Davion | Davian, Davien
**Meaning:** Little Dark/Black One
**Origin Language:** Old Irish

Davis | Davys
**Meaning:** Beloved
**Origin Language:** Hebrew

Davorin | Davor
**Meaning:** Joy / Sorrow
**Origin Language:** Common Slavic

Davos
**Meaning:** Beloved
**Origin Language:** Hebrew

Dawson | Daw
**Meaning:** Beloved
**Origin Language:** Hebrew

Dax | Dack, Dacks
**Meaning:** Badger
**Origin Language:** Old English

Daxton
**Meaning:** From Dæcca's Town / From A Town Of Badgers
**Origin Language:** Old English

Dayton
**Meaning:** From A Town With A Ditch
**Origin Language:** Old English

Dazelio | Dazellio, Dazello, Dazzello, Dazzelo
**Meaning:** Small Land
**Origin Language:** Latin

Deacon
**Meaning:** Deacon
**Origin Language:** English

Dean | Dene, Deno, Dino
**Meaning:** From A Valley
**Origin Language:** Old English

Deandre
**Meaning:** Manly / Brave Warrior
**Origin Language:** Ancient Greek

Deangelo | Diangelo
**Meaning:** Angel/Messenger
**Origin Language:** Latin

Dechen
**Meaning:** Happiness
**Origin Language:** Tibetan

Declan
**Meaning:** Full Of Goodness
**Origin Language:** Old Irish

Dederick | Dedrick
**Meaning:** Ruler Of The People
**Origin Language:** Ancient Germanic

Deimos
**Meaning:** Terror
**Origin Language:** Ancient Greek

Dekel
**Meaning:** Palm Tree
**Origin Language:** Hebrew

Delannoy | Delanoy
**Also:** Delano
**Meaning:** From Lannoy (A Commune In France)
**Origin Language:** French

Delbert
**Meaning:** Bright Noble
**Origin Language:** Ancient Germanic And Old English (Cognates)

Dell
**Meaning:** From A Valley
**Origin Language:** Old English

Delmar
**Meaning:** From Near A Pool Of Water
**Origin Language:** Old French

Delmin
**Meaning:** Protects His Father
**Origin Language:** Ancient Germanic

Delroy | Delroi
**Meaning:** The King
**Origin Language:** French

Delwyn | Delwin
**Meaning:** Pretty And Blessed
**Origin Language:** Welsh

Demarcus
**Meaning:** Of Mars (Mars Is The Name Of The Roman God Of War, Guardian Of Agriculture And The Roman People)
**Origin Language:** Latin

Demetrius | Demetrio, Demetrios, Demetry, Dimitar, Dimitri, Dimitrios, Dimitris, Dimitriy, Dmitar, Dmitrei, Dmitri, Dmitrie, Dmitrii, Dmitriy, Dmitry, Dmytro, Dymitr, Dzmitrie, Dzmitry
**Meaning:** Of Demeter (Demeter Is The Name Of The Greek Goddess Of The Harvest, Agriculture, Fertility, And Sacred Law)
**Origin Language:** Ancient Greek

Demid | Diomed, Diomedes, Diomid, Diomidis
**Meaning:** Of Zeus' Counsel (Zeus Is The Name Of The Roman God Of The Sky, Lightning, Thunder, Law, Order, And Justice)
**Origin Language:** Ancient Greek

Demir | Dimour, Dimur
**Meaning:** Iron
**Origin Language:** Ottoman Turkish

Denholm | Denolm
**Meaning:** From An Islet In A Valley (An Islet Is A Very Small, Often Unnamed Island)

**Origin Language:** Old English

Deniel
**Meaning:** God Is My Judge
**Origin Language:** Hebrew

Deniz
**Meaning:** Sea
**Origin Language:** Turkish

Dennis | Den, Denis, Dennie, Denny, Denys, Dinis, Diniz
**Meaning:** Of Dionysos (Dionysos Is The Name Of The Greek God Of Wine, Vegetation, Fertility, Festivity, Ritual Madness, Religious Ecstasy, And Theatre)
**Origin Language:** Ancient Greek

Denton
**Meaning:** From A Valley Town
**Origin Language:** Old English

Denver
**Meaning:** From Near A Ford Where Danish People Cross
**Origin Language:** Old English

Denzel | Denzil
**Meaning:** From Denzell (A Place In Cornwall, England)
**Origin Language:** Cornish

Deo | Dio
**Meaning:** God
**Origin Language:** Sanskrit

Deon | Deion, Dion
**Also:** Deonte
**Meaning:** Of Dionysos (Dionysos Is The Name Of The Greek God Of Wine, Vegetation, Fertility, Festivity, Ritual Madness, Religious Ecstasy, And Theatre)
**Origin Language:** Ancient Greek

Derek | Derick, Derrick, Deryck
**Meaning:** Ruler Of The People
**Origin Language:** Ancient Germanic

Dermot
**Meaning:** Unenvious
**Origin Language:** Old Irish

Derren | Deren, Derin, Derrin
**Meaning:** Of Airel (A Town In Normandy)
**Origin Language:** Old French

Derry | Derrie
**Meaning:** Unenvious
**Origin Language:** Old Irish

Derryl | Derell, Derrel, Derrell, Deryl
**Meaning:** Of Airel (A Town In Normandy)
**Origin Language:** Old French

Deryn
**Meaning:** Bird
**Origin Language:** Welsh

Deshaun | Dashawn, Deshawn
**Meaning:** Graced By God
**Origin Language:** Hebrew

Desmond | Des, Desmund, Dez, Dezmond, Dezmund
**Meaning:** From The Kingdom Of Desmond (A Historic Kingdom In Ireland)
**Origin Language:** Old Irish

Dev
**Meaning:** God
**Origin Language:** Sanskrit

Devante | Davonte, Devanté, Devonte, Devontea
**Meaning:** Little Dark/Black One
**Origin Language:** Old Irish

Deveraux | Devereu, Devereux
**Meaning:** From Évreux (A Commune In

Normandy, France) / Yew Tree / Wields
Weapons Made From A Yew Tree
**Origin Language:** Gaulish

Devlin | Devlyn
**Meaning:** Unlucky
**Origin Language:** Old Irish

Devon | Devan, Deven, Devin,
Devyn
**Meaning:** Little Dark/Black One
**Origin Language:** Old Irish

Dewey | Dewi, Dewy
**Meaning:** Beloved
**Origin Language:** Hebrew

Dexter | Dex
**Meaning:** Cloth Dyer
**Origin Language:** Old English

Deyan | Diyan
**Meaning:** Acts / Does
**Origin Language:** South Slavic

Dian | Dyan
**Meaning:** Candle
**Origin Language:** Indonesian

Dibri | Dibriy
**Meaning:** Eloquent
**Origin Language:** Hebrew

Didier
**Meaning:** Desire
**Origin Language:** Latin

Diego | Diogo
**Meaning:** Of Saint Iago
**Origin Language:** Hebrew And Latin
(In Combination)

Dietrich
**Meaning:** Ruler Of The People
**Origin Language:** Ancient Germanic

Digby | Digbie

**Meaning:** From A Town Near A Ditch
**Origin Language:** Old English And Old
Norse (A Mix Of Both)

Diggory | Diggorie
**Meaning:** Lost One
**Origin Language:** French

Dilan
**Meaning:** Love
**Origin Language:** Turkish

Dilbert
**Meaning:** Bright Noble
**Origin Language:** Ancient Germanic
And Old English (Cognates)

Dilwyn | Dilwen
**Meaning:** Genuine And Blessed
**Origin Language:** Welsh

Diodore | Diodoros, Diodorus
**Meaning:** Gift Of Zeus (Zeus Is The
Name Of The Roman God Of The Sky,
Lightning, Thunder, Law, Order, And
Justice)
**Origin Language:** Ancient Greek

Dior
**Meaning:** Animal
**Origin Language:** Old English

Dixon
**Meaning:** Rich And Hardy
**Origin Language:** Ancient Germanic

Dodge
**Meaning:** Famous Spear
**Origin Language:** Ancient Germanic

Dominic | Dom, Domen,
Domenic, Domenico, Domingo,
Dominick, Dominicus, Dominik,
Dominique
**Meaning:** Of The Lord/Church
**Origin Language:** Latin

Domitian | Domitianus, Domitius
**Meaning:** Tamed
**Origin Language:** Latin

Donald | Don, Donal, Donaldo, Donnie, Donny
**Meaning:** Chief/Ruler Of The World
**Origin Language:** Old Irish

Donar
**Meaning:** Thunder
**Origin Language:** Old Norse

Donatello
**Also:** Donatien
**Also:** Donato | Donat, Donatus
**Meaning:** Given (To The Church Or Monastery)
**Origin Language:** Latin

Donn
**Meaning:** Brown
**Origin Language:** Old Irish

Donovan
**Meaning:** Has Black-Brown Hair
**Origin Language:** Old Irish

Dontae | Dontay
**Meaning:** Enduring
**Origin Language:** Latin

Dontos
**Meaning:** Given (To The Church Or Monastery)
**Origin Language:** Latin

Doran
**Meaning:** Little Wanderer
**Origin Language:** Old Irish

Dorando | Dorand
**Meaning:** Adoring
**Origin Language:** Latin

Dorian | Doriano

**Also:** Dorinel | Dorin
**Meaning:** Of The Dorian People (The Name Of An Ancient Greek Tribe)
**Origin Language:** Ancient Greek

Dougal | Dugal
**Meaning:** Dark Stranger
**Origin Language:** Old Irish

Douglas | Doug, Dougie, Douglass
**Meaning:** Dark Water
**Origin Language:** Old Irish

Dovid | Dovyd
**Meaning:** Beloved
**Origin Language:** Hebrew

Doyle
**Meaning:** Dark Stranger
**Origin Language:** Old Irish

Draco | Drako
**Also:** Drake
**Meaning:** Dragon
**Origin Language:** Old English

Draven
**Also:** Dray | Drae, Draye, Dreye
**Meaning:** Precious (Common Slavic) / Phantom (English)
**Origin Language:** Common Slavic And Old English

Drew | Dre
**Meaning:** Manly / Brave Warrior
**Origin Language:** Ancient Greek

Driscoll | Driskoll
**Meaning:** Bearer Of News
**Origin Language:** Old Irish

Dritan | Driton
**Meaning:** Light
**Origin Language:** Albanian

Drogo

**Meaning:** Precious (Common Slavic) / Phantom (English)
**Origin Language:** Common Slavic And Old English

Drummond | Drumond
**Meaning:** From Near A Ridge
**Origin Language:** Scottish Gaelic

Drusus
**Meaning:** Dew / Dewy-Eyed
**Origin Language:** Latin

Drystan | Drest, Drestan, Drust, Drustan, Dryst
**Meaning:** Tumultuous
**Origin Language:** Ancient Celtic

Duarte
**Meaning:** Guardian Of Riches
**Origin Language:** Old English

Dudley | Dudlie
**Meaning:** From Dudda's Meadow / From A Round Meadow
**Origin Language:** Old English

Duff
**Meaning:** Black/Dark
**Origin Language:** Old Irish

Dugald
**Meaning:** Dark Stranger
**Origin Language:** Old Irish

Duilius | Duilio
**Meaning:** Warrior
**Origin Language:** Latin

Duncan
**Meaning:** Brunette Battler
**Origin Language:** Old Irish

Dunstan
**Meaning:** Dark Stone
**Origin Language:** Old English

Durans
**Also:** Durante
**Meaning:** Enduring
**Origin Language:** Latin

Durward
**Meaning:** Door Warden
**Origin Language:** Old English

Dustin | Dustie, Dusty
**Meaning:** Thor's Stone / Stone Of Thunder (Thor Is The Name Of The Norse God Of Thunder And Lightning)
**Origin Language:** Old Norse

Dwayne | Dewaine, Dewayne, Duane, Duwain, Duwaine, Dwain, Dwaine, Dwane
**Meaning:** Little Dark/Black One
**Origin Language:** Old Irish

Dwight
**Meaning:** Of Dionysos (Dionysos Is The Name Of The Greek God Of Wine, Vegetation, Fertility, Festivity, Ritual Madness, Religious Ecstasy, And Theatre)
**Origin Language:** Ancient Greek

Dylan | Dillan, Dillon
**Meaning:** Heads Towards The Tide Of The Sea
**Origin Language:** Welsh

# Chapter 5 - Names For Boys Beginning With E

Eadric | Eadrik, Edric, Edrik
**Meaning:** Wealth And Riches
**Origin Language:** Ancient Germanic And Old English And Old Norse (Cognates)

Ealair | Ealar, Eallair, Ellair
**Meaning:** Temple Chapel
**Origin Language:** Latin

Eamon | Eyman
**Meaning:** Wealthy Protector
**Origin Language:** Old English

Eaque | Eac, Eaco, Eacus, Eak,
Eako, Eakos
**Meaning:** Bewailing
**Origin Language:** Ancient Greek

Earl | Earle, Erle
**Meaning:** Noble / Earl
**Origin Language:** Old English

Easton
**Meaning:** From An Eastern Town
**Origin Language:** Old English

Ebden | Ebdon
**Meaning:** From A Farm With An Abbey
**Origin Language:** Old English

Eber
**Meaning:** The Region Beyond
**Origin Language:** Hebrew

Eberard | Ebbe, Eberardo,
Eberhard
**Meaning:** Hardy As A Boar
**Origin Language:** Ancient Germanic

Ebner | Ebnar, Ebnor, Ebnur
**Meaning:** My Father Is The Light
**Origin Language:** Hebrew

Ebrahim
**Meaning:** High Father Of Many
**Origin Language:** Hebrew

Ebron | Hebron
**Meaning:** Alliance
**Origin Language:** Hebrew

Eckart | Eckehard, Eckhard,
Eckhart, Ekkehard, Ekkehardt
**Meaning:** The Edge Of His Sword Is
Hardy
**Origin Language:** Ancient Germanic

Edber | Edbur
**Meaning:** Wealthy Castle
**Origin Language:** Old English

Eddard | Eddart, Eddeard,
Eddeart, Edeard, Edeart, Eidard,
Eidart, Eiddard, Eiddart, Eideard,
Eideart
**Meaning:** Warden Of Wealth
**Origin Language:** Old English

Eddie | Ed, Eddy
**Meaning:** A Short Form Of Any Of The
Numerous Names Beginning With Ed
**Origin Language:** Various

Edeel | Edeil, Edil
**Meaning:** Unbiased
**Origin Language:** Arabic

Eden
**Meaning:** Delight
**Origin Language:** Hebrew

Edgar | Eadgar, Eadgard,
Eadgardo, Edgard, Edgardo
**Meaning:** Spear Of Wealth
**Origin Language:** Old English

Edion
**Meaning:** Ode To A Hero
**Origin Language:** Ancient Greek

Edison | Eddison
**Meaning:** Wealthy Warrior
**Origin Language:** Old English

Edmund | Eadmond, Eadmund,
Edmond, Edmondo, Edmundo
**Meaning:** Wealthy Protector

**Origin Language:** Old English

Edmure | Edmer, Edmur
**Meaning:** Wealthy And Famous
**Origin Language:** Old English

Edon
**Meaning:** Shining One
**Origin Language:** Ancient Greek

Eduney
**Meaning:** From Eadwynn's Island / From A Rich And Friendly Island
**Origin Language:** Old English

Edur
**Meaning:** Snow
**Origin Language:** Basque

Edvart | Edevard, Edevart, Edvard, Edvardas, Edvardo, Edvards, Edvardt, Edvardus, Edvarto
**Meaning:** Warden Of Wealth
**Origin Language:** Old English

Edvin | Eadvin
**Meaning:** Wealthy And Friendly
**Origin Language:** Old English And Old Norse (Cognates)

Edwald | Eadwald, Edvaldo
**Meaning:** Wealthy Ruler
**Origin Language:** Old English

Edward | Eadward, Eadweard, Edi, Edo, Edoardo, Edouard, Edouard, Eduar, Eduard, Eduardas, Eduardito, Eduardo, Eduards, Eduardus, Eduart, Edwardt
**Meaning:** Warden Of Wealth
**Origin Language:** Old English

Edwin | Eadwin Eadwyn, Edwyn
**Meaning:** Wealthy And Friendly

**Origin Language:** Old English And Old Norse (Cognates)

Eero
**Meaning:** Ruler Of Forever
**Origin Language:** Old Norse

Egbert | Ecgberht, Ecgbert, Egberht
**Meaning:** The Bright Edge Of A Sword
**Origin Language:** Ancient Germanic And Old English (Cognates)

Egil | Egill
**Meaning:** Terror
**Origin Language:** Old Norse

Egon | Egan, Egano, Egen, Egeno, Eghan, Eghen, Eghon
**Meaning:** Sword's Edge
**Origin Language:** Ancient Germanic

Ehmet | Ehmed
**Meaning:** Praiseworthy
**Origin Language:** Arabic

Eike
**Meaning:** The Edge Of His Sword Is Hardy
**Origin Language:** Ancient Germanic

Eilam | Eylam
**Meaning:** Eternity
**Origin Language:** Hebrew

Eilert
**Meaning:** The Edge Of His Sword Is Hardy
**Origin Language:** Ancient Germanic

Eilian
**Meaning:** Sun
**Origin Language:** Ancient Greek

Einar | Einarr
**Meaning:** Solo Army
**Origin Language:** Old Norse

Eindrid
**Meaning:** Solo Rider
**Origin Language:** Old Norse

Einion | Enniaun
**Meaning:** Anvil
**Origin Language:** Old Welsh

Eiran
**Meaning:** Watchful
**Origin Language:** Hebrew

Eirian
**Meaning:** Beautiful
**Origin Language:** Welsh

Eitan | Eytan
**Also:** Eithan | Eythan
**Meaning:** Enduring
**Origin Language:** Hebrew

Eivind | Eyvind
**Meaning:** Victor Of Good Fortune
**Origin Language:** Old Norse

Ekain
**Meaning:** June
**Origin Language:** Basque

Ekbert | Ecberht, Ecbert, Ecgberht, Ecgbert, Ekberht
**Meaning:** The Bright Edge Of A Sword
**Origin Language:** Ancient Germanic And Old English (Cognates)

Ekin
**Meaning:** Harvest
**Origin Language:** Turkish

Eladio
**Meaning:** From Greece
**Origin Language:** Ancient Greek

Elam
**Meaning:** Eternity / Hidden

**Origin Language:** Hebrew

Elazar | Eleazar, Eliezer
**Meaning:** Helped By God
**Origin Language:** Hebrew

Elbert | Elberto
**Meaning:** Bright Noble
**Origin Language:** Ancient Germanic And Old English (Cognates)

Elbuin | Elbewin, Elboin, Elbuwin
**Meaning:** Friendly Elven One
**Origin Language:** Ancient Germanic

Eldar | Eldor
**Meaning:** Country Possessor
**Origin Language:** Ottoman Turkish And Persian (Cognates)

Eldon
**Meaning:** From An Old Homestead
**Origin Language:** Old English

Eldred
**Meaning:** Old Counsel
**Origin Language:** Old English

Eldridge
**Meaning:** Old And Rich / Noble And Rich
**Origin Language:** Ancient Germanic

Eldwin | Ealden, Ealdin, Ealdon, Ealdwin, Elden, Eldin, Eldo, Eldwen
**Meaning:** Friendly Old One
**Origin Language:** Ancient Germanic And Old English (Cognates)

Elfred | Elfredo, Elfrid
**Meaning:** Elven Counsel
**Origin Language:** Old English

Elham | Ealham, Ealhom, Elhom, Ellam, Ellom

**Meaning:** From A Homestead Near A Temple
**Origin Language:** Old English

**Elhanan | Elchanan**
**Meaning:** God Is Gracious
**Origin Language:** Hebrew

**Eli | Eliy, Ely**
**Meaning:** Ascending
**Origin Language:** Hebrew

**Eliah**
**Meaning:** My God Is God
**Origin Language:** Hebrew

**Eliakim | Eliakeim**
**Meaning:** God Rises
**Origin Language:** Hebrew

**Eliam | Eliyam, Elyam**
**Meaning:** Of God's People
**Origin Language:** Hebrew

**Elian | Elion**
**Meaning:** God Is My Light
**Origin Language:** Hebrew

**Elias**
**Meaning:** My God Is God
**Origin Language:** Hebrew

**Eliav | Eliab**
**Meaning:** God Is My Father
**Origin Language:** Hebrew

**Elidor | Eliodor, Eliodoro**
**Meaning:** The Sun's Gift
**Origin Language:** Ancient Greek

**Elidyr | Elidir, Elidor, Elidur**
**Meaning:** Steel
**Origin Language:** Old Welsh

**Eliel**
**Meaning:** My God Is God
**Origin Language:** Hebrew

**Eligio | Eligius**
**Meaning:** Chosen
**Origin Language:** Latin

**Elijah**
**Meaning:** My God Is God
**Origin Language:** Hebrew

**Elio**
**Meaning:** Sun
**Origin Language:** Ancient Greek

**Eliod | Eliodo**
**Meaning:** The Sun's Gift
**Origin Language:** Ancient Greek

**Elior**
**Meaning:** God Is My Light
**Origin Language:** Hebrew

**Eliou**
**Also:** Elis
**Meaning:** My God Is God
**Origin Language:** Hebrew

**Eliseo | Eliseus**
**Also:** Elisha | Elishua, Eliysha
**Meaning:** My God Is Salvation
**Origin Language:** Hebrew

**Eliud | Elioud**
**Meaning:** God Is Grandeur
**Origin Language:** Hebrew

**Elkan | Elkanah**
**Meaning:** Acquired By God
**Origin Language:** Hebrew

**Elland | Ealand, Ealant, Ealland, Eallant, Eland, Elant, Ellant**
**Meaning:** From An Island
**Origin Language:** Old English

**Ellard | Elard**
**Meaning:** Noble Guard

**Origin Language:** Ancient Germanic

**Ellgar | Elgar, Elger, Ellger**
**Meaning:** Noble Spear
**Origin Language:** Ancient Germanic

**Ellington**
**Meaning:** From Ealda's Town / From An Old Town
**Origin Language:** Old English

**Elliott | Eliot, Eliott, Elliot**
**Meaning:** My God Is God
**Origin Language:** Hebrew

**Ellis**
**Meaning:** Kind
**Origin Language:** Old Welsh

**Ellison**
**Meaning:** My God Is God
**Origin Language:** Hebrew

**Ellvar | Elvar**
**Meaning:** Elven Army
**Origin Language:** Ancient Germanic And Old English And Old Norse (Cognates)

**Ellyre | Ellar, Ellerie, Ellery**
**Meaning:** Light-Hearted
**Origin Language:** Ancient Greek

**Elmer | Elmar, Elmaro, Elmero, Elmir, Elmiro**
**Meaning:** Famous Noble
**Origin Language:** Ancient Germanic And Old English (Cognates)

**Elmere**
**Meaning:** From Near A Lake With Eels
**Origin Language:** Old English

**Elnathan**
**Meaning:** God Has Given
**Origin Language:** Hebrew

**Elon**
**Meaning:** Oak Tree
**Origin Language:** Hebrew

**Elouan**
**Meaning:** Light
**Origin Language:** Old Breton

**Elov | Elof, Eluf**
**Meaning:** Preserving His Heritage Always
**Origin Language:** Old Norse

**Eloy | Eloi**
**Meaning:** Chosen
**Origin Language:** Latin

**Elred**
**Meaning:** Noble Counsel
**Origin Language:** Old English

**Elric | Elrick, Elrik**
**Meaning:** Rich Noble
**Origin Language:** Ancient Germanic And Old English (Cognates)

**Elrond**
**Meaning:** Star Dome
**Origin Language:** Sindarian (Fictional Language Devised By J. R. R. Tolkien For Use In His Fantasy Stories, Such As Lord Of The Rings)

**Elroy | Elroi**
**Meaning:** The King
**Origin Language:** French

**Elsdon**
**Meaning:** From Elli's Valley / From An Old Valley
**Origin Language:** Old English

**Elstan**
**Meaning:** Stone Of Nobility
**Origin Language:** Old English

**Elton**

**Meaning:** From Aethelflaed's Town / From A Noble Beauty's Town
**Origin Language:** Old English

Eluar
**Meaning:** Elven Army
**Origin Language:** Ancient Germanic And Old English And Old Norse (Cognates)

Eluin | Eluino, Eluwin
**Meaning:** Friendly Noble
**Origin Language:** Ancient Germanic And Old English (Cognates)

Eluney
**Meaning:** Gives
**Origin Language:** Mapuche

Elvan
**Meaning:** Hues
**Origin Language:** Turkish

Elver | Elv, Elvi, Elvie, Elvy
**Meaning:** Elven
**Origin Language:** Ancient Germanic And Old English And Old Norse (Cognates)

Elvin | Elvyn
**Meaning:** Friendly Noble
**Origin Language:** Ancient Germanic And Old English (Cognates)

Elvio | Elvius
**Meaning:** Has Hair The Shade Of Honey
**Origin Language:** Latin

Elvis | Elvise, Elviss, Elvys
**Meaning:** All Wise
**Origin Language:** Old Norse

Elward | Elweard
**Meaning:** Noble Warden
**Origin Language:** Ancient Germanic

Elwin | Elwyn
**Meaning:** Friendly Noble
**Origin Language:** Ancient Germanic And Old English (Cognates)

Elwood
**Meaning:** From The Elder Tree Woods
**Origin Language:** Old English

Emelric | Emelrich, Emelrik
**Meaning:** Rich Worker
**Origin Language:** Ancient Germanic

Emerens | Emerentius
**Meaning:** Has Earned What He Deserves
**Origin Language:** Latin

Emeric | Emmerich
**Also:** Emerson | Emmerson
**Also:** Emery | Emerie, Emorie, Emory
**Meaning:** King Of The Homeland
**Origin Language:** Ancient Germanic

Emidio | Emidius
**Meaning:** Almond Tree
**Origin Language:** Latin

Emil | Emiel, Emile
**Also:** Emiliano | Emilian, Emilien, Emiliyan
**Also:** Emilio | Emilios
**Meaning:** Rival
**Origin Language:** Latin

Emin | Emeen
**Meaning:** Trustworthy
**Origin Language:** Arabic

Emir
**Meaning:** Commander / Prince
**Origin Language:** Arabic

Emlyn | Emlen, Emlin
**Meaning:** From Emlyn (An Ancient

Region In Wales) / Follows After Another
**Origin Language:** Welsh

Emmanuel | Emanouel, Emanouil, Emanuel, Emanuele, Emanuil, Emmanouel, Emmanouil, Emmanuele, Emmanuhel, Emmanuil
**Meaning:** God Is With Us
**Origin Language:** Hebrew

Emmett | Emmet, Emmit, Emmitt
**Meaning:** Universal
**Origin Language:** Ancient Germanic

Emory | Emorie
**Meaning:** Home Ruler
**Origin Language:** Ancient Germanic

Emre
**Meaning:** Friend
**Origin Language:** Turkish

Emrys | Emris
**Meaning:** Immortal
**Origin Language:** Ancient Greek

Emyr
**Meaning:** King
**Origin Language:** Welsh

Endel
**Meaning:** Manly / Brave Warrior
**Origin Language:** Ancient Greek

Ender
**Meaning:** Very Rare
**Origin Language:** Turkish

Endre | Endri
**Meaning:** Solo Rider
**Origin Language:** Old Norse

Endrit
**Meaning:** Light

**Origin Language:** Albanian

Enfred
**Meaning:** Eagle Of Peace
**Origin Language:** Ancient Germanic

Engel
**Meaning:** Angle (The Name Of A Germanic Tribe)
**Origin Language:** Ancient Germanic

Engram
**Meaning:** Raven Of The Angles (The Name Of A Germanic Tribe)
**Origin Language:** Ancient Germanic

Enis | Enes
**Meaning:** Friendly
**Origin Language:** Arabic

Ennis
**Meaning:** From An Island
**Origin Language:** Old Irish

Enoch | Enok
**Meaning:** Dedicated
**Origin Language:** Hebrew

Enos | Enosh
**Meaning:** Mortal
**Origin Language:** Hebrew

Enrique | Emric, Emrico, Emrik, Enric, Enrico, Enrik
**Meaning:** Sovereign Of The Homeland
**Origin Language:** Ancient Germanic

Ensio
**Meaning:** First
**Origin Language:** Finnish

Enver
**Meaning:** Illuminated
**Origin Language:** Arabic

Enzo | Anzo
**Meaning:** Giant

**Origin Language:** Ancient Germanic

**Ephraim** | Efraim, Efrayim, Efrem, Ephrayim, Ephrem
**Meaning:** Fruitful
**Origin Language:** Hebrew

**Eraldo** | Erald
**Meaning:** Of The Ruling Army
**Origin Language:** Old English

**Eran**
**Meaning:** Watchful
**Origin Language:** Hebrew

**Erasmus** | Erasmo, Erasmos, Erazem, Ermo
**Meaning:** Beloved
**Origin Language:** Ancient Greek

**Erast** | Erastos, Erastus, Rastus
**Meaning:** Beloved
**Origin Language:** Ancient Greek

**Erbert** | Erb, Erberto, Erbie, Erbrecht, Erby, Eribert, Eriberto
**Meaning:** Bright Warrior
**Origin Language:** Ancient Germanic

**Ercole**
**Meaning:** Hera's Glory (Hera Is The Name Of The Greek Goddess Of Marriage, Women, Marital Harmony, And The Protector Of Women During Childbirth)
**Origin Language:** Ancient Greek

**Ereald** | Erealdo, Eriald, Erialdo
**Meaning:** Of The Ruling Army
**Origin Language:** Old English

**Erebus** | Erebos
**Meaning:** Darkness
**Origin Language:** Ancient Greek

**Eren**

**Meaning:** Saint
**Origin Language:** Turkish

**Erez**
**Meaning:** Cedar Tree
**Origin Language:** Hebrew

**Erhard**
**Meaning:** Respectful And Hardy
**Origin Language:** Ancient Germanic

**Eric** | Eiric, Eirik, Erec, Erek, Erich, Erick, Erico, Erik, Eryk
**Meaning:** Ruler Of Forever
**Origin Language:** Old Norse

**Erion** | Eryon
**Meaning:** Our Wind
**Origin Language:** Albanian

**Erkell** | Erkill
**Meaning:** Stirrer Of The Divine Cauldron
**Origin Language:** Old Norse

**Erland** | Erlend
**Meaning:** Foreigner
**Origin Language:** Old Norse

**Erlewin** | Erluin, Erlwin
**Meaning:** Friendly Warrior
**Origin Language:** Ancient Germanic

**Erling** | Erlin
**Meaning:** Descendant Of The Jarl
**Origin Language:** Old Norse

**Erlott** | Erlotto
**Meaning:** Rascal
**Origin Language:** Old French

**Erman** | Ermano
**Also:** Ermand
**Meaning:** Army Man
**Origin Language:** Ancient Germanic

## Ermias
**Meaning:** God Will Uplift
**Origin Language:** Hebrew

## Ermin
**Meaning:** Universal
**Origin Language:** Ancient Germanic

## Ermir
**Meaning:** Good Wind
**Origin Language:** Albanian

## Ermis | Ermes
**Meaning:** Of Hermes (Hermes Is The Name Of The Greek God Of Boundaries, Roads And Travelers, Thieves, Athletes, Shepherds, Commerce, Speed, Cunning, Wit And Sleep, Psychopomp And Divine Messenger)
**Origin Language:** Ancient Greek

## Ermon
**Meaning:** Army Man
**Origin Language:** Ancient Germanic

## Ernest | Earnest, Earnesto, Earnestus, Ern, Ernesto, Ernestus, Ernie, Ernst, Ernust, Erny
**Meaning:** Earnest
**Origin Language:** Ancient Germanic

## Ernold
**Meaning:** From A Valley Of Eagles
**Origin Language:** Old English

## Erod | Erodion
**Meaning:** Ode To A Hero
**Origin Language:** Ancient Greek

## Erol
**Meaning:** Brave
**Origin Language:** Turkish

## Eros
**Meaning:** Love
**Origin Language:** Ancient Greek

## Errol
**Meaning:** From Errol (Scotland) / Man Of Courage
**Origin Language:** Scottish Gaelic

## Ervin | Ervyn
**Meaning:** Friend Of The Boars
**Origin Language:** Ancient Germanic And Old English (Cognates)

## Erwan | Erwann
**Meaning:** Yew Tree
**Origin Language:** Ancient Germanic

## Erwin | Erwyn
**Meaning:** Friend Of The Boars
**Origin Language:** Ancient Germanic And Old English (Cognates)

## Esaias
**Meaning:** God Is Salvation
**Origin Language:** Hebrew

## Esben
**Also:** Esber
**Meaning:** Bear Deity
**Origin Language:** Old Norse

## Esdras | Ezdras
**Meaning:** Helper
**Origin Language:** Hebrew

## Eser
**Meaning:** Achievement
**Origin Language:** Turkish

## Eskender | Eskandar
**Meaning:** Mankind's Defender
**Origin Language:** Ancient Greek

## Esmail | Esmaeel, Esmaeil
**Meaning:** God Hears
**Origin Language:** Hebrew

## Esmond | Esmond, Esmund
**Meaning:** Graceful Protector
**Origin Language:** Old English

Espen
**Meaning:** Bear Deity
**Origin Language:** Old Norse

Esteban
**Also:** Estevo
**Meaning:** Wears The Conqueror's Wreath
**Origin Language:** Ancient Greek

Eteris | Etere, Eterie, Etero
**Meaning:** Ether / Heaven
**Origin Language:** Ancient Greek

Ethan | Etan
**Meaning:** Enduring
**Origin Language:** Hebrew

Ethon
**Meaning:** Fiery
**Origin Language:** Ancient Greek

Euan
**Meaning:** Well-Born
**Origin Language:** Ancient Greek

Euander | Euandros, Euandrus
**Meaning:** The Good Of Mankind
**Origin Language:** Ancient Greek

Euarist | Euaristo, Euaristos, Euaristus
**Meaning:** Well-Pleasing
**Origin Language:** Ancient Greek

Eudes
**Meaning:** Wealthy
**Origin Language:** Ancient Germanic And Old English And Old Norse (Cognates)

Eudox | Eudoxos
**Meaning:** Good Reputation
**Origin Language:** Ancient Greek

Eugene | Eugen, Eugenio, Eugenios, Eugenius
**Meaning:** Well-Born
**Origin Language:** Ancient Greek

Eumon | Euman, Eumann
**Meaning:** Wealthy Protector
**Origin Language:** Old English

Euric | Eurico, Eurik, Euriko
**Meaning:** Ruler Of Forever
**Origin Language:** Old Norse

Euryal | Euryalos, Euryalus
**Meaning:** Broad Halo
**Origin Language:** Ancient Greek

Eustace | Eustache, Eustachie, Eustachio, Eustachius, Eustachy, Eustachys
**Meaning:** Grows/Harvests Grain Well
**Origin Language:** Ancient Greek

Eustath | Eustathios, Eustathius
**Meaning:** Stable
**Origin Language:** Ancient Greek

Evan
**Meaning:** Graced By God
**Origin Language:** Hebrew

Evander | Evandros, Evandrus
**Meaning:** The Good Of Mankind
**Origin Language:** Ancient Greek

Evangelos | Evangelus
**Meaning:** Bringer Of Good News
**Origin Language:** Ancient Greek

Evaric | Evarik
**Meaning:** Ruler Of Forever
**Origin Language:** Old Norse

Evarist | Evaristo, Evaristos, Evaristus
**Meaning:** Well-Pleasing

**Origin Language:** Ancient Greek

Even
**Meaning:** Victor Of Good Fortune
**Origin Language:** Old Norse

Everard | Everart, Evrard
**Meaning:** Hardy As A Boar
**Origin Language:** Ancient Germanic

Everest | Everist
**Meaning:** From Évreux (A Commune In Normandy, France) / Yew Tree / Wields Weapons Made From A Yew Tree
**Origin Language:** Gaulish

Everett | Everet
**Meaning:** Hardy As A Boar
**Origin Language:** Ancient Germanic

Evereux | Evreux, Evreux
**Meaning:** From Évreux (A Commune In Normandy, France) / Yew Tree / Wields Weapons Made From A Yew Tree
**Origin Language:** Gaulish

Everitt | Evert
**Meaning:** Hardy As A Boar
**Origin Language:** Ancient Germanic

Everix
**Meaning:** From Évreux (A Commune In Normandy, France) / Yew Tree / Wields Weapons Made From A Yew Tree
**Origin Language:** Gaulish

Evren
**Meaning:** Cosmos / The Universe
**Origin Language:** Turkish

Evron
**Meaning:** Servitude
**Origin Language:** Hebrew

Ewald
**Meaning:** The Law That Rules
**Origin Language:** Ancient Germanic

Ewan | Ewann, Ewen, Ewenn
**Meaning:** Born Of The Yew Tree
**Origin Language:** Old Irish

Ewart | Uwart
**Meaning:** From An Enclosure With A River
**Origin Language:** Old English

Ewell | Ewel, Ewil, Ewill
**Meaning:** Well / Spring (Of Water)
**Origin Language:** Old English

Eyalon | Eyal
**Meaning:** Gazelle
**Origin Language:** Hebrew

Eydan | Eyden, Eydin
**Meaning:** Fire
**Origin Language:** Old Irish

Eymard | Eimard
**Meaning:** From A Hardy Home
**Origin Language:** Ancient Germanic

Eymen
**Meaning:** Lucky
**Origin Language:** Arabic

Ezechias | Ezekias
**Meaning:** God Strengthens
**Origin Language:** Hebrew

Ezekiel | Ezechiel, Ezequiel
**Meaning:** God Will Strengthen
**Origin Language:** Hebrew

Ezio | Esio
**Meaning:** Eagle
**Origin Language:** Latin

Ezra | Ezrah, Ezras
**Meaning:** Helper
**Origin Language:** Hebrew

# Chapter 6 - Names For Boys Beginning With F

Fabian | Fabiano, Fabianus, Fabien, Fabio, Fabius
**Meaning:** Shaped Like A Bean
**Origin Language:** Latin

Faizel | Faisal, Faisel, Faizal, Faysal, Faysel
**Meaning:** Arbiter
**Origin Language:** Arabic

Fakhri
**Meaning:** Intellectual / Glorious
**Origin Language:** Arabic

Falk
**Meaning:** Falcon
**Origin Language:** German

Fane
**Meaning:** Wears The Conqueror's Crown
**Origin Language:** Ancient Greek

Faramond | Faramund, Faramundo
**Meaning:** Journeying For Protection
**Origin Language:** Ancient Germanic

Faris
**Meaning:** Horseman / Knight
**Origin Language:** Arabic

Farley | Farlee, Farleigh, Farlie, Farly
**Meaning:** From A Meadow Of Ferns
**Origin Language:** Old English

Faron | Faro
**Meaning:** Journey
**Origin Language:** Ancient Germanic

Farooq | Farouk, Faruk, Faruq
**Meaning:** Knows Right From Wrong
**Origin Language:** Arabic

Farquhar | Fearchar, Ferchar
**Meaning:** Friend Of Man
**Origin Language:** Old Irish

Farrell | Farell
**Meaning:** Man Of Boldness
**Origin Language:** Old Irish

Farrukh | Farrokh
**Meaning:** Happy
**Origin Language:** Persian

Federico | Federigo, Federiko
**Meaning:** Peaceful And Rich
**Origin Language:** Ancient Germanic

Fedor | Fedir
**Meaning:** God's Gift
**Origin Language:** Ancient Greek

Felicien | Feliciano, Felicianus, Felicius
**Meaning:** Lucky
**Origin Language:** Latin

Felin | Felinus, Felyn
**Meaning:** Of Cats
**Origin Language:** Latin

Felipe | Felip, Filip, Filipe, Filipp, Filippo, Filippos, Filippu
**Meaning:** Lover Of Horses
**Origin Language:** Ancient Greek

Felix | Feliks, Felis, Phelix
**Meaning:** Lucky
**Origin Language:** Latin

Fen
**Meaning:** Perfume / Strive
**Origin Language:** Chinese

Fenris

**Meaning:** Marsh Wolf / Swamp Wolf
**Origin Language:** Old Norse

Fenton
**Meaning:** From A Marshy Town
**Origin Language:** Old English

Feodor | Fyodor
**Meaning:** God's Gift
**Origin Language:** Ancient Greek

Feofil | Feophil, Fiofil, Fiophil
**Meaning:** Loves God
**Origin Language:** Ancient Greek

Ferdinand | Ferdie, Ferdinando,
Ferdo, Ferdy, Ferdynand
**Meaning:** On A Daring Journey
**Origin Language:** Ancient Germanic

Fergal | Fearghal
**Meaning:** Man Of Boldness
**Origin Language:** Old Irish

Fergus | Fearghas, Fearghus,
Fergie, Fergy
**Meaning:** Man Of Strength
**Origin Language:** Old Irish

Feridun | Faridoon, Fereydoun,
Feridon
**Meaning:** The Third
**Origin Language:** Persian

Fernando | Fernand
**Also:** Ferran
**Meaning:** On A Daring Journey
**Origin Language:** Ancient Germanic

Ferrer
**Meaning:** Blacksmith
**Origin Language:** Catalan

Ferro
**Meaning:** Iron
**Origin Language:** Italian

Fidelis | Fedele, Fidel
**Meaning:** Faithful
**Origin Language:** Latin

Filbert | Filibert, Filiberto
**Meaning:** Very Bright
**Origin Language:** Ancient Germanic

Fillib | Filib
**Meaning:** Lover Of Horses
**Origin Language:** Ancient Greek

Fillin
**Meaning:** Little Wolf
**Origin Language:** Old Irish

Finbar | Finbarr, Finnbar,
Finnbarr, Fionnbarr, Fionnbharr
**Meaning:** Fair Haired / Bright Headed
**Origin Language:** Old Irish

Findlay | Findley
**Meaning:** Blessed Warrior / Bright
Warrior
**Origin Language:** Scottish Gaelic

Fingal | Fingall
**Meaning:** Blessed Courage / Bright
Courage
**Origin Language:** Old Irish

Finian | Finien, Finion, Finnian,
Finnien, Finnion
**Meaning:** Blessed / Bright
**Origin Language:** Old Irish

Finley | Finlay, Finnlay, Finnley
**Meaning:** Blessed Warrior / Bright
Warrior
**Origin Language:** Scottish Gaelic

Finn | Finnr, Finnur
**Meaning:** From Finland
**Origin Language:** Old Norse

Finnegan | Finegan
**Meaning:** Blessed / Bright
**Origin Language:** Old Irish

Fintan | Fionntan, Fiontan
**Meaning:** Old And Blessed / Old And Bright / Blessed Fire / Bright Fire
**Origin Language:** Old Irish

Fionn | Fion
**Meaning:** Blessed / Bright
**Origin Language:** Old Irish

Fisher
**Meaning:** Fisher
**Origin Language:** English

Fitzroy | Fitz
**Meaning:** Son Of The King
**Origin Language:** Old French

Flanagan | Flan, Flann, Flannagan
**Meaning:** Blood Red
**Origin Language:** Old Irish

Flavian | Flaviano, Flavianus, Flavien, Flavio, Flavius
**Meaning:** Has Golden/Yellow Hair
**Origin Language:** Latin

Fletcher | Fletch
**Meaning:** Arrow Maker
**Origin Language:** Old English

Flint
**Meaning:** Flint
**Origin Language:** English

Florent | Florens, Florentin, Florentino, Florentinus, Florentius, Florenz
**Meaning:** Flourishing
**Origin Language:** Latin

Florian | Floriano, Florianus, Florin, Florinus, Florus

**Meaning:** Flower
**Origin Language:** Latin

Floyd
**Meaning:** Grey/Gray
**Origin Language:** Welsh

Flynn | Flin, Flinn, Flyn
**Meaning:** Blood Red
**Origin Language:** Old Irish

Folant
**Meaning:** Healthy
**Origin Language:** Latin

Foley
**Meaning:** Pirate
**Origin Language:** Old Irish

Folker | Folcher
**Meaning:** Of The People's Army
**Origin Language:** Ancient Germanic

Forbes
**Meaning:** Lives In A Field
**Origin Language:** Scottish Gaelic

Ford
**Meaning:** From Near A Ford
**Origin Language:** Old English

Forrest | Forest
**Meaning:** Forest
**Origin Language:** English

Foster
**Meaning:** From A Forest
**Origin Language:** Old French

Fox
**Meaning:** Fox
**Origin Language:** English

Fraener
**Meaning:** Embracer
**Origin Language:** Old Norse

Francis | Ffransis
**Also:** Francisco | Francesco,
Franciscus, Francisque
**Also:** Frank | Franc, Frankey,
Frankie, Franko, Franky
**Meaning:** Of The Franks (The Name Of
A Germanic Tribe) (Ancient Germanic) /
Javelin-Like (Latin)
**Origin Language:** Ancient Germanic
And Latin

Franklin | Franklina, Franklyn
**Meaning:** Freeman
**Origin Language:** Old English

Franz | Frans
**Meaning:** Of The Franks (The Name Of
A Germanic Tribe) (Ancient Germanic) /
Javelin-Like (Latin)
**Origin Language:** Ancient Germanic
And Latin

Fraser | Frazier
**Meaning:** From Fresel (Unknown
Location Most Likely Once Existed
Somewhere In France)
**Origin Language:** Scottish Gaelic

Fredenand
**Meaning:** Strives For Peace
**Origin Language:** Ancient Germanic

Frederick | Fred, Freddie, Freddy,
Frederic, Frederico, Frederik,
Fredo, Fredric, Fredrick, Fredrik,
Friderik, Friduric
**Meaning:** Peaceful And Rich
**Origin Language:** Ancient Germanic

Frediano
**Meaning:** Cold
**Origin Language:** Latin

Frey
**Meaning:** Lord
**Origin Language:** Old Norse

Fritz
**Meaning:** Peaceful And Rich
**Origin Language:** Ancient Germanic

Fulbert
**Meaning:** The People's Bright One
**Origin Language:** Ancient Germanic

Fulke | Folke, Fulco, Fulk
**Meaning:** Of The People
**Origin Language:** Ancient Germanic
And Old Norse (Cognates)

Fulton
**Meaning:** From A Hill Where Birds
Frequent
**Origin Language:** Old English

Fynn | Finn
**Meaning:** Blessed / Bright
**Origin Language:** Old Irish

# Chapter 7 - Names For Boys Beginning With G

Gabe
**Meaning:** God Is My Strength
**Origin Language:** Hebrew

Gabin | Gabino, Gabinus
**Meaning:** From Gabii (An Ancient
Town Located Just Outside Of Rome)
**Origin Language:** Latin

Gabriel | Gabirel, Gabrail, Gabrel,
Gabri, Gabrie, Gabrielus, Gabrilo,
Gabriyel
**Meaning:** God Is My Strength
**Origin Language:** Hebrew

Gaddiel | Gaddiyel, Gadiel
**Meaning:** God Is My Fortune

**Origin Language:** Hebrew

Gage | Gaige, Gayge
**Meaning:** Pledger / Moneylender
**Origin Language:** Old French

Gaheris | Gaherys
**Meaning:** Courage
**Origin Language:** Welsh

Gai | Guy
**Meaning:** From A Ravine
**Origin Language:** Hebrew

Gair | Gare, Garey
**Meaning:** Spear
**Origin Language:** Ancient Germanic And Old Norse (Cognates)

Gaius | Gaios
**Meaning:** Rejoice
**Origin Language:** Latin

Galen | Galenos
**Meaning:** Calm
**Origin Language:** Ancient Greek

Galileo | Gailiee, Galil, Galilaeus, Galilaios, Galilee
**Meaning:** Galilean / From Galilee (A Mountainous Region In Israel)
**Origin Language:** Hebrew

Gallagher
**Meaning:** Fond Of Strangers
**Origin Language:** Old Irish

Garen
**Meaning:** Spear
**Origin Language:** Ancient Germanic And Old Norse (Cognates)

Gareth | Gaz
**Meaning:** Courage
**Origin Language:** Welsh

Garfield

**Meaning:** From A Triangular Piece Of Land
**Origin Language:** Old English

Garnier
**Meaning:** Wary Soldier
**Origin Language:** Ancient Germanic

Garrett | Garret, Garrit
**Meaning:** Spear Of Hardiness
**Origin Language:** Ancient Germanic

Garrick | Garick, Garric, Garrik
**Meaning:** Oak Tree Grove
**Origin Language:** Occitan

Garsea
**Meaning:** Young
**Origin Language:** Basque

Garth
**Meaning:** Gardener
**Origin Language:** Old Norse

Garvan
**Meaning:** Little Rough One
**Origin Language:** Old Irish

Gary | Garie, Garrie, Garry
**Meaning:** Spear
**Origin Language:** Ancient Germanic And Old Norse (Cognates)

Gaspard | Gaspar, Gaspare, Gasparo
**Meaning:** Treasurer
**Origin Language:** Hebrew

Gaston | Gasto, Gastone
**Meaning:** Guest
**Origin Language:** Ancient Germanic

Gaultier | Gualterio, Gualtiero
**Also:** Gauthier | Gautier
**Meaning:** Army Ruler
**Origin Language:** Ancient Germanic

**Gautvin**
**Meaning:** Friendly Goth (The Name Of A Germanic Tribe)
**Origin Language:** Ancient Germanic

**Gavin | Gauvain, Gauvin, Gavain**
**Meaning:** Hawk Of May / From A Field Where Hawks Frequent
**Origin Language:** Welsh

**Gavriel | Gavirel, Gavrail, Gavrel, Gavri, Gavrie, Gavrielus, Gavrilo, Gavriyel**
**Meaning:** God Is My Strength
**Origin Language:** Hebrew

**Gedeon | Gedion**
**Also:** Gedon | Gedown
**Meaning:** He Who Cuts Down (Other People Or Things)
**Origin Language:** Hebrew

**Geirr | Geir**
**Meaning:** Spear
**Origin Language:** Ancient Germanic And Old Norse (Cognates)

**Gemariah | Gemaryah**
**Meaning:** God Has Completed
**Origin Language:** Hebrew

**Gendrick | Gendric, Gendrik**
**Also:** Gendrix
**Also:** Gendry | Gendrie
**Meaning:** King Of The Homeland
**Origin Language:** Ancient Germanic

**Gene | Geno**
**Meaning:** Well-Born
**Origin Language:** Ancient Greek

**Genesis | Genesio, Genesius**
**Meaning:** Origin / Horoscope
**Origin Language:** Latin

**Gennady | Genadi, Gennadi,**

**Gennadie, Gennadios, Gennadius, Gennadiy, Ghenadie**
**Meaning:** Calm
**Origin Language:** Ancient Greek

**Gentian | Genti, Gentius**
**Meaning:** Gentian (A Flowering Plant)
**Origin Language:** Albanian

**Geoffrey | Geffrey, Geoff, Geofferie, Geoffery, Geoffre, Geoffrie, Geoffroi, Geoffroy, Geoffry**
**Meaning:** Divine Peace
**Origin Language:** Ancient Germanic

**Geordie | Geordey, Geordi, Geordy**
**Also:** George | Georg, Georgei, Georges, Georgi, Georgie, Georgii, Georgios, Georgius, Georgiy, Georgo, Georgy, Giorgi, Giorgino, Giorgio, Giorgos, Gorgi
**Meaning:** Farmer
**Origin Language:** Ancient Greek

**Geraint**
**Meaning:** Of The Elders
**Origin Language:** Latin

**Gerald | Geraldo, Geraldus, Gerhold, Gerold, Girald, Giraldo**
**Meaning:** Spear Of Power
**Origin Language:** Ancient Germanic

**Gerard | Gerardo, Gerhard, Gerhardt, Gerhart, Gerrard, Gerrardo, Gherard, Gherardo**
**Meaning:** Spear Of Hardiness
**Origin Language:** Ancient Germanic

**Geraud**
**Meaning:** Spear Of Power
**Origin Language:** Ancient Germanic

Gerbern | Gerben
**Meaning:** Spear Of The Bear
**Origin Language:** Ancient Germanic

Gereon
**Meaning:** Of The Elders
**Origin Language:** Latin

Gerlach
**Meaning:** Plays With A Spear
**Origin Language:** Ancient Germanic

Germain | Germano, Germanus
**Meaning:** Brother
**Origin Language:** Latin

Gernot
**Meaning:** Crushes With Spears
**Origin Language:** Ancient Germanic

Gero | Gerro
**Meaning:** Spear
**Origin Language:** Ancient Germanic And Old Norse (Cognates)

Gerolt | Gearalt, Gearolt, Gerallt, Gerollt, Girallt, Giralt, Girollt, Girolt
**Meaning:** Spear Of Power
**Origin Language:** Ancient Germanic

Geront | Gerontius
**Meaning:** Of The Elders
**Origin Language:** Latin

Gerry | Geri, Gerrie, Gery
**Meaning:** Spear Of Power
**Origin Language:** Ancient Germanic

Gerulf | Garulf, Girulf
**Meaning:** Spear Of The Wolf
**Origin Language:** Ancient Germanic

Gervais | Gervaas, Gervas, Gervase, Gervasi, Gervasio, Gervasios, Gervasius
**Meaning:** Strong Spear
**Origin Language:** Ancient Germanic

Gianni | Gian, Gianis, Giannino, Giannis
**Meaning:** God Is Gracious
**Origin Language:** Hebrew

Gideon | Gidion, Gidon, Gidown
**Meaning:** He Who Cuts Down (Other People Or Things)
**Origin Language:** Hebrew

Giffard
**Meaning:** Gifted With Hardiness
**Origin Language:** Ancient Germanic

Gil | Gyl
**Meaning:** Happiness
**Origin Language:** Hebrew

Gilbert | Gib, Gilberto
**Meaning:** Pledge Of Brightness
**Origin Language:** Ancient Germanic

Gildo
**Meaning:** Universal Sacrifice
**Origin Language:** Ancient Germanic

Gilead | Gilad
**Meaning:** Heaped Stones Of Testimony
**Origin Language:** Hebrew

Gilen
**Meaning:** Desires Protection
**Origin Language:** Ancient Germanic

Giles | Gyles
**Meaning:** Young Goat
**Origin Language:** Latin

Gilford
**Meaning:** From A Golden Ford
**Origin Language:** Old English

Gillespie
**Meaning:** Bishop's Servant

**Origin Language:** Old Irish

Gillis | Gilles
**Meaning:** Young Goat
**Origin Language:** Latin

Gilmar
**Meaning:** Pledge Of Fame
**Origin Language:** Ancient Germanic

Gilmore | Gilmer, Gilmor
**Meaning:** Servant Of Mary
**Origin Language:** Old Irish

Gilroy | Gillaruad
**Meaning:** Red-Haired Boy
**Origin Language:** Old Irish

Giovanni
**Meaning:** God Is Gracious
**Origin Language:** Hebrew

Gisbert
**Meaning:** Pledge Of Brightness
**Origin Language:** Ancient Germanic

Gislen | Gisil, Gislenus, Gislin
**Meaning:** Pledge
**Origin Language:** Ancient Germanic

Giuseppe | Josepe
**Meaning:** God Will Add
**Origin Language:** Hebrew

Gladwin | Gladwyn
**Meaning:** Bright And Friendly
**Origin Language:** Old English

Glendower | Glyndwr
**Meaning:** Valley Water
**Origin Language:** Welsh

Glenn | Glen
**Meaning:** From A Valley
**Origin Language:** Welsh

Glynd | Glind, Glynde
**Meaning:** From A Fenced Enclosure
**Origin Language:** Old English

Glynn | Glin, Glinn, Glyn
**Meaning:** From A Valley
**Origin Language:** Welsh

Goddard | Godehard, Gotthard
**Meaning:** Divine And Hardy
**Origin Language:** Ancient Germanic

Godfrey | Godferie, Godfery, Godfre, Godfrie, Godfroi, Godfroy, Godfry
**Meaning:** Godly Peace
**Origin Language:** Ancient Germanic

Godric | Godrik
**Meaning:** God's Ruler
**Origin Language:** Old English

Godwin | Godwyn
**Meaning:** God's Friend
**Origin Language:** Old English

Gomer
**Meaning:** Complete
**Origin Language:** Hebrew

Gomes | Gomez
**Meaning:** Man
**Origin Language:** Ancient Germanic

Goran
**Meaning:** Man Of The Mountains
**Origin Language:** Common Slavic

Gordan
**Meaning:** Dignified
**Origin Language:** Common Slavic

Gordian | Gordianus
**Meaning:** From Gordium (Which Means "City" In Phrygian) (An Ancient Anatolian City Which Was Located In What Is Now Northwestern Turkey)
**Origin Language:** Latin

Gordon | Gord, Gorden, Gordie, Gordy
**Meaning:** From A Spacious Fortress
**Origin Language:** Scottish Gaelic

Govannon | Gofannon
**Meaning:** Smith
**Origin Language:** Old Welsh

Grady | Gradie
**Meaning:** Noble / Illustrious
**Origin Language:** Old Irish

Graham | Graeme, Grahame
**Meaning:** From A Gravelly Homestead
**Origin Language:** Old English

Granger | Grangier
**Meaning:** Farm Bailiff
**Origin Language:** Old French

Grant
**Meaning:** Great
**Origin Language:** Old French

Grantham
**Meaning:** From A Gravelly Homestead
**Origin Language:** Old English

Gratian | Graciano, Gratianus, Gratien, Graziano
**Meaning:** Grace
**Origin Language:** Latin

Grayne | Grane, Grein
**Meaning:** Branch
**Origin Language:** Old Norse

Grayson | Graysen, Greyson
**Meaning:** Steward's Son
**Origin Language:** Old English

Greger | Greg, Gregers, Gregg, Gregoire, Gregor, Gregur, Grigor
**Also:** Gregory | Greg, Gregg,

Gregoire, Gregorie, Gregorio, Gregorios, Gregorius, Grigori, Grigorie, Grigorios, Grigoris, Grigoriy, Grigory
**Meaning:** Watchful
**Origin Language:** Ancient Greek

Gren | Grenn
**Meaning:** Branch
**Origin Language:** Old Norse

Gresham
**Meaning:** From A Grassy Homestead
**Origin Language:** Old English

Grey | Gray
**Meaning:** Grey/Gray
**Origin Language:** English

Griffin | Griffith
**Also:** Grifud | Gruffud, Gruffudd, Gruffydd
**Meaning:** Strong Lord
**Origin Language:** Old Welsh

Grover
**Meaning:** From A Grove Of Trees
**Origin Language:** Old English

Guillermo | Guilermo, Guilherme, Gwilherm
**Meaning:** Desires Protection
**Origin Language:** Ancient Germanic

Gundar | Gundahar, Gundhar
**Meaning:** Army Warrior
**Origin Language:** Ancient Germanic

Gunnar | Gunari, Gunder, Gunnarr, Gunne, Gunner
**Meaning:** Army Battle
**Origin Language:** Old Norse

Gustav | Gus, Gustaf, Gustave, Gustavo
**Meaning:** Staff Of The Goths (The

Name Of A Germanic Tribe)
**Origin Language:** Old Norse

Gutierre
**Also:** Gwallter
**Meaning:** Army Ruler
**Origin Language:** Ancient Germanic

Gwilim | Guillelmus, Guillem,
Gwil, Gwilem, Gwill, Gwillym,
Gwilym
**Meaning:** Desires Protection
**Origin Language:** Ancient Germanic

Gwydion
**Meaning:** Born Of The Trees / Born In
The Wild
**Origin Language:** Welsh

Gwyn | Gwynn
**Meaning:** Blessed / White
**Origin Language:** Old Welsh

# Chapter 8 - Names For Boys Beginning With H

Habriel | Habirel, Habrail, Habrel,
Habri, Habrie, Habrielus, Habrilo,
Habriyel
**Meaning:** God Is My Strength
**Origin Language:** Hebrew

Hades | Haides
**Meaning:** Unseen
**Origin Language:** Ancient Greek

Hadley | Hadlee, Hadleigh
**Meaning:** From A Meadow Of Heather
**Origin Language:** Old English

Hadrian | Haddrian, Haddriano,
Haddrianus, Haddrien, Haddrion,

Hadriano, Hadriano, Hadrianus,
Hadrianus, Haidrian, Haidriano,
Haidrianus, Haidrien, Haidrion,
Haydrian, Haydriano, Haydrianus,
Haydrien, Haydrion
**Meaning:** From Hadria (The Name Of
Two Ancient Roman Settlements Which
Were Located In What Are Now
Northern Italy And Central Italy) / From
The Water
**Origin Language:** Latin

Hadwin
**Meaning:** Friend Of War
**Origin Language:** Old English

Hagen | Hagan, Hagano, Hageno,
Haghan, Haghen, Haghon, Hagon
**Meaning:** Hawthorn
**Origin Language:** Ancient Germanic

Haim | Haimir, Haimo
**Meaning:** Homely
**Origin Language:** Ancient Germanic

Haimon | Haemon
**Meaning:** Bloody
**Origin Language:** Ancient Greek

Hakeem | Hakim
**Meaning:** Wise
**Origin Language:** Arabic

Hal
**Meaning:** Boulder
**Origin Language:** Old Norse

Halbert | Halbertus
**Meaning:** Bright Noble
**Origin Language:** Ancient Germanic
And Old English (Cognates)

Haldor | Haldur, Halldor
**Meaning:** Thor's Boulder (Thor Is The
Name Of The Norse God Of Thunder
And Lightning)

**Origin Language:** Old Norse

Hale
**Meaning:** From A Nook
**Origin Language:** Old English

Halim
**Meaning:** Patient
**Origin Language:** Arabic

Hallagan | Halagan, Halegan, Haligan, Hallegan, Halligan
**Meaning:** Beauty / Mild Noble
**Origin Language:** Old Irish

Hallam
**Meaning:** From A Nook
**Origin Language:** Old English

Hallsten | Hallstein, Hallsteinn, Halstein, Halsten
**Meaning:** Boulder Stone
**Origin Language:** Old Norse

Halvard | Hallvar, Hallvard, Hallvor, Halvar, Halvor
**Meaning:** Guardian Of The Boulder
**Origin Language:** Old Norse

Hamilcar
**Meaning:** Brother Of Melqart (Melqart Is The Name Of A Semitic God Known As The King Of The Underworld, And Protector Of The Universe)
**Origin Language:** Phoenician

Hamilton
**Meaning:** From A Crooked Hill
**Origin Language:** Old English

Hamish
**Meaning:** Supplanter (Wrongfully Seizes And Holds The Place Of Another)
**Origin Language:** Hebrew

Hamlet

**Meaning:** Botherer Of Odin (Odin Is The Name Of A Norse God)
**Origin Language:** Old Norse

Hammond
**Meaning:** High Protector
**Origin Language:** Old Norse

Hamnet
**Also:** Hamon
**Meaning:** Homely
**Origin Language:** Ancient Germanic

Hamuel
**Meaning:** Raised By God
**Origin Language:** Hebrew

Hanan | Hanani
**Meaning:** Gracious
**Origin Language:** Hebrew

Hanlee | Hanleigh, Hanley, Hanlie
**Meaning:** From A High Meadow
**Origin Language:** Old English

Hans | Hann, Hannes
**Meaning:** God Is Gracious
**Origin Language:** Hebrew

Harald | Hareld, Harild, Harold
**Meaning:** Of The Powerful Army
**Origin Language:** Old Norse

Harard | Harward, Harweard
**Meaning:** Army Warden
**Origin Language:** Old English

Harbin
**Meaning:** Bright Warrior
**Origin Language:** Ancient Germanic

Harcourt
**Meaning:** From A Falconer's Hut
**Origin Language:** Old English

Hardwin | Hardouin, Harduin,

Harduino, Harduinus, Hartwin
**Meaning:** Hardy And Friendly
**Origin Language:** Ancient Germanic

Harel
**Meaning:** Altar
**Origin Language:** Hebrew

Hari
**Meaning:** Yellow / Tawny / Monkey / Horse / Lion
**Origin Language:** Sanskrit

Haris | Harris
**Meaning:** King Of The Homeland
**Origin Language:** Ancient Germanic

Harith
**Meaning:** Cultivator
**Origin Language:** Arabic

Harlan | Harland
**Meaning:** From A Land Full Of Hares
**Origin Language:** Old English

Harlem | Haarlam, Haarlem, Harlam
**Meaning:** From A Settlement On A Sandy Ridge
**Origin Language:** Old Dutch

Harley | Harlee, Harleigh, Harlie, Harrlee, Harrleigh, Harrley, Harrlie
**Meaning:** From A Meadow Of Hares
**Origin Language:** Old English

Harlin | Harlewin, Harling, Harluin, Harlwin
**Meaning:** Friendly Warrior
**Origin Language:** Ancient Germanic

Harlow
**Meaning:** From A Rocky Hill
**Origin Language:** Old English

Harman | Harmano

**Also:** Harmand
**Also:** Harmon
**Meaning:** Army Man
**Origin Language:** Ancient Germanic

Harold | Haroldo
**Meaning:** Of The Ruling Army
**Origin Language:** Old English

Harper
**Meaning:** Harp Maker / Harp Player
**Origin Language:** Old English

Harrick | Harric, Harrik
**Meaning:** Rich Army
**Origin Language:** Ancient Germanic

Harrison
**Also:** Harry | Harri, Harrie
**Meaning:** Sovereign Of The Homeland
**Origin Language:** Ancient Germanic

Harshal
**Meaning:** Happiness
**Origin Language:** Sanskrit

Hartley | Hartlee, Hartleigh, Hartlie
**Meaning:** From A Meadow Where Deer Roam
**Origin Language:** Old English

Harun | Haron, Haroun, Harron, Harroun, Harrun
**Meaning:** Exalted / Enlightened
**Origin Language:** Hebrew

Harvey | Haervey, Haervie, Haervy, Harve, Harvie, Harvy, Herve, Hervey
**Meaning:** Battle Worthy
**Origin Language:** Old Breton

Harvin
**Also:** Harwin
**Meaning:** Friendly Soldier

**Origin Language:** Ancient Germanic

## Hauke
**Meaning:** Mind And Spirit
**Origin Language:** Ancient Germanic

## Havel
**Meaning:** Rooster (Latin) / From Gaul (An Ancient Region Of Western Europe) (Ancient Celtic) / An Outlander (Ancient Celtic)
**Origin Language:** Latin And Ancient Celtic

## Havriel | Havirel, Havrail, Havrel, Havri, Havrie, Havrielus, Havrilo, Havriyel
**Meaning:** God Is My Strength
**Origin Language:** Hebrew

## Hayden | Hadyn, Haiden, Haidyn
**Meaning:** From A Valley Where Hay Is Grown
**Origin Language:** Old English

## Hayder | Haidar, Haider, Haydar, Heydar, Hydar, Hyder
**Meaning:** Lion / Warrior
**Origin Language:** Arabic

## Hayes | Haze
**Meaning:** Fire
**Origin Language:** Old Irish

## Haymard | Haimard
**Meaning:** From A Hardy Home
**Origin Language:** Ancient Germanic

## Haytham
**Meaning:** Young Hawk
**Origin Language:** Arabic

## Haywood
**Meaning:** From An Enclosed Woodland
**Origin Language:** Old English

## Heath
**Meaning:** Heath (Shrub)
**Origin Language:** English

## Heathcliff
**Meaning:** From A Cliff With Heath
**Origin Language:** Old English

## Hebel | Habel, Habil, Hebil
**Meaning:** Breath
**Origin Language:** Hebrew

## Hebron
**Meaning:** Alliance
**Origin Language:** Hebrew

## Heck | Heckie, Hecky
**Also:** Hector | Hektor
**Meaning:** Holding Fast
**Origin Language:** Ancient Greek

## Hedeon | Hedion, Hedon
**Meaning:** He Who Cuts Down (Other People Or Things)
**Origin Language:** Hebrew

## Hedley | Headley
**Meaning:** From A Meadow Of Heather
**Origin Language:** Old English

## Hedvard | Hedevard, Hedevart, Hedeward, Hedewart, Hedvart, Hedward, Hedwart
**Meaning:** Guardian Of Riches
**Origin Language:** Old English

## Heim | Heimir, Heimo
**Meaning:** Homely
**Origin Language:** Ancient Germanic

## Heimdall
**Meaning:** Pride Of The World / Radiance Of The World
**Origin Language:** Old Norse

## Hein | Heino

**Meaning:** Homely
**Origin Language:** Ancient Germanic

Helder
**Meaning:** Hell's Door
**Origin Language:** Old Dutch

Helias
**Meaning:** My God Is God
**Origin Language:** Hebrew

Helier
**Meaning:** Light-Hearted / Jovial
**Origin Language:** Ancient Greek

Helios | Helio
**Meaning:** Sun
**Origin Language:** Ancient Greek

Helmold | Helmald
**Meaning:** Protected Ruler
**Origin Language:** Ancient Germanic

Helvio | Helvius
**Meaning:** Has Hair The Shade Of Honey
**Origin Language:** Latin

Henderson
**Also:** Hendrick | Hendric, Hendrik
**Also:** Hendrix
**Also:** Hendry | Hendrie
**Meaning:** King Of The Homeland
**Origin Language:** Ancient Germanic

Henlie | Henlee, Henleigh, Henley
**Meaning:** From A High Meadow
**Origin Language:** Old English

Hennady
**Meaning:** At Peace
**Origin Language:** Ancient Greek

Henrik | Hemric, Hemrico, Hemrik, Henric, Henrico, Henrique

**Also:** Henry | Henri, Henrie
**Meaning:** King Of The Homeland
**Origin Language:** Ancient Germanic

Herard | Hereward, Herward
**Meaning:** Army Warden
**Origin Language:** Old English

Herbert | Harbert, Haribert, Herb, Herberto, Herbertus, Herbie, Herbrecht, Herby, Heribert, Heriberto
**Meaning:** Bright Warrior
**Origin Language:** Ancient Germanic

Hercule | Hercules
**Meaning:** Hera's Glory (Hera Is The Name Of The Greek Goddess Of Marriage, Women, Marital Harmony, And The Protector Of Women During Childbirth)
**Origin Language:** Ancient Greek

Hereald
**Meaning:** Of The Ruling Army
**Origin Language:** Old English

Herlewin | Herlin, Herling, Herluin, Herlwin
**Meaning:** Friendly Warrior
**Origin Language:** Ancient Germanic

Herman | Hermano
**Also:** Hermand
**Also:** Hermani | Hermanni
**Meaning:** Army Man
**Origin Language:** Ancient Germanic

Hermes
**Also:** Hermin | Herminio, Herminius
**Meaning:** Of Hermes (Hermes Is The Name Of The Greek God Of Boundaries, Roads And Travelers, Thieves, Athletes, Shepherds, Commerce, Speed, Cunning, Wit And Sleep,

Psychopomp And Divine Messenger)
**Origin Language:** Ancient Greek

Hermon
**Meaning:** Army Man
**Origin Language:** Ancient Germanic

Hernand | Hernando
**Meaning:** On A Daring Journey
**Origin Language:** Ancient Germanic

Hero | Hiro
**Meaning:** Hero
**Origin Language:** Ancient Greek

Herod | Herodion
**Meaning:** Ode To A Hero
**Origin Language:** Ancient Greek

Heron
**Meaning:** Hero
**Origin Language:** Ancient Greek

Herrick | Herric, Herrik
**Meaning:** Rich Army
**Origin Language:** Ancient Germanic

Herry | Herri, Herrie
**Meaning:** Home Ruler
**Origin Language:** Ancient Germanic

Herschel | Hersh, Hershel,
Heschel, Heshel, Hirsh, Hirshel
**Meaning:** Deer
**Origin Language:** Yiddish

Hesekiel | Hiezecihel
**Meaning:** God Will Strengthen
**Origin Language:** Hebrew

Hesiod | Hesiodos
**Meaning:** He That Sings Odes
**Origin Language:** Ancient Greek

Hevel
**Meaning:** Breath
**Origin Language:** Hebrew

Hezekiah | Hizkiah
**Meaning:** God Strengthens
**Origin Language:** Hebrew

Hieremias
**Meaning:** God Shall Uplift
**Origin Language:** Hebrew

Hieronymus | Hieronim,
Hieronym, Hieronymos
**Meaning:** Sacred Name
**Origin Language:** Ancient Greek

Hilbert
**Meaning:** Bright Battler
**Origin Language:** Ancient Germanic

Hodge
**Meaning:** Famous Spear
**Origin Language:** Ancient Germanic

Holden
**Meaning:** From A Deep Valley
**Origin Language:** Old English

Holgan | Hollgan
**Meaning:** Beauty / Mild Noble
**Origin Language:** Old Irish

Holger
**Meaning:** The Island's Spear
**Origin Language:** Old Norse

Holland
**Meaning:** From A Forested Land
**Origin Language:** Old Dutch

Hollis
**Meaning:** Holly Trees
**Origin Language:** Old English

Homer | Homeros
**Meaning:** Hostage
**Origin Language:** Ancient Greek

Hopkin | Hopcyn
**Meaning:** Famous And Bright
**Origin Language:** Ancient Germanic

Horace
**Also:** Horatio | Horacio, Horatius
**Meaning:** Timekeeper
**Origin Language:** Latin

Horst
**Meaning:** Thicket
**Origin Language:** German

Hosea | Hosee
**Also:** Hoshea, Howshea
**Meaning:** Salvation
**Origin Language:** Hebrew

Houston
**Meaning:** From Hugh's Town / From A Spirited Town
**Origin Language:** Old English

Howard | Haward
**Also:** Howie, Howy
**Meaning:** High Warden
**Origin Language:** Old Norse

Howell
**Meaning:** Prominent
**Origin Language:** Old Welsh

Hoyt
**Meaning:** Stick Thin
**Origin Language:** Old English

Hubert | Hubertus
**Meaning:** Bright Spirit
**Origin Language:** Ancient Germanic

Hudson | Hudde
**Also:** Huey | Hewie, Hewy, Hughie, Hughy
**Also:** Hugh | Hew, Huw
**Also:** Hugo | Huguo
**Meaning:** Mind And Spirit

**Origin Language:** Ancient Germanic

Humbert | Humberto, Hunberct, Hunbert, Hunberto
**Meaning:** Bright Bear Cub
**Origin Language:** Ancient Germanic

Humfred | Humfredo, Humfrid, Humfrido, Hunfred, Hunfredo, Hunfrid, Hunfrido
**Also:** Humphry | Humphrey, Humphrie
**Meaning:** Peaceful Bear Cub
**Origin Language:** Ancient Germanic

Hunter
**Meaning:** Hunter
**Origin Language:** English

Hurley
**Meaning:** From A Meadow With A Bend
**Origin Language:** Old English

Huxley
**Meaning:** From A Scorned Meadow
**Origin Language:** Old English

Hywel
**Meaning:** Prominent
**Origin Language:** Old Welsh

# Chapter 9 - Names For Boys Beginning With I

Iair | Iairos, Iairus
**Meaning:** He Shines
**Origin Language:** Hebrew

Ian | Ean, Iain, Ianis
**Meaning:** Graced By God
**Origin Language:** Hebrew

Ibrahim | Ibraheem

**Meaning:** High Father Of Many
**Origin Language:** Hebrew

## Icarus | Icaros, Ikaros, Ikarus
**Meaning:** Floating
**Origin Language:** Etruscan

## Idan | Edan
**Meaning:** An Era
**Origin Language:** Hebrew

## Ido | Iddo
**Meaning:** Timely
**Origin Language:** Hebrew

## Idris | Idriss
**Meaning:** Interpreter
**Origin Language:** Arabic

## Idwal
**Meaning:** Ruler Of Lords
**Origin Language:** Old Welsh

## Iefan | Ifan
**Meaning:** God Is Gracious
**Origin Language:** Hebrew

## Ifor
**Meaning:** From An Army That Dwells Within The Yew Trees
**Origin Language:** Old Norse

## Ignacio | Iggie, Iggy, Ignac, Ignace, Ignacie, Ignacy, Ignas, Ignat, Ignatios, Ignatius, Ignatiy, Ignatz, Ignaz, Ignazio, Nace, Nacho, Nacio
**Meaning:** Fire
**Origin Language:** Latin

## Igon
**Meaning:** Ascension
**Origin Language:** Basque

## Igor
**Meaning:** Army Of Ing/Yngvi

(Ing/Yngvi Is Another Name Of The God Freyr In Norse Mythology)
**Origin Language:** Old Norse

## Ike
**Meaning:** He Will Laugh
**Origin Language:** Hebrew

## Ilai
**Meaning:** Ascending
**Origin Language:** Hebrew

## Ilan
**Meaning:** Tree
**Origin Language:** Hebrew

## Ilarion | Ilar, Ilario, Ilariy, Illar, Illario, Illarion
**Meaning:** Light-Hearted / Jovial
**Origin Language:** Ancient Greek

## Ilbert
**Meaning:** Bright Battler
**Origin Language:** Ancient Germanic

## Ildor | Ildar
**Meaning:** Country Possessor
**Origin Language:** Ottoman Turkish And Persian (Cognates)

## Ilham
**Meaning:** Inspiration
**Origin Language:** Arabic

## Ilias | Ilyas, Ilyes
**Also:** Ilin | Ilyn
**Meaning:** My God Is God
**Origin Language:** Hebrew

## Illiam
**Meaning:** Desires Protection
**Origin Language:** Ancient Germanic

## Ilmar | Ilmari, Ilmo
**Meaning:** Air
**Origin Language:** Finnish

**Iman**
**Meaning:** Faith
**Origin Language:** Arabic

**Imani**
**Meaning:** Faith
**Origin Language:** Swahili

**Immanuel | Imanouel, Imanouil, Imanuel, Imanuele, Imanuil, Immanouel, Immanouil, Immanuele, Immanuhel, Immanuil**
**Meaning:** God Is With Us
**Origin Language:** Hebrew

**Imri | Imriy**
**Meaning:** Eloquent
**Origin Language:** Hebrew

**Indiana | Indie, Indy**
**Meaning:** From Indiana (United States)
**Origin Language:** English

**Indigo**
**Meaning:** Indigo
**Origin Language:** English

**Indy | Indie**
**Meaning:** From India (English) / River (Sanskrit)
**Origin Language:** English And Sanskrit

**Ingram**
**Meaning:** Raven Of The Angles (The Name Of A Germanic Tribe)
**Origin Language:** Ancient Germanic

**Innes**
**Meaning:** One Strength
**Origin Language:** Old Irish

**Innis**
**Meaning:** Island
**Origin Language:** Scottish Gaelic

**Ion**

**Meaning:** Violet
**Origin Language:** Ancient Greek

**Ira | Iyra**
**Meaning:** Watchful
**Origin Language:** Hebrew

**Iraklis | Irakliy**
**Meaning:** Hera's Glory (Hera Is The Name Of The Greek Goddess Of Marriage, Women, Marital Harmony, And The Protector Of Women During Childbirth)
**Origin Language:** Ancient Greek

**Irmin**
**Meaning:** Universal
**Origin Language:** Ancient Germanic

**Irodion | Irod**
**Meaning:** Ode To A Hero
**Origin Language:** Ancient Greek

**Irvin | Irvyn**
**Also:** Irvine
**Also:** Irving
**Meaning:** Green Water
**Origin Language:** Scottish Gaelic

**Irwin | Irwyn**
**Meaning:** Friend Of The Boars
**Origin Language:** Ancient Germanic And Old English (Cognates)

**Isaac | Isaak, Isac, Isacco, Isak, Isaque, Issac, Izaac, Izaak, Izac, Izak**
**Meaning:** He Will Laugh
**Origin Language:** Hebrew

**Isaiah | Isaia, Isaias, Isiah, Izaia, Izaiah, Iziah**
**Meaning:** God Is Salvation
**Origin Language:** Hebrew

**Ishaan**

**Meaning:** Wealthy / Owning Many Possessions / Ruler
**Origin Language:** Sanskrit

Ishmael
**Meaning:** God Hears
**Origin Language:** Hebrew

Ishmerai
**Meaning:** Preserver
**Origin Language:** Hebrew

Isidor | Isador, Isadore, Isidore, Isidoro, Isidoros, Isidorus, Isidro, Izidor
**Meaning:** Gift Of Isis (Isis Is The Name Of An Egyptian Goddess (Her Original Egyptian Name Is Aset, Isis Is The Name The Ancient Greeks Gave Her) She Was One Of The Most Important Goddesses Of Ancient Egypt)
**Origin Language:** Ancient Greek

Iskender | Iskandar, Iskander, Iskendar
**Meaning:** Mankind's Defender
**Origin Language:** Ancient Greek

Islay
**Meaning:** From The Island Of Islay (Scotland)
**Origin Language:** Scottish Gaelic

Islwyn | Islwin
**Meaning:** Below The Grove
**Origin Language:** Welsh

Ismail | Ismaeel, Ismael, Ismael, Ismaele, Ismahel
**Meaning:** God Hears
**Origin Language:** Hebrew

Israel | Israhel
**Meaning:** God Contends
**Origin Language:** Hebrew

Ithai
**Meaning:** With Me
**Origin Language:** Hebrew

Ithiel | Itiel, Iythiyel
**Meaning:** God Is With Me
**Origin Language:** Hebrew

Ivah
**Meaning:** Ruin
**Origin Language:** Hebrew

Ivailo | Ivaylo
**Meaning:** Wolf
**Origin Language:** Bulgar

Ivan | Ivane, Ivano, Ivans
**Meaning:** Graced By God
**Origin Language:** Hebrew

Ivar | Ivarr, Iver, Iverr, Ivor, Ivorr
**Meaning:** From An Army That Dwells Within The Yew Trees
**Origin Language:** Old Norse

Ives
**Meaning:** Yew Tree
**Origin Language:** Ancient Germanic

Ivis
**Meaning:** From An Army That Dwells Within The Yew Trees
**Origin Language:** Old Norse

Ivon
**Meaning:** Yew Tree
**Origin Language:** Ancient Germanic

Iwan
**Meaning:** God Is Gracious
**Origin Language:** Hebrew

Izan
**Meaning:** Enduring
**Origin Language:** Hebrew

Izar

**Meaning:** Star
**Origin Language:** Basque

# Chapter 10 - Names For Boys Beginning With J

Jabin
**Meaning:** Observed By God
**Origin Language:** Hebrew

Jabriel | Jabe, Jabirel, Jabrail, Jabrel, Jabri, Jabrie, Jabrielus, Jabrilo, Jabriyel
**Also:** Jabril | Jibril
**Meaning:** My Strength Is God
**Origin Language:** Hebrew

Jace | Jaese, Jaise, Jayce, Jayse
**Meaning:** Healer
**Origin Language:** Ancient Greek

Jack | Jac, Jacques, Jak
**Also:** Jackson
**Meaning:** Graced By God
**Origin Language:** Hebrew

Jacob | Giacobbe, Jacobi, Jacobie, Jacobo, Jacobus, Jacoby, Jakab, Jakob, Jakobe, Jakobi, Jakub, Jaycob
**Also:** Jacques
**Meaning:** Supplanter (Wrongfully Seizes And Holds The Place Of Another)
**Origin Language:** Hebrew

Jada
**Meaning:** He Knows
**Origin Language:** Hebrew

Jaden | Jadin, Jadyn, Jaeden, Jaedin, Jaedon, Jaiden, Jaidon, Jayden, Jaydin, Jaydon

**Meaning:** Thankful
**Origin Language:** Hebrew

Jadiel
**Meaning:** Praise Of God
**Origin Language:** Hebrew

Jadrian | Jaddrian, Jaddriano, Jaddrianus, Jaddrien, Jaddrion, Jadriano, Jadriano, Jadrianus, Jadrianus, Jaidrian, Jaidriano, Jaidrianus, Jaidrien, Jaidrion, Jaydrian, Jaydriano, Jaydrianus, Jaydrien, Jaydrion
**Meaning:** From Hadria (The Name Of Two Ancient Roman Settlements Which Were Located In What Are Now Northern Italy And Central Italy) / From The Water
**Origin Language:** Latin

Jagger
**Meaning:** One Who Carts Packs Around For A Living
**Origin Language:** Middle English

Jahan
**Meaning:** The World
**Origin Language:** Persian

Jahleel | Jahliel
**Meaning:** God Waits
**Origin Language:** Hebrew

Jair | Jairos, Jairus
**Meaning:** He Shines
**Origin Language:** Hebrew

Jakari
**Also:** Jake
**Meaning:** Supplanter (Wrongfully Seizes And Holds The Place Of Another)
**Origin Language:** Hebrew

Jalmari | Jalmar, Jari
**Meaning:** Protected By The Army

**Origin Language:** Old Norse

Jalon
**Meaning:** God Lodges
**Origin Language:** Hebrew

Jamal | Jamaal
**Meaning:** Beauty
**Origin Language:** Arabic

Jamar | Jamaar, Jamarr
**Meaning:** Beautiful Man That Dwells Near A Pool Of Water (A Combination Of Jamal And Lamar)
**Origin Language:** Arabic And Old French (In Combination)

Jamarcus
**Meaning:** Of Mars (Mars Is The Name Of The Roman God Of War, Guardian Of Agriculture And The Roman People)
**Origin Language:** Latin

Jamarion | Jamaarion
**Meaning:** Beautiful Man That Dwells Near A Pool Of Water (A Combination Of Jamal And Lamar)
**Origin Language:** Arabic And Old French (In Combination)

Jameel | Jamil
**Meaning:** Beautiful
**Origin Language:** Arabic

James | Jaymes
**Also:** Jameson | Jamison
**Also:** Jamie | Jaime, Jamey, Jamy, Jayme
**Meaning:** Supplanter (Wrongfully Seizes And Holds The Place Of Another)
**Origin Language:** Hebrew

Jamir | Jameer, Jamiri
**Meaning:** Beautiful Man That Dwells Near A Pool Of Water (A Combination Of Jamal And Lamar)
**Origin Language:** Arabic And Old

French (In Combination)

Janus | Janos
**Meaning:** Gate / Doorway
**Origin Language:** Latin

Japheth
**Meaning:** Enlarged
**Origin Language:** Hebrew

Jaqen | Jaqan
**Meaning:** This Name Has No Meaning (Jaqen Is A Fictional Character Featuring In The TV Series Game Of Thrones)
**Origin Language:** Invented

Jaquan
**Meaning:** Spring (Of Water) (Chinese) / Sea Spirit (Old Irish)
**Origin Language:** Chinese And Old Irish

Jarah
**Meaning:** Honeycomb / Honeysuckle
**Origin Language:** Hebrew

Jareb
**Meaning:** Contender
**Origin Language:** Hebrew

Jared | Jairyd, Jarad, Jarid, Jarod, Jarrad, Jarred, Jarrid, Jarrod
**Meaning:** Descent
**Origin Language:** Hebrew

Jarek | Jarik
**Meaning:** Fierce And Glorious
**Origin Language:** Common Slavic

Jaren
**Meaning:** He That Sings Or Shouts
**Origin Language:** Hebrew

Jareth
**Meaning:** Courage
**Origin Language:** Welsh

Jarlaith | Jarlaithe, Jarlath
**Meaning:** Dark Lord
**Origin Language:** Old Irish

Jarmil
**Meaning:** Dear Fierce One
**Origin Language:** Common Slavic

Jaromil
**Meaning:** Adored Of Spring
**Origin Language:** Common Slavic

Jaromir
**Meaning:** Peace Of Spring
**Origin Language:** Common Slavic

Jaron
**Meaning:** He That Sings Or Shouts
**Origin Language:** Hebrew

Jarrit | Jarret, Jarrett, Jarritt
**Meaning:** Spear Of Hardiness
**Origin Language:** Ancient Germanic

Jarvis | Jervis
**Meaning:** Strong Spear
**Origin Language:** Ancient Germanic

Jasiah | Jaziah
**Meaning:** God Supports
**Origin Language:** Hebrew

Jason | Jase, Jayceon, Jayson
**Meaning:** Healer
**Origin Language:** Ancient Greek

Jasper | Jesper,
**Meaning:** Treasurer
**Origin Language:** Hebrew

Javan
**Meaning:** Greece
**Origin Language:** Hebrew

Javed | Javaid, Javid
**Meaning:** Eternal
**Origin Language:** Persian

Javier | Javi, Javior
**Meaning:** From Etxeberria (Navarre, Spain)
**Origin Language:** Basque

Javion
**Also:** Javon
**Also:** Javonte
**Meaning:** Greece
**Origin Language:** Hebrew

Javriel | Jave, Javirel, Javrail, Javrel, Javri, Javrie, Javrielus, Javrilo, Javriyel
**Meaning:** My Strength Is God
**Origin Language:** Hebrew

Jax | Jaxx
**Also:** Jaxon | Jaxson, Jaxxon
**Also:** Jaxton | Jaxtan, Jaxten, Jaxtin, Jaxtyn
**Meaning:** Graced By God
**Origin Language:** Hebrew

Jay | Jae, Jai, Jaye
**Meaning:** Supplanter (Wrongfully Seizes And Holds The Place Of Another)
**Origin Language:** Hebrew

Jayant
**Meaning:** Victorious
**Origin Language:** Sanskrit

Jaydran | Jadran
**Meaning:** From Hadria (The Name Of Two Ancient Roman Settlements Which Were Located In What Are Now Northern Italy And Central Italy) / From The Water
**Origin Language:** Latin

Jaylani | Jaylaani
**Also:** Jaylen | Jaelan, Jaelan, Jaelen, Jaelon, Jailan, Jailen, Jailon, Jalen, Jalon, Jaylon

**Meaning:** Healer
**Origin Language:** Ancient Greek

Jayred
**Meaning:** Descent
**Origin Language:** Hebrew

Jaziel | Jahzeel
**Meaning:** God Waits
**Origin Language:** Hebrew

Jeconiah
**Meaning:** God Will Establish
**Origin Language:** Hebrew

Jedidiah | Jed
**Meaning:** God's Beloved
**Origin Language:** Hebrew

Jefferson
**Also:** Jeffrey | Jeff, Jefferie, Jeffery, Jeffrie, Jeffroi, Jeffroy, Jeffry, Jefre
**Meaning:** Divine Peace
**Origin Language:** Ancient Germanic

Jehiel
**Meaning:** God Will Live
**Origin Language:** Hebrew

Jelani | Jilani
**Meaning:** From Gilan (A Town Near Baghdad)
**Origin Language:** Arabic

Jemmy | Jem, Jemmie
**Meaning:** God Will Uplift
**Origin Language:** Hebrew

Jenaro | Genaro, Gennarino, Gennaro, Jennarino, Jennaro
**Meaning:** January
**Origin Language:** Latin

Jenesis | Jenesio, Jenesius
**Meaning:** Origin / Horoscope
**Origin Language:** Latin

Jensen | Jens, Jenson
**Meaning:** God Is Gracious
**Origin Language:** Hebrew

Jeor | Jior
**Also:** Jeordie | Jeordey, Jeordi, Jeordy
**Also:** Jeorge | Jeorg, Jeorgei, Jeorges, Jeorgi, Jeorgie, Jeorgii, Jeorgios, Jeorgius, Jeorgiy, Jeorgo, Jeorgy, Jiorgi, Jiorgino, Jiorgio, Jiorgos, Jorgi
**Meaning:** Farmer
**Origin Language:** Ancient Greek

Jepson | Jep
**Meaning:** Divine Peace
**Origin Language:** Ancient Germanic

Jeraint
**Meaning:** Of The Elders
**Origin Language:** Latin

Jerald | Jeraldo, Jeraldus, Jerhold, Jerold, Jirald, Jiraldo
**Also:** Jeralt | Jearalt, Jearolt, Jerallt, Jerollt, Jerolt, Jirallt, Jiralt, Jirollt, Jirolt
**Meaning:** Spear Of Power
**Origin Language:** Ancient Germanic

Jere | Jeri, Jerrie, Jerry, Jery
**Also:** Jeremiah | Geremia, Jeremias
**Meaning:** God Will Uplift
**Origin Language:** Hebrew

Jeremiel | Jerahmeel, Jerahmiel
**Meaning:** God Will Have Pity
**Origin Language:** Hebrew

Jeremy | Jeremi, Jeremie
**Meaning:** God Will Uplift
**Origin Language:** Hebrew

Jeriah
**Meaning:** Taught By God
**Origin Language:** Hebrew

Jericho
**Meaning:** From Jericho (Israel) / Moon
**Origin Language:** Hebrew

Jermain | Jermano, Jermanus
**Meaning:** Brother
**Origin Language:** Latin

Jeroboam
**Meaning:** The People Contend
**Origin Language:** Hebrew

Jerome
**Also:** Jeronim
**Meaning:** Sacred Name
**Origin Language:** Ancient Greek

Jerrard | Jerard, Jerardo, Jerhard, Jerhardt, Jerhart, Jerrardo
**Meaning:** Spear Of Hardiness
**Origin Language:** Ancient Germanic

Jerrick | Jeric, Jerick, Jerik, Jerric, Jerrik
**Meaning:** Ruler Of Forever
**Origin Language:** Old Norse

Jerrod | Jerad, Jerahd, Jered, Jerid, Jerod, Jerrad, Jerred, Jerrid
**Meaning:** Descent
**Origin Language:** Hebrew

Jerry | Jere, Jeri, Jerrie, Jery
**Meaning:** Spear Of Power
**Origin Language:** Ancient Germanic

Jesaiah
**Also:** Jeshaiah
**Meaning:** God Is Salvation
**Origin Language:** Hebrew

Jeshimon | Jeshemon
**Meaning:** Wilderness / The Desert
**Origin Language:** Hebrew

Jeshua | Jesh
**Meaning:** God Is Salvation
**Origin Language:** Hebrew

Jesiah | Jeziah
**Meaning:** God Supports
**Origin Language:** Hebrew

Jesimiel
**Meaning:** God Establishes
**Origin Language:** Hebrew

Jesse | Jess, Jessi, Jessie, Jessy, Jessye
**Meaning:** A Gift
**Origin Language:** Hebrew

Jether
**Meaning:** Abundance / Surplus
**Origin Language:** Hebrew

Jethro
**Meaning:** Observant
**Origin Language:** Hebrew

Jett
**Meaning:** Jet Black / Jet (Aircraft)
**Origin Language:** English

Jezza | Jez
**Meaning:** God Will Uplift
**Origin Language:** Hebrew

Jian
**Meaning:** Establish
**Origin Language:** Chinese

Jimmy | Jim, Jimi, Jimmie
**Meaning:** Supplanter (Wrongfully Seizes And Holds The Place Of Another)
**Origin Language:** Hebrew

Jiraiya | Jiraya
**Meaning:** Lightning Child

**Origin Language:** Japanese

Joab
**Meaning:** God Is Father
**Origin Language:** Hebrew

Joah
**Meaning:** God Is Brother
**Origin Language:** Hebrew

Joaquin | Joachim, Joakim, Joaquim, Jochim
**Meaning:** God Establishes
**Origin Language:** Hebrew

Joash
**Meaning:** Fire Of God
**Origin Language:** Hebrew

Joby | Giob, Giobb, Giobbe, Gioby, Job, Jobey, Jobie
**Meaning:** Hated
**Origin Language:** Hebrew

Jochen
**Meaning:** God Establishes
**Origin Language:** Hebrew

Joel | Giole
**Meaning:** God Is God
**Origin Language:** Hebrew

Joeri
**Meaning:** Farmer
**Origin Language:** Ancient Greek

Joey | Jo, Joe, Jojo
**Meaning:** God Will Add
**Origin Language:** Hebrew

Joffrey | Joff, Jofferie, Joffery, Joffrie, Joffroi, Joffroy, Joffry, Jofre
**Meaning:** Divine Peace
**Origin Language:** Ancient Germanic

Johan | Jehan, Jehohanan,

Johanan, Johann, Johannes
**Also:** John | Johnie, Johnnie, Johnny, Johny, Jon, Jonnie, Jonny
**Meaning:** God Is Gracious
**Origin Language:** Hebrew

Jonah
**Also:** Jonas | Jonus
**Meaning:** Dove
**Origin Language:** Hebrew

Jonathan | Johnathan, Johnathon, Jonatan, Jonathon
**Meaning:** God Has Given
**Origin Language:** Hebrew

Jones | Jone, Jonesy
**Also:** Jonty | Jontie
**Meaning:** God Is Gracious
**Origin Language:** Hebrew

Jools | Jules
**Meaning:** Downy (Down As In Soft Fluffy Hairs)
**Origin Language:** Latin

Jophiel
**Meaning:** Beauty Of God
**Origin Language:** Hebrew

Jorah
**Meaning:** Rainy
**Origin Language:** Hebrew

Joram
**Meaning:** Exalted By God
**Origin Language:** Hebrew

Joran | Joren
**Meaning:** Farmer
**Origin Language:** Ancient Greek

Jordan | Jordon
**Also:** Jordane | Jordanes, Jourdain
**Meaning:** Descending Flow
**Origin Language:** Semitic

Jordie | Jordi, Jordy
**Also:** Jorge | Jorgi, Jorgie, Jorj, Jorji, Jorjie
**Also:** Joris
**Also:** Jory | Jori, Jorie, Joriy, Jure
**Meaning:** Farmer
**Origin Language:** Ancient Greek

Jose | Joses
**Also:** Joseph | Josef, Josephus, Josif, Jozef, Jusef, Jusuf
**Meaning:** God Will Add
**Origin Language:** Hebrew

Joshua | Josh
**Meaning:** God Is Salvation
**Origin Language:** Hebrew

Josiah | Joziah
**Meaning:** God Supports
**Origin Language:** Hebrew

Joss
**Meaning:** Of The Goths (The Name Of A Germanic Tribe)
**Origin Language:** Ancient Germanic

Jost
**Meaning:** Lord
**Origin Language:** Old Breton

Jostein
**Meaning:** Stone Horse
**Origin Language:** Old Norse

Jotham
**Meaning:** God Is Perfect
**Origin Language:** Hebrew

Jovanni | Jovan
**Meaning:** Graced By God
**Origin Language:** Hebrew

Jove
**Meaning:** Of Jove (Jove Is An Alternate Name Of Jupiter The Name Of The Roman God of the sky and lightning)
**Origin Language:** Latin

Jovi | Jovie, Jovy
**Meaning:** Jovial
**Origin Language:** English

Jovian
**Also:** Jovis
**Meaning:** Of Jove (Jove Is An Alternate Name Of Jupiter The Name Of The Roman God of the sky and lightning)
**Origin Language:** Latin

Jowan
**Also:** Juan | Juanito
**Meaning:** God Is Gracious
**Origin Language:** Hebrew

Judas
**Meaning:** Praised
**Origin Language:** Hebrew

Judd
**Meaning:** Descending Flow
**Origin Language:** Semitic

Jude
**Meaning:** Praised
**Origin Language:** Hebrew

Judhael | Judhail
**Meaning:** Generous Lord
**Origin Language:** Old Welsh

Judicael
**Meaning:** Generous Lord
**Origin Language:** Old Breton

Judoc | Jodocus, Judocus
**Meaning:** Lord
**Origin Language:** Old Breton

Judson
**Meaning:** Descending Flow
**Origin Language:** Semitic

Julian | Giuliano, Jiulian, Jiuliano, Jiulien, Julen, Juliano, Julien, Julyan
**Also:** Julius | Giulio, Jiulio, Julio
**Meaning:** Downy (Down As In Soft Fluffy Hairs)
**Origin Language:** Latin

Junior
**Meaning:** Junior
**Origin Language:** English

Junius
**Meaning:** Of Juno (Juno Is The Name Of The Roman Goddess Of Marriage And Childbirth) / June
**Origin Language:** Latin

Jurian | Jurien, Jurion, Jurrian, Jurrien, Jurrion
**Also:** Juris
**Meaning:** Farmer
**Origin Language:** Ancient Greek

Justice
**Meaning:** Justice
**Origin Language:** English

Justin | Giustino, Giusto, Jiustino, Jiusto, Juste, Justie, Justinas, Justinian, Justino, Justinus, Justo, Justus, Justy, Justyn
**Meaning:** Just
**Origin Language:** Latin

# Chapter 11 - Names For Boys Beginning With K

Kaan
**Meaning:** Khan
**Origin Language:** Turkish

Kabil
**Meaning:** Acquired
**Origin Language:** Hebrew

Kade | Kaed, Kaid, Kayde
**Meaning:** Round
**Origin Language:** Old English

Kader | Kadir
**Meaning:** Powerful
**Origin Language:** Arabic

Kadmus | Kadmos
**Meaning:** Man From The East
**Origin Language:** Ancient Greek

Kadri
**Meaning:** Value
**Origin Language:** Turkish

Kaelan | Kalen, Kaylen
**Meaning:** Little Slender One
**Origin Language:** Old Irish

Kahal
**Meaning:** Chief Of Battle
**Origin Language:** Old Irish

Kai | Khai, Ky, Kye
**Meaning:** Sea
**Origin Language:** Hawaiian

Kaiden | Kadan, Kaden, Kaedan, Kaeden, Kaidan, Kaydan, Kayden
**Meaning:** Place Of Battle
**Origin Language:** Welsh

Kaimbe
**Meaning:** Warrior
**Origin Language:** Old Frisian

Kain | Kaen, Kaeno, Kaino, Kayn, Kayno
**Meaning:** Acquired
**Origin Language:** Hebrew

Kainan | Kaenan, Kaenen, Kainam, Kainen, Keinan, Keinen, Kenan, Kenen, Keynan
**Meaning:** Possession
**Origin Language:** Hebrew

Kairo | Kyro
**Meaning:** From Cairo (Egypt) (English) / The Strong (Arabic)
**Origin Language:** English And Arabic

Kais
**Meaning:** Measurement
**Origin Language:** Arabic

Kaiser | Kaisar, Kaizar, Kaizer
**Meaning:** Has Long Flowing Hair / Has Beautiful Hair
**Origin Language:** Latin

Kaleb | Kalev
**Meaning:** Wholehearted / Dog
**Origin Language:** Hebrew

Kalel | Kal-El, Kal-L
**Meaning:** This Name Has No Meaning (Kal-El Is The Birth Name Of Fictional Comic Book Character Superman)
**Origin Language:** Invented

Kaleo
**Meaning:** The Voice
**Origin Language:** Hawaiian

Kalil
**Meaning:** Friend
**Origin Language:** Arabic

Kalin
**Meaning:** Viburnum Tree
**Origin Language:** Bulgarian And Macedonian (Cognates)

Kalisto | Kallisto, Kallistus
**Meaning:** Beautiful
**Origin Language:** Ancient Greek

Kallan | Kallen
**Meaning:** Chief Of Battle
**Origin Language:** Old Irish

Kallias
**Meaning:** Beauty
**Origin Language:** Ancient Greek

Kallum | Kalum, Kalumb
**Meaning:** Dove
**Origin Language:** Latin

Kalvin | Kal, Kalvino, Kalvinus
**Meaning:** Bald
**Origin Language:** Latin

Kalyan
**Meaning:** Amiable
**Origin Language:** Sanskrit

Kalydon
**Meaning:** From Kalydon/Calydon (A Greek City In Ancient Aetolia)
**Origin Language:** Ancient Greek

Kamal | Kemal
**Meaning:** Perfection
**Origin Language:** Arabic

Kamari
**Meaning:** Moon
**Origin Language:** Arabic

Kamden | Kamdin, Kamdon, Kamdyn
**Meaning:** From An Enclosed Valley
**Origin Language:** Old English

Kamen
**Meaning:** Stone
**Origin Language:** Bulgarian

Kameron | Kam, Kamren, Kamron, Kamryn, Kamryn
**Meaning:** Crooked Nose
**Origin Language:** Scottish Gaelic

Kamil
**Meaning:** Perfect
**Origin Language:** Arabic

Kane | Kaen, Kaene, Kain, Kaine, Kayne
**Meaning:** Little Battler
**Origin Language:** Old Irish

Kannan
**Meaning:** Dark Black
**Origin Language:** Sanskrit

Kannon
**Meaning:** Clergy
**Origin Language:** Old English

Kaolin
**Meaning:** Little Slender One
**Origin Language:** Old Irish

Kapriel
**Meaning:** My Strength Is God
**Origin Language:** Hebrew

Karam
**Meaning:** Generous
**Origin Language:** Arabic

Karayan
**Meaning:** Dark
**Origin Language:** Armenian

Kareem | Karim, Kerem, Kerim
**Meaning:** Generous
**Origin Language:** Arabic

Karey | Karie, Kary
**Meaning:** Dark
**Origin Language:** Old Irish

Kari
**Meaning:** Beloved
**Origin Language:** Latin

Karl | Karlo
**Meaning:** Has Freedom
**Origin Language:** Ancient Germanic

Karlisle | Karlyle
**Meaning:** Stronghold Of Lugus (Lugus Is The Name Of A Celtic God)
**Origin Language:** Gaulish

Karlman | Karlmann
**Meaning:** Manly And Free
**Origin Language:** Ancient Germanic

Karlos | Karlito, Karlitos, Karlo, Karolus
**Meaning:** Has Freedom
**Origin Language:** Ancient Germanic

Karlton | Karleton
**Meaning:** From A Town Of Freedom
**Origin Language:** Old English

Karson | Karsen, Karsin, Karsyn
**Meaning:** Rock
**Origin Language:** Scottish Gaelic

Karsten
**Meaning:** Christ / The Anointed One / Messiah
**Origin Language:** Ancient Greek

Karter | Kartier
**Meaning:** Carter
**Origin Language:** Norman French

Kase | Kasey
**Meaning:** Vigilant
**Origin Language:** Old Irish

Kaseem | Kasim, Kassim
**Meaning:** Sharer
**Origin Language:** Arabic

Kash | Kashton
**Meaning:** Case Maker
**Origin Language:** Old French

Kasimir | Kasim, Kasimiro, Kazim, Kazimir
**Meaning:** Destroyer Of Peace
**Origin Language:** Slavic

Kasper | Kaspar
**Meaning:** Treasurer
**Origin Language:** Hebrew

Kassander | Kassandro, Kassandros
**Meaning:** Surpasses Other Men
**Origin Language:** Ancient Greek

Kassian | Kassianus
**Also:** Kassius
**Meaning:** Empty/Hollow
**Origin Language:** Latin

Kastor
**Meaning:** Shining
**Origin Language:** Ancient Greek

Katello | Katellus
**Meaning:** Small
**Origin Language:** Latin

Kathal
**Meaning:** Chief Of Battle
**Origin Language:** Old Irish

Kay
**Meaning:** A Short Form Of Any Of The Numerous Names Beginning With K
**Origin Language:** Various

Kayne | Kaine
**Meaning:** Next In Line To Be Chieftain
**Origin Language:** Yoruba

Kayson | Kaesen, Kaeson, Kaisen, Kaison, Kasen, Kason, Kaysen
**Meaning:** From Kálfr's Town / From A Town Where Calves Reside
**Origin Language:** Old English And Old Norse (A Mix Of Both)

Keane | Kean, Keyn
**Meaning:** Little Battler
**Origin Language:** Old Irish

Keanu | Keano
**Meaning:** The Cool Breeze
**Origin Language:** Hawaiian

Keaton
**Meaning:** From A Town With Many Sheds
**Origin Language:** Old English

Keegan | Kegan
**Meaning:** Fire
**Origin Language:** Old Irish

Keelan
**Meaning:** Little Slender One
**Origin Language:** Old Irish

Keenan
**Meaning:** Long-Lasting
**Origin Language:** Old Irish

Kei
**Meaning:** Intelligent / Gemstone / Congratulate
**Origin Language:** Japanese

Keir
**Meaning:** From Near A Marshland
**Origin Language:** Old Norse

Keith
**Meaning:** From The Woods
**Origin Language:** Scottish Gaelic

Kelcey
**Meaning:** From Cenel's Island / From A Fierce Island
**Origin Language:** Old English

Kelechi
**Meaning:** Thank God
**Origin Language:** Igbo

Kelemen
**Meaning:** Clemency
**Origin Language:** Latin

Kellan | Kelan, Kelen, Kellen
**Meaning:** From A Swamp
**Origin Language:** Ancient Germanic

Kelvin
**Meaning:** From Near The River Kelvin (Scotland)
**Origin Language:** Scottish Gaelic

Kemen
**Meaning:** Courage
**Origin Language:** Basque

Kemp
**Meaning:** Champion / Athlete
**Origin Language:** Old English

Kemuel
**Meaning:** Raised By God
**Origin Language:** Hebrew

Ken
**Meaning:** Healthy / Strong
**Origin Language:** Japanese

Kenaniah | Kenanyah
**Meaning:** God Establishes
**Origin Language:** Hebrew

Kendal | Kendall
**Meaning:** From A Coastal Valley
**Origin Language:** Old English

Kendrick | Kendric, Kendrik, Keneric, Keneric, Kenerick, Kenerik, Kenric, Kenrick, Kenrik
**Meaning:** Keen And Rich
**Origin Language:** Old English

Kenelm
**Meaning:** Keen Protector
**Origin Language:** Old English

Kenith | Kenyth
**Meaning:** Handsome
**Origin Language:** Old Irish

Kenji
**Meaning:** Healthy Two / Strong Two / Study Two
**Origin Language:** Japanese

Kennard | Kenard
**Meaning:** Royal And Hardy
**Origin Language:** Old English

Kennedy | Kennedie
**Meaning:** Ugly
**Origin Language:** Old Irish

Kennet | Kennett
**Also:** Kenneth | Kennith
**Meaning:** Born Of Fire
**Origin Language:** Old Irish

Kenny | Kennie
**Meaning:** Handsome
**Origin Language:** Old Irish

Kenric | Kenrik
**Meaning:** Royal And Rich
**Origin Language:** Old English

Kensley | Kenslee, Kensleigh, Kenslie
**Meaning:** From Cyne's Meadow / From A Royal Meadow
**Origin Language:** Old English

Kent
**Meaning:** From The Coast
**Origin Language:** Old English

Kenton
**Meaning:** From A Royal Town
**Origin Language:** Old English

Kenward | Kennward, Kenweard
**Meaning:** Royal Warden
**Origin Language:** Old English

Kenyon
**Also:** Kenzey | Kensey, Kensie, Kenzie
**Meaning:** Handsome
**Origin Language:** Old Irish

Kenzo
**Meaning:** Healthy Three / Strong Three / Study Three
**Origin Language:** Japanese

Keone
**Meaning:** The Homeland / The Sand
**Origin Language:** Hawaiian

Keoni
**Meaning:** God Is Gracious
**Origin Language:** Hebrew

Kerr
**Meaning:** From Near A Marshland
**Origin Language:** Old Norse

Keshaun | Keshawn
**Meaning:** Graced By God
**Origin Language:** Hebrew

Kester
**Meaning:** Christ / The Anointed One / Messiah
**Origin Language:** Ancient Greek

Kevin | Kev, Kevan, Keven, Kevyn
**Meaning:** Homely Birth
**Origin Language:** Old Irish

Khalid | Khaled
**Meaning:** Eternal
**Origin Language:** Arabic

Khalil | Khaleel
**Meaning:** Friend
**Origin Language:** Arabic

Khaliq
**Meaning:** Creator
**Origin Language:** Arabic

Khamis | Khamisi
**Meaning:** Born On A Thursday
**Origin Language:** Arabic And Swahili (Cognate)

Khayri
**Meaning:** Charitable
**Origin Language:** Arabic

Khris | Kris
**Also:** Khrister | Krister
**Meaning:** Christ / The Anointed One / Messiah
**Origin Language:** Ancient Greek

Khristoph | Khristoff, Khristoff, Khristophe, Kristoff, Kristoph, Krystoff, Krystoph
**Meaning:** Bearer Of Christ
**Origin Language:** Late Greek

Khristos | Kristos
**Meaning:** Christ / The Anointed One / Messiah
**Origin Language:** Ancient Greek

Kian | Keyaan, Keyan
**Meaning:** King / Symbol Of Pride
**Origin Language:** Persian

Kiar
**Meaning:** Dark
**Origin Language:** Old Irish

Kiefer
**Meaning:** Pine Tree
**Origin Language:** German

Kieran | Keiran, Keiren, Keiron,

Kiaran, Kiaren, Kiaron, Kieren, Kieron
**Meaning:** Dark
**Origin Language:** Old Irish

Killian | Kilian, Kylian, Kyllian
**Meaning:** Little Church
**Origin Language:** Irish

Kilmer | Kilmar
**Meaning:** Servant Of Mary
**Origin Language:** Old Irish

Kilroy
**Meaning:** Red-Haired Boy
**Origin Language:** Old Irish

Kimbal | Kimball, Kimbel
**Meaning:** Bold Royalty
**Origin Language:** Old English

Kimon
**Meaning:** Sleepy
**Origin Language:** Ancient Greek

Kingsley
**Meaning:** From A King's Meadow
**Origin Language:** Old English

Kingston
**Meaning:** From A King's Town
**Origin Language:** Old English

Kinsley | Kinslee, Kinsleigh, Kinslie, Kynslee, Kynsleigh, Kynsley, Kynslie
**Meaning:** From Cyne's Meadow / From A Royal Meadow
**Origin Language:** Old English

Kinzey | Kincey, Kincie, Kinsey, Kinsie, Kinzie
**Meaning:** Royal And Victorious
**Origin Language:** Old English

Kipling

**Meaning:** From Cyppel's/Cybbel's Town (It Is Unknown What The Old English Personal Names Cyppel Or Cybbel Mean)
**Origin Language:** Old English

Kir
**Meaning:** Shepherd / Protector
**Origin Language:** Old Persian

Kiran
**Meaning:** Sunbeam
**Origin Language:** Sanskrit

Kirby | Kirbie
**Meaning:** From A Settlement With A Church
**Origin Language:** Old Norse

Kirk
**Meaning:** Church
**Origin Language:** Old Norse

Kiro
**Meaning:** Lord
**Origin Language:** Ancient Greek

Kit
**Meaning:** Christ / The Anointed One / Messiah
**Origin Language:** Ancient Greek

Kitchi
**Meaning:** Brave
**Origin Language:** Algonquin

Klaud | Klaude
**Meaning:** Limps / Stumbles / Wavers / Hesitates
**Origin Language:** Latin

Klaus
**Meaning:** Victory Of The People
**Origin Language:** Ancient Greek

Klement | Klem, Klem, Klemen, Klemente, Klementius, Klements, Klim, Klimen, Kliment

**Meaning:** Clemency
**Origin Language:** Latin

Kleon | Klion
**Meaning:** Glory
**Origin Language:** Ancient Greek

Kletus | Kleitis, Kleitos, Kleitus, Kleitus, Kletis
**Meaning:** Famous
**Origin Language:** Ancient Greek

Knox
**Meaning:** From A Round Hill
**Origin Language:** Scottish Gaelic

Kobe | Kobi, Kobie, Kobus, Koby
**Meaning:** Supplanter (Wrongfully Seizes And Holds The Place Of Another)
**Origin Language:** Hebrew

Koda
**Meaning:** Friend
**Origin Language:** Sioux

Kody | Kodey, Kodie
**Meaning:** Rich
**Origin Language:** Ancient Germanic And Old English And Old Norse (Cognates)

Koen
**Meaning:** Brave Counsellor
**Origin Language:** Ancient Germanic

Kohen
**Meaning:** Priest
**Origin Language:** Hebrew

Kolbert | Kolobert
**Meaning:** Calm And Bright
**Origin Language:** Ancient Germanic

Kolby | Kolbie
**Meaning:** From Koli's Town / From A Coal Town
**Origin Language:** Old Norse

Kole
**Meaning:** Charcoal
**Origin Language:** Old English

Koleman | Kolman, Koloman
**Meaning:** Dove
**Origin Language:** Latin

Kolter
**Meaning:** One Who Looks After Horses
**Origin Language:** Old English

Kolton | Koltan, Kolten, Koltin, Koltyn
**Meaning:** From Cola's Town / From A Coal Town
**Origin Language:** Old English

Kolumbo | Kolm, Kolombano, Kolombo, Kolumbanus
**Meaning:** Dove
**Origin Language:** Latin

Konnor | Konner, Konor
**Meaning:** Dog Lover
**Origin Language:** Old Irish

Konrad | Konrado
**Meaning:** Brave Counsellor
**Origin Language:** Ancient Germanic

Koralo
**Meaning:** Coral
**Origin Language:** Ancient Greek

Koray
**Meaning:** Ember Moon
**Origin Language:** Turkish

Korbin | Korbinus
**Also:** Korbinian
**Also:** Korbus
**Meaning:** Raven
**Origin Language:** Latin

**Korey | Korie, Kory**
**Meaning:** Trooper
**Origin Language:** Old Norse

**Korin | Koryn**
**Meaning:** Armed With A Spear
**Origin Language:** Latin

**Kornel | Kornell**
**Also:** Kornelius | Korneille,
Kornelio, Kornelios, Kornelis,
Kornello
**Meaning:** Horned
**Origin Language:** Latin

**Korrad | Kord, Korradino,
Korrado**
**Meaning:** Brave Counsellor
**Origin Language:** Ancient Germanic

**Korvin | Korvinus**
**Also:** Korvus
**Meaning:** Raven
**Origin Language:** Latin

**Korwin | Korwyn**
**Meaning:** Maker Of Shoes From
Cordovan Leather (The Name Of The
Leather Was Named From The City Of
Cordova In Spain)
**Origin Language:** Old English

**Kosmas | Cosmos, Kosimo,
Kosme, Kosmo**
**Also:** Kosmin
**Meaning:** The Universe / The Cosmos
**Origin Language:** Ancient Greek

**Kostantino | Kostanzo**
**Also:** Kostas
**Also:** Kostin
**Meaning:** Constant (Unchanging)
**Origin Language:** Latin

**Koty | Kotey, Kotie**
**Meaning:** Rich

**Origin Language:** Ancient Germanic
And Old English And Old Norse
(Cognates)

**Krispian | Krispin, Krispino,
Krispinus, Krispus, Kryspin**
**Meaning:** Curly-Haired
**Origin Language:** Latin

**Kristian | Khristian, Khristianos,
Khristianus, Kristiano, Krystian**
**Meaning:** A Christian
**Origin Language:** Latin

**Kristopher | Khristoffer,
Khristoforos, Khristopher,
Khristophoros, Khristophorus,
Kristoffer, Krystoffer, Krystopher**
**Meaning:** Bearer Of Christ
**Origin Language:** Late Greek

**Krius | Kreios, Krios**
**Meaning:** Ram
**Origin Language:** Ancient Greek

**Krosby | Krosbie, Krossbie,
Krossby, Krozbie, Krozby**
**Meaning:** From A Village With A Cross
**Origin Language:** Old Norse

**Kurt | Koert**
**Meaning:** Brave Counsellor
**Origin Language:** Ancient Germanic

**Kurtis | Kurt**
**Meaning:** Courteous
**Origin Language:** Old French

**Kuthbert**
**Meaning:** Famous And Bright
**Origin Language:** Old English

**Kylan | Kylen**
**Also:** Kyle
**Also:** Kyler
**Also:** Kylo

**Meaning:** Slender
**Origin Language:** Old Irish

Kynaston
**Meaning:** From Cynefrið's Town /
From A Royal And Peaceful Town
**Origin Language:** Old English

Kyran | Kiran
**Meaning:** Dark
**Origin Language:** Old Irish

Kyree | Kyri, Kyrie, Kyry
**Also:** Kyrie | Kyry
**Meaning:** Sovereign / Lord
**Origin Language:** Ancient Greek

Kyros
**Meaning:** Shepherd / Protector
**Origin Language:** Old Persian

Kyson
**Meaning:** Slender
**Origin Language:** Old Irish

# Chapter 12 - Names For Boys Beginning With L

Lachlan | Lachie, Lachlainn,
Lachlann, Lachy, Lackie
**Meaning:** Viking
**Origin Language:** Old Irish

Ladon
**Meaning:** From A Barn
**Origin Language:** Old Norse

Lael
**Meaning:** Of God
**Origin Language:** Hebrew

Laelius | Lail, Lailius, Lailo, Leil,
Lelio
**Meaning:** Inept
**Origin Language:** Latin

Laios | Laius
**Meaning:** The Left (Opposite Of Right)
/ Awkward
**Origin Language:** Ancient Greek

Laird
**Meaning:** Landowner
**Origin Language:** Scots

Lamar
**Meaning:** From Near A Pool Of Water
**Origin Language:** Old French

Lambert | Lamberto
**Meaning:** From A Beautiful Land
**Origin Language:** Ancient Germanic

Lamont
**Meaning:** Man Of The Law
**Origin Language:** Old Norse

Lance
**Also:** Lancelot | Lancel
**Also:** Lando
**Meaning:** Of The Land
**Origin Language:** Ancient Germanic

Landon | Landen
**Meaning:** From A Long Hill
**Origin Language:** Old English

Landric | Landrick, Landrik
**Also:** Landry | Landrie
**Meaning:** From A Rich Land
**Origin Language:** Ancient Germanic

Lane | Layne
**Meaning:** Lives On A Lane
**Origin Language:** English

Lanford
**Meaning:** From Near A Long Ford
**Origin Language:** Old English

Langdon | Langden
**Meaning:** From A Long Hill
**Origin Language:** Old English

Langston | Langstan
**Meaning:** From Near Where A Long Stone Lies
**Origin Language:** Old English

Lanny | Lannie
**Also:** Lanzo
**Meaning:** Of The Land
**Origin Language:** Ancient Germanic

Lari
**Meaning:** From Larissa (A City In Thessaly Greece)
**Origin Language:** Ancient Greek

Larkin
**Also:** Larry | Larrie
**Also:** Lars | Larz
**Meaning:** Laurel
**Origin Language:** Latin

Larus
**Meaning:** Laurel Tree
**Origin Language:** English

Lashawn | Leshawn
**Meaning:** God Is Gracious
**Origin Language:** Hebrew

Lassi
**Meaning:** Young Girl
**Origin Language:** English

Lathom | Lathum
**Meaning:** From A Barn
**Origin Language:** Old Norse

Launce | Launcelot
**Meaning:** Of The Land
**Origin Language:** Ancient Germanic

Laurent | Laurentin, Laurentino, Laurentinus, Laurentius
**Also:** Laurits | Lauritz
**Also:** Laurus | Lauris, Lauro
Lawrence | Laurence, Laurenz, Lawrie, Lawry
**Also:** Lawson
**Meaning:** From Laurentum (An Ancient Roman City That Was Considered The Capital Of Italy) / Laurel Tree
**Origin Language:** Latin

Layton | Leighton, Leyton
**Meaning:** From A Town Where Leeks Are Grown
**Origin Language:** Old English

Laz
**Meaning:** From Laurentum (An Ancient Roman City That Was Considered The Capital Of Italy) / Laurel Tree
**Origin Language:** Latin

Leander | Leandre
**Also:** Leandro | Leandros
**Meaning:** Has The Qualities Of A Lion
**Origin Language:** Ancient Greek

Leary | Learie, Leirey, Leiry
**Meaning:** Calf Herder
**Origin Language:** Old Irish

Lee | Leigh
**Meaning:** From A Meadow
**Origin Language:** Old English

Leif | Leifr, Leifur, Leiv
**Meaning:** Heir
**Origin Language:** Old Norse

Leir | Lear
**Meaning:** The Sea
**Origin Language:** Old Welsh

Leith | Laith
**Meaning:** From A Damp Town

**Origin Language:** Scottish Gaelic

## Leland
**Meaning:** From A Fallow Land
**Origin Language:** Old English

## Lemek
**Meaning:** Powerful
**Origin Language:** Hebrew

## Lemoine
**Meaning:** The Monk
**Origin Language:** French

## Lemuel | Lemuwel
**Meaning:** For God
**Origin Language:** Hebrew

## Lennart | Lenart, Leonart, Leonhart
**Meaning:** Hardy Lion
**Origin Language:** Ancient Germanic

## Lennon
**Meaning:** Lover / Sweetheart
**Origin Language:** Old Irish

## Lennox | Lenox
**Meaning:** From Lennox (Scotland)
**Origin Language:** Scottish Gaelic

## Lenny | Len, Lenn, Lenne, Lenni, Lennie
**Meaning:** Hardy Lion
**Origin Language:** Ancient Germanic

## Leo | Lio
**Meaning:** Lion
**Origin Language:** Latin

## Leolin
**Meaning:** Of Lugus And Belenos (Lugus And Belenos Are The Names Of Two Celtic Gods)
**Origin Language:** Ancient Celtic

## Leon | Leonas, Leone
**Meaning:** Lion
**Origin Language:** Ancient Greek

## Leonard | Lenard, Lennard, Leonhard
**Also:** Leonardo | Leonard
**Meaning:** Hardy Lion
**Origin Language:** Ancient Germanic

## Leonce | Leoncio
**Meaning:** Lion
**Origin Language:** Ancient Greek

## Leonidas | Leanid, Leonid, Leonida, Leonide, Leonides
**Meaning:** Son Of A Lion
**Origin Language:** Ancient Greek

## Leonius | Leon
**Meaning:** Lion
**Origin Language:** Latin

## Leonty | Leonti, Leontie, Leontinus, Leontios, Leontius, Leontiy
**Meaning:** Lion
**Origin Language:** Ancient Greek

## Leopold | Leopoldo
**Meaning:** Of The Bold People
**Origin Language:** Ancient Germanic

## Leroy | Leeroy, Leroi
**Meaning:** The King
**Origin Language:** French

## Lester
**Meaning:** From Leicester (England) / From A Camp On The River Ligore (England)
**Origin Language:** Latin

## Leucadio
**Also:** Leucas
**Meaning:** From Leucadia/Leukas (An

Ancient Greek Island Now Known As
Lefkada)
**Origin Language:** Latin

Leuis | Leui, Lewi
**Meaning:** Attached
**Origin Language:** Hebrew

Leukas
**Meaning:** From Leukas/Leucadia (An
Ancient Greek Island Now Known As
Lefkada)
**Origin Language:** Ancient Greek

Leukos
**Meaning:** Bright White
**Origin Language:** Ancient Greek

Lev
**Meaning:** Heart
**Origin Language:** Hebrew

Levent
**Meaning:** Handsome / Roguish
**Origin Language:** Turkish

Levi | Leviy
**Meaning:** Attached
**Origin Language:** Hebrew

Levin
**Meaning:** Beloved Friend
**Origin Language:** Ancient Germanic
And Old English (Cognates)

Levon | Levan
**Meaning:** Lion
**Origin Language:** Ancient Greek

Lew
**Meaning:** Lion
**Origin Language:** Polish

Lewin
**Meaning:** Beloved Friend
**Origin Language:** Ancient Germanic
And Old English (Cognates)

Lewis | Lluis, Loic, Lois, Loois,
Looys, Louis, Luis, Luiz
**Meaning:** Famous Battler
**Origin Language:** Ancient Germanic

Lex
**Meaning:** Defender
**Origin Language:** Ancient Greek

Liam | Liem, Lyam
**Meaning:** Desires Protection
**Origin Language:** Ancient Germanic

Lian
**Meaning:** Lotus / Water Lily / Waterfall
**Origin Language:** Chinese

Lias
**Meaning:** My God Is God
**Origin Language:** Hebrew

Lieven
**Meaning:** Beloved Friend
**Origin Language:** Ancient Germanic
And Old English (Cognates)

Lincoln
**Meaning:** From A Lake Colony
**Origin Language:** Brythonic And Latin
(A Mix Of Both)

Linden
**Meaning:** Linden Tree
**Origin Language:** Ancient Germanic

Lindon | Lyndon
**Meaning:** From A Hill With Linden
Trees
**Origin Language:** Old English

Linford
**Meaning:** From A Ford Where Linseed
Grows
**Origin Language:** Old English

Linos | Linas, Lino, Linus

**Meaning:** Linseed
**Origin Language:** Ancient Greek

Linton | Lynton
**Meaning:** From A Town Where Linseed Grows
**Origin Language:** Old English

Linwood | Lynwood
**Meaning:** From A Linden Tree Forest
**Origin Language:** Old English

Lionel | Leonel
**Meaning:** Lion
**Origin Language:** Ancient Greek

Lior
**Meaning:** My Light
**Origin Language:** Hebrew

Lir
**Meaning:** The Sea
**Origin Language:** Old Irish

Liridon
**Meaning:** Desires Freedom
**Origin Language:** Albanian

Liron
**Meaning:** A Song For Me
**Origin Language:** Hebrew

Livian | Livianus, Livio, Livius
**Meaning:** Envious
**Origin Language:** Latin

Lleu | Lugh
**Meaning:** Skillful
**Origin Language:** Gaulish

Llew
**Meaning:** Lion
**Origin Language:** Welsh

Llewellyn | Llewelin, Llewellin, Llewelyn, Llywelin, Llywellin,

Llywellyn, Llywelyn
**Meaning:** Of Lugus And Belenos (Lugus And Belenos Are The Names Of Two Celtic Gods)
**Origin Language:** Ancient Celtic

Lloyd | Llwyd, Loyd
**Meaning:** Grey/Gray
**Origin Language:** Welsh

Llyr
**Meaning:** The Sea
**Origin Language:** Old Welsh

Lochan
**Meaning:** The Eye
**Origin Language:** Sanskrit

Lochlan | Lauchlan, Lochlainn, Lochlann, Lockie, Locky
**Meaning:** Viking
**Origin Language:** Old Irish

Logan
**Meaning:** From A Little Hollow
**Origin Language:** Old English

Lohan
**Meaning:** Light
**Origin Language:** Old Breton

Loki | Loke
**Meaning:** Entangler
**Origin Language:** Old Norse

Loman | Lomanus, Lommy
**Also:** Lonan
**Meaning:** Little Blackbird
**Origin Language:** Old Irish

Lonny | Lon, Lonnie
**Meaning:** Ready For Nobility
**Origin Language:** Ancient Germanic

Lorcan | Lorccan
**Meaning:** Little Fierce One

**Origin Language:** Old Irish

Lorenzo | Lorencio, Lorens, Lorenz
**Also:** Loris | Loras, Loros, Lorys
**Meaning:** From Laurentum (An Ancient Roman City That Was Considered The Capital Of Italy) / Laurel Tree
**Origin Language:** Latin

Lothar | Lotario, Lothair, Lothaire, Lothario, Lotharius, Lothur, Lotterio
**Meaning:** Famous Soldier
**Origin Language:** Ancient Germanic

Louie | Lou, Loui, Louy
**Meaning:** Famous Battler
**Origin Language:** Ancient Germanic

Lovell | Louvel, Lovel
**Meaning:** Wolf
**Origin Language:** Latin

Lowe | Lowie
**Meaning:** Famous Battler
**Origin Language:** Ancient Germanic

Lowell | Louwel, Lowel
**Meaning:** Wolf
**Origin Language:** Latin

Lowen
**Meaning:** Beloved Friend
**Origin Language:** Ancient Germanic And Old English (Cognates)

Luca | Louka, Luka
**Meaning:** From Lucania (Italy) (Ancient Greek) / From The Sacred Woods (Latin)
**Origin Language:** Ancient Greek And Latin

Lucan | Lucanus
**Meaning:** From Luca (An Ancient Roman City Now Lucca In Tuscany)

**Origin Language:** Latin

Lucca
**Meaning:** From A Swampy Place
**Origin Language:** Ancient Celtic

Lucian | Luciano, Lucianus, Lucien
**Also:** Lucilio | Lucilius, Lucio
**Also:** Lucius
**Meaning:** Light
**Origin Language:** Latin

Lucky | Luckie
**Meaning:** Lucky
**Origin Language:** English

Lucretius
**Meaning:** Lucrative
**Origin Language:** Latin

Luigi | Luigino
**Meaning:** Famous Battler
**Origin Language:** Ancient Germanic

Lukas | Loukas, Lucas
**Also:** Luke | Lluc, Luc
**Meaning:** From Lucania (Italy) (Ancient Greek) / From The Sacred Woods (Latin)
**Origin Language:** Ancient Greek And Latin

Luken | Loukianos, Loukios, Lukian, Lukien, Lukyan
**Meaning:** Light
**Origin Language:** Latin

Luther | Leuthar, Leuther, Lewthar, Lewther, Luthar
**Meaning:** Of The People's Army
**Origin Language:** Ancient Germanic

Lyall | Liel, Liell, Liolle, Lyal, Lyel, Lyell
**Meaning:** Wolven
**Origin Language:** Old Norse

Lycaon | Lykaon
**Also:** Lycus | Lykos
**Meaning:** Wolf
**Origin Language:** Ancient Greek

Lydos
**Meaning:** Noble One / Beautiful One / From Lydia (An Ancient Kingdom In Western Anatolia)
**Origin Language:** Ancient Greek

Lyle
**Meaning:** The Island
**Origin Language:** Old French

Lysander | Lisander, Lisandro, Lysandros
**Meaning:** Liberator
**Origin Language:** Ancient Greek

# Chapter 13 - Names For Boys Beginning With M

Mabon | Mapon
**Meaning:** Great Son
**Origin Language:** Ancient Celtic

Mac | Mack
**Meaning:** Son
**Origin Language:** Irish

Macario | Macarius, Makario, Makarios
**Meaning:** Blessed
**Origin Language:** Ancient Greek

Macaulay | Macauley
**Meaning:** Unknown Meaning
**Origin Language:** Old Irish

Maccius
**Meaning:** Unknown Meaning
**Origin Language:** Latin

Macdara
**Meaning:** Son Of The Oak Tree
**Origin Language:** Old Irish

Mace
**Meaning:** Mace (Spice)
**Origin Language:** English

Machli | Machliy
**Meaning:** Sick / Weak
**Origin Language:** Hebrew

Mackenzy | Mackenzie, Mckenzie, Mckenzy
**Meaning:** Handsome
**Origin Language:** Old Irish

Macsen | Maksen
**Meaning:** The Greatest
**Origin Language:** Latin

Madden | Maddan, Maddon
**Meaning:** Mastiff
**Origin Language:** Old Irish

Maddox
**Meaning:** Little Fortunate One
**Origin Language:** Old Welsh

Madigan | Madigen, Madigon
**Meaning:** Mastiff
**Origin Language:** Old Irish

Madison
**Meaning:** Mighty Battler
**Origin Language:** Ancient Germanic

Madoc
**Meaning:** Little Fortunate One
**Origin Language:** Old Welsh

Mael
**Meaning:** Noble
**Origin Language:** Old Breton

Magni | Magne, Magny
**Meaning:** Mighty
**Origin Language:** Old Norse

Magnus
**Meaning:** Great
**Origin Language:** Latin

Mahli
**Also:** Mahlon
**Meaning:** Sick / Weak
**Origin Language:** Hebrew

Mahon
**Meaning:** Bear Cub
**Origin Language:** Old Irish

Maitland
**Meaning:** Bad And Talented / Evil Genius
**Origin Language:** Anglo-Norman French

Makai
**Meaning:** Seaward
**Origin Language:** Hawaiian

Makari | Macar, Macari, Makar, Makariy
**Meaning:** Blessed
**Origin Language:** Ancient Greek

Malachi | Malach, Malachai, Malachie, Malachy, Malakai, Malakiy
**Meaning:** My Angel / My Messenger
**Origin Language:** Hebrew

Malak
**Meaning:** Angel
**Origin Language:** Arabic

Malcolm | Malcom
**Meaning:** Devoted To Colum (The Name Of A Saint)
**Origin Language:** Scottish Gaelic

Malik
**Meaning:** Wave
**Origin Language:** Greenlandic

Malone | Maylone
**Meaning:** Devoted To Eoin (Saint John)
**Origin Language:** Old Irish

Manfred | Manfredi, Manfredo
**Meaning:** Mighty And Peaceful
**Origin Language:** Ancient Germanic

Mani | Maney
**Meaning:** Jewel
**Origin Language:** Sanskrit

Manuel | Manel, Mannie, Manny, Manoel, Manolo, Manouel, Manu, Manuele
**Meaning:** God Is With Us
**Origin Language:** Hebrew

Marceau
**Also:** Marcel | Marceli, Marcell, Marcello, Marcellus, Marcelo
**Also:** Marcelin | Marcelino, Marcellin, Marcellino, Marcellinus
**Also:** Marcial | Martial, Martialis
**Also:** Marcin
**Also:** Marcius | Marcio
**Also:** Marcus | Marcas, Marcio, Marco, Marcos, Markas, Marko, Markos, Markus
**Also:** Marin | Marinus, Maryn
**Also:** Mario
**Meaning:** Of Mars (Mars Is The Name Of The Roman God Of War, Guardian Of Agriculture And The Roman People)
**Origin Language:** Latin

Marion
**Meaning:** Rebellious
**Origin Language:** Hebrew

Marius | Marios
**Also:** Mark | Marc
**Meaning:** Of Mars (Mars Is The Name Of The Roman God Of War, Guardian Of Agriculture And The Roman People)
**Origin Language:** Latin

Marlon
**Meaning:** From A Famous Land
**Origin Language:** Ancient Germanic

Marlow | Marlowe
**Meaning:** From Near The Remnants Of A Lake
**Origin Language:** Old English

Marlyn | Marlin, Marlynn
**Meaning:** Citadel On The Sea
**Origin Language:** Welsh

Marnix
**Meaning:** From Marnix (Historical Place Of Unknown Location, Perhaps Once Existed In Belgium)
**Origin Language:** Dutch

Marrok | Marok, Marroc, Marrock
**Meaning:** Of Mars (Mars Is The Name Of The Roman God Of War, Guardian Of Agriculture And The Roman People)
**Origin Language:** Latin

Marshall | Marshal
**Meaning:** Horse Groom
**Origin Language:** Latin

Martin | Marten, Martino, Martinus, Martyn
**Also:** Marty | Mart, Marte, Martie
**Meaning:** Of Mars (Mars Is The Name Of The Roman God Of War, Guardian Of Agriculture And The Roman People)
**Origin Language:** Latin

Marvin | Marvyn
**Also:** Marwin | Marwyn

**Meaning:** Famous And Friendly
**Origin Language:** Old English

Marzell | Marzel
**Meaning:** Of Mars (Mars Is The Name Of The Roman God Of War, Guardian Of Agriculture And The Roman People)
**Origin Language:** Latin

Mason | Mayson
**Meaning:** Mason / Stone Worker
**Origin Language:** English

Massimo | Massimiliano
**Meaning:** The Greatest
**Origin Language:** Latin

Mathias | Mateus, Matheus, Maththaios, Maththias, Matteus, Matthaios, Matthei, Mattheus, Matthias, Mattias
**Also:** Matt | Matei, Mateo, Matio, Mato, Mats, Matteo, Matti, Mattie, Mattio, Mattis, Matts, Matty
**Also:** Matthos
**Meaning:** God's Gift
**Origin Language:** Hebrew

Mattaniah | Mattanyah
**Meaning:** God's Gift
**Origin Language:** Hebrew

Matthew | Mathew, Mathieu, Matthieu
**Meaning:** God's Gift
**Origin Language:** Hebrew

Mattin | Mattyn
**Meaning:** Of Mars (Mars Is The Name Of The Roman God Of War, Guardian Of Agriculture And The Roman People)
**Origin Language:** Latin

Mattis | Matis, Mattys, Matys
**Meaning:** God's Gift
**Origin Language:** Hebrew

Maurice | Mauricio, Mauricius, Mauritius, Maurits, Maurizio, Moritz
**Also:** Maury | Mauri, Maurie, Maurus
**Meaning:** From Mauretania (An Ancient Kingdom On The Coast Of North West Africa)
**Origin Language:** Latin

Maverick
**Meaning:** A Maverick
**Origin Language:** English

Max | Macs, Maks
**Also:** Maxen
**Also:** Maxence
**Also:** Maxent | Maxentius
**Also:** Maxim | Maksim, Maksym, Maximo
**Also:** Maximilian | Maksimilian, Maksymilian, Maximiliano, Maximilianus, Maximilien, Maximillian
**Also:** Maximus | Maximiano, Maximianus, Maximino, Maximinus
**Meaning:** The Greatest
**Origin Language:** Latin

Maxton
**Meaning:** From Macca's Town / From A Town With A Boundary Stone
**Origin Language:** Old English

Maxwell
**Meaning:** From Near Magnus' Well / From Near A Great Well
**Origin Language:** Old English

Maylon
**Meaning:** Devoted To Eoin (Saint John)
**Origin Language:** Old Irish

Maynard | Maynerd, Maynhard, Meinard, Meinerd, Meinhard
**Meaning:** Mighty And Hardy
**Origin Language:** Ancient Germanic

Mazin
**Meaning:** Rain Clouds
**Origin Language:** Arabic

Mccoy | Mckoy
**Also:** Mcgee
**Also:** Mckay | Mccay, Mckey
**Also:** Mckee | Mckey, Mckie
**Meaning:** Son Of Fire
**Origin Language:** Old Gaelic

Mckinley | Mckinlee, Mckinleigh, Mckinlie, Mckinly
**Meaning:** Blessed Warrior / Bright Warrior
**Origin Language:** Scottish Gaelic

Meinrad
**Meaning:** Mighty Counsellor
**Origin Language:** Ancient Germanic

Meirion | Marion
**Meaning:** Of Mars (Mars Is The Name Of The Roman God Of War, Guardian Of Agriculture And The Roman People)
**Origin Language:** Latin

Mekhi
**Meaning:** "Who Is Like God?"
**Origin Language:** Hebrew

Melbourne
**Meaning:** From A Mill Near A Stream
**Origin Language:** Old English

Melchor | Melchior, Melchiorre, Melker
**Meaning:** King Of Light
**Origin Language:** Hebrew

Melek | Melech

**Meaning:** King
**Origin Language:** Hebrew

Mellan
**Meaning:** Little Delightful One
**Origin Language:** Old Irish

Melle
**Meaning:** Meeting
**Origin Language:** Ancient Germanic

Melville | Mel
**Also:** Melvin | Mel, Melvyn
**Meaning:** From A Bad Town
**Origin Language:** Old French

Memphis
**Meaning:** Enduring Beauty
**Origin Language:** Ancient Egyptian

Mendel
**Meaning:** Comforter
**Origin Language:** Hebrew

Merdan
**Meaning:** Masculine
**Origin Language:** Persian

Mergen
**Meaning:** Sharp Eyed
**Origin Language:** Turkmen

Merit | Merritt
**Meaning:** From Near The Boundary Gate
**Origin Language:** Old English

Merrick | Merric, Merrik, Meuric, Meurick, Meurik
**Meaning:** From Mauretania (An Ancient Kingdom On The Coast Of North West Africa)
**Origin Language:** Latin

Merrill
**Meaning:** Bright Sea
**Origin Language:** Old Irish

Merton | Merten
**Meaning:** From A Town On A Lake
**Origin Language:** Old English

Mervin | Merfin, Merfyn, Merv, Mervyn, Mirvin, Mirvyn
**Meaning:** Eminent Marrow
**Origin Language:** Old Welsh

Meyer | Meir
**Meaning:** Light Giver
**Origin Language:** Hebrew

Micah | Micha, Michah, Mikhah, Miyka, Miykah
**Also:** Micaiah | Michaeas, Michaiah, Michaias, Micheas
**Also:** Michael | Maikel, Meical, Micael, Michail, Michal, Micheal, Michel, Michiel, Mickael
**Also:** Michalis
**Meaning:** "Who Is Like God?"
**Origin Language:** Hebrew

Michelangelo
**Meaning:** The Angel That Asks "Who Is Like God?" (A Combination Of Michael And Angelo)
**Origin Language:** Hebrew And Latin (In Combination)

Michi
**Meaning:** Path
**Origin Language:** Japanese

Micky | Mick, Mickie
**Meaning:** "Who Is Like God?"
**Origin Language:** Hebrew

Midian | Midyan
**Meaning:** Strife
**Origin Language:** Hebrew

Miguel | Miguelito
**Also:** Mihael | Mihail, Mihailo

**Also:** Mihalis | Mihalys
**Meaning:** "Who Is Like God?"
**Origin Language:** Hebrew

Mikalai | Mikalay
**Meaning:** The People's Victory
**Origin Language:** Ancient Greek

Mikey | Mike
**Also:** Mikkel | Mikaeel, Mikael, Mikail, Mikel, Mikhael, Mikhail, Mikhailo, Mikheil, Mykhail, Mykhailo, Mykhaylo
**Also:** Miko | Mikko
**Meaning:** "Who Is Like God?"
**Origin Language:** Hebrew

Milan | Milann, Milen, Mylan, Mylann
**Meaning:** Gracious
**Origin Language:** Common Slavic

Milburn
**Meaning:** From A Mill Near A Brook
**Origin Language:** Old English

Miles | Myles
**Meaning:** Gracious (Ancient Germanic) / Crusher Of Things (A Miller) (Ancient Greek
**Origin Language:** Ancient Germanic And Ancient Greek

Milford
**Meaning:** From A Ford By A Mill
**Origin Language:** Old English

Milian | Milien, Millian
**Meaning:** The Greatest
**Origin Language:** Latin

Millard
**Meaning:** Warden Of A Mill
**Origin Language:** Old English

Miller
**Meaning:** Mill Worker
**Origin Language:** Middle English

Milo | Mylo
**Meaning:** Gracious (Ancient Germanic) / Crusher Of Things (A Miller) (Ancient Greek
**Origin Language:** Ancient Germanic And Ancient Greek

Milton
**Meaning:** From A Town With A Mill
**Origin Language:** Old English

Minos
**Meaning:** King
**Origin Language:** Ancient Greek

Miran
**Meaning:** Peace / The World
**Origin Language:** Common Slavic

Mirche
**Meaning:** Peace
**Origin Language:** Common Slavic

Mirco | Mirko
**Meaning:** World Glory
**Origin Language:** Common Slavic

Miro
**Meaning:** Peace / The World
**Origin Language:** Common Slavic

Misael
**Also:** Mitchell | Mitch
**Meaning:** "Who Is Like God?"
**Origin Language:** Hebrew

Mnason
**Meaning:** Reminding
**Origin Language:** Ancient Greek

Moe | Mo
**Meaning:** From Mauretania (An Ancient Kingdom On The Coast Of North West Africa)

**Origin Language:** Latin

Molan | Molin, Mollan, Mollen, Mollin, Mollyn, Molyn
**Meaning:** From A Mill
**Origin Language:** Old English

Monro | Monroe
**Meaning:** From The Mouth Of A River
**Origin Language:** Old Irish

Montague
**Meaning:** Pointed Mountain
**Origin Language:** French

Montgomery | Montgomerie
**Also:** Monty | Monte, Montie
**Meaning:** From Gumarich's Hill / From A Hill With A Lot Of Man Power
**Origin Language:** Ancient Germanic And Old French (A Mix Of Both)

Morcant
**Meaning:** Bright Sea / Together With The Sea
**Origin Language:** Old Welsh

Mordechai | Mordecai, Mordekai, Mordekay, Mordokhay
**Meaning:** Servant Of Marduk (Marduk Is The Name Of The Babylonian God Of Creation, Water, Agriculture, Justice, Medicine, And Magic)
**Origin Language:** Hebrew

Mordred | Modred
**Meaning:** Moderated
**Origin Language:** Latin

Moreno
**Meaning:** Dark Skinned
**Origin Language:** Spanish

Morgen | Morgan
**Meaning:** Bright Sea / Together With The Sea
**Origin Language:** Old Welsh

Morley | Morlee, Moreleigh
**Meaning:** From A Marshy Meadow
**Origin Language:** Old English

Morpheus
**Meaning:** Shape Within A Dream
**Origin Language:** Ancient Greek

Morris | Muiris
**Meaning:** From Mauretania (An Ancient Kingdom On The Coast Of North West Africa)
**Origin Language:** Latin

Morten
**Meaning:** Of Mars (Mars Is The Name Of The Roman God Of War, Guardian Of Agriculture And The Roman People)
**Origin Language:** Latin

Mortimer
**Meaning:** Still Water
**Origin Language:** Old French

Morton | Mort, Mortan, Morten, Mortie, Morty
**Meaning:** From A Town Near A Moor
**Origin Language:** Old English

Moses | Moises, Moisey, Mose, Mouses, Moyses
**Meaning:** Rescued
**Origin Language:** Hebrew

Mosi
**Meaning:** First Born Child / Number One
**Origin Language:** Swahili

Moss
**Meaning:** Rescued
**Origin Language:** Hebrew

Mostyn | Mostin
**Meaning:** From A Town Where Moss Grows

**Origin Language:** Old English

Moyne | Moine
**Meaning:** Alone / Monkish
**Origin Language:** Ancient Greek

Muhammad | Mihammad,
Mohamed, Mohammad,
Mohammed, Muhamed,
Muhammed
**Meaning:** Praised
**Origin Language:** Arabic

Munroe | Munro
**Meaning:** From The Mouth Of A River
**Origin Language:** Old Irish

Murad
**Meaning:** Desire
**Origin Language:** Arabic

Murchad
**Meaning:** Battler At Sea
**Origin Language:** Old Irish

Murdanie | Murdani, Murdany
**Also:** Murdock | Murdoch
**Meaning:** Chieftain
**Origin Language:** Old Irish

Murphy | Murphie
**Meaning:** Battler At Sea
**Origin Language:** Old Irish

Murray | Moray
**Meaning:** From The Seashore
**Origin Language:** Scottish Gaelic

Murrough
**Meaning:** Battler At Sea
**Origin Language:** Old Irish

Myron | Mayron, Miron
**Meaning:** Perfumed
**Origin Language:** Ancient Greek

# Chapter 14 - Names For Boys Beginning With N

Nael
**Meaning:** God Has Given
**Origin Language:** Hebrew

Napoleon
**Meaning:** From Napoli/Naples (Italy)
**Origin Language:** Italian

Nash
**Meaning:** At The Ash Tree
**Origin Language:** Old English

Nataleo | Natalio, Natalius
**Meaning:** Birthday Of The Lord / Christmas Day
**Origin Language:** Latin

Nate
**Also:** Nathan | Natan, Natham
**Meaning:** He Gave
**Origin Language:** Hebrew

Nathaniel | Natanael, Natanaele,
Natanail, Nataniel, Nathanael,
Nathanahel, Netanel, Nethaneel,
Nethanel
**Meaning:** God Has Given
**Origin Language:** Hebrew

Naum | Naoum
**Meaning:** Comforter
**Origin Language:** Hebrew

Nayden
**Meaning:** Found
**Origin Language:** Bulgarian

Nazaire
**Also:** Nazaren | Nazar, Nazareno,

Nazarenus, Nazario, Nazarius, Nazariy, Nazzareno
**Meaning:** From Nazareth (The Childhood Home Of Jesus)
**Origin Language:** Latin

Neacel
**Meaning:** Victory Of The People
**Origin Language:** Ancient Greek

Neil | Neal
**Meaning:** Champion
**Origin Language:** Old Irish

Nedabiah | Nedabyah
**Meaning:** Impelled By God
**Origin Language:** Hebrew

Neely | Neelie
**Meaning:** The Poet's Son
**Origin Language:** Scottish Gaelic

Nehemiah | Nechemyah
**Meaning:** God Comforts
**Origin Language:** Hebrew

Neilos | Nil, Nilo, Nilus
**Meaning:** Of The Nile (River)
**Origin Language:** Ancient Greek

Neirin | Neurin
**Meaning:** Dignity
**Origin Language:** Latin

Neizan
**Meaning:** He Gave
**Origin Language:** Hebrew

Nelson
**Meaning:** Surpasses All Rivals
**Origin Language:** Old Irish

Neo
**Meaning:** Gifting
**Origin Language:** Tswana

Neraiah | Neriah
**Meaning:** Light Of The Lord
**Origin Language:** Hebrew

Nereo | Nereus, Nerio
**Meaning:** Water
**Origin Language:** Ancient Greek

Nero
**Meaning:** Manly
**Origin Language:** Latin

Nestor
**Meaning:** Returner
**Origin Language:** Ancient Greek

Nethaniah | Nethanyah
**Meaning:** God Has Given
**Origin Language:** Hebrew

Nev | Nevio
**Meaning:** Birth-Marked
**Origin Language:** Latin

Nevada
**Meaning:** Snowcapped
**Origin Language:** Spanish

Nevan | Nevin
**Meaning:** Little Holy One
**Origin Language:** Irish And Scottish Gaelic (Cognates)

Neven
**Meaning:** Marigold
**Origin Language:** South Slavic

Neville | Nevil
**Meaning:** From A New Town
**Origin Language:** Old French

Newton | Newt
**Meaning:** From A New Town
**Origin Language:** Old English

Niall | Nial, Nyal, Nyall
**Meaning:** Champion

**Origin Language:** Old Irish

Nicander | Nicandros, Nicanor, Nikander, Nikandros, Nikanor
**Meaning:** Victorious Man
**Origin Language:** Ancient Greek

Nichol | Nicol
**Also:** Nick | Nic, Nickie, Nicky, Nico, Nik, Nyk
**Also:** Nico | Niko, Nikos
**Also:** Nicolas | Nicholas, Nicklas, Nickolas, Nickolaus, Niclas, Nicolaos, Nicolau, Nicolaus, Niklas, Nikolaos, Nikolas, Nikolaus
**Also:** Niels | Nils
**Meaning:** Victory Of The People
**Origin Language:** Ancient Greek

Nigel | Nigellus
**Meaning:** Champion
**Origin Language:** Old Irish

Nikolai | Nicolai, Nikolay, Nikolay
**Meaning:** Victory Of The People
**Origin Language:** Ancient Greek

Nilam
**Meaning:** Dark Blue
**Origin Language:** Sanskrit

Nilas | Nylas
**Meaning:** The People's Victory
**Origin Language:** Ancient Greek

Niles | Nyles
**Meaning:** Winner
**Origin Language:** Old Irish

Niv
**Meaning:** Fruit
**Origin Language:** Hebrew

Nivan | Niven, Nivin
**Meaning:** Little Holy One
**Origin Language:** Irish And Scottish

Gaelic (Cognates)

Nixon
**Meaning:** Victory Of The People
**Origin Language:** Ancient Greek

Niyol
**Meaning:** Wind
**Origin Language:** Navajo

Noah | Noa
**Meaning:** In Motion
**Origin Language:** Hebrew

Noak | Noach
**Meaning:** Resting
**Origin Language:** Hebrew

Noam | Noham
**Meaning:** Pleasantness
**Origin Language:** Hebrew

Noel
**Meaning:** Christmas
**Origin Language:** Old French

Nolan | Noland
**Meaning:** Little Loud One
**Origin Language:** Old Irish

Norbert | Norberto
**Meaning:** Bright Northerner
**Origin Language:** Ancient Germanic

Norman | Norm, Normand, Normann, Normund, Normy
**Meaning:** Viking / Northman
**Origin Language:** Ancient Germanic

Norris
**Meaning:** Wet Nurse
**Origin Language:** Old French

Norton
**Meaning:** From A Town In The North
**Origin Language:** Old English

Norwood
**Meaning:** From A Northern Woodland
**Origin Language:** Old English

Nova | Novah
**Meaning:** New
**Origin Language:** Latin

Novak
**Meaning:** New
**Origin Language:** Serbian

Nowell | Nowel
**Meaning:** Christmas
**Origin Language:** Old French

# Chapter 15 - Names For Boys Beginning With O

Oakley | Oaklee, Oakleigh, Oaklie
**Meaning:** From An Oak Tree Meadow
**Origin Language:** Old English

Obadiah | Obadyah
**Meaning:** In Servitude To God
**Origin Language:** Hebrew

Oberic | Oberich, Oberico, Obericus, Oberigo, Oberik, Obiric, Obirich, Obirico, Obirik
**Also:** Oberon | Oberin, Oberyn, Obirin, Obiron, Obiryn
**Meaning:** Elven Ruler
**Origin Language:** Ancient Germanic

Obi
**Meaning:** Heart
**Origin Language:** Igbo

Octavius | Octavian, Octavianus, Octavio
**Meaning:** Eighth

**Origin Language:** Latin

Odalis | Odalys
**Meaning:** Wealthy
**Origin Language:** Ancient Germanic And Old English And Old Norse (Cognates)

Odell
**Meaning:** From A Hill Where Woad Grows
**Origin Language:** Old English

Odilon | Odilo
**Meaning:** Wealthy
**Origin Language:** Ancient Germanic And Old English And Old Norse (Cognates)

Odin | Oden, Odinn, Odyn
**Meaning:** The Mad One
**Origin Language:** Old English And Old Norse (Cognates)

Odion
**Meaning:** The Older Twin
**Origin Language:** Esan

Odo | Oddo, Ode
**Meaning:** Wealthy
**Origin Language:** Ancient Germanic And Old English And Old Norse (Cognates)

Odran
**Meaning:** Little Grayish-Brown One
**Origin Language:** Old Irish

Oduard | Odoard, Odoardo, Odoart, Oduardo, Oduart, Odward, Odwart
**Meaning:** Guardian Of Riches
**Origin Language:** Old English

Ogden
**Meaning:** From A Valley Of Oak Trees
**Origin Language:** Old English

Ohan | Ohann, Ohanne, Ohannes
**Meaning:** God Is Gracious
**Origin Language:** Hebrew

Okan
**Meaning:** Archer
**Origin Language:** Turkish

Olaf | Olav, Olev, Olof, Olov, Oluf
**Meaning:** Remainder Of The Ancestors
**Origin Language:** Old Norse

Olam | Oulam
**Meaning:** Perpetual
**Origin Language:** Hebrew

Olander | Ollander
**Meaning:** From A Forested Land
**Origin Language:** Old Dutch

Olbry | Olberie, Olbery, Olbri, Olbrie
**Meaning:** Elven Ruler
**Origin Language:** Ancient Germanic

Oleg
**Meaning:** Holy
**Origin Language:** Old Norse

Oleksander | Olexandar, Olexande, Olexander, Olexandre, Olexandreus, Olexandro, Olexandros, Olexandru, Olexandrus, Olexandur
**Meaning:** Defender Of Mankind
**Origin Language:** Ancient Greek

Olf | Olph
**Meaning:** Wolf
**Origin Language:** Old Norse

Oliver | Olivar, Olivero, Olivier, Oliviero, Oliviro, Olyvar, Olyvero, Olyvier, Olyviro

**Meaning:** Olive Tree
**Origin Language:** Latin

Olligan | Oligan
**Meaning:** Beauty / Mild Noble
**Origin Language:** Old Irish

Olly | Oli, Olle, Olli, Ollie
**Meaning:** Olive Tree
**Origin Language:** Latin

Olric | Olrich, Olrick, Olrik
**Meaning:** Rich Heritage
**Origin Language:** Ancient Germanic

Omar | Omari, Oumar
**Meaning:** Life
**Origin Language:** Arabic

Ombert | Omberto
**Meaning:** Bright Bear Cub
**Origin Language:** Ancient Germanic

Omer
**Meaning:** Omer (An Ancient Israelite Unit Of Dry Measure)
**Origin Language:** Hebrew

Omid
**Meaning:** Hope
**Origin Language:** Persian

Omiros
**Meaning:** Hostage
**Origin Language:** Ancient Greek

Omondi
**Meaning:** Born Early In The Morning
**Origin Language:** Luo

Omri | Omriy
**Meaning:** Life
**Origin Language:** Hebrew

Onan
**Meaning:** Pain
**Origin Language:** Hebrew

Onni
**Meaning:** Luck
**Origin Language:** Finnish

Onslow | Onslo, Onslowe
**Meaning:** From Near The Burial Mound Of A Man Called Andhere / From Near A Brave Warriors Burial Mound
**Origin Language:** Old English

Onyx
**Meaning:** Onyx
**Origin Language:** English

Opher | Ofir, Ophir
**Meaning:** From Ophir (The Name Of A Port Mentioned In The Bible Of Unknown Location)
**Origin Language:** Hebrew

Ophion | Ophioneus
**Meaning:** Serpent
**Origin Language:** Ancient Greek

Oran
**Meaning:** Little Grayish-Brown One
**Origin Language:** Old Irish

Orazio
**Meaning:** Timekeeper
**Origin Language:** Latin

Orbil | Orbilius
**Meaning:** Bereaved
**Origin Language:** Latin

Oren
**Meaning:** Pine Tree
**Origin Language:** Hebrew

Oreste | Orestes
**Meaning:** Maker Of The Mountains
**Origin Language:** Ancient Greek

Orfiel | Orifiel
**Meaning:** On God's Neck

**Origin Language:** Hebrew

Ori
**Meaning:** My Light
**Origin Language:** Hebrew

Origen | Origene, Origenes
**Meaning:** Born Of Horus (Horus Is The Name Of The Ancient Egyptian God Of Kingship And The Sky)
**Origin Language:** Ancient Greek

Oriol
**Meaning:** Golden-Haired
**Origin Language:** Catalan

Orion
**Meaning:** Light Of Heaven
**Origin Language:** Ancient Greek

Orlando
**Meaning:** Famous Throughout The Land
**Origin Language:** Ancient Germanic

Ormar | Ormarr
**Meaning:** Army Of Serpents
**Origin Language:** Old Norse

Ormaro
**Meaning:** Famous Father
**Origin Language:** Ancient Germanic

Ormond
**Meaning:** Red
**Origin Language:** Old Irish And Scottish Gaelic (Cognates)

Orpheus | Orfeas, Orfeo
**Meaning:** Darkness Of The Night
**Origin Language:** Ancient Greek

Orrell | Orell
**Meaning:** From A Hill Where Ore Is Found
**Origin Language:** Old English

Orrin
**Meaning:** Little Ash-Brown One
**Origin Language:** Old Irish

Orson
**Meaning:** Bear
**Origin Language:** Latin

Orvar
**Meaning:** Arrow
**Origin Language:** Old Norse

Orville | Orval
**Meaning:** Golden City
**Origin Language:** French

Orwell | Orewel, Orewell, Orwel
**Meaning:** From Near The Branch Of A River
**Origin Language:** Old English

Osbert | Osberht
**Meaning:** Bright And Divine
**Origin Language:** Ancient Germanic And Old English (Cognates)

Osborn | Osbeorn, Osborne, Osbourne
**Meaning:** Divine Bear
**Origin Language:** Old English

Oscar | Oksari, Oscari, Oscarino, Osgar, Oskar
**Meaning:** Divine Spear
**Origin Language:** Ancient Germanic And Old English And Old Norse (Cognates)

Oshea | Osea, Osee
**Meaning:** Salvation
**Origin Language:** Hebrew

Osheen | Osian, Ossian
**Meaning:** Little Deer
**Origin Language:** Old Irish

Osiris
**Meaning:** Mighty / Eye
**Origin Language:** Ancient Egyptian

Osman
**Meaning:** Baby Bustard (A Type Of Bird)
**Origin Language:** Arabic

Osmond | Osmund
**Meaning:** Divine Protector
**Origin Language:** Old English

Osvin | Osvyn
**Meaning:** Divine And Friendly / God's Friend
**Origin Language:** Ancient Germanic And Old English (Cognates)

Oswald
**Meaning:** Divine Ruler
**Origin Language:** Ancient Germanic And Old English And Old Norse (Cognates)

Oswin | Osuine, Osuinus, Oswen, Oswine, Oswinn, Oswino, Oswyn, Oswynn
**Meaning:** Divine And Friendly / God's Friend
**Origin Language:** Ancient Germanic And Old English (Cognates)

Othello | Otello, Othell, Otho
**Meaning:** Wealthy
**Origin Language:** Latin

Othmar
**Meaning:** Wealthy And Famous
**Origin Language:** Ancient Germanic And Old Norse (Cognates)

Othniel | Othniyel
**Meaning:** Lion Of God
**Origin Language:** Hebrew

Otieno

**Meaning:** Born At Night
**Origin Language:** Luo

Otis
**Meaning:** Wealthy
**Origin Language:** Ancient Germanic And Old English And Old Norse (Cognates)

Otmar | Ottmar, Ottomar
**Meaning:** Wealthy And Famous
**Origin Language:** Ancient Germanic And Old Norse (Cognates)

Otniel
**Meaning:** Lion Of God
**Origin Language:** Hebrew

Ottavian | Otavio, Ottavante, Ottaviano, Ottavio, Ottavo
**Meaning:** Eighth
**Origin Language:** Latin

Otto | Oto
**Also:** Ottorin | Ottorino
**Meaning:** Wealthy
**Origin Language:** Ancient Germanic And Old English And Old Norse (Cognates)

Ovadiah
**Meaning:** In Servitude To God
**Origin Language:** Hebrew

Ovid | Ofydd, Ovidio, Ovidius
**Meaning:** Shepherd
**Origin Language:** Latin

Owain
**Meaning:** Well-Born
**Origin Language:** Ancient Greek

Owen | Owan
**Meaning:** Born Of The Yew Tree
**Origin Language:** Old Irish

Ozaziah | Ozazias

**Meaning:** God Is Strong
**Origin Language:** Hebrew

Ozi | Ozzi
**Meaning:** My Power
**Origin Language:** Hebrew

Ozias
**Meaning:** God Is Strong
**Origin Language:** Hebrew

Oziel | Ozihel
**Meaning:** God Is My Strength
**Origin Language:** Hebrew

Ozzy | Oz, Ozzie
**Meaning:** Strength
**Origin Language:** Hebrew

# Chapter 16 - Names For Boys Beginning With P

Pablo
**Meaning:** Humble
**Origin Language:** Latin

Pace | Payce
**Meaning:** Peace
**Origin Language:** Old English

Paden
**Meaning:** Patrician / Aristocrat
**Origin Language:** Latin

Paeon | Paian, Paion
**Meaning:** Healer
**Origin Language:** Ancient Greek

Palaemon | Palaimon
**Meaning:** Wrestler
**Origin Language:** Ancient Greek

Pallas

**Meaning:** Brandishes (A Weapon)
**Origin Language:** Ancient Greek

Palmer | Palmiro
**Meaning:** Pilgrim / Palm Tree
**Origin Language:** Italian

Paolo | Paolino
**Meaning:** Humble
**Origin Language:** Latin

Paris | Parris, Parriss, Parys
**Meaning:** Combative
**Origin Language:** Ancient Greek

Parker
**Meaning:** Keeper Of The Park
**Origin Language:** Old English

Parry | Parrie
**Meaning:** Sovereign Of The Homeland
**Origin Language:** Ancient Germanic

Parzival | Parsifal, Parzifal
**Meaning:** Pierces The Valley
**Origin Language:** Old French

Pascal | Pascual, Paskal
**Also:** Paschalis | Paschal
**Also:** Pasquale | Pasqualino
**Meaning:** Easter
**Origin Language:** Latin

Patrick | Pat, Patraicc, Patricio, Patricius, Patrik, Patrikios, Patrizio, Patryk
**Also:** Patton
**Meaning:** Patrician / Aristocrat
**Origin Language:** Latin

Paul | Paulie, Paulinus, Paulo, Paulos, Paulus, Pauly, Poul
**Also:** Pavel | Paval, Paviel, Pavle, Pavol
**Also:** Pavlin

**Also:** Pavlo | Pavlos
**Meaning:** Small / Humble
**Origin Language:** Latin

Paxton
**Meaning:** From Pœcc's Town (The Meaning Of The Old English Personal Name Pœcc Is Unknown)
**Origin Language:** Old English

Pearce | Pierce
**Also:** Pedro
**Meaning:** Stone
**Origin Language:** Ancient Greek

Pepe | Pepito, Peppe, Peppi, Peppino
**Meaning:** God Will Add
**Origin Language:** Hebrew

Perceval | Percevel, Percival, Percivel
**Also:** Percy | Perce, Percie
**Meaning:** Pierces The Valley
**Origin Language:** Old French

Peregrin | Peregrine, Peregrinus
**Meaning:** Pilgrim
**Origin Language:** Latin

Perez | Peretz
**Meaning:** He That Bursts Forth
**Origin Language:** Hebrew

Perrin
**Meaning:** Stone
**Origin Language:** Ancient Greek

Perry
**Meaning:** Ruler Of The Homeland
**Origin Language:** Ancient Germanic

Perun
**Meaning:** Thunder
**Origin Language:** Common Slavic

Peter | Peeter, Petar, Pete, Petr, Petre, Petter, Petur, Petyr
**Also:** Peterkin
**Also:** Petro | Petras, Petros, Petru, Petrus
**Meaning:** Stone
**Origin Language:** Ancient Greek

Peyton | Paityn, Payton
**Meaning:** From Pæga's Town / From A Rural Town
**Origin Language:** Old English

Phaedrus | Phaidros
**Meaning:** Luminous
**Origin Language:** Ancient Greek

Phane | Phanes
**Meaning:** Appears
**Origin Language:** Ancient Greek

Pharamond | Pharamund, Pharamundo
**Meaning:** Journeying For Protection
**Origin Language:** Ancient Germanic

Pharell | Pharel
**Meaning:** Man Of Boldness
**Origin Language:** Old Irish

Pharez | Phares
**Meaning:** He That Bursts Forth
**Origin Language:** Hebrew

Pherick | Pheric, Pherik
**Meaning:** Patrician / Aristocrat
**Origin Language:** Latin

Philbert | Philibert
**Meaning:** Very Bright
**Origin Language:** Ancient Germanic

Philip | Phil, Philipp, Philippe, Philippos, Philippus, Phillip
**Meaning:** Lover Of Horses
**Origin Language:** Ancient Greek

Philon | Philo
**Meaning:** Lover / Friend
**Origin Language:** Ancient Greek

Phineas | Phinehas
**Meaning:** Mouth Of The Serpent
**Origin Language:** Hebrew

Phineus
**Meaning:** Vulture
**Origin Language:** Ancient Greek

Phirun
**Meaning:** Rain
**Origin Language:** Khmer

Phoebus | Phoibos
**Meaning:** Radiant
**Origin Language:** Ancient Greek

Phoenix | Phoinix
**Meaning:** Phoenix
**Origin Language:** English

Phrix | Phrixos, Phrixus
**Meaning:** Causes Shivers
**Origin Language:** Ancient Greek

Pierre | Pierino, Piero
**Also:** Pierrick
**Also:** Piers | Peers
**Meaning:** Stone
**Origin Language:** Ancient Greek

Piran
**Meaning:** Dark
**Origin Language:** Old Irish

Porter
**Meaning:** Door Keeper
**Origin Language:** Old French

Presley | Preslee, Presleigh, Preslie, Presly
**Meaning:** From A Priest's Meadow

**Origin Language:** Old English

Preston
**Meaning:** From A Priest's Town
**Origin Language:** Old English

Prince
**Meaning:** Prince
**Origin Language:** English

Pryce | Price
**Meaning:** Ardent
**Origin Language:** Old Welsh

# Chapter 17 - Names For Boys Beginning With Q

Qainan | Qaenan, Qaenen, Qainam, Qainen, Qeinan, Qeinen, Qenan, Qenen, Qeynan
**Meaning:** Possession
**Origin Language:** Hebrew

Quade
**Meaning:** Ruler Of The Army
**Origin Language:** Ancient Germanic

Quan
**Meaning:** Spring (Of Water) (Chinese) / Sea Spirit (Old Irish)
**Origin Language:** Chinese And Old Irish

Quant
**Meaning:** Prankster / Rogue
**Origin Language:** Ancient Germanic

Quantrell | Quantrill
**Meaning:** Attractive
**Origin Language:** Old French

Quarlis | Quarles, Quarless, Quarliss, Quarlys

**Meaning:** From Near A Circle Made Of Stones
**Origin Language:** Old English

Quenby | Quinby
**Meaning:** From The Queens Manor
**Origin Language:** Old English

Quentin
**Meaning:** Fifth
**Origin Language:** Latin

Quim
**Meaning:** God Establishes
**Origin Language:** Hebrew

Quimby | Quemby
**Meaning:** From The Queens Manor
**Origin Language:** Old English

Quince | Quincey, Quincie, Quinctilius, Quinctius, Quinctus, Quincy
**Meaning:** Fifth
**Origin Language:** Latin

Quinlan
**Meaning:** Of A Beautiful Appearance
**Origin Language:** Old Irish

Quinn | Quin
**Meaning:** The Head (The Most Important Person)
**Origin Language:** Old Irish

Quintilian | Quinctilius, Quintilianus, Quintilius, Quintillus
**Also:** Quinton | Quinten, Quintin, Quintino
**Also:** Quintus | Quintius
**Meaning:** Fifth
**Origin Language:** Latin

Quirin | Quirino, Quirinus
**Meaning:** Armed With A Spear
**Origin Language:** Latin

Quixley | Quixlee, Quixleigh, Quixlie
**Meaning:** From Cwichelm's Meadow / From A Meadow Of Living Elm Trees / From The Living Protector's Meadow
**Origin Language:** Old English

# Chapter 18 - Names For Boys Beginning With R

Raban
**Meaning:** Raven
**Origin Language:** Ancient Germanic

Radcliff | Radcliffe, Radclyff, Radclyffe
**Meaning:** From A Red Cliff
**Origin Language:** Old English

Radley | Radlee, Radleigh, Radlie
**Meaning:** From A Red Meadow
**Origin Language:** Old English

Raeburn
**Meaning:** From Near A Stream Where Roebuck Frequent
**Origin Language:** Old English

Rafael | Rafail, Raffael, Raffaello, Raphael, Refael, Rephael, Rhaphael
**Meaning:** God Has Healed
**Origin Language:** Hebrew

Rafferty | Raffertie
**Meaning:** Spring Tide / Flood
**Origin Language:** Old Irish

Raiden | Rayden
**Meaning:** Thunder And Lightning
**Origin Language:** Japanese

Raleigh

**Meaning:** From A Meadow Where Roebuck Roam
**Origin Language:** Old English

Ralph | Ralf, Ralphie, Ralphy
**Meaning:** Counsel Of The Wolf
**Origin Language:** Ancient Germanic

Rambert
**Meaning:** Bright Raven
**Origin Language:** Ancient Germanic

Ramiel
**Meaning:** God's Thunder
**Origin Language:** Arabic

Ramiro | Ramirus
**Meaning:** Famous Governor
**Origin Language:** Ancient Germanic

Ramon
**Meaning:** Protecting Governor
**Origin Language:** Ancient Germanic

Ramsay | Ramsey
**Meaning:** From An Island Where Garlic Is Grown
**Origin Language:** Old English

Ramses | Rameses, Ramesses, Ramessu, Rhamesses
**Meaning:** Born Of Ra (Ra Is The Name Of The Egyptian God Of The Sun, Order, Kings, And The Sky)
**Origin Language:** Ancient Egyptian

Ranald
**Meaning:** Ruling Governor
**Origin Language:** Ancient Germanic And Old Norse (Cognates)

Randall | Randal, Randel, Randell, Randyl, Randyll
**Also:** Randolph | Randolf, Randulf, Ranolf, Ranulf, Ranulph
**Meaning:** Looks Over The Rim Of His

Wolven Shield
**Origin Language:** Old Norse

Randy | Rand
**Meaning:** The Rim Of A Shield
**Origin Language:** Ancient Germanic

Raniero | Rainerio, Rainier, Reinier
**Meaning:** Army Governor
**Origin Language:** Ancient Germanic And Old Norse (Cognates)

Rasmus | Rasmo, Rasmos
**Meaning:** Beloved
**Origin Language:** Ancient Greek

Rauf
**Meaning:** Compassionate
**Origin Language:** Arabic

Raul | Raoul
**Meaning:** Counsel Of The Wolf
**Origin Language:** Ancient Germanic

Ray
**Meaning:** Ray Of Light
**Origin Language:** English

Rayan | Rayaan, Rayyan
**Meaning:** Luxuriant
**Origin Language:** Arabic

Raylan
**Meaning:** Ray Of Light
**Origin Language:** English

Raymond | Raimon, Raimond, Raimondo, Raimund, Raimundo, Raymund, Raymundo, Reimond, Reimund
**Meaning:** Protecting Governor
**Origin Language:** Ancient Germanic

Raynard | Rainard, Reinard, Reinhard, Reinhardt, Renard, Reynard, Reynhard
**Meaning:** Hardy Governor
**Origin Language:** Ancient Germanic

Rayner | Rainer, Reiner
**Meaning:** Army Governor
**Origin Language:** Ancient Germanic And Old Norse (Cognates)

Raziel
**Meaning:** God Is My Secret
**Origin Language:** Hebrew

Reagan | Regan
**Meaning:** Little King
**Origin Language:** Old Irish

Redd | Red
**Meaning:** Red
**Origin Language:** English

Redmond | Redmund
**Meaning:** Protecting Governor
**Origin Language:** Ancient Germanic

Reggie | Reg, Reggy
**Meaning:** Ruling Governor
**Origin Language:** Ancient Germanic And Old Norse (Cognates)

Regin
**Meaning:** Advisor / Governor
**Origin Language:** Ancient Germanic

Reginald | Reginold
**Meaning:** Ruling Governor
**Origin Language:** Ancient Germanic And Old Norse (Cognates)

Reid | Reed
**Meaning:** Red / Red-Haired
**Origin Language:** Old English

Reign | Reyne
**Meaning:** Reign
**Origin Language:** English

Reilly | Reillie

**Meaning:** Of The Social People / Of The Warring People / Of The Church People
**Origin Language:** Old Irish

Reinald | Reinaldo, Reinhold, Reynaldo, Reynaldus, Reynold, Rinaldo
**Meaning:** Ruling Governor
**Origin Language:** Ancient Germanic And Old Norse (Cognates)

Rembrandt
**Meaning:** Sword Advisor
**Origin Language:** Ancient Germanic

Remiel
**Meaning:** God Will Have Pity
**Origin Language:** Hebrew

Remington
**Meaning:** From A Town By The Boundary Of A Stream
**Origin Language:** Old English

Remus | Remo
**Meaning:** Oar
**Origin Language:** Latin

Remy | Remi, Remie
**Meaning:** Rower
**Origin Language:** Latin

Ren
**Meaning:** Lotus / Love
**Origin Language:** Japanese

Renart | Renarto
**Meaning:** Hardy Governor
**Origin Language:** Ancient Germanic

Renatus | Renat, Renato
**Meaning:** Reborn
**Origin Language:** Latin

Renaud | Reynaud
**Meaning:** Ruling Governor

**Origin Language:** Ancient Germanic And Old Norse (Cognates)

Rene | René
**Meaning:** Reborn
**Origin Language:** Latin

Renfry | Renfree, Renfreu, Renfrew
**Meaning:** The Point At The Current (Of Water)
**Origin Language:** Old Welsh

Renley | Renlee, Renleigh, Renlie, Renly
**Meaning:** From A Meadow Of Wrens
**Origin Language:** Old English

Renzo
**Meaning:** From Laurentum (An Ancient Roman City That Was Considered The Capital Of Italy) / Laurel Tree
**Origin Language:** Latin

Reuben | Reuven, Reuwben, Rhouben, Rouben, Rube, Ruben
**Meaning:** Behold A Son
**Origin Language:** Hebrew

Rex
**Meaning:** Monarch
**Origin Language:** Latin

Reyes
**Meaning:** Royal
**Origin Language:** Latin

Rezart | Rezar
**Meaning:** Golden Ray
**Origin Language:** Albanian

Rhett
**Meaning:** Advisor
**Origin Language:** Dutch

Rhisiart

**Meaning:** Rich And Hardy
**Origin Language:** Ancient Germanic

## Rhodri | Rhodrie, Rhodry
**Meaning:** King Of Chariots
**Origin Language:** Old Welsh

## Rhyderch | Rhydderch, Riderch, Ryderch
**Meaning:** Has The Aspect Of A King
**Origin Language:** Old Welsh

## Rhys | Reece, Rees, Reese, Ris
**Meaning:** Ardent
**Origin Language:** Old Welsh

## Riad
**Also:** Riaz
**Meaning:** Meadows
**Origin Language:** Arabic

## Ricardo | Ricard, Riccard, Riccardo, Rickard, Rikard, Rikkard
**Also:** Richard
**Also:** Richmal
**Meaning:** Rich And Hardy
**Origin Language:** Ancient Germanic

## Richmond
**Meaning:** From A Rich Hill
**Origin Language:** Old French

## Ricky | Rick, Rickey, Ricki, Rickie, Rik, Rikkie, Rikky, Rikky
**Also:** Rickon | Ricon, Rikon
**Also:** Rico
**Meaning:** Rich
**Origin Language:** Ancient Germanic

## Ridley | Ridleigh, Ridlie
**Meaning:** From A Meadow With Reeds
**Origin Language:** Old English

## Rigby | Rigbie
**Meaning:** From A Farm On A Ridge
**Origin Language:** Old Norse

## Riggs | Rigge, Rigges, Riggey
**Meaning:** From Near A Ridge Of Land
**Origin Language:** Old English

## Rihard
**Meaning:** Rich And Hardy
**Origin Language:** Ancient Germanic

## Riley | Rylee, Ryley, Rylie, Ryly
**Meaning:** From A Meadow Of Rye
**Origin Language:** Old English

## Rino
**Meaning:** Youthful
**Origin Language:** Albanian

## Rio
**Meaning:** River
**Origin Language:** Spanish

## Riordan | Reardan, Rearden, Riorden
**Meaning:** The King's Little Poet
**Origin Language:** Old Irish

## Ripley | Riplea, Ripleigh, Riplie
**Meaning:** From A Divided Meadow
**Origin Language:** Old English

## Ritchie | Rich, Richie, Richy, Ritchy
**Meaning:** Rich
**Origin Language:** Ancient Germanic

## River
**Meaning:** River
**Origin Language:** English

## Roald
**Meaning:** Famous Ruler
**Origin Language:** Old Norse

## Robby | Rob, Robbie, Robi
**Also:** Robert | Roberto
**Also:** Robin | Robyn

**Meaning:** Famous And Bright
**Origin Language:** Ancient Germanic

Rocco | Roc, Roch, Rok, Rokko, Roko
**Also:** Rocky | Rockie, Rokkie, Rokky
**Meaning:** Rook
**Origin Language:** Ancient Germanic

Roddy | Rod, Roddie
**Also:** Roderick | Roderic, Roderik
**Meaning:** Famous And Rich
**Origin Language:** Ancient Germanic

Rodion
**Meaning:** Ode To A Hero
**Origin Language:** Ancient Greek

Rodney
**Meaning:** From Hroda's Island / From A Famous Island
**Origin Language:** Old English

Rodolph | Rodolf, Rodolfe, Rodolfito, Rodolfo, Rodolphe
**Meaning:** Famous Wolf
**Origin Language:** Ancient Germanic

Rodrigo | Rodrigue
**Meaning:** Famous And Rich
**Origin Language:** Ancient Germanic

Roel
**Meaning:** Famous Throughout The Land
**Origin Language:** Ancient Germanic

Roger | Rodge, Rodger, Rogerio, Rogerius, Rogier
**Meaning:** Famous Spear
**Origin Language:** Ancient Germanic

Rohan
**Meaning:** Ascending
**Origin Language:** Sanskrit

Rolan
**Also:** Roland | Rolando, Rolland, Rowland
**Meaning:** Famous Throughout The Land
**Origin Language:** Ancient Germanic

Rollo | Rolo
**Also:** Rolph | Rolf
**Meaning:** Famous Wolf
**Origin Language:** Ancient Germanic

Romain | Romayn, Romayne, Romein
**Also:** Roman | Romano, Romanos, Romanus
**Also:** Romeo | Romaeus, Romeu
**Also:** Romilius
**Also:** Romolo | Romollo
**Also:** Romulus
**Meaning:** From Rome
**Origin Language:** Latin

Romuald | Romualdo
**Meaning:** Famous Ruler
**Origin Language:** Ancient Germanic

Ron
**Meaning:** Song
**Origin Language:** Hebrew

Ronald | Ronaldo
**Meaning:** Ruling Governor
**Origin Language:** Ancient Germanic And Old Norse (Cognates)

Ronan
**Meaning:** Little Seal
**Origin Language:** Old Irish

Ronen
**Meaning:** Song
**Origin Language:** Hebrew

## Ronin
**Meaning:** A Masterless Samurai
**Origin Language:** Japanese

## Ronny | Ronnie
**Meaning:** Ruling Governor
**Origin Language:** Ancient Germanic And Old Norse (Cognates)

## Roosevelt | Roose
**Meaning:** Field Of Roses
**Origin Language:** Dutch

## Roque
**Meaning:** Rook
**Origin Language:** Ancient Germanic

## Rory | Rorie
**Meaning:** Red-Haired King
**Origin Language:** Old Irish

## Rosario | Rozario
**Meaning:** Rosary
**Origin Language:** Spanish

## Roscoe | Rosco
**Meaning:** From A Forest Where Roebuck Frequent
**Origin Language:** Old Norse

## Rosendo | Rozendo
**Meaning:** Walks The Path Towards Fame
**Origin Language:** Ancient Germanic

## Ross
**Meaning:** From Near The Promontory
**Origin Language:** Scottish Gaelic

## Roswell
**Meaning:** From Near A Water Spring On A Promontory
**Origin Language:** Old English

## Rotem
**Meaning:** White Broom (The Name Of A Flowering Shrub)

**Origin Language:** Hebrew

## Roul
**Meaning:** Famous Wolf
**Origin Language:** Ancient Germanic

## Rowan | Rowen
**Meaning:** Little Red-Haired One
**Origin Language:** Old Irish

## Rowley
**Meaning:** Famous Throughout The Land
**Origin Language:** Ancient Germanic

## Roy
**Meaning:** Red
**Origin Language:** Old Irish And Scottish Gaelic (Cognates)

## Royce
**Meaning:** Rose
**Origin Language:** Latin

## Roydon
**Meaning:** From A Hill Where Rye Is Grown
**Origin Language:** Old English

## Royle
**Meaning:** From A Hill Where Rye Is Grown
**Origin Language:** Old English

## Royston
**Meaning:** From Royse's Town / From A Town With Many Roses
**Origin Language:** Old English

## Ru
**Meaning:** Scholar
**Origin Language:** Chinese

## Ruarc | Ruarcc
**Meaning:** Famous And Rich
**Origin Language:** Ancient Germanic

Rudolph | Rudolf, Rudolfe, Rudolfo, Rudolphe, Rudolphus
**Also:** Rudy | Rudi, Rudie, Ruedi
**Meaning:** Famous Wolf
**Origin Language:** Ancient Germanic

Rudyard
**Meaning:** From A Yard Where Rue Is Grown
**Origin Language:** Old English

Rufus | Ruphus
**Meaning:** Red Haired
**Origin Language:** Latin

Rui
**Meaning:** Famous And Rich
**Origin Language:** Ancient Germanic

Rumen
**Meaning:** Red-Cheeked
**Origin Language:** Bulgarian And Macedonian (Cognates)

Rupert | Ruperto
**Meaning:** Famous And Bright
**Origin Language:** Ancient Germanic

Rurik | Ruric
**Meaning:** Famous And Rich
**Origin Language:** Ancient Germanic

Russell | Russ, Russel
**Meaning:** Little Red One
**Origin Language:** Old French

Rusty | Rustie
**Meaning:** Rusty / Red-Haired
**Origin Language:** English

Ryan | Rian, Rie, Ry
**Meaning:** Little King
**Origin Language:** Old Irish

Ryder
**Meaning:** Mounted Warrior
**Origin Language:** Old English

Ryker
**Meaning:** Rich
**Origin Language:** Low German

Rylan | Rylen
**Also:** Ryland
**Meaning:** From Land Where Rye Is Grown
**Origin Language:** Old English

Ryo
**Meaning:** Cool / Refreshing / Distant / Reality
**Origin Language:** Japanese

# Chapter 19 - Names For Boys Beginning With S

Sacha | Sascha, Sasha
**Meaning:** Mankind's Defender
**Origin Language:** Ancient Greek

Sachairi
**Meaning:** God Remembers
**Origin Language:** Hebrew

Sacheverell
**Meaning:** Leaping Roebuck
**Origin Language:** Old French

Saint
**Meaning:** Saint
**Origin Language:** English

Salem
**Meaning:** Safe
**Origin Language:** Arabic

Salvador | Sal, Salvator
**Meaning:** Rescuer
**Origin Language:** Latin

**Sam | Saam**
**Meaning:** Dark
**Origin Language:** Old Avestan

**Samael | Sammael**
**Meaning:** Severity Of God
**Origin Language:** Hebrew

**Sami**
**Meaning:** Elevated
**Origin Language:** Arabic

**Samil**
**Meaning:** Severity Of God
**Origin Language:** Hebrew

**Sammy | Sammi, Sammie**
**Meaning:** His Name Is "El" (His Name Is God)
**Origin Language:** Hebrew

**Sampson**
**Also:** Samson | Samsoni, Samzun
**Meaning:** Sun Child
**Origin Language:** Hebrew

**Samuel | Samoil, Samouel, Samual, Samuhel, Samuil**
**Meaning:** His Name Is "El" (His Name Is God)
**Origin Language:** Hebrew

**Sancho**
**Meaning:** Saintly
**Origin Language:** Latin

**Sanders | Sandor, Sandro**
**Meaning:** Mankind's Defender
**Origin Language:** Ancient Greek

**Sandford**
**Meaning:** From Near A Sandy Ford Sand
**Origin Language:** Old English

**Sanford**
**Meaning:** From Near A Sandy Ford Sand
**Origin Language:** Old English

**Sanson**
**Meaning:** Sun Child
**Origin Language:** Hebrew

**Santana**
**Meaning:** Of Saint Anna
**Origin Language:** Spanish

**Santeri**
**Meaning:** Defender Of Mankind
**Origin Language:** Ancient Greek

**Santiago**
**Meaning:** Of Saint Iago
**Origin Language:** Hebrew And Latin (In Combination)

**Santino | Sante, Santi, Santo**
**Meaning:** Saint
**Origin Language:** Latin

**Saral**
**Meaning:** Straight
**Origin Language:** Sanskrit

**Saraph**
**Meaning:** Serpent
**Origin Language:** Hebrew

**Saul | Saoul, Saulos**
**Meaning:** He That Was Asked For
**Origin Language:** Hebrew

**Sawney**
**Meaning:** Mankind's Defender
**Origin Language:** Ancient Greek

**Sawyer**
**Meaning:** Wood Sawyer
**Origin Language:** Old English

**Saxon**

**Meaning:** Of The Saxons (The Name Of A Germanic Tribe)
**Origin Language:** Ancient Germanic

Schuyler
**Meaning:** Student
**Origin Language:** German

Scott | Scot, Scottie, Scotty
**Meaning:** From Scotland
**Origin Language:** Scottish Gaelic

Scout
**Meaning:** Scout
**Origin Language:** English

Sean | Shaun, Shawn
**Meaning:** Graced By God
**Origin Language:** Hebrew

Sebastian | Sebastiano, Sebastianus, Sebastien, Sebastyan
**Meaning:** From Sebaste (An Ancient City In Asia Minor) / Venerable
**Origin Language:** Latin

Seff
**Meaning:** Wolf
**Origin Language:** Yiddish

Sefton
**Meaning:** From A Town Where Rushes Grow
**Origin Language:** Old English

Seir | Seiyr
**Meaning:** Rough / Hairy
**Origin Language:** Hebrew

Selby | Selbie
**Meaning:** From A Farmstead With Willow Trees
**Origin Language:** Old Norse

Selim
**Meaning:** Safe
**Origin Language:** Arabic

Selwyn | Selwin
**Meaning:** Friendly Manor Dweller
**Origin Language:** Old English

Semion | Semyon
**Meaning:** He Has Heard
**Origin Language:** Hebrew

Serafim | Serafeim, Serafin, Serafino, Seraphin, Seraphinus
**Meaning:** Burning / Glowing / Seraphim
**Origin Language:** Latin

Sergio | Serge, Sergei, Sergey, Sergianus, Sergios, Sergius, Sergo
**Meaning:** Protected
**Origin Language:** Latin

Seth
**Meaning:** Appointed
**Origin Language:** Hebrew

Sevan
**Meaning:** Lake
**Origin Language:** Armenian

Sevastian | Sevastien, Sevastyan
**Meaning:** From Sebaste (An Ancient City In Asia Minor) / Venerable
**Origin Language:** Latin

Seven | Sevyn
**Meaning:** Seven
**Origin Language:** English

Severin | Severiano, Severianus, Severino, Severinus
**Meaning:** Severe/Stern
**Origin Language:** Latin

Seward | Seweard, Siward, Siweard
**Meaning:** Victorious Warden
**Origin Language:** Ancient Germanic And Old English (Cognates)

Seymour
**Meaning:** Of Saint Maurus
**Origin Language:** Latin

Shadi
**Meaning:** Singer
**Origin Language:** Arabic

Shae | Shay, Shaye, Shea
**Meaning:** Approvable
**Origin Language:** Old Irish

Shai
**Meaning:** Gift
**Origin Language:** Hebrew

Shakeel | Shakil, Shaquille
**Meaning:** Handsome
**Origin Language:** Arabic

Shakir
**Meaning:** Thankful
**Origin Language:** Arabic

Shallum | Shalluwm
**Meaning:** Retribution
**Origin Language:** Hebrew

Shamus | Seumas, Sheamus
**Meaning:** Supplanter (Wrongfully Seizes And Holds The Place Of Another)
**Origin Language:** Hebrew

Shane | Shaine, Shayne
**Meaning:** God Is Gracious
**Origin Language:** Hebrew

Shani
**Meaning:** Scarlet Red
**Origin Language:** Hebrew

Shaw
**Meaning:** From Near A Thicket
**Origin Language:** Old English

Shelach

**Meaning:** Javelin
**Origin Language:** Hebrew

Shelby | Shelbie
**Meaning:** From A Farmstead With Willow Trees
**Origin Language:** Old Norse

Sheldon | Sheldan, Shelden
**Meaning:** From A Flat Topped Hill
**Origin Language:** Old English

Shelton
**Meaning:** From A Town On A Shelf
**Origin Language:** Old English

Shem
**Meaning:** Sigma / Name
**Origin Language:** Hebrew

Shemaiah | Shemayah
**Also:** Shemuel | Shemuwel
**Meaning:** Heard By God
**Origin Language:** Hebrew

Shepard | Shepherd
**Meaning:** Shepherd
**Origin Language:** English

Sheridan
**Meaning:** Seeker
**Origin Language:** Old Irish

Sherlock
**Meaning:** Sheared Locks Of Hair
**Origin Language:** Old English

Sherman
**Meaning:** Cloth Cutter
**Origin Language:** Old English

Sherwood
**Meaning:** From A Bright Forest
**Origin Language:** Old English

Shet
**Meaning:** Appointed

**Origin Language:** Hebrew

Shikoba
**Meaning:** Feather
**Origin Language:** Choctaw

Shiloh | Shiyloh
**Meaning:** Tranquil
**Origin Language:** Hebrew

Shimon | Shimown
**Meaning:** He Has Heard
**Origin Language:** Hebrew

Shimson | Shimshon, Shimshown
**Meaning:** Sun Child
**Origin Language:** Hebrew

Shion
**Meaning:** Aster / Sound
**Origin Language:** Japanese

Shiori
**Meaning:** Weave / Bookmark / Bending
**Origin Language:** Japanese

Shon
**Meaning:** Graced By God
**Origin Language:** Hebrew

Shyam | Shyamal
**Meaning:** Dark Blue
**Origin Language:** Sanskrit

Siarl
**Meaning:** Has Freedom
**Origin Language:** Ancient Germanic

Sibald | Sibbe, Sybald
**Meaning:** Bold And Victorious
**Origin Language:** Old English

Sidney | Sid, Syd, Sydney
**Meaning:** From A Wide Island
**Origin Language:** Old English

Silas | Sylas

**Also:** Silvanus | Sylvanus
**Meaning:** Of The Forest
**Origin Language:** Latin

Silver
**Meaning:** Silver
**Origin Language:** English

Silvius | Silvio
**Meaning:** Forest
**Origin Language:** Latin

Simeon | Simion, Symeon
**Meaning:** He Has Heard
**Origin Language:** Hebrew

Simiel
**Meaning:** God Establishes
**Origin Language:** Hebrew

Simon | Sime, Simen, Simo, Symon, Szymon
**Meaning:** He Has Heard
**Origin Language:** Hebrew

Simpson | Simson
**Meaning:** Sun Child
**Origin Language:** Hebrew

Simund | Semond, Semund, Simond
**Meaning:** Victorious Protector
**Origin Language:** Old Norse

Sirius
**Meaning:** Burning
**Origin Language:** Latin

Siwart | Siverd, Sivert
**Meaning:** Victorious Warden
**Origin Language:** Ancient Germanic And Old English (Cognates)

Sky
**Meaning:** Sky
**Origin Language:** English

Skyler | Skylar
**Meaning:** Student
**Origin Language:** German

Sloan
**Meaning:** Little Raider
**Origin Language:** Old Irish

Smith
**Meaning:** Metal Worker
**Origin Language:** Old English

Sofron | Sophron
**Meaning:** Sensible
**Origin Language:** Ancient Greek

Sohan
**Meaning:** God Is Gracious
**Origin Language:** Hebrew

Solomon | Salomo, Salomon,
Salomone, Sol, Sollie, Solly
**Meaning:** Peace
**Origin Language:** Hebrew

Sondre
**Meaning:** Sun
**Origin Language:** Old Norse

Sonny | Sonnie
**Meaning:** Little Son
**Origin Language:** English

Soren
**Meaning:** Severe/Stern
**Origin Language:** Latin

Sorin
**Meaning:** The Sun
**Origin Language:** Romanian

Sorley
**Meaning:** Wanders Through The
Summer
**Origin Language:** Old Norse

Sovann
**Meaning:** Gold
**Origin Language:** Khmer

Sparrow
**Meaning:** Sparrow
**Origin Language:** English

Spencer
**Meaning:** Dispenser Of Provisions
**Origin Language:** Old English

Spiridon | Spyridon
**Meaning:** Spirit
**Origin Language:** Ancient Greek

Stafford
**Meaning:** From Near A Ford With A
Port
**Origin Language:** Old English

Stanford
**Meaning:** From Near A Stony Ford
**Origin Language:** Old English

Stanley | Stan, Stanlee, Stanleigh,
Stanlie, Stanly
**Meaning:** From A Stony Meadow
**Origin Language:** Old English

Stannos | Stanos
**Meaning:** This Name Has No Meaning
(Stannos Is A Fictional Character
Featuring In The TV Series Game Of
Thrones)
**Origin Language:** Invented

Stathis
**Meaning:** Stable
**Origin Language:** Ancient Greek

Steenie | Steeny
**Also:** Stefan | Staffan, Stefano,
Stefanos, Stefanus, Steffan, Steffen
**Meaning:** Wears The Conqueror's
Crown

**Origin Language:** Ancient Greek

Steinar | Steinarr
**Meaning:** Stone Army
**Origin Language:** Old Norse

Steinn | Stein
**Meaning:** Stone
**Origin Language:** Old Norse

Stelian | Stelios
**Meaning:** Pillar
**Origin Language:** Ancient Greek

Stellan
**Meaning:** Calm
**Origin Language:** Old Norse

Stepan
**Meaning:** Wears The Conqueror's Crown
**Origin Language:** Ancient Greek

Sterling | Stirling
**Meaning:** Sterling (Excellent)
**Origin Language:** English

Stetson
**Meaning:** Young Wild One
**Origin Language:** Old English

Steven | Stephan, Stephanas, Stephane, Stephanos, Stephanus, Stephen, Stevan
**Also:** Stevie | Ste, Steve, Stevo, Stevy
**Meaning:** Wears The Conqueror's Crown
**Origin Language:** Ancient Greek

Stian
**Meaning:** Wanderer / He Who Treads
**Origin Language:** Old Norse

Stig
**Meaning:** The Path

**Origin Language:** Old Norse

Stipan
**Meaning:** Wears The Conqueror's Crown
**Origin Language:** Ancient Greek

Straton
**Meaning:** Of The Army
**Origin Language:** Ancient Greek

Stuart | Stew, Stewart, Stu
**Meaning:** Guard Of The House
**Origin Language:** Old English

Stylian | Stylianos
**Meaning:** Pillar
**Origin Language:** Ancient Greek

Sullivan | Sulivan, Sullie, Sully
**Meaning:** Dark-Eyed
**Origin Language:** Old Irish

Sunny | Sunnie
**Meaning:** Sunny
**Origin Language:** English

Sutton
**Meaning:** From A Southern Town
**Origin Language:** Old English

Sven | Svein, Sveinn
**Meaning:** Attendant / Boy
**Origin Language:** Old Norse

Sweeney | Sweeny
**Meaning:** Joyful
**Origin Language:** Old Irish

Sylas
**Meaning:** He That Was Asked For
**Origin Language:** Hebrew

Sylvain | Silvain, Silvan, Sylvan, Sylvanus
**Also:** Sylvester | Silvester, Silvestre,

Silvestro, Sylvestre
**Meaning:** Of The Forest
**Origin Language:** Latin

# Chapter 20 - Names For Boys Beginning With T

Tacit | Tacito, Tacitus
**Meaning:** Silent
**Origin Language:** Latin

Tadeo | Tad, Taddeo, Tadeos, Tadeu, Tadzio
**Meaning:** Heart
**Origin Language:** Old Aramaic

Tai
**Meaning:** Extreme
**Origin Language:** Chinese

Talbot
**Meaning:** Destroyer Of Messages
**Origin Language:** Ancient Germanic And Old English (Cognates)

Talon
**Meaning:** Talon
**Origin Language:** English

Tamir
**Meaning:** Date Palm
**Origin Language:** Hebrew

Taniel
**Meaning:** God Is My Judge
**Origin Language:** Hebrew

Tanner
**Meaning:** Hide Tanner
**Origin Language:** Old English

Taranis
**Meaning:** Thunder

**Origin Language:** Ancient Celtic

Taras | Tarasios
**Meaning:** From Taras (An Ancient Greek City Now Taranto Italy)
**Origin Language:** Ancient Greek

Tarben
**Meaning:** Thor's Bear / Thundering Bear (Thor Is The Name Of The Norse God Of Thunder And Lightning)
**Origin Language:** Old Norse

Tariq | Tarec, Tarek, Tareq, Tarik
**Meaning:** Knocks At The Door
**Origin Language:** Arabic

Tarly | Tarling
**Meaning:** Of Tyrhtel's People (The Meaning Of The Old English Name Tyrhtel Is Unknown)
**Origin Language:** Old English

Taro
**Meaning:** Great Son
**Origin Language:** Japanese

Taron
**Meaning:** From Taron (Historical Region In Armenia Now Turkey)
**Origin Language:** Armenian

Tarquin | Tarquinius
**Meaning:** From Tarquinii (An Ancient Etruscan City Now Known As Tarquinia Italy)
**Origin Language:** Latin

Taskell | Taskill
**Meaning:** Stirrer Of The Divine Cauldron
**Origin Language:** Old Norse

Tate
**Meaning:** Cheerful
**Origin Language:** Old Norse

Tatum | Taytum
**Meaning:** From Tata's Homestead (The Meaning Of The Old English Personal Name Tata Is Unknown)
**Origin Language:** Old English

Tavish
**Meaning:** Twin
**Origin Language:** Old Aramaic

Tavor
**Meaning:** Misfortune
**Origin Language:** Old Aramaic

Taylan
**Meaning:** Tall
**Origin Language:** Turkish

Taylor | Tailor, Tayler
**Meaning:** Tailor
**Origin Language:** English

Teague | Teige, Teigue, Tighe
**Meaning:** Poet
**Origin Language:** Old Irish

Teddy | Ted, Teddie
**Meaning:** God's Gift
**Origin Language:** Ancient Greek

Teman
**Meaning:** Right Hand / South
**Origin Language:** Hebrew

Temeni
**Meaning:** Southerner
**Origin Language:** Hebrew

Temir | Timour, Timur
**Meaning:** Iron
**Origin Language:** Ottoman Turkish

Tennyson | Tenney
**Meaning:** Of Dionysos (Dionysos Is The Name Of The Greek God Of Wine, Vegetation, Fertility, Festivity, Ritual Madness, Religious Ecstasy, And Theatre)

**Origin Language:** Ancient Greek

Tenzin
**Meaning:** Upholder Of Teachings
**Origin Language:** Tibetan

Teo | Tio
**Meaning:** God
**Origin Language:** Ancient Greek

Teodor | Teodoro, Tiodor, Tiodoro
**Meaning:** God's Gift
**Origin Language:** Ancient Greek

Teon | Tion
**Meaning:** God
**Origin Language:** Ancient Greek

Teophil | Teofil, Tiofil, Tiophil
**Meaning:** Loves God
**Origin Language:** Ancient Greek

Terell | Terrell
**Meaning:** Stubborn
**Origin Language:** Old French

Terrance | Terance, Terence, Terrence
**Also:** Terry | Terrie
**Meaning:** Treader / Earth (Soil)
**Origin Language:** Latin

Tevin
**Meaning:** Homely Birth
**Origin Language:** Old Irish

Tex
**Meaning:** From Texas (United States) (English) / Friend (Spanish)
**Origin Language:** English And Spanish

Teyman
**Meaning:** On The Right / In The South
**Origin Language:** Hebrew

**Thaddeus | Thad, Thaddaeus, Thaddai, Thaddaios, Thadeus**
**Meaning:** Heart
**Origin Language:** Old Aramaic

**Thamir**
**Meaning:** Fruitful
**Origin Language:** Arabic

**Thanasis**
**Meaning:** Immortal
**Origin Language:** Ancient Greek

**Thane**
**Meaning:** Thane (A Noble Title)
**Origin Language:** English

**Thanos**
**Meaning:** Death
**Origin Language:** Ancient Greek

**Thatcher**
**Meaning:** Maker Of Thatched Roofs
**Origin Language:** Old English

**Thelonius**
**Meaning:** Ruler Of The People
**Origin Language:** Ancient Germanic

**Theo | Thio**
**Meaning:** God
**Origin Language:** Ancient Greek

**Theobald | Thiobald**
**Meaning:** Of The Bold People
**Origin Language:** Ancient Germanic

**Theodore | Theodor, Theodoros, Theodorus, Thiodor, Thiodore, Thiodore, Thiodoros, Thiodorus**
**Meaning:** God's Gift
**Origin Language:** Ancient Greek

**Theodos | Teodosio, Theodo, Theodosios, Theodosius**
**Meaning:** Given By God

**Origin Language:** Ancient Greek

**Theon | Thion**
**Meaning:** God
**Origin Language:** Ancient Greek

**Theophil | Theofilos, Theophilos, Theophilus, Thiofilos, Thiophil**
**Meaning:** Loves God
**Origin Language:** Ancient Greek

**Therias | Thereios, Thereus**
**Also:** **Therinon | Therino, Therinos**
**Meaning:** Summer / Harvester
**Origin Language:** Ancient Greek

**Theron**
**Meaning:** Hunter
**Origin Language:** Ancient Greek

**Thiago | Tiago**
**Meaning:** Of Saint Iago
**Origin Language:** Hebrew And Latin (In Combination)

**Thierry | Thierrie**
**Meaning:** The People's Ruler
**Origin Language:** Ancient Germanic

**Thomas | Thoma, Tomas, Tomaso, Tomos**
**Meaning:** Twin
**Origin Language:** Old Aramaic

**Thor | Thoros, Thorus**
**Meaning:** Thunder
**Origin Language:** Old Norse

**Thorbern | Thorben, Thorbernus, Thorburn**
**Meaning:** Thor's Bear / Thundering Bear (Thor Is The Name Of The Norse God Of Thunder And Lightning)
**Origin Language:** Old Norse

**Thorley | Thorlee, Thorleigh**

**Meaning:** From A Thorny Meadow
**Origin Language:** Old English

## Thormod
**Meaning:** The Mind Of Thor /
Thundering Mind (Thor Is The Name Of
The Norse God Of Thunder And
Lightning)
**Origin Language:** Old Norse

## Thornton
**Meaning:** From A Thorny Town
**Origin Language:** Old English

## Thorsten | Thorstein, Thorsteinn, Thurstan, Thurstein, Thursteinn, Thursten, Thurston
**Meaning:** Thor's Stone / Stone Of
Thunder (Thor Is The Name Of The
Norse God Of Thunder And Lightning)
**Origin Language:** Old Norse

## Thorvald
**Meaning:** Ruled By Thor / Ruled By
Thunder (Thor Is The Name Of The
Norse God Of Thunder And Lightning)
**Origin Language:** Old Norse

## Thyam | Thiam
**Meaning:** From Near The River Thyamis
(Greece)
**Origin Language:** Ancient Greek

## Tian | Tien, Tyan
**Meaning:** A Christian
**Origin Language:** Latin

## Tielo
**Meaning:** The People's Ruler
**Origin Language:** Ancient Germanic

## Tiernan
**Meaning:** Little Lord
**Origin Language:** Old Irish

## Tierney
**Meaning:** Lord

**Origin Language:** Old Irish

## Tilen
**Meaning:** Young Goat
**Origin Language:** Latin

## Timeo | Timio, Timo
**Also:** Timeus | Timaeus, Timaios
**Meaning:** Has Strong Moral Principles
**Origin Language:** Ancient Greek

## Timmy | Tim, Timmie
**Meaning:** Respects God
**Origin Language:** Ancient Greek

## Timon
**Meaning:** Has Strong Moral Principles
**Origin Language:** Ancient Greek

## Timotheus | Timotei, Timoteo, Timoteus, Timotheos
**Also:** Timothy | Timofei, Timofey, Timothe, Timothee, Timothei, Timothie, Tymofee, Tymofiy, Tymothy
**Meaning:** Respects God
**Origin Language:** Ancient Greek

## Tinsley | Tinsleigh,Tinsely, Tynsleigh, Tynsley
**Meaning:** From Tynni's Meadow (It Is
Unknown What The Meaning Of The
Old English Personal Name Tynni Is)
**Origin Language:** Old English

## Titan
**Meaning:** Revenge
**Origin Language:** Ancient Greek

## Titus | Tito, Titos, Tytus
**Meaning:** Titled
**Origin Language:** Latin

## Tobiah
**Also:** Tobias
**Also:** Tobin

**Meaning:** God Is Good
**Origin Language:** Hebrew

## Tobith
**Also:** Toby | Tobie, Tobih
**Meaning:** Good
**Origin Language:** Hebrew

## Todd | Tod
**Meaning:** Fox
**Origin Language:** Old English

## Tolbert
**Meaning:** Destroyer Of Messages
**Origin Language:** Ancient Germanic And Old English (Cognates)

## Tomer
**Meaning:** Palm Tree
**Origin Language:** Hebrew

## Tommen | Tommin
**Also:** Tommy | Thom, Tom, Tomi, Tommi, Tommie, Tomy
**Meaning:** Twin
**Origin Language:** Old Aramaic

## Tony | Toni, Tonie, Tonino, Tonio
**Meaning:** Of Ani (Ani Is The Name Of An Etruscan God, Thought To Be Equivalent To The Roman God Janus, The God Of Beginnings, Gates, Transitions, Time, Duality, Doorways, Passages, And Endings)
**Origin Language:** Latin

## Topher
**Meaning:** Bearer Of Christ
**Origin Language:** Late Greek

## Torben | Torbern, Torbernus, Torbun
**Meaning:** Thor's Bear / Thundering Bear (Thor Is The Name Of The Norse God Of Thunder And Lightning)

**Origin Language:** Old Norse

## Torin
**Meaning:** Thunder
**Origin Language:** Ancient Celtic

## Tormod
**Meaning:** The Mind Of Thor / Thundering Mind (Thor Is The Name Of The Norse God Of Thunder And Lightning)
**Origin Language:** Old Norse

## Tormund
**Meaning:** Protected By Thor / Protected By Thunder (Thor Is The Name Of The Norse God Of Thunder And Lightning)
**Origin Language:** Old Norse

## Torquil | Torcall, Torcuil, Torcull, Torkel
**Meaning:** Thor's Cauldron / Thundering Cauldron (Thor Is The Name Of The Norse God Of Thunder And Lightning)
**Origin Language:** Old Norse

## Torsten | Torstein
**Meaning:** Thor's Stone / Stone Of Thunder (Thor Is The Name Of The Norse God Of Thunder And Lightning)
**Origin Language:** Old Norse

## Torvald
**Meaning:** Ruled By Thor / Ruled By Thunder (Thor Is The Name Of The Norse God Of Thunder And Lightning)
**Origin Language:** Old Norse

## Tovi
**Meaning:** Good
**Origin Language:** Hebrew

## Toyin
**Meaning:** Worthy Of Praise
**Origin Language:** Yoruba

## Trafford

**Meaning:** From A Ford Where Fish Are Caught
**Origin Language:** Old English

Trahern | Trahaearn, Traherne
**Meaning:** Very Iron-Like
**Origin Language:** Old Welsh

Traian | Traianus
**Meaning:** Transporter
**Origin Language:** Latin

Tranter
**Meaning:** Walks / Peddles For A Living
**Origin Language:** Old English

Travers
**Also:** Travis | Traviss, Travys
**Meaning:** Gatekeeper / Toll Collector
**Origin Language:** Old French

Trayan
**Meaning:** Enduring
**Origin Language:** South Slavic

Trent
**Meaning:** From Near The River Trent (England)
**Origin Language:** English

Trenton
**Meaning:** From Trent's Town / From A Town Near The River Trent
**Origin Language:** Old English

Trevelyan
**Meaning:** From A Homestead On A Hill
**Origin Language:** Cornish

Trevor | Trefor, Trev
**Meaning:** From A Big Village
**Origin Language:** Welsh

Trey
**Meaning:** Three
**Origin Language:** Old English

Tripp | Trip
**Meaning:** Professional Dancer
**Origin Language:** Old French

Tristan | Tristane, Tristen, Tristin, Triston, Trystan, Trystane
**Meaning:** Tumultuous
**Origin Language:** Ancient Celtic

Triton | Tritonos
**Meaning:** Of The Third
**Origin Language:** Ancient Greek

Troy | Troi
**Meaning:** From Troia/Troy (An Ancient City In Anatolia)
**Origin Language:** Ancient Greek

Tru | True
**Meaning:** True
**Origin Language:** English

Truett | Truet
**Meaning:** From A Meadow In A Resinous Wood
**Origin Language:** Old Norse

Truman | Trueman
**Meaning:** A True Man
**Origin Language:** Old English

Tryfon | Trifon, Triphon, Tryphon
**Meaning:** Delicate
**Origin Language:** Ancient Greek

Trystram | Tristram
**Meaning:** Tumultuous
**Origin Language:** Ancient Celtic

Tucker
**Meaning:** Cloth Fuller
**Origin Language:** Old English

Tudor | Tudur
**Meaning:** The People's Ruler
**Origin Language:** Ancient Germanic

Tullian | Tullianus
**Also:** Tully | Tulio, Tullie, Tullio, Tullius, Tullus
**Meaning:** Waterfall
**Origin Language:** Latin

Turin
**Meaning:** Victorious Mood
**Origin Language:** Sindarian (Fictional Language Devised By J. R. R. Tolkien For Use In His Fantasy Stories, Such As Lord Of The Rings)

Turner | Torner
**Meaning:** Tournament Official
**Origin Language:** Old French

Tustin | Tustyn
**Meaning:** Thor's Stone / Stone Of Thunder (Thor Is The Name Of The Norse God Of Thunder And Lightning)
**Origin Language:** Old Norse

Tybalt | Tibalt
**Meaning:** Of The Bold People
**Origin Language:** Ancient Germanic

Tycho
**Meaning:** Thor's Cauldron / Thundering Cauldron (Thor Is The Name Of The Norse God Of Thunder And Lightning)
**Origin Language:** Old Norse

Tychon
**Meaning:** Fortune / Luck
**Origin Language:** Ancient Greek

Tye
**Meaning:** From A Pasture
**Origin Language:** Old English

Tyler | Tylar, Tylor
**Meaning:** Roof Tiler
**Origin Language:** Old English

Tymon
**Meaning:** Has Strong Moral Principles

**Origin Language:** Ancient Greek

Tynley | Tynleigh, Tynlie
**Meaning:** From Tynni's Meadow (It Is Unknown What The Meaning Of The Old English Personal Name Tynni Is)
**Origin Language:** Old English

Tyr
**Meaning:** Deity
**Origin Language:** Old Norse

Tyree
**Meaning:** The Carpenter's Son
**Origin Language:** Scottish Gaelic

Tyrion | Tyrian, Tyrien
**Meaning:** Of Tyre (An Ancient City That Once Sat Where Lebanon Is Now) / Rock
**Origin Language:** Latin

Tyrone | Tyron
**Meaning:** Born Of The Yew Tree
**Origin Language:** Old Irish

Tyrrell | Tyrell
**Meaning:** Stubborn
**Origin Language:** Old French

Tyson
**Meaning:** Firebrand
**Origin Language:** Old French

Tywin | Tywyn
**Meaning:** This Name Has No Meaning (Tywin Is A Fictional Character Featuring In The TV Series Game Of Thrones)
**Origin Language:** Invented

# Chapter 21 - Names For Boys Beginning With U

Uberto
**Meaning:** Bright Mind
**Origin Language:** Ancient Germanic

Ugo
**Meaning:** Mind And Spirit
**Origin Language:** Ancient Germanic

Uilliam | Uilleam
**Meaning:** Desires Protection
**Origin Language:** Ancient Germanic

Ulf | Ulph
**Meaning:** Wolf
**Origin Language:** Old Norse

Ulfric
**Meaning:** Rich Wolf
**Origin Language:** Ancient Germanic

Ulrick | Ulric, Ulrich, Ulrik
**Meaning:** Rich Heritage
**Origin Language:** Ancient Germanic

Umar
**Meaning:** Life
**Origin Language:** Arabic

Umbert | Umberto
**Meaning:** Bright Bear Cub
**Origin Language:** Ancient Germanic

Urie | Uri
**Meaning:** My Flame
**Origin Language:** Hebrew

Uriel
**Meaning:** God Is My Flame
**Origin Language:** Hebrew

Urion | Urian, Urien, Uryan, Uryen, Uryon
**Meaning:** Born Into The Trust Of Another / Inherited Birth
**Origin Language:** Old Welsh

Uther | Uthyr
**Meaning:** Terrible
**Origin Language:** Welsh

# Chapter 22 - Names For Boys Beginning With V

Vahan
**Meaning:** Shield
**Origin Language:** Armenian

Valens
**Also:** Valent | Valente
**Also:** Valentin | Valentine, Valentinian, Valentino, Valentinus, Valentyn
**Meaning:** Strong / Healthy
**Origin Language:** Latin

Valerian | Valeri, Valeriano, Valerianus, Valerio, Valerius, Valeriy, Valero
**Meaning:** Strong Enough
**Origin Language:** Latin

Valter
**Meaning:** Army Ruler
**Origin Language:** Ancient Germanic

Vance | Van
**Meaning:** From A Swamp
**Origin Language:** Old English

Vangel | Vangelis, Vangelys
**Meaning:** Bringer Of Good News
**Origin Language:** Ancient Greek

Vanni | Vani, Vanno, Vano
**Meaning:** God Is Gracious
**Origin Language:** Hebrew

Vardan

**Meaning:** Rose
**Origin Language:** Armenian

Varin | Varinius
**Also:** Varius
**Also:** Varys | Varis
**Meaning:** Varied / Versatile
**Origin Language:** Latin

Vaughan | Vaughn
**Meaning:** Little
**Origin Language:** Welsh

Vedast | Vedastus
**Meaning:** Stranger From The Forest
**Origin Language:** Ancient Germanic

Velius
**Meaning:** Concealed
**Origin Language:** Latin

Vendel
**Meaning:** Of The Vandals (The Name Of A Germanic Tribe)
**Origin Language:** Ancient Germanic

Vergil | Vergilio, Vergilius, Virgil, Virgilio, Virgilius
**Meaning:** Of The Vergiliae (Vergilae Is The Name The Romans Used For The Star Constellation That Is Mostly Know Today As "The Pleiades")
**Origin Language:** Latin

Verne | Vere, Vern
**Meaning:** Alder Tree
**Origin Language:** Gaulish

Verner
**Meaning:** Wary Soldier
**Origin Language:** Ancient Germanic

Vernon
**Meaning:** Alder Tree
**Origin Language:** Gaulish

Verus
**Meaning:** Sincere
**Origin Language:** Latin

Vesper | Vesperus
**Meaning:** Of The Evening
**Origin Language:** Latin

Vester
**Meaning:** Of The Forest
**Origin Language:** Latin

Vibian | Vibianus
**Meaning:** Vibrating
**Origin Language:** Latin

Vico
**Meaning:** Famous Battler
**Origin Language:** Ancient Germanic

Victor | Vic, Viktar, Viktor
**Meaning:** Victory
**Origin Language:** Latin

Viggo | Vigge
**Meaning:** Warrior
**Origin Language:** Old Norse

Vilhelm | Vilhelmas, Vilhelmi, Vilhelmo, Vilhelms
**Also:** Viliam | Villiam
**Also:** Vilis | Vilys
**Also:** Villem | Vilem, Vilim, Villum
**Meaning:** Desires Protection
**Origin Language:** Ancient Germanic

Vince
**Also:** Vincent | Vincenc, Vincente, Vincentius, Vincenzo, Vinzent
**Also:** Vinnie | Vin, Vinko, Vinny
**Meaning:** The Winner
**Origin Language:** Latin

Viserys
**Meaning:** This Name Has No Meaning (Viserys Is A Fictional Character

Featuring In The TV Series Game Of Thrones)
**Origin Language:** Invented

Vitalis | Vitali, Vitaly, Vitalys
**Meaning:** Vital
**Origin Language:** Latin

Vivien | Vivian, Vivianus
**Meaning:** Alive
**Origin Language:** Latin

# Chapter 23 - Names For Boys Beginning With W

Wade | Waid, Waide, Wayd, Wayde
**Meaning:** From A Ford
**Origin Language:** Old English

Walker
**Meaning:** Cloth Fuller
**Origin Language:** Old English

Wallace
**Also:** Wallis
**Meaning:** Of The Walha People (The Name Of A Gallic Tribe)
**Origin Language:** Ancient Germanic

Walmar
**Meaning:** Famous Ruler
**Origin Language:** Ancient Germanic

Walter | Walt, Wolt, Wolter
**Meaning:** Army Ruler
**Origin Language:** Ancient Germanic

Walton
**Meaning:** From A Walled Town
**Origin Language:** Old English

Wardell

**Meaning:** From A Lookout's Hill
**Origin Language:** Old English

Warin | Warinn, Warrin, Warrinn
**Meaning:** Wary
**Origin Language:** Ancient Germanic

Warren
**Meaning:** Warren
**Origin Language:** English

Warrick | Warwick
**Meaning:** From A Village With A Dam
**Origin Language:** Old English

Wason | Wasson
**Meaning:** From A Western Town
**Origin Language:** Old English

Watson
**Meaning:** Army Ruler
**Origin Language:** Ancient Germanic

Wayland | Weyland
**Also:** Waylon | Wellon, Weylon
**Meaning:** Skilled
**Origin Language:** Ancient Germanic

Wayne | Wain, Waine, Wayn
**Meaning:** Wagon Maker
**Origin Language:** Old English

Weland | Welland
**Meaning:** Skilled
**Origin Language:** Ancient Germanic

Weldon
**Meaning:** From A Hill With A Well
**Origin Language:** Old English

Wells
**Meaning:** From Near A Well
**Origin Language:** Old English

Wendell | Wendel, Wendelin
**Meaning:** Of The Vandals (The Name Of A Germanic Tribe)

**Origin Language:** Ancient Germanic

Wenzel
**Meaning:** More Glorious
**Origin Language:** Czech

Werner | Warner
**Meaning:** Wary Soldier
**Origin Language:** Ancient Germanic

Werther
**Meaning:** Worthy Soldier
**Origin Language:** Ancient Germanic

Wesley | Wes, Weslee, Wesleigh, Weslie, Wesly
**Meaning:** From A Western Meadow
**Origin Language:** Old English

Wesson | Weson, Whesson
**Meaning:** From A Western Town
**Origin Language:** Old English

Westley | Wes, Westlee, Westleigh, Westlie, Westly
**Meaning:** From A Western Meadow
**Origin Language:** Old English

Weston | Westin
**Meaning:** From A Western Town
**Origin Language:** Old English

Wetzel
**Meaning:** Wary Soldier
**Origin Language:** Ancient Germanic

Whisson | Wison, Wisson
**Meaning:** From A Western Town
**Origin Language:** Old English

Whitaker | Whitacre
**Meaning:** From The White Acres
**Origin Language:** Old English

Wilber | Wilbor, Wilbur
**Meaning:** Wild Boar

**Origin Language:** Old English

Wilbern | Wilburn
**Meaning:** From Near A Stream Lined With Willow Trees
**Origin Language:** Old English

Wilder | Wylder
**Meaning:** Untamed
**Origin Language:** Old English

Wiley
**Meaning:** From A Willow Tree Meadow
**Origin Language:** Old English

Wilford | Wilferd, Wilfurd
**Meaning:** From A Ford With Willow Trees
**Origin Language:** Old English

Wilfred | Wilf, Wilfrid
**Meaning:** Desires Peace
**Origin Language:** Old English

Wilkin | Wilkie, Wilky
**Meaning:** Desires Protection
**Origin Language:** Ancient Germanic

Will | Wil
**Meaning:** Will / Desire
**Origin Language:** Ancient Germanic

Willard | Wilard, Wilheard, Wilheard
**Meaning:** Desired Hardiness
**Origin Language:** Ancient Germanic

Willem | Wilhelm, Wilhelmus, Willahelm, Willelm
**Also:** William | Williem
**Also:** Willis | Willi, Willie, Willy
**Meaning:** Desires Protection
**Origin Language:** Ancient Germanic

Wilmer | Wilmar, Wilmor, Wilmur
**Meaning:** Desires To Be Famous

**Origin Language:** Old English

Wilmot
**Also:** Wilson
**Meaning:** Desires Protection
**Origin Language:** Ancient Germanic

Wilton | Wilt, Wiltan
**Meaning:** From A Town With Willow Trees
**Origin Language:** Old English

Windsor
**Meaning:** From A Bank With A Windlass
**Origin Language:** Old English

Winfield
**Meaning:** From A Pasture Near A Field
**Origin Language:** Old English

Winfred | Winfrid, Wynfred, Wynfrid
**Meaning:** Friendly And Peaceful
**Origin Language:** Old English

Winslow | Winslo, Winsloe
**Meaning:** From Wine's Hill / From A Friendly Hill
**Origin Language:** Old English

Winston | Winstan, Wynnstan, Wynnston, Wynstan, Wynston
**Meaning:** Stone Of Joy
**Origin Language:** Old English

Winton
**Meaning:** From Wine's Town / From A Friendly Town
**Origin Language:** Old English

Wolfram
**Meaning:** Wolf Raven
**Origin Language:** Ancient Germanic

Wolfric | Wolfrik, Wulfric, Wulfrik

**Meaning:** Rich Wolf
**Origin Language:** Old English

Woodie | Woody
**Also:** Woodrow
**Meaning:** From A Row Of Homes Near Woodland
**Origin Language:** Old English

Wyatt | Wyat, Wyot, Wyott
**Meaning:** Hardy In Battle
**Origin Language:** Old English

Wybert
**Meaning:** Bright Battler
**Origin Language:** Old English

Wylie
**Meaning:** Desires Protection
**Origin Language:** Ancient Germanic

Wymond
**Meaning:** Protector In Battle
**Origin Language:** Old English

Wyn | Wynn
**Meaning:** Friendly
**Origin Language:** Ancient Germanic And Old English (Cognates)

Wystan
**Meaning:** Stone Of Battle
**Origin Language:** Old English

# Chapter 24 - Names For Boys Beginning With X

Xabier | Xaber, Xabior , Xzabier
**Meaning:** From Etxeberria (Navarre, Spain)
**Origin Language:** Basque

Xander

**Meaning:** Mankind's Defender
**Origin Language:** Ancient Greek

## Xaro
**Meaning:** This Name Has No Meaning (Xaro Is A Fictional Character Featuring In The TV Series Game Of Thrones)
**Origin Language:** Invented

## Xavier | Xaver, Xavior, Xzavier
**Meaning:** From Etxeberria (Navarre, Spain)
**Origin Language:** Basque

## Xenon
**Meaning:** Unusual / Foreign / Guest
**Origin Language:** Ancient Greek

# Chapter 25 - Names For Boys Beginning With Y

## Yadiel
**Meaning:** Praise Of God
**Origin Language:** Hebrew

## Yadon | Yadown
**Meaning:** Thankful
**Origin Language:** Hebrew

## Yair | Yairos, Yairus, Yaiyr
**Meaning:** He Shines
**Origin Language:** Hebrew

## Yale
**Meaning:** From A Glade
**Origin Language:** Welsh

## Yannick | Yanick
**Also:** Yannis | Yan, Yanis, Yann, Yanni, Yianni, Yiannis
**Meaning:** God Is Gracious
**Origin Language:** Hebrew

## Yarden
**Meaning:** Descending Flow
**Origin Language:** Semitic

## Yardley | Yardlee, Yardleigh, Yardlie
**Meaning:** From A Meadow Where Twigs Are Gathered
**Origin Language:** Old English

## Yared
**Meaning:** Descent
**Origin Language:** Hebrew

## Yarik | Yarek
**Meaning:** Fierce And Glorious
**Origin Language:** Common Slavic

## Yarle | Yarl, Yeorl, Yeorle, Yourl, Yourle
**Meaning:** From A Hill With A Muddy Spring
**Origin Language:** Old English

## Yaron
**Meaning:** He That Sings Or Shouts
**Origin Language:** Hebrew

## Yarrell | Yaral, Yarel, Yareli, Yarill, Yarrelly, Yarroll, Yerill, Yerll, Yerrall, Yerrell, Yerrelly, Yerrill, Yirrell, Yirrelly, Yourell
**Meaning:** From A Hill With A Muddy Spring
**Origin Language:** Old English

## Yateley | Yatelee, Yateleigh, Yatelie
**Meaning:** From A Meadow With A Gate
**Origin Language:** Old English

## Yauhen
**Meaning:** Well-Born
**Origin Language:** Ancient Greek

## Yeadon | Yeadan, Yeaden, Yeadun

**Meaning:** From A High Hill
**Origin Language:** Old English

Yeland | Yeeland, Yelland
**Meaning:** From A High Land
**Origin Language:** Old English

Yeshua
**Meaning:** God Is Salvation
**Origin Language:** Hebrew

Yishai | Yishay
**Meaning:** A Gift
**Origin Language:** Hebrew

Yishmael
**Meaning:** God Hears
**Origin Language:** Hebrew

Yoan | Yoann
**Meaning:** Graced By God
**Origin Language:** Hebrew

Yoel
**Meaning:** God Is God
**Origin Language:** Hebrew

Yohan | Yohanes, Yohann, Yohannes
**Meaning:** Graced By God
**Origin Language:** Hebrew

Yonah
**Meaning:** Dove
**Origin Language:** Hebrew

Yonatan
**Meaning:** God Has Given
**Origin Language:** Hebrew

Yoni
**Meaning:** God Is Gracious
**Origin Language:** Hebrew

Yorah
**Meaning:** Rainy
**Origin Language:** Hebrew

Yorath
**Meaning:** Worthy Lord
**Origin Language:** Old Welsh

Yordan
**Meaning:** Descending Flow
**Origin Language:** Semitic

Yoren
**Meaning:** Horse Lover
**Origin Language:** Old Norse

Yori
**Meaning:** Rely
**Origin Language:** Japanese

Yorick
**Also:** Yrian
**Meaning:** Farmer
**Origin Language:** Ancient Greek

Yulian | Yuli, Yulien, Yuliy
**Meaning:** Downy (Down As In Soft Fluffy Hairs)
**Origin Language:** Latin

Yunus | Younes, Younus
**Meaning:** Dove
**Origin Language:** Hebrew

Yury | Youri, Yuri, Yurie, Yuriy
**Meaning:** Farmer
**Origin Language:** Ancient Greek

Yvain
**Meaning:** Well-Born
**Origin Language:** Ancient Greek

Yvan
**Meaning:** Graced By God
**Origin Language:** Hebrew

Yves
**Also:** Yvo
**Also:** Yvon

**Meaning:** Yew Tree
**Origin Language:** Ancient Germanic

Ywain
**Meaning:** Well-Born
**Origin Language:** Ancient Greek

# Chapter 26 - Names For Boys Beginning With Z

Zabulon | Zaboulon, Zabulun
**Meaning:** Gift / Dowry
**Origin Language:** Hebrew

Zaccai | Zakkai, Zakkay
**Also:** Zaccheus | Zacchaeus,
Zakchaios
**Meaning:** Pure
**Origin Language:** Hebrew

Zachariah | Zakariah
**Also:** Zacharias | Zacarias,
Zaccharias
**Also:** Zachariel
**Meaning:** The Remembrance Of God
**Origin Language:** Hebrew

Zachary | Zacharie, Zacherie,
Zachery, Zackarie, Zackary,
Zackerie, Zackery, Zakarie, Zakary,
Zakerie, Zakery
**Also:** Zack | Zac, Zach, Zak
**Also:** Zahari
**Meaning:** God Remembers
**Origin Language:** Hebrew

Zahi
**Meaning:** Beautiful
**Origin Language:** Arabic

Zahir | Zaahir
**Meaning:** Shining / Blooming

**Origin Language:** Arabic

Zaid | Zayd
**Meaning:** Increasing
**Origin Language:** Arabic

Zakhar
**Meaning:** God Remembers
**Origin Language:** Hebrew

Zaki
**Meaning:** Pure
**Origin Language:** Arabic

Zal | Zaal
**Meaning:** Albino
**Origin Language:** Persian

Zalman | Zalmon
**Meaning:** Shady
**Origin Language:** Hebrew

Zander
**Meaning:** Defender Of Mankind
**Origin Language:** Ancient Greek

Zane | Zaen, Zaene, Zain, Zaine,
Zayne
**Meaning:** God Is Gracious
**Origin Language:** Hebrew

Zavier | Zaver, Zavior
**Meaning:** From Etxeberria (Navarre,
Spain)
**Origin Language:** Basque

Zayden | Zaiden
**Meaning:** Increasing
**Origin Language:** Arabic

Zayn | Zaian, Zain, Zayaan, Zayan,
Zayyan
**Meaning:** Grace / Beauty
**Origin Language:** Arabic

Zebadiah | Zebadyah, Zebedaios

**Also:** Zebedee | Zebedie
**Meaning:** God Has Bestowed
**Origin Language:** Hebrew

Zechariah | Zekaryah, Zekharyah
**Meaning:** God Remembers
**Origin Language:** Hebrew

Zedekiah | Zed
**Meaning:** God's Justice
**Origin Language:** Hebrew

Zef | Zeff
**Meaning:** Wolf
**Origin Language:** Hebrew

Zeke
**Meaning:** God Will Strengthen
**Origin Language:** Hebrew

Zeno
**Meaning:** Of Zeus (Zeus Is The Name Of The Roman God Of The Sky, Lightning, Thunder, Law, Order, And Justice)
**Origin Language:** Ancient Greek

Zenoby | Zenobi, Zenobios
**Meaning:** Life Of Zeus (Zeus Is The Name Of The Roman God Of The Sky, Lightning, Thunder, Law, Order, And Justice)
**Origin Language:** Ancient Greek

Zenon | Zinon
**Meaning:** Of Zeus (Zeus Is The Name Of The Roman God Of The Sky, Lightning, Thunder, Law, Order, And Justice)
**Origin Language:** Ancient Greek

Zephaniah | Zefaniah, Zephania
**Meaning:** God Has Hidden
**Origin Language:** Hebrew

Zephaniel
**Meaning:** Hiding God

**Origin Language:** Hebrew

Zephyr | Zeferino, Zephyrinus, Zephyro, Zephyros, Zephyrus
**Meaning:** West Wind
**Origin Language:** Ancient Greek

Zerach | Zerakh
**Meaning:** Shining
**Origin Language:** Hebrew

Zerachiel
**Meaning:** Command Of God
**Origin Language:** Hebrew

Zev | Zeev
**Meaning:** Wolf
**Origin Language:** Hebrew

Zevadiah | Zevadyah
**Meaning:** God Has Bestowed
**Origin Language:** Hebrew

Zevi | Tzevi, Zvi
**Meaning:** Gazelle
**Origin Language:** Hebrew

Zibeon
**Meaning:** Dyed
**Origin Language:** Hebrew

Zimri
**Meaning:** My Musician
**Origin Language:** Hebrew

Zinovy | Zinovie, Zinoviy
**Meaning:** Life Of Zeus (Zeus Is The Name Of The Roman God Of The Sky, Lightning, Thunder, Law, Order, And Justice)
**Origin Language:** Ancient Greek

Zion | Tzion, Zyon
**Meaning:** From Heaven
**Origin Language:** Hebrew

Ziv

**Meaning:** Glowing
**Origin Language:** Hebrew

Zohar
**Meaning:** Radiance
**Origin Language:** Hebrew

Zophai
**Meaning:** Overflowing
**Origin Language:** Hebrew

Zopyros
**Meaning:** Glowing
**Origin Language:** Ancient Greek

Zoran
**Meaning:** Dawn
**Origin Language:** Slavic

Zorion
**Meaning:** Happiness
**Origin Language:** Basque

Zsolt
**Meaning:** Sultan
**Origin Language:** Hungarian

Zuan
**Meaning:** Graced By God
**Origin Language:** Hebrew

Zuriel
**Meaning:** My Rock Is God
**Origin Language:** Hebrew

Zyair | Zaire, Zyaire
**Meaning:** A River That Swallows Other Rivers
**Origin Language:** Kikongo

# Chapter 27 - Names For Girls Beginning With A

Aaliyah | Aalia, Aaliya, Alaia, Alaiya, Alaya, Alayah, Alea, Aleah, Aliah, Alyah
**Meaning:** Exalted
**Origin Language:** Arabic

Aarna
**Meaning:** The Ocean
**Origin Language:** Sanskrit

Abby | Abaigh, Abbey, Abbi, Abbie, Abbye, Abi, Aby
**Meaning:** My Father Is Joyful
**Origin Language:** Hebrew

Abela | Abella
**Also:** Abelene | Abelena, Abelina, Abeline
**Also:** Abelia | Abellana
**Meaning:** Breath
**Origin Language:** Hebrew

Abena | Abene, Abeni, Abina
**Meaning:** Born On A Tuesday
**Origin Language:** Akan

Abia | Abiah, Abiha
**Meaning:** My Father Is God
**Origin Language:** Hebrew

Abigaia
**Also:** Abigail | Abagail, Abaigeal, Abbigail, Abbygail, Abegaelle, Abegail, Abegale, Abigael, Abigael, Abigaelle, Abigaila, Abigaile, Abigaille, Abigal, Abigale, Abigall, Abigayil, Abigayl, Abigayle, Abigel
**Meaning:** My Father Is Joyful
**Origin Language:** Hebrew

Abilene | Abilena
**Meaning:** Meadow
**Origin Language:** Hebrew

Abira | Aaberah, Aabeyra, Aabira, Aabireh, Aabiyrah, Aabiyreh, Aabyre, Aabyreh, Aberah, Abeyra, Abireh, Abiyrah, Abiyreh, Abyre, Abyreh
**Meaning:** Dream Interpreter
**Origin Language:** Arabic

Abital | Abitala, Abitla, Abiytal
**Meaning:** My Father Is The Dew
**Origin Language:** Hebrew

Abra
**Meaning:** Born On A Tuesday
**Origin Language:** Ewe

Abril
**Meaning:** April
**Origin Language:** Catalan And Portuguese And Spanish (Cognates)

Acacia | Acatia, Akacia, Akatia
**Meaning:** Acacia
**Origin Language:** English

Acantha | Acanta, Acanthe, Akanta, Akantha, Akanthe
**Meaning:** Thorn
**Origin Language:** Ancient Greek

Ackerlea | Ackerleigh, Ackerley, Ackerly, Akelea, Akeleigh, Akeley
**Meaning:** From An Oak Tree Meadow
**Origin Language:** Old English

Ada | Aada, Adah
**Meaning:** Island
**Origin Language:** Turkish

Adaiah | Adaya, Adaya, Adayah, Adayah, Adyah, Edya

**Meaning:** God Has Adorned Himself
**Origin Language:** Hebrew

Adaire | Adair
**Meaning:** Spear Of Wealth
**Origin Language:** Old English

Adala
**Meaning:** Noble
**Origin Language:** Ancient Germanic And Old English (Cognates)

Adalia
**Meaning:** Noble
**Origin Language:** Hebrew

Adalie | Adalea, Adalee, Adaleigh, Adaley
**Meaning:** From Ealdred's Meadow / From A Meadow Of Noble Strength
**Origin Language:** Old English

Adalinde | Adalind, Adalinda, Adelind, Adelinda, Adelinde
**Also:** Adalindis | Adalindys, Adallindis, Adallindys
**Also:** Adaline | Adalina, Adallina, Addilina, Adelina, Adeline, Adelyna, Adilene
**Meaning:** Tender Noble
**Origin Language:** Ancient Germanic

Adalis | Adalisa, Adalissa, Adalissa, Adalisza, Adalisza, Adaliz, Adaliza, Adaliza, Adalys, Adelis, Adelissa, Adelisza, Adeliza, Adellissa, Adelys, Adhalissa, Adhelissa, Adheliza
**Meaning:** Of The Noble Sort
**Origin Language:** Ancient Germanic

Adalynn | Adalin, Adalyn, Addilin, Addilyn, Adelin, Adelyn, Adelynn, Adilynn
**Meaning:** Tender Noble
**Origin Language:** Ancient Germanic

Adamina | Adamena, Adamene, Adamine
**Also:** Adamira | Adamera
**Meaning:** Of The Humankind
**Origin Language:** Hebrew

Adanna
**Meaning:** Father's Daughter
**Origin Language:** Igbo

Adara
**Meaning:** Noble
**Origin Language:** Hebrew

Adarina | Adarena
**Meaning:** Like A Fire
**Origin Language:** Old Persian

Addie | Addy
**Meaning:** A Short Form Of Any Of The Numerous Names Beginning With Ad
**Origin Language:** Various

Addira | Adira
**Meaning:** Strong
**Origin Language:** Hebrew

Addisyn | Addison, Addyson, Adyson
**Meaning:** Of The Humankind
**Origin Language:** Hebrew

Addriona | Addrionne
**Meaning:** From Hadria (The Name Of Two Ancient Roman Settlements Which Were Located In What Are Now Northern Italy And Central Italy) / From The Water
**Origin Language:** Latin

Adea | Adia
**Meaning:** Given By God
**Origin Language:** Latin

Adeelah | Adeela, Adela, Adelah,

Adila, Adilah
**Meaning:** Unbiased
**Origin Language:** Arabic

Adelaide | Adalaid, Adalaida, Adalaide, Adaleide, Adelaid, Adelaida, Adelaidis, Adeleide
**Also:** Adelais | Adalais, Adalaiz, Adaleis, Adaleiz, Adelaiz, Adeleis, Adeleiz
**Meaning:** Of The Noble Sort
**Origin Language:** Ancient Germanic

Adele | Addela, Adela, Adelia, Adelie, Adelie, Adeliya, Adell, Adella, Adelle, Adely, Adhela, Adila, Adilla
**Meaning:** Noble
**Origin Language:** Ancient Germanic And Old English (Cognates)

Adelice | Adelicia
**Also:** Adelina | Adaleine, Adalena, Adalina, Adalina, Adeleine, Adelena
**Meaning:** Of The Noble Sort
**Origin Language:** Ancient Germanic

Adelita
**Meaning:** Noble
**Origin Language:** Ancient Germanic And Old English (Cognates)

Adelitza | Adelitze, Adelitzse, Adlitza, Adlitze
**Meaning:** Like A Noble
**Origin Language:** Ancient Germanic

Adelma | Adalma, Adalmia, Adelmia
**Also:** Adelmina | Adalmena, Adalmina, Adelmena
**Meaning:** Father's Protector
**Origin Language:** Ancient Germanic

Adelonda
**Meaning:** Tender Noble
**Origin Language:** Ancient Germanic

Adelphia | Adelfa, Adelfia, Adelfina, Adelphe, Adelphie
**Meaning:** Born Of The Same Womb / Double
**Origin Language:** Ancient Greek

Ademara
**Also:** Ademira
**Meaning:** Famous Father
**Origin Language:** Ancient Germanic

Adena | Adenah, Adene
**Meaning:** Delicate
**Origin Language:** Hebrew

Adeona
**Meaning:** Approaching
**Origin Language:** Latin

Aderyn
**Meaning:** Bird
**Origin Language:** Welsh

Adina | Adena, Adene, Adine
**Meaning:** Delicate
**Origin Language:** Hebrew

Adla
**Meaning:** Noble
**Origin Language:** Ancient Germanic And Old English (Cognates)

Adleisha | Adleesha, Adlesha
**Meaning:** Like A Noble
**Origin Language:** Ancient Germanic

Adler | Addler, Adlar
**Meaning:** Eagle
**Origin Language:** German

Adleta | Adeletta, Adlette
**Meaning:** Of The Noble Sort

**Origin Language:** Ancient Germanic

**Adlie | Adley**
**Meaning:** Eagle
**Origin Language:** German

**Adnie | Adney**
**Meaning:** From Eadwynn's Island / From A Rich And Friendly Island
**Origin Language:** Old English

**Adoetta | Adoeete, Adoet, Adoeta, Adoete, Adoett, Adoette**
**Meaning:** Large Tree
**Origin Language:** Kiowa

**Adona**
**Also:** Adonella | Adonelle
**Meaning:** My Lord
**Origin Language:** Hebrew

**Adonia**
**Meaning:** My Lord Is God
**Origin Language:** Hebrew

**Adonica | Adonika**
**Meaning:** My Lord
**Origin Language:** Hebrew

**Adora | Ador, Adoria**
**Meaning:** Adoring
**Origin Language:** Latin

**Adorabella | Adorabell, Adorabelle**
**Meaning:** Adored Beauty
**Origin Language:** Latin

**Adoranda**
**Also:** Adorata
**Also:** Adorena | Adorene, Adorina, Adorine
**Also:** Adorette | Adoretta
**Also:** Adorinda
**Meaning:** Adoring
**Origin Language:** Latin

**Adorna**
**Meaning:** Adorned
**Origin Language:** Latin

**Adria | Adrea, Adreia, Aidrea, Aidreia, Aidria, Aydrea, Aydreia, Aydria**
**Also:** Adrianna | Addriana, Addrianne, Addriena, Addrienne, Adriana, Adrianne, Aidriana, Aidrianne, Aidriena, Aidrienne, Aydriana, Aydrianne, Aydriena, Aydrienne
**Meaning:** From Hadria (The Name Of Two Ancient Roman Settlements Which Were Located In What Are Now Northern Italy And Central Italy) / From The Water
**Origin Language:** Latin

**Adula**
**Meaning:** Noble
**Origin Language:** Ancient Germanic And Old English (Cognates)

**Aedona | Aedone, Aedoni, Aedonia**
**Meaning:** Shining
**Origin Language:** Ancient Greek

**Aeesha | Aeeshah, Aeisha, Aiesha, Aieshah, Aieysha, Ayeesah, Ayeesha, Ayeeshah, Ayeisha, Ayeishah, Ayesha, Ayisha, Ayishah**
**Meaning:** Alive
**Origin Language:** Arabic

**Aelia | Aileigh, Ailey, Ailia, Ailie**
**Also:** Aeliana
**Meaning:** Sun
**Origin Language:** Ancient Greek

**Aella | Aellae, Aellai, Aellia**
**Meaning:** Whirlwind
**Origin Language:** Ancient Greek

Aemiliana | Aemiliann, Aemilianna, Aemilianne, Aemiline, Aimiliana, Aimiliann, Aimilianna, Aimilianne, Aimiline
**Also:** Aemillia | Aemilia, Aemille, Aimilia, Aimille, Aimillia
**Meaning:** Rival
**Origin Language:** Latin

Aerona
**Meaning:** From Near The River Aeron (Wales)
**Origin Language:** Welsh

Aesyle | Aesile
**Meaning:** Shining
**Origin Language:** Ancient Greek

Aetia
**Meaning:** Eagle
**Origin Language:** Latin

Aferdita | Aferdite
**Meaning:** Daybreak / Morning
**Origin Language:** Albanian

Affery | Affrey, Affrie, Affrye
**Also:** Affra | Affia, Affie, Affrah, Aifra, Aifria
**Meaning:** Very Speckled
**Origin Language:** Old Irish

Afra | Afraa, Afrah, Afria, Afrya, Afryah
**Meaning:** Pink
**Origin Language:** Arabic

Agara
**Meaning:** Flight
**Origin Language:** Hebrew

Agata | Agaata, Agaate, Agate, Agota
**Also:** Agatha | Agathe, Agathi

**Meaning:** Good
**Origin Language:** Ancient Greek

Aglaea | Aglae, Aglaia, Aglaya
**Meaning:** Beauty
**Origin Language:** Ancient Greek

Aglaeca
**Meaning:** Misery
**Origin Language:** Old English

Agnes | Agnesa, Agnese, Agness, Agnessa, Agnez, Agneza, Agneze, Agnezz, Agnezza
**Also:** Agneta | Agnete, Agnetha, Agnethe, Agnetta, Agnette, Agnita, Agnite
**Also:** Agnia | Agna, Agneia
**Meaning:** Chaste
**Origin Language:** Ancient Greek

Aida | Ayda
**Meaning:** Returning Visitor
**Origin Language:** Arabic

Aidana | Aedana, Aedena, Aidena, Aydana, Aydena
**Meaning:** Fire
**Origin Language:** Old Irish

Aidee | Aidi, Aidie, Aidy, Aydee
**Meaning:** Reserved
**Origin Language:** Greek

Aideen
**Meaning:** Envy
**Origin Language:** Old Irish

Aidith | Aiditha, Aidyta, Aidyth, Aidytha, Aidythe
**Meaning:** Wealthy Warrior
**Origin Language:** Old English

Aifric | Affraic, Aifricci, Aithric, Aithrica
**Meaning:** Very Speckled

**Origin Language:** Old Irish

Aikaterine | Aikaterina, Aikaterini, Akatarini, Akaterina, Akaterine
**Meaning:** Pure
**Origin Language:** Ancient Greek

Aila | Aili
**Meaning:** Holy
**Origin Language:** Old Norse

Ailani | Aelani, Aelany, Ailana, Ailanah, Ailanea, Ailaneah, Ailanie, Ailany
**Meaning:** Chief
**Origin Language:** Hawaiian

Aileen | Ailene, Ayleen, Aylene
**Meaning:** Forever / Eternity
**Origin Language:** Ancient Germanic

Ailen | Ayelen, Aylen
**Meaning:** Happiness
**Origin Language:** Mapuche

Ailis | Ailys
**Also:** Ailise | Ailisa
**Also:** Ailish
**Meaning:** Like A Noble
**Origin Language:** Ancient Germanic

Ailith | Alyth
**Meaning:** Ascending
**Origin Language:** Scottish Gaelic

Ailsa
**Meaning:** From Ailsa Craig (Scotland)
**Origin Language:** Scottish Gaelic

Aimi
**Meaning:** Beautiful Love
**Origin Language:** Japanese

Ainara | Ainhara
**Meaning:** Swallow (As In The Bird)
**Origin Language:** Basque

Ainhoa | Ainoa
**Meaning:** From Ainhoa (France)
**Origin Language:** Basque

Ainslie | Ainslea, Ainslee, Ainsleigh, Ainsley, Ainsly
**Meaning:** From A Lonely Meadow
**Origin Language:** Old English

Aira | Airi
**Meaning:** Herald
**Origin Language:** Finnish

Airah | Ayra, Ayrah
**Meaning:** Too Much For The Eye To See / Unowned
**Origin Language:** Arabic

Airin | Airina, Airine
**Meaning:** Peace
**Origin Language:** Ancient Greek

Airlann
**Meaning:** Ireland
**Origin Language:** Old Irish

Aisha | Aaisha, Aaishah, Aayshah, Aesha, Aeshah, Aeshia, Aiasha, Aischa, Aischa, Aishah, Aishia, Aishiah, Aiyesha, Aiyesha, Aiysha, Ayasha, Aysha, Ayshah
**Meaning:** Alive
**Origin Language:** Arabic

Aishling | Aishleen, Aishlene, Aishleyne, Aishlin, Aishlinn, Aishlyn
**Also:** Aisleen | Aislene, Aisleyne, Aislin, Aisling, Aislinn, Aislyn, Aislynn
**Meaning:** Dream
**Origin Language:** Irish

Aissa | Aisia, Aisiah, Aisyah

**Meaning:** Alive
**Origin Language:** Arabic

**Aitana | Aetana, Aita**
**Meaning:** From The Mountains
**Origin Language:** Spanish

**Aithra | Aifra, Aifria**
**Meaning:** Very Speckled
**Origin Language:** Old Irish

**Aitra**
**Meaning:** Ether / Heaven
**Origin Language:** Ancient Greek

**Aivana | Aivanna**
**Meaning:** Flower
**Origin Language:** Swahili

**Aivara | Aiva**
**Meaning:** From An Army That Dwells
Within The Yew Trees
**Origin Language:** Old Norse

**Aiza | Aizah**
**Meaning:** Noble
**Origin Language:** Arabic

**Akatta | Akaata**
**Meaning:** Good
**Origin Language:** Ancient Greek

**Akela | Akella**
**Meaning:** Noble
**Origin Language:** Ancient Germanic
And Old English (Cognates)

**Akira**
**Meaning:** Bright / Clear
**Origin Language:** Japanese

**Aksinia | Aksinya**
**Meaning:** Friendly To Guests/Strangers
(Hospitable)
**Origin Language:** Ancient Greek

**Alaia**

**Meaning:** Joyful
**Origin Language:** Basque

**Alaina | Alaine, Alayna, Alayne,
Allaina, Allaine, Alleyn, Alleyna,
Allina, Alline**
**Meaning:** Little Rock
**Origin Language:** Old Breton

**Alais**
**Meaning:** Of The Noble Sort
**Origin Language:** Ancient Germanic

**Alala**
**Meaning:** Warcry
**Origin Language:** Ancient Greek

**Alamea**
**Meaning:** Precious
**Origin Language:** Hawaiian

**Alameda | Alamida**
**Meaning:** Tree Lined Path
**Origin Language:** Spanish

**Alanda | Alanta, Allanda, Allande,
Allanta, Allante**
**Meaning:** From An Island
**Origin Language:** Old English

**Alani | Alahni, Alarni, Allani**
**Also:** Alanis | Alannis
**Also:** Alanna | Alana, Alanagh,
Alanah, Alannah, Allana, Allanah,
Allannah
**Meaning:** Little Rock
**Origin Language:** Old Breton

**Alaria | Allaria**
**Meaning:** Light-Hearted
**Origin Language:** Ancient Greek

**Alarica | Alarika**
**Meaning:** All Ruling
**Origin Language:** Ancient Germanic

Alastriona
**Meaning:** Mankind's Defender
**Origin Language:** Ancient Greek

Alaula
**Meaning:** Dawn
**Origin Language:** Hawaiian

Alaura | Allaura, Allora, Alora
**Meaning:** Laurel
**Origin Language:** Latin

Alba
**Meaning:** Elven
**Origin Language:** Ancient Germanic And Old English And Old Norse (Cognates)

Albena | Albina
**Meaning:** Albanian
**Origin Language:** Ancient Greek

Albera | Albira
**Meaning:** All True
**Origin Language:** Ancient Germanic

Alberica | Alberika
**Meaning:** Elven Ruler
**Origin Language:** Ancient Germanic

Alberie
**Meaning:** Albanian
**Origin Language:** Ancient Greek

Alberta | Albearta
**Meaning:** Bright Noble
**Origin Language:** Ancient Germanic And Old English (Cognates)

Alcera | Alcira, Alsera, Alsira
**Meaning:** God Is My Oath
**Origin Language:** Hebrew

Alda
**Meaning:** Wave
**Origin Language:** Icelandic

Aldara
**Meaning:** From An Army Of Old
**Origin Language:** Old Norse

Aldelma | Aldemia
**Meaning:** Father's Protector
**Origin Language:** Ancient Germanic

Aldena | Aldeana, Aldene, Aldina, Aldine
**Meaning:** Old And Friendly
**Origin Language:** Ancient Germanic And Old English (Cognates)

Aldera | Alderia, Aldira, Aldiria
**Meaning:** Old Warrior
**Origin Language:** Ancient Germanic

Aldith | Alditha, Aldyth, Aldytha
**Meaning:** Old Battler
**Origin Language:** Old English

Aldona
**Meaning:** Old And Friendly
**Origin Language:** Ancient Germanic And Old English (Cognates)

Aldora | Alldora
**Meaning:** Thor's Boulder (Thor Is The Name Of The Norse God Of Thunder And Lightning)
**Origin Language:** Old Norse

Aleandara | Aliandara
**Also:** Aleandra | Aliandra
**Meaning:** Defender Of Mankind
**Origin Language:** Ancient Greek

Alectra | Alectria, Alektra, Alektria
**Meaning:** Amber / The Shade Of The Sun / Incandescent
**Origin Language:** Ancient Greek

Aleena | Aleana, Aleane, Aleene, Alina, Aline, Allean, Alleana, Alleen, Alleena, Alleene, Allena,

Allene, Allina, Alline
**Meaning:** Little Rock
**Origin Language:** Old Breton

Alegra | Alegria, Allegra, Allegria
**Meaning:** Cheerful
**Origin Language:** Latin

Aleisha | Aleesha, Alesha, Alisha, Alishia, Alysha
**Also:** Aleita | Aleit, Alleyt, Alleyta
**Meaning:** Like A Noble
**Origin Language:** Ancient Germanic

Aleria | Alereia, Aliria, Alleria, Allyra
**Meaning:** Old Warrior
**Origin Language:** Ancient Germanic

Alesia | Alecia
**Meaning:** Of The Noble Sort
**Origin Language:** Ancient Germanic

Alessandra | Aleissandra, Aleissandre, Aleissandria, Aleissandrie, Aleissandrina, Aleissandrine, Alessandre, Alessandre, Alessandria, Alessandria, Alessandrie, Alessandrie, Alessandrina, Alessandrina, Alessandrine, Alessandrine, Alissandra, Alissandre, Alissandria, Alissandrie, Alissandrina, Alissandrine
**Meaning:** Mankind's Defender
**Origin Language:** Ancient Greek

Alessia | Alessa, Alesszia, Aleszia
**Meaning:** Defender
**Origin Language:** Ancient Greek

Aleta | Alita
**Also:** Alethia | Aleth, Aletha, Alethaia, Alethea, Aletheia
**Meaning:** Truth

**Origin Language:** Ancient Greek

Aletia | Alletia
**Also:** Aletta | Aleta, Alette, Alletta, Allette
**Meaning:** Of The Noble Sort
**Origin Language:** Ancient Germanic

Alettra | Aletra, Aletria, Alettria
**Meaning:** Amber / The Shade Of The Sun / Incandescent
**Origin Language:** Ancient Greek

Alexandra | Aleixandra, Aleixandre, Aleixandria, Aleixandrie, Aleixandrina, Aleixandrine, Aleksandra, Aleksandre, Aleksandria, Aleksandrie, Aleksandrina, Aleksandrine, Alexandre, Alexandria, Alexandrie, Alexandrina, Alexandrine, Alixandra, Alixandre, Alixandria, Alixandrie, Alixandrina, Alixandrine
**Meaning:** Mankind's Defender
**Origin Language:** Ancient Greek

Alexia | Aleksa, Aleksia, Alexia, Alexya, Aliks, Aliksya, Alix, Alixe, Alixia, Alyks, Alyx, Alyxia
**Also:** Alexina | Aleksena, Aleksene, Aleksina, Aleksine, Alexena, Alexene, Alexine, Alixena, Alixene , Alixina, Alixine
**Also:** Alexys | Aleksis, Alexis, Aliksys, Alixis, Alyxis
**Meaning:** Defender
**Origin Language:** Ancient Greek

Alfia | Alfaia, Alfeia, Alfhaia, Alfiya
**Meaning:** Healthy
**Origin Language:** Ancient Greek

Alia | Aliya, Aliyah
**Meaning:** Ascending
**Origin Language:** Hebrew

Alice | Aalis, Aalys, Alease, Alis,
Alise, Aliz, Allice, Allis, Allyce,
Alyce, Alys, Alyse
**Also:** Alicia | Alisia, Alissia, Alisya,
Allycia, Alycia, Alysia, Alyssia
**Also:** Alidea | Alida, Alide, Allida,
Allide, Allidea, Alyda
**Meaning:** Like A Noble
**Origin Language:** Ancient Germanic

Alidora
**Meaning:** Gift Of The Sun
**Origin Language:** Ancient Greek

Alienora | Alianora, Alianore,
Alienor
**Meaning:** Noble Of The North
**Origin Language:** Ancient Germanic

Alietta | Aliette
**Meaning:** My God Is God
**Origin Language:** Hebrew

Alima
**Meaning:** Scholar
**Origin Language:** Arabic

Alina | Aleena, Aleene, Alena,
Alene, Alin, Aline, Alleena, Alleene
**Meaning:** Torch
**Origin Language:** Ancient Greek

Alinda | Alindra
**Meaning:** Tender Noble
**Origin Language:** Ancient Germanic

Alioda
**Meaning:** Gift Of The Sun
**Origin Language:** Ancient Greek

Aliona | Alyona

**Meaning:** Torch
**Origin Language:** Ancient Greek

Aliora
**Meaning:** God Is My Light
**Origin Language:** Hebrew

Alisabeth | Alisabet, Alisabeta,
Alisabete, Alisabeti, Alisabetta,
Alizabet, Alizabeta, Alizabete,
Alizabeth, Alizabeti, Alizabetta,
Alysabeth Alyzabeth
**Also:** Alisaveta | Alisavet, Alizavet,
Alizaveta
**Meaning:** God Is My Oath
**Origin Language:** Hebrew

Alisende | Alisenda, Alissenda,
Alissende
**Meaning:** Journeys To A Temple
**Origin Language:** Ancient Germanic

Aliska | Alyska
**Also:** Alison | Alicen, Alisan,
Alisson, Allison, Allisson, Allyson,
Alycen, Alyson, Alysson
**Meaning:** Of The Noble Sort
**Origin Language:** Ancient Germanic

Alithea | Alith, Alitha, Alithaia,
Alitheia, Alithia
**Meaning:** Truth
**Origin Language:** Ancient Greek

Alivia
**Meaning:** Olive Tree
**Origin Language:** Latin

Aliyyah | Aliyya
**Meaning:** Exalted
**Origin Language:** Arabic

Aliza | Alisa, Alize, Alizia
**Meaning:** Joyful
**Origin Language:** Hebrew

Alizee
**Meaning:** Trade Wind
**Origin Language:** French

Allesia | Alesia, Alesya, Allesya
**Meaning:** Mankind's Defender
**Origin Language:** Ancient Greek

Allie | Alley, Alli, Ally
**Meaning:** A Short Form Of Any Of The Numerous Names Beginning With Al
**Origin Language:** Various

Alloma | Alhoma, Aloma
**Meaning:** From A Homestead Near A Temple
**Origin Language:** Old English

Alma
**Meaning:** Nourishing
**Origin Language:** Latin

Almara
**Meaning:** Famous Noble
**Origin Language:** Ancient Germanic And Old English (Cognates)

Almaria | Almariyah, Almeria, Almeriyah
**Meaning:** The Watchtower
**Origin Language:** Arabic

Almena | Almene, Almina, Almine
**Also:** Almica | Almika
**Meaning:** Nourishing
**Origin Language:** Latin

Almira | Almera
**Meaning:** Famous Noble
**Origin Language:** Ancient Germanic And Old English (Cognates)

Alnea | Alnia
**Meaning:** An Alder Tree
**Origin Language:** Latin

Alodie | Alodi, Alodia, Alody
**Meaning:** All Wealthy
**Origin Language:** Ancient Germanic

Aloma | Alomara
**Meaning:** Famous Noble
**Origin Language:** Ancient Germanic And Old English (Cognates)

Alona | Aallona, Aalona, Allona
**Meaning:** Oak Tree
**Origin Language:** Hebrew

Alondra
**Meaning:** Dark
**Origin Language:** Spanish

Alonza | Alonsa
**Meaning:** Ready For Nobility
**Origin Language:** Ancient Germanic

Alourdes | Alordes
**Meaning:** Laurel
**Origin Language:** Latin

Aloysia | Aloisa, Aloisia
**Meaning:** Famous Battler
**Origin Language:** Ancient Germanic

Alrica | Alrika
**Meaning:** All Ruling
**Origin Language:** Ancient Germanic

Alsa | Alsie, Alsy, Alza, Alzie, Alzy
**Also:** Alsabeth | Alzabeth
**Meaning:** My God Is An Oath
**Origin Language:** Hebrew

Alta | Alte
**Meaning:** Old
**Origin Language:** Yiddish

Althea | Altea, Altha, Althaea, Althaia, Altheia, Althia, Altia
**Meaning:** Healer
**Origin Language:** Ancient Greek

Altiera | Altera
**Meaning:** Old Warrior
**Origin Language:** Ancient Germanic

Altina | Altena
**Meaning:** Pure Gold
**Origin Language:** Ottoman Turkish

Aluara
**Meaning:** Elven Army
**Origin Language:** Ancient Germanic
And Old English And Old Norse
(Cognates)

Aluina | Aluinna, Aluinnia,
Aluwina
**Meaning:** Noble Friend
**Origin Language:** Ancient Germanic
And Old English (Cognates)

Alva | Alvah, Alvi, Alvia, Alvie
**Meaning:** Elven
**Origin Language:** Ancient Germanic
And Old English And Old Norse
(Cognates)

Alvania | Alvana
**Meaning:** Albanian
**Origin Language:** Ancient Greek

Alvara
**Meaning:** Elven Army
**Origin Language:** Ancient Germanic
And Old English And Old Norse
(Cognates)

Alvena | Alvina, Alvine, Alvinia,
Alvinna
**Meaning:** Noble Friend
**Origin Language:** Ancient Germanic
And Old English (Cognates)

Alvera | Alveria, Alvira, Alviria
**Meaning:** All True
**Origin Language:** Ancient Germanic

Alvery | Alveri, Alverie
**Meaning:** Elven Counsel
**Origin Language:** Old English

Alvida | Alveda
**Meaning:** Elven
**Origin Language:** Ancient Germanic
And Old English And Old Norse
(Cognates)

Alvilda | Alvilde
**Meaning:** Elven Battler
**Origin Language:** Old Norse

Alvisa | Alvissa
**Meaning:** All Wise
**Origin Language:** Old Norse

Alvoria | Alvora
**Meaning:** Albanian
**Origin Language:** Ancient Greek

Alwilda | Alwilde
**Meaning:** Elven Battler
**Origin Language:** Old Norse

Alwina | Alwena, Alwene, Alwine
**Meaning:** Noble Friend
**Origin Language:** Ancient Germanic
And Old English (Cognates)

Alya
**Meaning:** The Sky / Heaven
**Origin Language:** Arabic

Alyssa | Alisa, Alissa, Allisa,
Allissa, Allyssa, Alysa
**Meaning:** Of The Noble Sort
**Origin Language:** Ancient Germanic

Alyssum
**Meaning:** Alyssum (Flower)
**Origin Language:** English

Alzera | Alzira
**Meaning:** God Is My Oath
**Origin Language:** Hebrew

Ama
**Meaning:** Born On A Saturday
**Origin Language:** Akan

Amabel | Amabella, Amabilia, Amable
**Meaning:** Lovable
**Origin Language:** Latin

Amada
**Meaning:** Beloved
**Origin Language:** Latin

Amadea | Amadia, Amedea, Amidea, Amidia
**Meaning:** Loved By God
**Origin Language:** Latin

Amadora | Amadore
**Meaning:** Loves God
**Origin Language:** Latin

Amaia | Amaya, Amayah, Amiyah
**Meaning:** The End
**Origin Language:** Basque

Amal | Amaal, Amaali
**Meaning:** Hope
**Origin Language:** Arabic

Amala
**Meaning:** Pure
**Origin Language:** Sanskrit

Amalindis | Amalindys, Amelindis, Amelindys
**Meaning:** Gentle Worker
**Origin Language:** Ancient Germanic

Amalissa | Amalisa, Amelisa, Amelissa
**Also:** Amalsia | Amalcia, Amelcia, Amelsia
**Meaning:** Worker
**Origin Language:** Ancient Germanic

Amalthea | Amalfea, Amalfia, Amaltea, Amaltheia, Amalthia, Amaltia
**Meaning:** Soothing
**Origin Language:** Ancient Greek

Amanda
**Meaning:** Worthy Of Love
**Origin Language:** Latin

Amani
**Meaning:** Wish / Desire
**Origin Language:** Arabic

Amanta | Amante, Amantia
**Also:** Amanza | Amanzia
**Meaning:** Loving
**Origin Language:** Latin

Amara | Amarah
**Meaning:** Eternal
**Origin Language:** Sanskrit

Amaranda | Amarande
**Also:** Amaranthe | Amaranta, Amarante, Amarantha
**Meaning:** Amaranth Flower / Unfading
**Origin Language:** Ancient Greek

Amari
**Meaning:** Long Living
**Origin Language:** Arabic

Amaris | Amariss, Amarys, Amaryss
**Meaning:** God Has Said
**Origin Language:** Hebrew

Amaryllis | Amarilis, Amarillis, Amarylis
**Also:** Amaryssa | Amarisa, Amarise, Amarissa, Amarysa
**Meaning:** Sparkling
**Origin Language:** Ancient Greek

Amata
**Meaning:** Beloved
**Origin Language:** Latin

Amber | Amba, Ambie, Ambre, Ambyr
**Meaning:** Amber (English And Latin) / The River (Old English)
**Origin Language:** English And Latin And Old English

Amberlie | Amberlea, Amberlee, Amberleigh, Amberly
**Also:** Amberlina | Amberlena, Amberlyn, Amberlynn
**Meaning:** From A Meadow Where Yellowhammers Frequent (A Yellowhammer Is A Type Of Bird)
**Origin Language:** Old English

Ambra
**Also:** Ambrette | Ambretta, Ambritt
**Meaning:** Amber
**Origin Language:** Latin

Ambrogena | Ambrogia, Ambrogina,
**Also:** Ambrosia | Ambroisie, Ambrosena, Ambrosene, Ambrosina, Ambrosine, Ambrozena, Ambrozene, Ambrozia, Ambrozie, Ambrozina, Ambrozine
**Meaning:** Immortal
**Origin Language:** Ancient Greek

Amelie | Amali, Amalia, Amalie, Amaliya, Amaly, Amele, Ameli, Amelia, Amélie, Amely
**Meaning:** Worker
**Origin Language:** Ancient Germanic

Amelinda | Amalinda, Amalinde,

Amelind, Amelinde
**Also:** Amelin | Amelyn, Amelynn
**Also:** Ameline | Amelina, Amelyne, Amelyne
**Meaning:** Gentle Worker
**Origin Language:** Ancient Germanic

Amelita | Amalita
**Meaning:** Worker
**Origin Language:** Ancient Germanic

America | Ameriga, Amerika
**Also:** Amerie | Amery
**Meaning:** Rich Worker
**Origin Language:** Ancient Germanic

Ami
**Meaning:** Beautiful Asia
**Origin Language:** Japanese

Amia | Aimea, Aimia, Amea, Aymea, Aymia
**Meaning:** Beloved
**Origin Language:** Latin

Amica
**Meaning:** Friendly
**Origin Language:** Latin

Amice | Amisa, Amise, Amisi, Amisia
**Meaning:** Friend
**Origin Language:** Old French

Amilia | Amillia
**Meaning:** Rival
**Origin Language:** Latin

Amilla | Amila, Amyla, Amylla
**Meaning:** Worker
**Origin Language:** Ancient Germanic

Amina | Aamina, Aaminah, Aamine, Ameena, Amenah, Aminah, Amine, Aminia
**Meaning:** Feels Safe

**Origin Language:** Arabic

Aminta | Amintah, Amynta, Amyntah
**Meaning:** Defender
**Origin Language:** Ancient Greek

Amirah | Ameera, Amira
**Meaning:** Commander
**Origin Language:** Arabic

Amisha | Ameesh, Ameesha, Ameish, Ameisha
**Meaning:** Desire
**Origin Language:** Sanskrit

Amita
**Meaning:** Infinite
**Origin Language:** Sanskrit

Amity | Amitie
**Meaning:** Amity
**Origin Language:** English

Amla
**Meaning:** Amla Tree
**Origin Language:** Sanskrit

Amleta | Amaleta, Amaletta, Amalette, Amletta, Amlette
**Also:** Amleth | Amaleth, Amaletha, Amletha
**Also:** Amloda | Amlodha, Amlotha
**Meaning:** Annoyer Of Odin (Odin Is The Name Of A Norse God)
**Origin Language:** Old Norse

Amma
**Meaning:** Grandmother
**Origin Language:** Old Norse

Ammia
**Meaning:** Mother
**Origin Language:** Ancient Greek

Amodia | Amodea

**Meaning:** Loved By God
**Origin Language:** Latin

Amona | Amoena, Amoene
**Meaning:** Lovely
**Origin Language:** Latin

Amora | Amor, Amore, Amour, Amoura
**Also:** Amorana | Amourana
**Also:** Amoretta | Amorette, Amouretta, Amourette
**Also:** Amorina | Amorena, Amourena, Amourina
**Also:** Amorosa | Amourosa
**Meaning:** Love
**Origin Language:** Latin

Amra
**Meaning:** Immortal
**Origin Language:** Sanskrit

Amy | Aimee, Aimie, Aimy, Amee, Amie
**Meaning:** Beloved
**Origin Language:** Latin

Anacaria | Anacara, Anachara, Anacharia, Anakara, Anakaria, Anakhara, Anakharia
**Meaning:** With Grace
**Origin Language:** Ancient Greek

Anaelle | Anaella
**Meaning:** Care
**Origin Language:** Arabic

Anahera
**Meaning:** Angel
**Origin Language:** Maori

Anahi | Anahei, Annahi
**Meaning:** Maize
**Origin Language:** Tupi

Anahis | Anahys, Annahis,
Annahys
**Meaning:** Gracious
**Origin Language:** Hebrew

Anahita
**Meaning:** Immaculate
**Origin Language:** Persian

Anais
**Meaning:** Gracious
**Origin Language:** Hebrew

Anaitis
**Meaning:** Immaculate
**Origin Language:** Persian

Analia | Anelia, Aneliya
**Meaning:** Gracious
**Origin Language:** Hebrew

Analyn | Anelyn, Annalyn,
Annelyn
**Meaning:** Tender Grace (A Combination
Of Anne And Linda)
**Origin Language:** Ancient Germanic
And Hebrew (In Combination)

Ananda | Anandi
**Meaning:** Bliss
**Origin Language:** Sanskrit

Anantha | Ananta, Ananth,
Ananthe, Ananthia, Anathia
**Meaning:** Infinite
**Origin Language:** Sanskrit

Anara | Anar
**Meaning:** Pomegranate
**Origin Language:** Kazakh And Kyrgyz
(Cognates)

Anastasia | Anastacia, Anastase,
Anastasie, Anastassia, Anastasy,
Anastazia, Anastazie, Anastazy,
Anastya

**Meaning:** Resurrected
**Origin Language:** Ancient Greek

Anatola | Anatolia, Anatoliya
**Meaning:** Rising Sun
**Origin Language:** Ancient Greek

Anavay | Anavae, Anavaia,
Anavaya, Anavey, Anaveya
**Meaning:** Complete
**Origin Language:** Pali

Ancharia | Ancaria, Ankaria,
Ankharia
**Meaning:** With Grace
**Origin Language:** Ancient Greek

Andeana | Andiana, Andiane,
Andianna, Andianne, Andieane
**Also:** Andi | Andee, Andy
**Also:** Andina | Andena
**Meaning:** Brave Warrior
**Origin Language:** Ancient Greek

Andora
**Meaning:** Thor's Eagle (Thor Is The
Name Of The Norse God Of Thunder
And Lightning)
**Origin Language:** Old Norse

Andra
**Also:** Andrada
**Also:** Andrea | Andraia, Andreia,
Andria
**Also:** Andrella
**Also:** Andriana | Andreana,
Andriane, Andrianna, Andrianne,
Andrieane
**Also:** Andrietta | Andriette
**Also:** Andrina | Andreina,
Andreine, Andrena, Andrene,
Andrine
**Meaning:** Brave Warrior
**Origin Language:** Ancient Greek

Androna | Andronia
**Also:** Andronica | Andronika
**Meaning:** Mankind's Victory
**Origin Language:** Ancient Greek

Aneira
**Meaning:** Dignity
**Origin Language:** Latin

Anella | Anelia, Anelle, Anellie,
Annela, Annelia, Annelia, Annelie,
Annella, Annelle, Annellia
**Also:** Anelma | Anelme
**Meaning:** Begged For
**Origin Language:** Finnish

Anese | Aneese, Anise, Annisa,
Annise, Annissa
**Meaning:** Anise (Herb)
**Origin Language:** Latin

Angel | Aingeal, Ainjel
**Also:** Angela | Ange, Angele,
Angelea, Angelia, Angelie, Angella,
Angie, Angiola, Angy, Anjela,
Anngela, Annjela
**Also:** Angelica | Angelca, Angelika,
Angelike, Angeliki, Angelique,
Angelka, Angyalka, Anjelica,
Anjelika
**Also:** Angelina | Angelien,
Angeline, Angellina
**Also:** Angelita | Anjelita
**Also:** Aniella | Aniela, Anielka
**Meaning:** Angel/Messenger
**Origin Language:** Latin

Aniette | Aniet, Anieta, Anietta
**Also:** Anina | Anine, Annina,
Annine
**Meaning:** Gracious
**Origin Language:** Hebrew

Anisa | Anisah, Anisia, Anisiya,

Anissa, Annisa
**Meaning:** Friendly
**Origin Language:** Arabic

Anisha
**Meaning:** Sleepless
**Origin Language:** Sanskrit

Anison | Annison
**Meaning:** Anise (Herb)
**Origin Language:** Latin

Anita | Anite, Anitta, Anitte
**Meaning:** Gracious
**Origin Language:** Hebrew

Aniya | Anaia, Anaya, Anayah,
Ania, Aniyah
**Meaning:** Care
**Origin Language:** Arabic

Anizette | Anisetta, Anisette,
Anizetta
**Meaning:** Anise (Herb)
**Origin Language:** Latin

Anna | Ahna, Ana, Ane, Ann,
Anne
**Meaning:** Gracious
**Origin Language:** Hebrew

Annabelle | Anabel, Anabela,
Anabell, Anabella, Anabelle,
Annabel, Annabela, Annabell,
Annabella
**Meaning:** Lovable
**Origin Language:** Latin

Annalee | Analee
**Meaning:** From A Graced Meadow (A
Combination Of Anna And Lee)
**Origin Language:** Old English And
Hebrew (In Combination)

Annalina | Analina, Anelina,
Aneline, Anlina, Annaline,

Annelina, Anneline
**Also:** Annalinda | Anelinda,
Anelinde, Anlinda, Annelinda,
Annelinde
**Meaning:** Tender Grace (A Combination
Of Anne And Linda)
**Origin Language:** Ancient Germanic
And Hebrew (In Combination)

Annalisa | Anelie, Aneliese,
Anelise, Anelisse, Anely, Annalise,
Anneli, Annelie, Annelies,
Anneliese, Annelise, Annely
**Meaning:** God Is My Oath And I Am
Gracious (A Combination Of Anna And
Lisa)
**Origin Language:** Hebrew

Annea | Anea, Ania, Annia
**Meaning:** Gracious
**Origin Language:** Hebrew

Annemarie | Anamara, Anamaria,
Anmaria, Annamaria, Annemary,
Annmarie, Annmary
**Meaning:** Gracious Rebel (A
Combination Of Anne And Marie)
**Origin Language:** Hebrew

Annette | Aneta, Anett, Anetta,
Anette, Annet, Anneta, Annett,
Annetta
**Also:** Annie | Ani, Anni, Anny
**Also:** Annika | Anica, Anika,
Anneca, Anneka, Anneke, Annica,
Annick
**Meaning:** Gracious
**Origin Language:** Hebrew

Annora | Anora
**Meaning:** Dignity
**Origin Language:** Latin

Annushka | Annuska, Anoushka,
Anouska, Anuschka, Anushka

**Meaning:** Gracious
**Origin Language:** Hebrew

Annwyn | Annwin, Annwn,
Annwvyn, Annwynn, Anwin,
Anwn, Anwvyn, Anwyn, Anwynn
**Meaning:** Very Deep / Otherworldly
**Origin Language:** Middle Welsh

Anona | Annona
**Meaning:** Corn / Grain
**Origin Language:** Latin

Anori
**Meaning:** Affectionate Village
**Origin Language:** Japanese

Anoushe | Annosha, Anooshe,
Anoosheh, Anousheh, Anusheh
**Meaning:** Immortal
**Origin Language:** Persian

Anslea | Anslee, Ansleigh, Ansley,
Anslie, Ansly
**Meaning:** From A Lonely Meadow
**Origin Language:** Old English

Anteia | Antaea, Antaia, Antia
**Meaning:** Opponent
**Origin Language:** Ancient Greek

Anthea | Anfaia, Anfea, Anfeia,
Anfia, Anfiya, Annthaia, Annthea,
Anntheia, Annthia, Anthaia,
Antheia, Anthia
**Meaning:** Flower
**Origin Language:** Ancient Greek

Anthora | Antora
**Meaning:** Thor's Eagle (Thor Is The
Name Of The Norse God Of Thunder
And Lightning)
**Origin Language:** Old Norse

Antica | Antika
**Also:** Antoinette | Antoinetta

**Also:** Antonella | Antonela
**Also:** Antonette | Antonetta,
Antonieta, Antonietta, Antoniette
**Also:** Antonia | Antoniya
**Meaning:** Of Ani (Ani Is The Name Of
An Etruscan God, Thought To Be
Equivalent To The Roman God Janus,
The God Of Beginnings, Gates,
Transitions, Time, Duality, Doorways,
Passages, And Endings)
**Origin Language:** Latin

Anya
**Meaning:** Gracious
**Origin Language:** Hebrew

Anzelda | Ansalda, Anselda,
Anzalda
**Meaning:** Mighty God
**Origin Language:** Ancient Germanic

Aolani
**Meaning:** Heavenly Cloud
**Origin Language:** Hawaiian

Aphra | Aphrah, Aphria, Aphrya,
Aphryah
**Meaning:** Pink
**Origin Language:** Arabic

Aphrodite | Afrodita, Afrodite,
Afroditi, Aphrodita, Aphroditi
**Meaning:** Born From The Foam Of The
Sea
**Origin Language:** Ancient Greek

Apolena | Apolene, Apollena,
Apollene, Apollin, Apollina,
Apolline, Apollonia, Apollyn,
Apolonia
**Meaning:** Of Apollo (Apollo Is The
Name Of The Greek God Of Oracles,
Healing, Archery, Music And Arts,
Sunlight, Knowledge, Herds And Flocks,
And Protection Of The Young)
**Origin Language:** Ancient Greek

April
**Meaning:** April
**Origin Language:** English

Aprilis | Aprilisa, Aprilys
**Meaning:** Opening (Referring To The
Opening Of Flowers And Trees In
Spring)
**Origin Language:** Latin

Ara
**Meaning:** Plougher
**Origin Language:** Latin

Arabella | Arabel, Arabela, Arabell,
Arabelle
**Meaning:** Lovable
**Origin Language:** Latin

Araceli | Aracela, Aracelie,
Aracelis, Aracely, Arazela, Arazeli,
Arazelis
**Meaning:** Altar Of The Sky
**Origin Language:** Latin

Araci | Aracia, Aracy
**Meaning:** Dawn
**Origin Language:** Tupi

Aradia
**Meaning:** Ode To A Heroine
**Origin Language:** Ancient Greek

Aralda | Aralde, Araldia, Arelda,
Arelde, Areldia, Arilda, Arilde,
Arildia
**Meaning:** Of The Ruling Army
**Origin Language:** Old English

Aramia | Aramaea, Aramea,
Aramea, Arameia
**Meaning:** Highlands
**Origin Language:** Hebrew

Araminta

**Meaning:** Valley
**Origin Language:** Basque

Ararie | Araria
**Meaning:** Plougher
**Origin Language:** Latin

Aratia | Arata
**Also:** Aratona | Aratonia
**Meaning:** Prayed For
**Origin Language:** Ancient Greek

Arbelle | Arbela, Arbella
**Meaning:** Lovable
**Origin Language:** Latin

Ardala
**Meaning:** Of High Gallantry
**Origin Language:** Old Irish

Ardena | Arda, Ardene, Ardina, Ardine
**Meaning:** Valley Of The Eagle
**Origin Language:** Old English

Ardita
**Meaning:** Golden Day
**Origin Language:** Albanian

Ardith | Ardath, Ardatha, Ardathe, Ardathia, Ardeth, Ardetha, Ardethe, Ardethia, Arditha, Ardithe, Ardithia, Ardytha, Ardythe
**Meaning:** Flowering Field
**Origin Language:** Hebrew

Areca | Arecea, Areci, Arecia
**Meaning:** Areca (Type Of Palm)
**Origin Language:** English

Arenzia | Arensa, Arense, Arensia, Arenza, Arenze
**Meaning:** Ruler Of The Eagles
**Origin Language:** Ancient Germanic

Arete | Areta, Areti, Aretia, Arita

**Meaning:** Virtue
**Origin Language:** Ancient Greek

Aretha | Aritha
**Meaning:** The Waterer
**Origin Language:** Ancient Greek

Aria | Aaria, Aarya, Ariah, Ariya, Ariyah, Arya, Aryia
**Meaning:** Song / Air
**Origin Language:** Italian

Ariadne | Ariadna, Ariadni
**Meaning:** Very Pure / Very Holy
**Origin Language:** Ancient Greek

Arialda
**Meaning:** Of The Ruling Army
**Origin Language:** Old English

Arianna | Areanna, Ariana, Ariane, Arianne, Arriana, Aryana, Aryanna
**Meaning:** Very Pure / Very Holy
**Origin Language:** Ancient Greek

Arielle | Ariel, Ariella, Aryiel
**Meaning:** Lion Of God
**Origin Language:** Hebrew

Arienne | Ariena, Ariene, Arienna
**Meaning:** Of The Star Sign Aries
**Origin Language:** English

Arin | Aryn
**Meaning:** Ireland
**Origin Language:** Old Irish

Arine | Arena, Arene, Arina
**Meaning:** Peace
**Origin Language:** Ancient Greek

Arioni | Aironie, Ariona, Arione, Arionna, Ariony, Aryona, Aryonna
**Meaning:** Spiritual / Noble
**Origin Language:** Sanskrit

Arisa | Aresa, Aresia, Arezia
**Meaning:** Ruin
**Origin Language:** Ancient Greek

Arisha
**Meaning:** Peace
**Origin Language:** Ancient Greek

Arista
**Meaning:** Ear Of Grain
**Origin Language:** Latin

Aristea | Aristia
**Meaning:** The Best
**Origin Language:** Ancient Greek

Aristona
**Meaning:** The Best (First) Meal / Breakfast
**Origin Language:** Ancient Greek

Arla
**Meaning:** Early In The Morning
**Origin Language:** Swedish

Arlea | Arlee, Arleigh, Arley, Arlie
**Meaning:** From A Meadow Of Hares
**Origin Language:** Old English

Arlene | Arleen, Arleene, Arlena
**Meaning:** Friendly Warrior
**Origin Language:** Ancient Germanic

Arleth | Arletha
**Also:** Arlette | Arlet, Arlett, Arletta, Arletty
**Meaning:** Noble Heritage
**Origin Language:** Ancient Germanic

Arlina | Arla, Arline
**Meaning:** Friendly Warrior
**Origin Language:** Ancient Germanic

Arlinda | Arlinde, Arlindi, Arlindia
**Meaning:** Born Of Gold
**Origin Language:** Albanian

Arlotta | Arlotte
**Meaning:** Rascal
**Origin Language:** Old French

Arluina | Arlewina, Arlewine, Arluine
**Meaning:** Friendly Warrior
**Origin Language:** Ancient Germanic

Armella | Armelle
**Meaning:** Princess Of Bears
**Origin Language:** Old Welsh

Armida | Armide
**Meaning:** Army Woman
**Origin Language:** Ancient Germanic

Armina | Armena, Armene, Armine
**Meaning:** Whole
**Origin Language:** Ancient Germanic

Arnella | Arnelle, Arnellia
**Also:** Arnetta | Arenette, Arneta, Arnita
**Also:** Arnina | Arnena
**Meaning:** Eagle
**Origin Language:** Ancient Germanic And Old Norse (Cognates)

Arnora
**Meaning:** Thor's Eagle (Thor Is The Name Of The Norse God Of Thunder And Lightning)
**Origin Language:** Old Norse

Aroa
**Meaning:** Era / Time
**Origin Language:** Basque

Arodia
**Meaning:** Ode To A Heroine
**Origin Language:** Ancient Greek

Arosa | Arrosa, Arosia, Arrosia

**Meaning:** Rose
**Origin Language:** Latin

Artemis | Artemys
**Meaning:** Safe
**Origin Language:** Ancient Greek

Artia
**Meaning:** Bear
**Origin Language:** Old Welsh

Aruna
**Meaning:** Dawn
**Origin Language:** Sanskrit

Arvana | Arvania
**Meaning:** Albanian
**Origin Language:** Ancient Greek

Arveda | Arvedia, Arvida, Arvidia
**Also:** Arvia
**Meaning:** Tree Of The Eagle
**Origin Language:** Old Norse

Arwen
**Meaning:** Noble Maiden
**Origin Language:** Sindarian (Fictional Language Devised By J. R. R. Tolkien For Use In His Fantasy Stories, Such As Lord Of The Rings)

Arzella | Arcelia, Arzelia, Arzelle
**Meaning:** Altar Of The Sky
**Origin Language:** Latin

Asceline | Acelina, Aceline, Ascelin, Ascelina, Ascelyn, Ascelynn
**Meaning:** Gentle Noble
**Origin Language:** Ancient Germanic

Asellia | Asella
**Meaning:** Young Donkey
**Origin Language:** Latin

Asha

**Meaning:** Hope / Desire
**Origin Language:** Sanskrit

Ashanti
**Meaning:** Warlike
**Origin Language:** Twi

Ashia | Ashiah, Asiah
**Meaning:** Alive
**Origin Language:** Arabic

Ashleen | Ashlena, Ashlene, Ashlin, Ashlina, Ashline, Ashlyn, Ashlynn
**Meaning:** Dream
**Origin Language:** Irish

Ashleigh | Ash, Ashlea, Ashlee, Ashley, Ashlie, Ashly
**Meaning:** From An Ash Tree Meadow
**Origin Language:** Old English

Ashwyn | Ashwina, Ashwyna, Ashwynn, Ashwynna, Ashwynne
**Meaning:** Horse Possessor
**Origin Language:** Sanskrit

Asora | Asoria
**Meaning:** Azure / Lapis Lazuli / Sky Blue
**Origin Language:** Latin

Aspen | Aspyn
**Meaning:** Aspen Tree
**Origin Language:** English

Asra
**Meaning:** Nocturnal Wanderer
**Origin Language:** Arabic

Astarte
**Meaning:** Lady Of The Heavens / Lady Of The Sky
**Origin Language:** Akkadian

Astella | Astelle

**Meaning:** Star
**Origin Language:** Latin

Asteria | Astera, Asterie
**Meaning:** Star
**Origin Language:** Ancient Greek

Astoria
**Meaning:** Hawk
**Origin Language:** Occitan

Astra | Aster, Astree, Astri
**Also:** Astraea | Astraia, Astrea, Astreia, Astria
**Meaning:** Star
**Origin Language:** Ancient Greek

Astrelle | Astrella
**Meaning:** Star
**Origin Language:** Latin

Astrid | Astrida
**Meaning:** Beautiful And Divine
**Origin Language:** Old Norse

Atalia | Atala, Atalyah
**Meaning:** God Is Exalted
**Origin Language:** Hebrew

Atanasia | Atanasie, Attanasia, Attanasie
**Meaning:** Immortal
**Origin Language:** Ancient Greek

Atarah | Atara
**Meaning:** God Is Exalted
**Origin Language:** Hebrew

Atarina | Atarena
**Meaning:** Like A Fire
**Origin Language:** Old Persian

Ataya | Aatiya, Ataia, Atiya
**Meaning:** Bestowal
**Origin Language:** Arabic

Athala | Athela
**Meaning:** Noble
**Origin Language:** Ancient Germanic And Old English (Cognates)

Athaliah | Athalia, Athalie
**Meaning:** God Is Exalted
**Origin Language:** Hebrew

Athena | Afana, Afena, Afene, Afina, Afine, Athana, Athene, Athina, Athine
**Meaning:** Very Divine
**Origin Language:** Ancient Greek

Atria | Atra, Atrea
**Meaning:** Fearless
**Origin Language:** Ancient Greek

Attavia | Attaviana, Attavie
**Meaning:** Eighth
**Origin Language:** Latin

Auberta
**Meaning:** Bright Noble
**Origin Language:** Ancient Germanic And Old English (Cognates)

Aubrey | Aubree, Aubrie, Aubry
**Also:** Aubriella | Aubrielle
**Also:** Aubrina | Aubrena, Aubrene, Aubrine
**Meaning:** Elven Ruler
**Origin Language:** Ancient Germanic

Aude | Aud, Auda, Audie, Audy
**Meaning:** Rich
**Origin Language:** Ancient Germanic And Old English And Old Norse (Cognates)

Audence | Audenci, Audencia, Audenza, Audenzia
**Meaning:** Audacious
**Origin Language:** Latin

Audina | Audine, Awdina, Awdine
**Meaning:** Wealthy And Friendly
**Origin Language:** Old English And Old Norse (Cognates)

Audmara | Audamara
**Meaning:** Wealthy And Famous
**Origin Language:** Ancient Germanic And Old Norse (Cognates)

Audra
**Meaning:** Storm
**Origin Language:** Lithuanian

Audrette | Audretta
**Also:** Audrey | Audrea, Audri, Audria, Audrie
**Also:** Audria | Audrea, Audreia
**Meaning:** Noble Strength
**Origin Language:** Old English

Audrianna | Auddriana, Auddrianne, Auddriena, Auddrienne, Auddriona, Auddrionne, Audriana, Audrianne
**Meaning:** From Hadria (The Name Of Two Ancient Roman Settlements Which Were Located In What Are Now Northern Italy And Central Italy) / From The Water
**Origin Language:** Latin

Audrica | Audrika
**Meaning:** Wealth And Riches
**Origin Language:** Ancient Germanic And Old English And Old Norse (Cognates)

Audrina | Audrena, Audrene, Audrine
**Meaning:** Noble Strength
**Origin Language:** Old English

Audruna
**Meaning:** Wealthy Rune
**Origin Language:** Old Norse

August | Augusta, Auguste
**Also:** Augustina | Augustyna
**Meaning:** Exalted (Latin) / August (English)
**Origin Language:** Latin And English

Aulisa | Auli, Aulisia
**Meaning:** Helpful
**Origin Language:** Finnish

Aulona | Auloni, Aulonia
**Meaning:** Channel / Glen
**Origin Language:** Ancient Greek

Auna | Aune
**Meaning:** The Mad One
**Origin Language:** Old English And Old Norse (Cognates)

Aunaira | Aunaire
**Also:** Auncaria | Aunacaria, Aunakaria, Auncara, Aunkara, Aunkaria
**Meaning:** With Grace
**Origin Language:** Ancient Greek

Aundria | Aundraia, Aundrea, Aundreia
**Meaning:** Brave Warrior
**Origin Language:** Ancient Greek

Aura | Aurae, Aure, Auri, Auria, Aurie
**Meaning:** Breeze (Ancient Greek) / Aura (English)
**Origin Language:** Ancient Greek And English

Aurea
**Also:** Aureliana | Aureliann, Aurelianna, Aurelianne
**Also:** Aurica | Aurika
**Also:** Auriel | Aurelia, Aurelie, Aurella, Aurelle, Aurely, Auriella,

Aurielle
**Also:** Aurietta | Auriette
**Meaning:** Golden
**Origin Language:** Latin

Aurora
**Meaning:** Dawn
**Origin Language:** Latin

Ausra
**Meaning:** Dawn
**Origin Language:** Lithuanian

Austine | Austena, Austene, Austina
**Meaning:** Exalted
**Origin Language:** Latin

Austra
**Meaning:** Easter
**Origin Language:** Ancient Germanic And Old English (Cognates)

Autumn
**Meaning:** Autumn
**Origin Language:** English

Ava | Avah
**Also:** Avaline | Avalin, Avalina, Avalyn, Avalynn, Avelin, Avelina, Aveline, Avelyn
**Meaning:** Breathes (Hebrew) / Forever / Eternity (Ancient Germanic)
**Origin Language:** Hebrew And Ancient Germanic

Avalon | Avallon, Avalona, Avalonia, Avilon, Avilona, Avvallon, Avvalon
**Meaning:** Apple Tree
**Origin Language:** Welsh

Avana | Avania, Avannia
**Meaning:** Flower
**Origin Language:** Swahili

Avani
**Meaning:** Earth
**Origin Language:** Sanskrit

Avanti
**Meaning:** From Avanti (An Ancient Kingdom In India)
**Origin Language:** Sanskrit

Avarona | Avaron, Aviron, Avirona
**Meaning:** From Avalon (An Island In Arthurian Romance)
**Origin Language:** English

Avela | Avelia, Avella, Avellia
**Also:** Avelana | Avalana, Avallana, Avellana
**Meaning:** Forever / Eternity
**Origin Language:** Ancient Germanic

Averada | Avra, Avrada, Avrarda
**Meaning:** Hardy As A Boar
**Origin Language:** Ancient Germanic

Averie | Averi, Avery
**Meaning:** Elven Ruler
**Origin Language:** Ancient Germanic

Averill | Averhild, Averild
**Meaning:** Boar Battler
**Origin Language:** Old English

Averita
**Meaning:** Hardy As A Boar
**Origin Language:** Ancient Germanic

Avia | Aviya
**Meaning:** My Father Is God
**Origin Language:** Hebrew

Aviana | Avianna
**Meaning:** Very Pure / Very Holy
**Origin Language:** Ancient Greek

Avice | Avis, Avise

**Meaning:** Forever / Eternity
**Origin Language:** Ancient Germanic

Avigail | Avigayil
**Meaning:** My Father Is Joyful
**Origin Language:** Hebrew

Avila | Avilla
**Meaning:** Forever / Eternity
**Origin Language:** Ancient Germanic

Avira
**Meaning:** Spirit / Air
**Origin Language:** Old Aramaic

Avlona | Avloni, Avlonia
**Meaning:** Channel / Glen
**Origin Language:** Ancient Greek

Avon | Afon, Aven
**Meaning:** River
**Origin Language:** Welsh

Avonlea
**Meaning:** From A Meadow With A River (A Combination Of Avon And Lea)
**Origin Language:** Old English And Welsh (In Combination)

Avra | Avrea, Avri, Avria, Avrie
**Meaning:** Breeze
**Origin Language:** Ancient Greek

Avril
**Meaning:** April
**Origin Language:** French

Awintia | Awentia, Awinita
**Meaning:** Fawn
**Origin Language:** Cherokee

Awnice | Awnis
**Meaning:** Chaste
**Origin Language:** Ancient Greek

Axella | Axa, Axelle, Axelle
**Meaning:** My Father Is Peace

**Origin Language:** Hebrew

Aya | Aaea, Aaee, Aaia, Aaiah, Aaie, Aaieh, Aaya, Aayah, Aaye, Aea, Aeah, Aia, Aiah, Ayah, Ayeh
**Meaning:** A Sign (Arabic) / Truth (Japanese)
**Origin Language:** Arabic And Japanese

Ayalah | Ayala
**Meaning:** Gazelle
**Origin Language:** Hebrew

Ayana | Ayanna
**Meaning:** Flower
**Origin Language:** Swahili

Ayeesa, Ayeisa, Ayeisah, Ayisa, Ayisah, Aysia
**Meaning:** Alive
**Origin Language:** Arabic

Ayla | Aiyla
**Meaning:** Moonlight / Halo
**Origin Language:** Turkish

Aylana | Aylan
**Meaning:** Openness
**Origin Language:** Kurdish

Aylin | Aylina, Ayline
**Meaning:** Of The Moon
**Origin Language:** Turkish And Azerbaijani (Cognates)

Aynhara | Aynara
**Meaning:** Swallow (As In The Bird)
**Origin Language:** Basque

Ayonna
**Meaning:** Flower
**Origin Language:** Swahili

Ayshe | Aish, Aishe
**Meaning:** Alive
**Origin Language:** Arabic

Azahara | Azahar
**Meaning:** Orange Blossom
**Origin Language:** Spanish

Azalea | Azaleah, Azalee, Azalee,
Azalia, Azalia, Azaliah, Azaliya,
Azealia, Azelia, Azeliya
**Meaning:** Dry Earth
**Origin Language:** Ancient Greek

Azaria
**Meaning:** Helped By God
**Origin Language:** Hebrew

Azelia | Azela, Azele, Azelie,
Azella, Azelle, Azellia, Azellie,
Azzela, Azzele, Azzelia, Azzelie,
Azzella, Azzelle, Azzellia, Azzellie
**Meaning:** Small Land
**Origin Language:** Latin

Aziza | Azize
**Meaning:** Powerful
**Origin Language:** Arabic

Azra
**Meaning:** Virgin
**Origin Language:** Arabic

Azure | Azora, Azoria, Azura,
Azuria, Azzora, Azzura
**Also:** Azurina | Azurena, Azurene,
Azurine, Azzurrena, Azzurrina
**Meaning:** Azure / Lapis Lazuli / Sky
Blue
**Origin Language:** Latin

# Chapter 28 - Names For Girls Beginning With B

Bailee | Baile, Bailea, Baileigh,
Bailey, Bailie, Baily, Bayle, Baylea,
Baylee, Bayleigh, Bayley
**Meaning:** Bailiff
**Origin Language:** Old English

Bambi | Bambie, Bamby
**Meaning:** Young Girl
**Origin Language:** Italian

Barbara | Barb, Barbary, Barbe,
Barbora, Barbra, Barbs, Barebra
**Meaning:** Foreign
**Origin Language:** Latin

Bayla | Baila, Bailah, Baylah
**Meaning:** Bailiff
**Origin Language:** Old English

Bea | Bee, Bia
**Also:** Beatrice | Beatrise, Beatriz,
Beitris, Betrys
**Also:** Beatrix
**Meaning:** Female Voyager
**Origin Language:** Latin

Becca | Becci, Becka, Beckah,
Beckie, Becky, Bekka, Bekki
**Meaning:** Shackled By Her Own Beauty
**Origin Language:** Hebrew

Belinay
**Meaning:** Reflection Of The Moon On A Lake
**Origin Language:** Turkish

Belinda | Belinde, Bellinda,
Bellinde
**Meaning:** Beautiful Serpent / Beautiful And Gentle (A Combination Of Bella And Linda)
**Origin Language:** Ancient Germanic And Latin (In Combination)

Bella | Bell, Belle
**Meaning:** Beautiful

**Origin Language:** French

Bellamie | Bellamy
**Meaning:** Beautiful Friend
**Origin Language:** French

Bellatrix
**Meaning:** Female Warrior
**Origin Language:** Latin

Bellita | Belita
**Meaning:** Beautiful
**Origin Language:** French

Bellona
**Meaning:** Warrior
**Origin Language:** Latin

Benedetta | Benedette, Benedita, Beneditta
**Also:** Benedicta | Benedikta
**Also:** Benita
**Meaning:** Blessed
**Origin Language:** Latin

Berdine | Berdena, Berdene, Berdina
**Meaning:** Hardy As A Bear
**Origin Language:** Ancient Germanic

Beren
**Meaning:** Strong / Smart
**Origin Language:** Turkish

Berendine | Berendina
**Meaning:** Hardy As A Bear
**Origin Language:** Ancient Germanic

Berenice | Berenike
**Meaning:** Bringer Of Victory
**Origin Language:** Ancient Greek

Berit
**Meaning:** Prestige
**Origin Language:** Old Irish

Berlin
**Meaning:** From Berlin (Germany)
**Origin Language:** German

Berna
**Meaning:** Young
**Origin Language:** Turkish

Bernarda
**Also:** Bernardette | Bernadetta, Bernadette, Bernardetta
**Also:** Bernardine | Bernadina, Bernadine, Bernardina
**Also:** Bernardita | Bernadita
**Meaning:** Hardy As A Bear
**Origin Language:** Ancient Germanic

Bernetta | Bernette
**Also:** Bernice | Bernese, Berniece, Bernike, Bernise
**Meaning:** Bringer Of Victory
**Origin Language:** Ancient Greek

Bernie | Berny
**Meaning:** Hardy As A Bear
**Origin Language:** Ancient Germanic

Bertha | Berhta, Berta
**Also:** Bertilla
**Also:** Bertina | Bertena
**Meaning:** Bright
**Origin Language:** Ancient Germanic

Beryl | Beril, Berill, Beryll
**Meaning:** Beryl
**Origin Language:** English

Besiana | Besa
**Meaning:** Oath
**Origin Language:** Albanian

Bessie | Bess, Bessy
**Meaning:** God Is My Oath
**Origin Language:** Hebrew

Bethan
**Meaning:** My God Is An Oath
**Origin Language:** Hebrew

Bethany | Beth, Bethania, Bethanie, Bethney
**Meaning:** House Of Figs
**Origin Language:** Hebrew

Bethari
**Meaning:** Goddess
**Origin Language:** Indonesian

Bethel
**Meaning:** House Of God
**Origin Language:** Hebrew

Betisa
**Meaning:** Unending
**Origin Language:** Basque

Betlinda | Betlinde
**Meaning:** Bright Serpent
**Origin Language:** Ancient Germanic

Betony | Betonie
**Meaning:** Betony (Herb)
**Origin Language:** English

Betsy | Betsie, Betzie, Betzy
**Meaning:** God Is My Oath
**Origin Language:** Hebrew

Bettina | Betania, Bettania, Bettena, Bettene, Bettine
**Meaning:** House Of Figs
**Origin Language:** Hebrew

Betty | Bet, Beti, Bette, Bettie, Bettye
**Meaning:** God Is My Oath
**Origin Language:** Hebrew

Beulah | Beula
**Meaning:** Married
**Origin Language:** Hebrew

Beverley | Bev, Beverlea, Beverlee, Beverleigh, Beverlie, Beverly
**Meaning:** From Near A Stream Where Beavers Frequent
**Origin Language:** Old English

Bevin
**Meaning:** Blessed Woman / White Woman
**Origin Language:** Old Irish

Bexley | Bexlea, Bexlee, Bexleigh, Bexlie
**Meaning:** From A Wood Of Box Trees
**Origin Language:** Old English

Beyla | Baila, Beylah, Beyle
**Meaning:** White
**Origin Language:** Slavic

Beyoncé | Beyonce
**Meaning:** Unknown Meaning
**Origin Language:** Old French

Bianca | Bianka
**Meaning:** White
**Origin Language:** Ancient Germanic

Bidelia | Biddie, Biddy
**Meaning:** The Exalted One
**Origin Language:** Old Irish

Bindy | Bindie
**Meaning:** Beautiful Serpent / Beautiful And Gentle (A Combination Of Bella And Linda)(Bindy Is A Short Version Of Belinda)
**Origin Language:** Ancient Germanic And Latin (In Combination)

Birdie | Birdy
**Meaning:** Little Bird
**Origin Language:** English

Birta | Birita, Birte

**Also:** Birtha | Birthe
**Also:** Bithiah | Bethia, Bithia, Bithyah
**Meaning:** Daughter Of God
**Origin Language:** Hebrew

Blaire | Blair
**Meaning:** Battlefield
**Origin Language:** Scottish Gaelic

Blanche | Blanch
**Meaning:** White
**Origin Language:** Ancient Germanic

Blythe
**Meaning:** Cheerful
**Origin Language:** Old English

Bo
**Meaning:** Wave
**Origin Language:** Chinese

Boann
**Meaning:** White Cow
**Origin Language:** Old Irish

Bobbi | Bobbie
**Meaning:** Famous And Bright
**Origin Language:** Ancient Germanic

Bohdana | Bodana
**Meaning:** Given By God
**Origin Language:** Common Slavic

Bonita
**Meaning:** Pretty
**Origin Language:** Spanish

Bonnie | Bonny
**Meaning:** Pretty
**Origin Language:** Scottish Gaelic

Braelynn | Braelin, Braelina, Braelyn
**Meaning:** Briar
**Origin Language:** English

Braidie | Braidy
**Meaning:** Spirited
**Origin Language:** Old Irish

Brandy | Brandee, Brandi, Brandie
**Meaning:** Brandy
**Origin Language:** English

Branwen | Branwenn
**Meaning:** Blessed Raven
**Origin Language:** Welsh

Brava
**Meaning:** Valiant
**Origin Language:** Esperanto

Braylee | Braylea, Brayleigh, Brayley, Braylie
**Meaning:** From A Meadow Of Briars
**Origin Language:** Old English

Breana | Breann, Breanna, Breanne
**Meaning:** Power / Hill
**Origin Language:** Old Irish

Breda | Breeda
**Also:** Bree
**Also:** Breeshey
**Meaning:** Prestige
**Origin Language:** Old Irish

Brenda
**Meaning:** Princess
**Origin Language:** Old Irish

Brenna
**Meaning:** Little Raindrop
**Origin Language:** Old Irish

Bria | Brea, Breia
**Meaning:** Power / Hill
**Origin Language:** Old Irish

Briallen
**Meaning:** Primrose

**Origin Language:** Welsh

Briana | Brianna, Brianne, Bryana, Bryanna, Bryanne
**Meaning:** Power / Hill
**Origin Language:** Old Irish

Briar | Brier
**Meaning:** Briar
**Origin Language:** English

Bridget | Bridgette
**Also:** Bridy | Bride, Bridie
**Meaning:** Prestige
**Origin Language:** Old Irish

Briella | Brielle
**Meaning:** God Is My Strength
**Origin Language:** Hebrew

Briena | Brienna, Brienne, Bryena, Bryenna, Bryenne
**Meaning:** Power / Hill
**Origin Language:** Old Irish

Brigida | Brighid, Brigid, Bryghid, Brygid, Brygida
**Also:** Brigitta | Brigit, Brigita, Brigitte
**Meaning:** Prestige
**Origin Language:** Old Irish

Brina | Breena
**Meaning:** Juniper
**Origin Language:** Slovene

Briony | Brionie, Bryonie, Bryony
**Meaning:** Bryony (A Type Of Vine)
**Origin Language:** English

Briseida
**Meaning:** Insolence
**Origin Language:** Ancient Greek

Britannia | Brittania
**Meaning:** From The British Islands

**Origin Language:** Latin

Britta | Brit, Brita, Britt
**Meaning:** Prestige
**Origin Language:** Old Irish

Brittany | Britne, Britney, Britni, Brittani, Brittanie, Brittne, Brittney, Brittni, Brittnie, Brittny
**Meaning:** From The British Islands
**Origin Language:** Latin

Brooke | Brook
**Meaning:** Brook
**Origin Language:** Old English

Brooklynn | Brooklin, Brooklina, Brooklyn
**Meaning:** From Brooklyn (New York City)
**Origin Language:** Dutch

Bruna
**Also:** Brunella | Brunelle
**Meaning:** Protected / Brunette
**Origin Language:** Ancient Germanic

Brylee | Briarlea, Briarlee, Briarleigh, Briarley, Brierlea, Brierlee, Brierleigh, Brierley, Briley, Brylea, Bryleigh, Bryley, Brylie
**Meaning:** From A Meadow Of Briars
**Origin Language:** Old English

Brynlee | Brinlee, Brinley, Brynlea, Brynleigh
**Meaning:** From A Burnt Meadow
**Origin Language:** Old English

Brynn | Brin, Brinn, Brinne, Bryn, Brynne
**Meaning:** Hill
**Origin Language:** Welsh

Buffy | Buffie
**Meaning:** My God Is An Oath

Origin Language: Hebrew

# Chapter 29 - Names For Girls Beginning With C

Cadence | Caedence, Caedense, Caidence, Caidense, Caydence, Caydense
Meaning: Cadence (Rhythm)
Origin Language: English

Cadi | Cadee, Cadia, Cadie, Cady, Caidee, Caidi, Caidie, Caidy
Meaning: Pure
Origin Language: Ancient Greek

Caelina | Caelin, Caeline, Caelyn, Caelynn
Meaning: Heaven
Origin Language: Latin

Caetana | Caitana, Cayetana
Meaning: From Caieta (An Ancient Town On The Coast Of Latium, A District Located In West Central Italy)
Origin Language: Latin

Cahaya | Cahya
Meaning: Light
Origin Language: Malay

Caieta | Caeta
Meaning: From Caieta (An Ancient Town On The Coast Of Latium, A District Located In West Central Italy)
Origin Language: Latin

Cailla | Caila, Cayla, Cayla
Also: Cailly | Caeleigh, Caeley, Caelie, Caely, Caileigh, Cailey, Caillie, Cayleigh, Cayley, Caylie, Cayly

Also: Cailyn | Caelena, Caelene, Caelin, Caelina, Caelyn, Cailena, Cailene, Cailin, Cailina, Caylena, Caylene, Caylin, Caylina, Caylyn
Meaning: From Cailly (France)
Origin Language: Old French

Caisley | Caislea, Caislee, Caisleigh, Caislie, Caselea, Caselee, Caseleigh, Caseley, Caselie
Meaning: From A Meadow Where Cats Roam
Origin Language: Old English

Caitie | Cate, Catia, Catie, Caty
Also: Caitlyn | Caetlin, Caitlin, Catelin, Catelyn, Cattalin, Cattalyn
Also: Caitria | Caitra, Caitrie
Meaning: Pure
Origin Language: Ancient Greek

Calandra | Calandre, Callandra, Callandre
Meaning: Beauty Of Mankind / Invoker Of Mankind
Origin Language: Ancient Greek

Calantha | Calanthe, Calanthia
Meaning: Beautiful Flower
Origin Language: Ancient Greek

Calfuray
Meaning: Violet
Origin Language: Mapuche

Caliandra | Caliandre, Calliandra, Calliandre
Meaning: Beauty Of Mankind / Invoker Of Mankind
Origin Language: Ancient Greek

Calla
Meaning: Calla (Type Of Lily)
Origin Language: English

Callandria | Calandria
**Meaning:** Beauty Of Mankind / Invoker Of Mankind
**Origin Language:** Ancient Greek

Callene | Callena, Callina, Calline
**Also:** Callie | Caleigh, Cali, Calleigh, Cally
**Meaning:** From Cailly (France)
**Origin Language:** Old French

Callista | Calista, Caliste, Calliste, Callysta, Calysta
**Meaning:** Beautiful
**Origin Language:** Ancient Greek

Calluna | Caluna
**Meaning:** Calluna (Another Name For Heather, The Flowering Plant)
**Origin Language:** English

Caltha
**Meaning:** Caltha Flower
**Origin Language:** English

Calvina | Calvena
**Meaning:** Bald
**Origin Language:** Latin

Calypso
**Meaning:** She That Conceals Herself
**Origin Language:** Ancient Greek

Camarin
**Meaning:** Sheltered
**Origin Language:** Chamorro

Camelia | Camellia
**Meaning:** Camellia Flower
**Origin Language:** Latin

Cameo
**Meaning:** Cameo
**Origin Language:** English

Cameron | Cam, Camrin, Camryn
**Meaning:** Crooked Nose
**Origin Language:** Scottish Gaelic

Camille | Camilla, Camille, Cammila, Cammilla, Camylle
**Also:** Camiyah | Camiah
**Also:** Cammy | Cammi, Cammie
**Meaning:** Acolyte
**Origin Language:** Latin

Candace | Candase, Candee, Candice, Candis, Candise, Candyce, Candyse
**Meaning:** Queen Mother
**Origin Language:** Cushitic

Candela | Cande, Candelas
**Meaning:** Candlemas (A Christian Holiday)
**Origin Language:** Spanish

Candra
**Meaning:** The Moon
**Origin Language:** Sanskrit

Capri
**Meaning:** Capri (A Shade Of Blue)
**Origin Language:** English

Caprice | Capricia
**Meaning:** Whim
**Origin Language:** Italian

Caprine | Caprena, Caprene, Caprina
**Meaning:** Goats
**Origin Language:** Latin

Capucine
**Meaning:** Nasturtium (Flowering Plant)
**Origin Language:** French

Cara | Caraugh
**Meaning:** Beloved
**Origin Language:** Latin

Caramia
**Meaning:** My Beloved
**Origin Language:** Italian

Cardea
**Meaning:** Turning Point / A Critical Moment
**Origin Language:** Latin

Careen | Carreen
**Meaning:** Free Woman Of Peace (A Combination Of Carla And Irene)
**Origin Language:** Ancient Greek And Ancient Germanic (In Combination)

Carenza | Carensa, Cerensa, Cerenza
**Meaning:** Love
**Origin Language:** Cornish

Carey | Carie, Cary
**Meaning:** Dark
**Origin Language:** Old Irish

Carin | Caren, Caryn
**Meaning:** Pure
**Origin Language:** Ancient Greek

Carina | Carena, Carene, Carine
**Meaning:** Dear
**Origin Language:** Latin

Caris | Carys
**Meaning:** Loving
**Origin Language:** Old Welsh

Carissa | Charissa
**Meaning:** Kindness
**Origin Language:** Ancient Greek

Carita | Charita
**Meaning:** Charity
**Origin Language:** Latin

Carla
**Also:** Carlina | Carlena, Carlene,

Carline
**Meaning:** Has Freedom
**Origin Language:** Ancient Germanic

Carlisa
**Meaning:** God Is My Oath And I Am A Freewoman (A Combination Of Carla And Lisa)
**Origin Language:** Ancient Germanic And Hebrew (In Combination)

Carlotta | Carlota
**Also:** Carly | Carley, Carlie
**Also:** Carlynn | Carlynne
**Meaning:** Has Freedom
**Origin Language:** Ancient Germanic

Carme
**Meaning:** Shearer Of The Harvest
**Origin Language:** Ancient Greek

Carmel | Carmela, Carmella
**Also:** Carmelita
**Meaning:** Garden
**Origin Language:** Hebrew

Carmen
**Also:** Carmina | Carmena
**Meaning:** Song
**Origin Language:** Latin

Carol | Carola, Carole, Carrol, Caryl
**Also:** Caroline | Carolena, Carolene, Carolin, Carolina, Carolyn, Carolynn
**Meaning:** Has Freedom
**Origin Language:** Ancient Germanic

Caron
**Meaning:** From Caron (Wales)
**Origin Language:** Welsh

Carrie | Cari, Carri, Carry
**Meaning:** Has Freedom
**Origin Language:** Ancient Germanic

Casilda
**Meaning:** Poem
**Origin Language:** Arabic

Casley | Caslea, Caslee, Casleigh, Caslie
**Meaning:** From A Meadow Where Cats Roam
**Origin Language:** Old English

Cassandra | Casandra, Casandre, Cass, Cassandre, Cassie, Cassy
**Meaning:** Surpasses Men
**Origin Language:** Ancient Greek

Cassarah
**Meaning:** Che Sarà (What Will Be Will Be)
**Origin Language:** Italian

Cassia | Cassiah
**Meaning:** Cinnamon
**Origin Language:** Ancient Greek

Cassidy | Cass, Cassidie, Cassie, Cassy
**Meaning:** Curly Haired
**Origin Language:** Old Irish

Cassiopeia | Cassiopea, Cassiopia
**Meaning:** Throned
**Origin Language:** Ancient Greek

Cataleya | Cattleya
**Meaning:** Cattleya (A Genus Of Orchids)
**Origin Language:** English

Catalina | Caitlina, Caitline, Cataleen, Catalena, Catalene, Catalin, Cataline, Catalyn, Catalynn, Catelina, Cateline, Cattalina, Cattaline
**Also:** Catherine | Catharina, Catharine, Catherin, Catherina,

Catheryn
**Also:** Cathleen | Cathlena, Cathlene, Cathlin, Cathlina, Cathline, Cathlyn, Cathlynn
**Also:** Cathy | Cath, Cathee, Cathie
**Also:** Catica | Catika, Cattica, Cattika
**Meaning:** Pure
**Origin Language:** Ancient Greek

Catlea | Catlee, Catleigh, Catley, Catlie
**Meaning:** From A Cat's Meadow
**Origin Language:** Old English

Catrina | Catrena, Catrine, Catrine
**Also:** Catrinel | Catrinella, Catrinelle
**Also:** Catriona | Catreona, Catreone, Catri, Catrione
**Meaning:** Pure
**Origin Language:** Ancient Greek

Catsley | Catslea, Catslee, Catsleigh, Catslie
**Meaning:** From A Cat's Meadow
**Origin Language:** Old English

Cattalin | Cattalyn, Cattalynn
**Also:** Cattaline | Cattalina
**Meaning:** Pure
**Origin Language:** Ancient Greek

Caysie | Cacey, Cacie, Cacy, Casey, Casie, Caycee
**Meaning:** Vigilant
**Origin Language:** Old Irish

Cece
**Also:** Cecile | Cecily
**Also:** Cecilia | Caecilia, Cecelia, Cecilie, Cecylia
**Meaning:** Aimless / Without Sight
**Origin Language:** Latin

Cedar
**Meaning:** Cedar Tree
**Origin Language:** English

Celandine
**Meaning:** Celandine (Flower)
**Origin Language:** English

Celeste
**Also:** Celestine | Celestena, Celestene, Celestina
**Meaning:** Of The Sky / Celestial
**Origin Language:** Latin

Celia | Caelia
**Meaning:** Heaven
**Origin Language:** Latin

Celinda
**Meaning:** Soft Tender And Heavenly (A Combination Of Celine And Linda)
**Origin Language:** Ancient Germanic And Latin (In Combination)

Celine | Celena, Celene, Celin, Celina, Celyn, Celynn
**Meaning:** The Moon
**Origin Language:** Ancient Greek

Celosia
**Meaning:** Burned
**Origin Language:** Ancient Greek

Cemile
**Meaning:** Beautiful
**Origin Language:** Arabic

Ceren
**Meaning:** Baby Gazelle
**Origin Language:** Turkish

Ceres
**Meaning:** Food Grower
**Origin Language:** Latin

Ceri
**Meaning:** Loving
**Origin Language:** Old Welsh

Cerise
**Meaning:** Cherry
**Origin Language:** French

Cersei
**Meaning:** Hawk
**Origin Language:** Ancient Greek

Cerys | Ceris
**Meaning:** Loving
**Origin Language:** Old Welsh

Cesarina | Cesarena, Cesarene, Cesarine
**Meaning:** Has Long Flowing Hair / Has Beautiful Hair
**Origin Language:** Latin

Ceylan
**Meaning:** Gazelle
**Origin Language:** Turkish

Cezara | Cezaria
**Meaning:** Has Long Flowing Hair / Has Beautiful Hair
**Origin Language:** Latin

Chalice
**Meaning:** Chalice / Goblet
**Origin Language:** English

Chana | Chanah, Channa, Channah
**Meaning:** Gracious
**Origin Language:** Hebrew

Chandana
**Meaning:** Sandalwood
**Origin Language:** Sanskrit

Chandler
**Meaning:** Candle Seller

**Origin Language:** Old English

Chandra
**Meaning:** The Moon
**Origin Language:** Sanskrit

Chanel | Chanelle
**Meaning:** From Near A Channel Of Water
**Origin Language:** Old French

Channarie | Channary
**Meaning:** Moon Faced Girl
**Origin Language:** Khmer

Chantal | Chantalle, Chantel, Chantelle
**Meaning:** Stony / Song
**Origin Language:** French

Chantrea
**Meaning:** Moonlight
**Origin Language:** Khmer

Chara
**Meaning:** Happiness
**Origin Language:** Ancient Greek

Charis | Charys
**Meaning:** Kindness
**Origin Language:** Ancient Greek

Charise | Charice, Charisse
**Meaning:** The Shade Of A Cherry
**Origin Language:** Anglo-Norman French

Charisma
**Meaning:** Charisma
**Origin Language:** English

Charity | Charitie
**Meaning:** Charity
**Origin Language:** English

Charla

**Also:** Charlene | Charleen, Charlena, Charlina, Charline
**Also:** Charli | Charlea, Charlee, Charly
**Also:** Charlize
**Also:** Charlotte | Charlotta
**Also:** Charlynn | Charlin, Charlyn
**Meaning:** Has Freedom
**Origin Language:** Ancient Germanic

Charmaine | Charmaina, Charmian, Charmion
**Meaning:** Delight
**Origin Language:** Ancient Greek

Charnette
**Meaning:** Plain (Of Land)
**Origin Language:** Hebrew

Chastity | Chasitie, Chasity, Chastitie
**Meaning:** Chastity
**Origin Language:** English

Chaya
**Meaning:** Lives
**Origin Language:** Hebrew

Chea
**Meaning:** Healthy
**Origin Language:** Khmer

Chelle
**Meaning:** "Who Is Like God?"
**Origin Language:** Hebrew

Chelsea | Chelsey, Chelsie, Chelsy
**Meaning:** From Near A Chalk Port
**Origin Language:** Old English

Cher
**Also:** Cherette | Cheretta
**Also:** Cherie | Cheree, Cheri, Chery
**Also:** Cherilina | Cherilena, Cherilene, Cheriline

**Also:** Cherilyn | Cherilin, Cherilynn
**Meaning:** Darling
**Origin Language:** French

Cherise | Cherice, Cherisse
**Meaning:** The Shade Of A Cherry
**Origin Language:** Anglo-Norman French

Cheryl | Cherryl
**Meaning:** Darling
**Origin Language:** French

Chesleigh | Cheslea, Chesley, Cheslie, Chesly
**Meaning:** From A Meadow Where Soldiers Camp
**Origin Language:** Old English

Chevonne
**Meaning:** God Is Gracious
**Origin Language:** Hebrew

Cheyenne | Cheyanne
**Meaning:** Red Speakers
**Origin Language:** Dakota

Chiara
**Also:** Chiarine | Chiarena, Chiarene, Chiarina
**Meaning:** Bright And Clear
**Origin Language:** Latin

Chiela
**Meaning:** Heavenly
**Origin Language:** Esperanto

China | Chyna
**Meaning:** From China
**Origin Language:** English

Chloe | Chloie, Cloe, Cloie
**Meaning:** Yellow-Green Springtime Grass
**Origin Language:** Ancient Greek

Chloris | Chlorys
**Meaning:** Pale Green
**Origin Language:** Ancient Greek

Chosette
**Meaning:** Little Thing
**Origin Language:** French

Chrissy | Chrissie, Chryssie, Chryssy, Crissie, Crissy, Cryssie, Cryssy
**Meaning:** Christ / The Anointed One / Messiah
**Origin Language:** Ancient Greek

Christabelle | Christabel, Christabella, Christobel, Christobela, Christobella, Christobelle
**Meaning:** Beautiful Christian
**Origin Language:** Latin

Christel | Christella, Christelle, Chrystel, Chrystella, Chrystelle, Cristel, Cristella, Cristelle, Crystel, Crystella, Crystelle
**Meaning:** Christ / The Anointed One / Messiah (Ancient Greek) / Crystal (English)
**Origin Language:** Ancient Greek And English

Christen | Chrysten, Cristen, Cristyn, Crysten, Crystin
**Meaning:** Christ / The Anointed One / Messiah
**Origin Language:** Ancient Greek

Christiana | Christiane, Christianna, Christianne, Christianne, Cristiann, Cristianna, Cristianne, Crystiana
**Also:** Christina | Christine, Chrystina, Chrystine, Cristina, Cristine, Crystina, Crystine

**Meaning:** A Christian
**Origin Language:** Latin

Christy | Christa, Christi, Christie, Chrysta, Chrysti, Chrystie, Chrysty, Crista, Cristi, Cristie, Cristy, Crysta, Crysti, Crystie, Crysty
**Meaning:** Christ / The Anointed One / Messiah
**Origin Language:** Ancient Greek

Chrizanne | Chrizanna
**Meaning:** A Christian
**Origin Language:** Latin

Chrysa | Chryssa
**Also:** Chrysanta
**Also:** Chrysanthe | Chrysantha, Chrysanthi
**Meaning:** Golden Flower
**Origin Language:** Ancient Greek

Ciara | Ceara, Ceira, Ciarra, Ciera, Cierra
**Meaning:** Dark
**Origin Language:** Old Irish

Cicely | Cicelie
**Meaning:** Aimless / Without Sight
**Origin Language:** Latin

Ciel
**Meaning:** Sky
**Origin Language:** French

Cierra | Ciera
**Meaning:** Mountain Range
**Origin Language:** Spanish

Cilla | Cila, Cili, Cilka, Cille
**Meaning:** Aimless / Without Sight
**Origin Language:** Latin

Cindi | Cindee, Cindy
**Also:** Cindra
**Also:** Cinzia | Cinsia

**Meaning:** Woman From Kynthos / From Mount Cynthus (A Mountain On The Isle Of Delos, Part Of The Greek Cyclades)
**Origin Language:** Ancient Greek

Circe
**Meaning:** Hawk
**Origin Language:** Ancient Greek

Claire | Clare
**Also:** Clara
**Meaning:** Illustrious / Clear And Gleaming
**Origin Language:** Latin

Clarencia
**Meaning:** Clarence (A British Ducal Title)
**Origin Language:** Latin

Clarette | Claretta
**Meaning:** Illustrious / Clear And Gleaming
**Origin Language:** Latin

Claribel
**Meaning:** Illustrious Beauty
**Origin Language:** Latin

Clarice
**Also:** Clarinda
**Also:** Clarissa | Clarisa, Clarisse
**Also:** Claritia
**Meaning:** Illustrious / Clear And Gleaming
**Origin Language:** Latin

Clarity | Claritie
**Meaning:** Clarity
**Origin Language:** English

Clarke | Clark
**Meaning:** Cleric / Scribe
**Origin Language:** Old English

Claudette | Claudetta
**Also:** Claudia | Claudie
**Also:** Claudine | Claudena, Claudene, Claudina
**Meaning:** Limps / Stumbles / Wavers / Hesitates
**Origin Language:** Latin

Clelia | Clelie, Clely
**Meaning:** Illustrious
**Origin Language:** Latin

Clematis
**Meaning:** Clematis (Flower)
**Origin Language:** English

Clemence | Clemencie, Clemency, Climence, Climencie, Climency
**Also:** Clementia | Climentia
**Also:** Clementine | Clementina, Climentina, Climentine
**Meaning:** Clemency
**Origin Language:** Latin

Cleo | Clea, Cleio, Clio, Clio
**Also:** Cleona | Cliona
**Meaning:** Glory
**Origin Language:** Ancient Greek

Cleopatra
**Meaning:** A Father's Glory
**Origin Language:** Ancient Greek

Cloelia
**Meaning:** Illustrious
**Origin Language:** Latin

Clover
**Meaning:** Clover
**Origin Language:** English

Coco
**Meaning:** Diminutive Of Names Beginning With Co / Cocoa (Chocolate) (English)
**Origin Language:** English

Coleen | Colena, Colene, Colina, Coline, Colleen, Collene, Collina
**Meaning:** Girl
**Origin Language:** Irish

Colette
**Meaning:** Victory Of The People
**Origin Language:** Ancient Greek

Conny | Connie
**Also:** Constance | Constancia, Constanta, Constantena, Constantia, Constantina, Constanza, Constanze
**Meaning:** Constant (Unchanging)
**Origin Language:** Latin

Cora
**Meaning:** Maiden
**Origin Language:** Ancient Greek

Coral
**Meaning:** Coral
**Origin Language:** English

Coralie | Coralia, Coraly
**Also:** Coraline | Coralin, Coralina, Coralyn, Coralynn
**Meaning:** Coral
**Origin Language:** Ancient Greek

Cordelia | Cordeilla, Cordie, Cordy
**Meaning:** Bloody Flood / Fierce Flood
**Origin Language:** Old Welsh

Cordula
**Meaning:** Heart
**Origin Language:** Latin

Corentina | Corentine
**Meaning:** Hurricane
**Origin Language:** Old Breton

Coretta | Corette
**Meaning:** Maiden

**Origin Language:** Ancient Greek

Cornelia | Corneliya
**Meaning:** Horned
**Origin Language:** Latin

Corrina | Coreen, Corie, Corina,
Corine, Corinna, Corinne, Corrie,
Corrine, Corry, Cory, Corynn
**Meaning:** Maiden
**Origin Language:** Ancient Greek

Cosima | Cosma, Cosmia
**Also:** Cosmina | Cosmena,
Cosmene, Cosmine
**Meaning:** The Universe / The Cosmos
**Origin Language:** Ancient Greek

Courtney | Cortney, Courteney
**Meaning:** Short Nosed
**Origin Language:** Old French

Cressida | Creseida, Creseyde,
Crisede, Criseida, Criseyde,
Crissida, Cryseida, Cryseide
**Meaning:** Golden
**Origin Language:** Ancient Greek

Cruz | Cruza
**Also:** Cruzita
**Meaning:** Cross (Of Crucifixion)
**Origin Language:** Spanish And
Portuguese (Cognates)

Crysia | Chrisia, Chrysia, Crisia
**Meaning:** Christ / The Anointed One /
Messiah
**Origin Language:** Ancient Greek

Crystal | Christal, Chrystal, Cristal,
Crystelle, Crystle
**Meaning:** Crystal
**Origin Language:** English

Csilla | Cilla, Silla
**Meaning:** Star

**Origin Language:** Hungarian

Cyanea| Cyan, Cyana, Cyania
**Meaning:** Dark Blue
**Origin Language:** Ancient Greek

Cybil | Cybella, Cybelle, Cybill,
Cybilla, Cybille, Cybyl, Cybylla,
Cybylle
**Meaning:** Prophetess / Oracle
**Origin Language:** Latin

Cynthia | Cynthaia, Cynthea,
Cyntheia
**Meaning:** Woman From Kynthos /
From Mount Cynthus (A Mountain On
The Isle Of Delos, Part Of The Greek
Cyclades)
**Origin Language:** Ancient Greek

# Chapter 30 - Names For Girls Beginning With D

Daciana
**Meaning:** From Dacia (An Old Name
For The Region That Is Now Romania
And Moldova)
**Origin Language:** Romanian

Daenerys
**Meaning:** This Name Has No Meaning
(Daenerys Is A Fictional Character
Featuring In The TV Series Game Of
Thrones)
**Origin Language:** Invented

Dafina | Dafine, Daphina,
Daphine
**Meaning:** Laurel
**Origin Language:** Ancient Greek

Dagney | Dagnie, Dagny
**Meaning:** New Day

**Origin Language:** Old Norse

**Dahlia | Dahlie, Darhlia, Darhlie, Darlia, Darlie**
**Meaning:** Dahlia (Flower)
**Origin Language:** English

**Daina | Daine**
**Meaning:** Song
**Origin Language:** Lithuanian

**Daisy | Daisie**
**Meaning:** Daisy
**Origin Language:** English

**Daiva**
**Meaning:** Destiny
**Origin Language:** Sanskrit

**Dakota**
**Meaning:** Allies
**Origin Language:** Dakota

**Dalena | Dalina**
**Meaning:** Fights The Distance
**Origin Language:** Common Slavic

**Daleyza | Dalaiza, Daleaza**
**Also:** Dalia
**Meaning:** Dahlia (Flower)
**Origin Language:** English

**Dalida**
**Meaning:** Delicate
**Origin Language:** Hebrew

**Dalinda**
**Meaning:** Soft And Tender
**Origin Language:** Ancient Germanic

**Dalisay**
**Meaning:** Pure
**Origin Language:** Tagalog

**Dallas**
**Meaning:** From A Homestead In A

Meadow
**Origin Language:** Scottish Gaelic

**Dalma**
**Meaning:** Sheep
**Origin Language:** Illyrian

**Dalya | Dalia**
**Meaning:** The Branch That Hangs
**Origin Language:** Hebrew

**Damaris | Damari**
**Meaning:** Calf
**Origin Language:** Ancient Greek

**Damia**
**Also:** Damiana | Damianna, Damianne
**Meaning:** Tamer
**Origin Language:** Ancient Greek

**Damira**
**Meaning:** Given The World
**Origin Language:** Slavic

**Dana | Daena, Daina, Dayna**
**Meaning:** Wise
**Origin Language:** Persian

**Danae | Danaë, Danai**
**Meaning:** Of The Danaans (The Most Ancient Greek Tribe)
**Origin Language:** Ancient Greek

**Danai**
**Meaning:** Summoned
**Origin Language:** Shona

**Danelle | Danella**
**Also:** Danette | Danetta
**Also:** Dani | Danii, Danni, Dannii
**Also:** Danica | Danika, Danitsa
**Meaning:** Morning Star / Venus
**Origin Language:** Common Slavic

**Danielle | Daniela, Daniella,**

Danila
**Also:** Danique
**Also:** Danita
**Meaning:** My Judge Is God
**Origin Language:** Hebrew

Daniyah | Dania
**Meaning:** Near
**Origin Language:** Arabic

Danya
**Meaning:** Judged By God
**Origin Language:** Hebrew

Daphne | Dafna, Dafne, Dafnee, Dafni, Dafnie, Daphnee, Daphney, Daphnie
**Meaning:** Laurel
**Origin Language:** Ancient Greek

Dara
**Meaning:** Oak Tree Grove / Fruitful
**Origin Language:** Old Irish

Darbie | Darby, Derbie, Derby
**Meaning:** From A Deer Farm
**Origin Language:** Old Norse

Darcie | Darcey, Darcy
**Meaning:** Of Arcy (A Town In France)
**Origin Language:** Old French

Dardana
**Meaning:** Of The Dardani People (An Illyrian Tribe That Lived On The Balkan Peninsula)
**Origin Language:** Albanian

Daria | Dareia, Dariya
**Meaning:** Possesses Goodness
**Origin Language:** Old Persian

Darina | Darena, Darene, Darine
**Meaning:** Gift
**Origin Language:** Slavic

Darla
**Also:** Darlene | Darlaina, Darlaine, Darleen, Darlena, Darlina
**Meaning:** Darling
**Origin Language:** English

Darshana
**Meaning:** Philosophy
**Origin Language:** Sanskrit

Darya | Derya
**Meaning:** The Ocean
**Origin Language:** Persian

Dasha
**Meaning:** Possesses Goodness
**Origin Language:** Old Persian

Dashurie
**Meaning:** Intimacy
**Origin Language:** Albanian

Davida
**Also:** Davina | Davena, Davine, Davinia
**Meaning:** Beloved
**Origin Language:** Hebrew

Davora
**Also:** Davorina | Davorena, Davorene, Davorine
**Meaning:** Joy / Sorrow
**Origin Language:** Common Slavic

Dawn
**Meaning:** Dawn
**Origin Language:** English

Dayana | Dayan
**Meaning:** Goddess
**Origin Language:** Latin

Daylie | Daley, Dalie, Daly
**Meaning:** Of The Assembly
**Origin Language:** Old Irish

Deana | Deanna, Deanne, Deeann, Deena, Dena, Dene
**Meaning:** From A Valley
**Origin Language:** Old English

Deborah | Deb, Debbi, Debbie, Debbora, Debby, Debi, Debora, Debowrah, Debra
**Meaning:** Bee
**Origin Language:** Hebrew

Dede
**Meaning:** Locust
**Origin Language:** Luo

Defne | Dephne
**Meaning:** Laurel
**Origin Language:** Ancient Greek

Deianira | Deianeira
**Meaning:** Slayer Of Men
**Origin Language:** Ancient Greek

Deidre | Deidra, Deirdre
**Meaning:** Raging / Sorrowful
**Origin Language:** Old Irish

Deinara | Dinara
**Meaning:** Judged
**Origin Language:** Hebrew

Deitra
**Meaning:** Raging / Sorrowful
**Origin Language:** Old Irish

Deja
**Meaning:** Already
**Origin Language:** French

Delaney | Delanee, Delanie
**Meaning:** Dark And Healthy
**Origin Language:** Old Irish

Delara | Dilara
**Meaning:** Decorated Heart
**Origin Language:** Persian

Delcisa
**Meaning:** Pledge Of Nobility
**Origin Language:** Ancient Germanic

Delfia | Delfa, Delfie, Delpha, Delphia, Delphie
**Meaning:** From Delphi (An Ancient Town In Central Greece, It Was A Sacred Precinct That Served As The Seat Of The Oracle Pythia)
**Origin Language:** Latin

Delia
**Meaning:** From Delos (An Island In Greece)
**Origin Language:** Ancient Greek

Delice | Delicia
**Meaning:** Delicious
**Origin Language:** English

Delight
**Meaning:** Delight
**Origin Language:** English

Delilah | Dalila, Dalilah, Daliylah, Delila, Deliylah
**Meaning:** Delicate
**Origin Language:** Hebrew

Delinda
**Also:** Deline | Deleen, Delene
**Meaning:** Soft And Tender
**Origin Language:** Ancient Germanic

Della
**Meaning:** Noble
**Origin Language:** Ancient Germanic And Old English (Cognates)

Delma
**Also:** Delmina | Delmena
**Meaning:** Father's Protector
**Origin Language:** Ancient Germanic

Delmira
**Meaning:** Famous Noble
**Origin Language:** Ancient Germanic And Old English (Cognates)

Delores | Delora, Deloris, Dollie, Dolly, Dolores, Dolors, Dores
**Meaning:** Sorrows
**Origin Language:** Spanish

Delphie | Delfa, Delfia, Delphia
**Meaning:** Born Of The Same Womb / Double
**Origin Language:** Ancient Greek

Delphine | Delfina, Delfine, Delphina, Delphinia
**Also:** Delphis
**Meaning:** From Delphi (An Ancient Town In Central Greece, It Was A Sacred Precinct That Served As The Seat Of The Oracle Pythia)
**Origin Language:** Latin

Delta
**Meaning:** The Fourth Letter Of The Greek Alphabet
**Origin Language:** Ancient Greek

Delyth | Delith
**Meaning:** Pretty
**Origin Language:** Welsh

Demelza
**Meaning:** Fort Of Maeldaf
**Origin Language:** Cornish

Demeter
**Meaning:** Earth Mother
**Origin Language:** Ancient Greek

Demetria | Demetra, Dimetra, Dimetria, Dimitra, Dumitra, Dumitria
**Also:** Demi | Dimi
**Meaning:** Of Demeter (Demeter Is The Name Of The Greek Goddess Of The Harvest, Agriculture, Fertility, And Sacred Law)
**Origin Language:** Ancient Greek

Denica | Denika, Denitsa
**Meaning:** Morning Star / Venus
**Origin Language:** Common Slavic

Denice | Deniece, Denisa, Denise, Denisse
**Meaning:** Of Dionysos (Dionysos Is The Name Of The Greek God Of Wine, Vegetation, Fertility, Festivity, Ritual Madness, Religious Ecstasy, And Theatre)
**Origin Language:** Ancient Greek

Derin
**Meaning:** Deep / Profound
**Origin Language:** Turkish

Dervila | Dervla
**Meaning:** A Poet's Daughter
**Origin Language:** Old Irish

Desdemona | Desdemone, Disdemona, Disdemone
**Meaning:** Ill-Fated
**Origin Language:** Ancient Greek

Desideria | Desiderina, Desiderine
**Meaning:** Desire
**Origin Language:** Latin

Desiree | Desirae, Deziree
**Meaning:** Desired
**Origin Language:** Latin

Destiny | Destinee, Destinie
**Meaning:** Destiny
**Origin Language:** English

Detta
**Meaning:** A Short Form Of Any Of The Numerous Names Ending In Detta (It Also Can Mean "Falling" In Old Norse, This However Is Not The Original

Meaning Of The Name)
**Origin Language:** Various

Deverose
**Meaning:** From Évreux (A Commune In Normandy, France) / Yew Tree / Wields Weapons Made From A Yew Tree
**Origin Language:** Gaulish

Devi
**Meaning:** Goddess
**Origin Language:** Sanskrit

Devon
**Meaning:** Little Dark/Black One
**Origin Language:** Old Irish

Devora | Devorah, Dvora, Dvorah
**Meaning:** Bee
**Origin Language:** Hebrew

Dezirinda
**Meaning:** Desirable
**Origin Language:** Esperanto

Dharma | Darma
**Meaning:** Virtue
**Origin Language:** Sanskrit

Diamanda | Diamande, Diamanta, Diamante
**Also:** Diamond
**Meaning:** Diamond
**Origin Language:** Ancient Greek

Diana | Dea, Dee, Di, Diane, Diann, Dianna, Dianne, Dianne, Dyan, Dyana
**Meaning:** Goddess
**Origin Language:** Latin

Diantha | Dianthe
**Meaning:** Dianthus (Flower)
**Origin Language:** Ancient Greek

Dido

**Meaning:** Beloved
**Origin Language:** Hebrew

Diellza
**Meaning:** Sunny
**Origin Language:** Albanian

Dimona
**Meaning:** South
**Origin Language:** Hebrew

Dinah | Deina, Dina, Diynah
**Meaning:** Judged
**Origin Language:** Hebrew

Diona | Dione
**Meaning:** Goddess / Of Zeus (Zeus Is The Name Of The Roman God Of The Sky, Lightning, Thunder, Law, Order, And Justice)
**Origin Language:** Ancient Greek

Dionne | Deonne
**Also:** Dionysia
**Meaning:** Of Dionysos (Dionysos Is The Name Of The Greek God Of Wine, Vegetation, Fertility, Festivity, Ritual Madness, Religious Ecstasy, And Theatre)
**Origin Language:** Ancient Greek

Dior
**Meaning:** Animal
**Origin Language:** Old English

Dita | Ditte
**Meaning:** He Will Be Praised
**Origin Language:** Hebrew

Divina | Divena, Divene, Divine
**Meaning:** Goddess
**Origin Language:** Latin

Dixie | Dixy
**Meaning:** Ten
**Origin Language:** French

Docia | Dosia

**Meaning:** Given By God
**Origin Language:** Ancient Greek

Dodie | Dodi, Dody
**Meaning:** Gift Of God
**Origin Language:** Ancient Greek

Domenica | Domenika,
Domeniqua, Dominica, Dominika,
Dominiqua, Domnica, Domnika
**Meaning:** Of The Lord/Church
**Origin Language:** Latin

Domitia
**Also:** Domitilla | Domitila,
Domitille
**Meaning:** Tamed
**Origin Language:** Latin

Domnina | Domna, Domnine
**Meaning:** Mistress Of The Domain
**Origin Language:** Latin

Donata
**Also:** Donatella
**Also:** Donatienne | Donatienna
**Meaning:** Given (To The Church Or
Monastery)
**Origin Language:** Latin

Donella | Donelle
**Also:** Donna
**Meaning:** Chief/Ruler Of The World
**Origin Language:** Old Irish

Dora | Dorie, Dory
**Meaning:** Gift
**Origin Language:** Ancient Greek

Dorcas | Dorkas
**Meaning:** Gazelle
**Origin Language:** Ancient Greek

Doreen | Dorean, Dorena,
Dorene, Dorina, Dorine
**Meaning:** Gift

**Origin Language:** Ancient Greek

Doretta | Doreta, Dorette, Dorit,
Dorita
**Meaning:** Gift Of God
**Origin Language:** Ancient Greek

Doria | Dorea, Doreah, Doriah
**Also:** Dorina | Doriane, Dorine
**Meaning:** Of The Dorian People (The
Name Of An Ancient Greek Tribe)
**Origin Language:** Ancient Greek

Dorinda
**Meaning:** Gift
**Origin Language:** Ancient Greek

Doris | Dorris
**Meaning:** Of The Dorian People (The
Name Of An Ancient Greek Tribe)
**Origin Language:** Ancient Greek

Dorota | Dorotea, Doroteia,
Doroteya, Dorotia
**Also:** Dorothy | Dorothea,
Dorothee, Dorothee, Dorothie
**Also:** Dorrit | Dorete
**Also:** Dortha | Dorte, Dorthe,
Dorthea, Dorthie, Dorthy
**Also:** Dottie | Dot, Dotty
**Meaning:** Gift Of God
**Origin Language:** Ancient Greek

Dove
**Meaning:** Dove
**Origin Language:** English

Dovilia | Dovilla
**Meaning:** Warrior
**Origin Language:** Latin

Draven
**Meaning:** Precious (Common Slavic) /
Phantom (English)
**Origin Language:** Common Slavic And
Old English

Drea | Draia, Draya, Dreia, Dria
**Meaning:** Brave Warrior
**Origin Language:** Ancient Greek

Drita
**Meaning:** Light
**Origin Language:** Albanian

Dua
**Meaning:** Prayer
**Origin Language:** Arabic

Duana | Dwaina
**Meaning:** Little Dark/Black One
**Origin Language:** Old Irish

Duffy
**Meaning:** Black/Dark
**Origin Language:** Old Irish

Duilia
**Meaning:** Warrior
**Origin Language:** Latin

Dulce | Dolcie, Dolcy, Duce, Dulcie, Dulcy
**Meaning:** Sweet
**Origin Language:** Latin

Dulcibella | Duclibelle
**Meaning:** Sweet And Beautiful
**Origin Language:** Latin

Dulcinea
**Meaning:** Sweet
**Origin Language:** Spanish

Dustie | Dusty
**Meaning:** Thor's Stone / Stone Of Thunder (Thor Is The Name Of The Norse God Of Thunder And Lightning)
**Origin Language:** Old Norse

Dyan | Dian
**Meaning:** Candle
**Origin Language:** Indonesian

# Chapter 31 - Names For Girls Beginning With E

Eadie | Eady, Edie, Edy
**Meaning:** Rich
**Origin Language:** Ancient Germanic And Old English And Old Norse (Cognates)

Earlina | Earleen, Earlene, Earlin, Earline, Earlyn
**Meaning:** Noble
**Origin Language:** Old English

Ebony | Ebonie
**Meaning:** Ebony
**Origin Language:** English

Ecaterina | Ecaterine, Ecaterini, Ekaterina, Ekaterine, Ekaterini
**Meaning:** Pure
**Origin Language:** Ancient Greek

Echo
**Meaning:** Echo
**Origin Language:** English

Eda
**Meaning:** Well-Mannered
**Origin Language:** Turkish

Edana
**Meaning:** Envy
**Origin Language:** Old Irish

Edda
**Meaning:** Great Grandmother
**Origin Language:** Old Norse

Edeilah | Edeeleh, Edielah, Edila, Edileh
**Meaning:** Unbiased

**Origin Language:** Arabic

Edeline | Edelene, Edelena,
Edelin, Edelina, Edelyn
**Meaning:** Like A Noble
**Origin Language:** Ancient Germanic

Edelle | Edela, Edele, Edelia,
Edella, Edila, Edilla
**Meaning:** Noble
**Origin Language:** Ancient Germanic
And Old English (Cognates)

Edelmira
**Meaning:** Famous Noble
**Origin Language:** Ancient Germanic
And Old English (Cognates)

Eden
**Meaning:** Delight
**Origin Language:** Hebrew

Ederne
**Meaning:** Beautiful
**Origin Language:** Basque

Edetana
**Meaning:** From The Mountains
**Origin Language:** Spanish

Edina | Edena, Edene, Edine
**Meaning:** Delicate
**Origin Language:** Hebrew

Edith | Edita, Edite, Editha,
Edyta, Edytha, Edythe
**Meaning:** Wealthy Warrior
**Origin Language:** Old English

Edmee
**Meaning:** Wealthy Protector
**Origin Language:** Old English

Edna
**Meaning:** Pleasure
**Origin Language:** Hebrew

Eduarda
**Meaning:** Warden Of Wealth
**Origin Language:** Old English

Edurna | Edurne
**Meaning:** Snow
**Origin Language:** Basque

Edvina | Edvena
**Also:** Edwina | Edweena, Edwena,
Edwine, Edwyna
**Meaning:** Wealthy And Friendly
**Origin Language:** Old English And Old
Norse (Cognates)

Edya
**Meaning:** God Has Adorned Himself
**Origin Language:** Hebrew

Effie | Effy
**Also:** Effimia
**Meaning:** Well-Spoken
**Origin Language:** Ancient Greek

Efia | Efua
**Meaning:** Born On A Friday
**Origin Language:** Akan

Eila
**Meaning:** Oak Tree
**Origin Language:** Hebrew

Eileen | Eilene
**Meaning:** Forever / Eternity
**Origin Language:** Ancient Germanic

Eilish
**Meaning:** God Is My Oath
**Origin Language:** Hebrew

Eiluned | Eluned
**Meaning:** Idol
**Origin Language:** Welsh

Eira

**Meaning:** Snow
**Origin Language:** Welsh

Eireann
**Meaning:** Ireland
**Origin Language:** Old Irish

Eirene | Eireen, Eirini
**Meaning:** Peace
**Origin Language:** Ancient Greek

Eirlys | Eirlis
**Meaning:** Snowdrop
**Origin Language:** Welsh

Eirwen
**Meaning:** White As Snow
**Origin Language:** Welsh

Eithra | Eithria
**Also:** Eithrica | Eithric
**Meaning:** Very Speckled
**Origin Language:** Old Irish

Ekeila | Ekeile, Ekela, Ekele, Ekila,
Ekile, Ekyla, Ekyle
**Meaning:** Wise
**Origin Language:** Arabic

Ekin
**Meaning:** Harvest
**Origin Language:** Turkish

Ela
**Meaning:** Hazel
**Origin Language:** Turkish

Elaide | Elaida, Elayda, Elayde
**Meaning:** Of The Noble Sort
**Origin Language:** Ancient Germanic

Elaine | Elain , Elaina, Elayna,
Elayne, Ellaina, Ellaine, Ellayna,
Ellayne
**Meaning:** Torch
**Origin Language:** Ancient Greek

Elaira | Ealaira, Eallaira, Ellaira
**Meaning:** Temple Chapel
**Origin Language:** Latin

Elanda | Ealanda, Ealanta,
Eallanda, Eallande, Eallanta,
Eallante, Elanta, Ellanda, Ellande,
Ellanta, Ellante
**Meaning:** From An Island
**Origin Language:** Old English

Elanor
**Meaning:** Star Sun
**Origin Language:** Sindarian (Fictional
Language Devised By J. R. R. Tolkien For
Use In His Fantasy Stories, Such As Lord
Of The Rings)

Elaria | Ellaria
**Meaning:** Light-Hearted
**Origin Language:** Ancient Greek

Elaura | Ellaura, Ellora, Elora
**Meaning:** Laurel
**Origin Language:** Latin

Elba
**Meaning:** Elven
**Origin Language:** Ancient Germanic
And Old English And Old Norse
(Cognates)

Elbera | Elbira
**Meaning:** All True
**Origin Language:** Ancient Germanic

Elcera | Elcira, Elsera, Elsira
**Meaning:** God Is My Oath
**Origin Language:** Hebrew

Eldena | Eldina
**Meaning:** Friendly Old One
**Origin Language:** Ancient Germanic
And Old English (Cognates)

**Eldreda**
**Meaning:** Noble Strength
**Origin Language:** Old English

**Eleanor | Eleanora, Eleanore, Elenoire, Elenora, Eleonor, Eleonora, Eleonore, Eléonore, Elianora, Elianore, Elinor, Elionora, Elionore, Ellinor**
**Meaning:** Noble Of The North
**Origin Language:** Ancient Germanic

**Electra | Electria, Elektra, Elektria**
**Meaning:** Amber / The Shade Of The Sun / Incandescent
**Origin Language:** Ancient Greek

**Elena | Elene, Eleni, Eliena, Elina, Eline**
**Meaning:** Torch
**Origin Language:** Ancient Greek

**Eleri**
**Meaning:** From Near The River Leri (Wales)
**Origin Language:** Welsh

**Eleria | Elleria, Ellerie, Ellery, Ellyra**
**Meaning:** Light-Hearted
**Origin Language:** Ancient Greek

**Elettra | Eletra, Eletria, Elettria**
**Meaning:** Amber / The Shade Of The Sun / Incandescent
**Origin Language:** Ancient Greek

**Elfra | Elfria**
**Meaning:** Elven
**Origin Language:** Ancient Germanic And Old English And Old Norse (Cognates)

**Elfrida | Elfrada, Elfreda, Elfrede**
**Meaning:** Elven Counsel
**Origin Language:** Old English

**Elia | Elea**
**Meaning:** Noble Of The North
**Origin Language:** Ancient Germanic

**Elianna | Eliana, Elliana, Ellianna**
**Meaning:** My God Answered
**Origin Language:** Hebrew

**Elicia | Elisia**
**Meaning:** Like A Noble
**Origin Language:** Ancient Germanic

**Elidora**
**Meaning:** The Sun's Gift
**Origin Language:** Ancient Greek

**Elietta | Eliette**
**Meaning:** My God Is God
**Origin Language:** Hebrew

**Elioda**
**Meaning:** The Sun's Gift
**Origin Language:** Ancient Greek

**Eliora**
**Meaning:** God Is My Light
**Origin Language:** Hebrew

**Elisaveta | Elisavet, Elizavet, Elizaveta**
**Also:** Elise | Elisa, Ellisa, Ellise
**Meaning:** God Is My Oath
**Origin Language:** Hebrew

**Elisende | Elisenda, Elissenda, Elissende**
**Meaning:** Journeys To A Temple
**Origin Language:** Ancient Germanic

**Elissa**
**Meaning:** Goddess
**Origin Language:** Phoenician

**Elita**
**Meaning:** A Short Form Of Any Of The

Numerous Names Ending In Elita
**Origin Language:** Various

Elithyia | Ileithyia, Ilithyia
**Meaning:** The Deliverer (In Regards To Childbirth)
**Origin Language:** Ancient Greek

Eliza | Elyza
**Also:** Elizabeth | Elisabet, Elisabeta, Elisabete, Elisabeth, Elisabeti, Elisabetta, Elizabet, Elizabeta, Elizabete, Elizabeti, Elizabetta, Elysabeth Elyzabeth
**Also:** Ella | Elle, Elli, Ellie, Elly
**Meaning:** God Is My Oath
**Origin Language:** Hebrew

Ellen | Elen, Elin, Ellin, Ellyn, Ellynn, Elyn, Elynn
**Meaning:** Torch
**Origin Language:** Ancient Greek

Elliana
**Meaning:** Sun
**Origin Language:** Ancient Greek

Ellitze | Ellitza
**Meaning:** Of The Noble Sort
**Origin Language:** Ancient Germanic

Elma
**Meaning:** Desires Protection
**Origin Language:** Ancient Germanic

Elmira
**Meaning:** Famous Noble
**Origin Language:** Ancient Germanic And Old English (Cognates)

Elna | Elnia
**Meaning:** Torch
**Origin Language:** Ancient Greek

Elnora
**Meaning:** Noble Of The North

**Origin Language:** Ancient Germanic

Elodie | Elodi, Elodia, Elody
**Meaning:** All Wealthy
**Origin Language:** Ancient Germanic

Eloise | Eloisa, Elouisa, Elouise
**Meaning:** Her Holiness Goes Far And Wide
**Origin Language:** Ancient Germanic

Eloma | Ealhoma, Ealloma, Elama, Elhoma, Ellama, Elloma
**Meaning:** From A Homestead Near A Temple
**Origin Language:** Old English

Elowen
**Meaning:** Elm Tree
**Origin Language:** Cornish

Eloya | Eloia
**Meaning:** Chosen
**Origin Language:** Latin

Elsa | Els, Elz, Elza
**Also:** Elsabeth | Elzabeth
**Also:** Elsie | Els, Else, Elsy, Elz, Elze, Elzie, Elzy
**Also:** Elspeth | Elspet, Elzpet, Elzpeth
**Meaning:** God Is My Oath
**Origin Language:** Hebrew

Eluara
**Meaning:** Elven Army
**Origin Language:** Ancient Germanic And Old English And Old Norse (Cognates)

Eluina | Eluinna, Eluinnia, Eluwina
**Meaning:** Friendly Noble
**Origin Language:** Ancient Germanic And Old English (Cognates)

Eluney | Elunie
**Meaning:** Gives
**Origin Language:** Mapuche

Elva | Elvah, Elvi, Elvia, Elvie
**Meaning:** Elven
**Origin Language:** Ancient Germanic And Old English And Old Norse (Cognates)

Elvara
**Meaning:** Elven Army
**Origin Language:** Ancient Germanic And Old English And Old Norse (Cognates)

Elvia
**Meaning:** Has Hair The Shade Of Honey
**Origin Language:** Latin

Elvina | Elvena, Elvine
**Meaning:** Friendly Noble
**Origin Language:** Ancient Germanic And Old English (Cognates)

Elvira | Elvera, Elveria, Elvire, Elviria
**Meaning:** All True
**Origin Language:** Ancient Germanic

Elvissa | Elvisa
**Meaning:** All Wise
**Origin Language:** Old Norse

Elyasa
**Meaning:** My God Is God
**Origin Language:** Hebrew

Elysia
**Meaning:** Blissful
**Origin Language:** Latin

Ema
**Meaning:** Benefit / Bay / Inlet / Flax
**Origin Language:** Japanese

Emanuelle | Emanuela, Emanuella, Emmanuele, Emmanuella, Emmanuelle
**Meaning:** God Is With Us
**Origin Language:** Hebrew

Ember
**Also:** Emberly | Emberlie
**Also:** Emberlynn | Emberlyn
**Meaning:** Ember
**Origin Language:** English

Embla
**Meaning:** Elm Tree
**Origin Language:** Old Norse

Emelia
**Meaning:** Worker
**Origin Language:** Ancient Germanic

Emerald
**Meaning:** Emerald
**Origin Language:** English

Emersyn | Emersin
**Meaning:** Sovereign Of The Homeland
**Origin Language:** Ancient Germanic

Emi
**Meaning:** Beautiful Picture / Beautiful Painting
**Origin Language:** Japanese

Emilienne | Emiliana, Emiliann, Emilianna Emilienn, Emilianne, Emilienna
**Also:** Emilita
**Also:** Emily | Emalee, Emelie, Emely, Emilee, Emili, Emilia, Emilie, Emilie, Emiliya, Emille
**Meaning:** Rival
**Origin Language:** Latin

Emina
**Meaning:** Feels Safe

**Origin Language:** Arabic

Emine
**Meaning:** Trustworthy
**Origin Language:** Arabic

Emira
**Meaning:** Commander
**Origin Language:** Arabic

Emma | Em, Emie, Emmi,
Emmie, Emmy, Emy
**Meaning:** Universal
**Origin Language:** Ancient Germanic

Emmalyn | Emelin, Emelyn,
Emelynn, Emmalin, Emmelin,
Emmelyn
**Also:** Emmeline | Emalina,
Emelena, Emelene, Emeline,
Emmalina, Emmaline, Emmelina
**Meaning:** Gentle Worker
**Origin Language:** Ancient Germanic

Emorie | Emerie, Emery, Emory
**Meaning:** Ruler Of The Homeland
**Origin Language:** Ancient Germanic

Enara | Ehnhara, Enhara
**Meaning:** Swallow (As In The Bird)
**Origin Language:** Basque

Encarna | Encarnita
**Meaning:** Incarnation
**Origin Language:** Spanish

Endis
**Meaning:** Eagle Deity
**Origin Language:** Old Norse

Endla
**Meaning:** Brave Warrior
**Origin Language:** Ancient Greek

Endrita
**Meaning:** Light

**Origin Language:** Albanian

Enea | Enia
**Also:** Eneida
**Meaning:** Praise
**Origin Language:** Ancient Greek

Enfreda | Enfrida
**Meaning:** Eagle Of Peace
**Origin Language:** Ancient Germanic

Enid | Enida, Enyd, Enyda
**Meaning:** The Soul
**Origin Language:** Welsh

Enisa | Enisah, Enisia, Enisiya,
Enissa, Ennisa
**Meaning:** Friendly
**Origin Language:** Arabic

Enola
**Meaning:** Alone (Backwards)
**Origin Language:** English

Enora | Ennora
**Meaning:** Esteem
**Origin Language:** Latin

Enrica | Enrika
**Also:** Enriqueta | Enrichetta,
Enrichette, Enriquetta, Enriquette
**Meaning:** Sovereign Of The Homeland
**Origin Language:** Ancient Germanic

Ensley | Enslea, Enslee, Ensleigh,
Enslie, Ensly
**Meaning:** From A Lonely Meadow
**Origin Language:** Old English

Enya | Enia
**Meaning:** Kernel
**Origin Language:** Old Irish

Eowyn
**Meaning:** Horse Joy
**Origin Language:** Old English

Eppie | Eppy
**Meaning:** Well-Spoken
**Origin Language:** Ancient Greek

Era
**Meaning:** Wind
**Origin Language:** Albanian

Eradia
**Meaning:** Ode To A Heroine
**Origin Language:** Ancient Greek

Eralda | Eraldia, Erelda, Ereldia,
Erilda, Erildia
**Meaning:** Of The Ruling Army
**Origin Language:** Old English

Erica | Eerica, Eerika, Eirica,
Eirika, Ericka, Erika, Eryca, Eryka
**Meaning:** Ruler Of Forever
**Origin Language:** Old Norse

Erin | Eryn
**Meaning:** Ireland
**Origin Language:** Old Irish

Eris
**Meaning:** Strife
**Origin Language:** Ancient Greek

Erlea
**Meaning:** Bee
**Origin Language:** Basque

Erleth | Erletha
**Also:** Erlette | Erlet, Erlett, Erletta,
Erletty
**Also:** Erleva
**Meaning:** Army Heritage
**Origin Language:** Ancient Germanic

Erlida
**Meaning:** From Near A Gravelly Slope
**Origin Language:** Old English

Erlina | Erlena, Erlene, Erline
**Meaning:** Friendly Warrior
**Origin Language:** Ancient Germanic

Erlith | Erlitha
**Meaning:** From Near A Gravelly Slope
**Origin Language:** Old English

Erlotta | Erlotte
**Meaning:** Rascal
**Origin Language:** Old French

Erluina | Erlewina, Erlewine,
Erluine
**Meaning:** Friendly Warrior
**Origin Language:** Ancient Germanic

Erma
**Meaning:** Universal
**Origin Language:** Ancient Germanic

Ermalinda | Ermalinde, Ermelinda,
Ermelinde
**Meaning:** Completely Tender
**Origin Language:** Ancient Germanic

Ermana
**Also:** Ermanda
**Meaning:** Army Woman
**Origin Language:** Ancient Germanic

Ermina | Ermena
**Meaning:** Universal
**Origin Language:** Ancient Germanic

Erminia
**Meaning:** Of Hermes (Hermes Is The
Name Of The Greek God Of
Boundaries, Roads And Travelers,
Thieves, Athletes, Shepherds, Commerce,
Speed, Cunning, Wit And Sleep,
Psychopomp And Divine Messenger)
**Origin Language:** Ancient Greek

Ermona
**Meaning:** Army Woman

**Origin Language:** Ancient Germanic

**Erna**
**Meaning:** Healthy
**Origin Language:** Old Norse

**Ernestine | Earnesta, Earnestina, Earnestine, Ernesta, Ernestina, Ernsta**
**Meaning:** Earnest
**Origin Language:** Ancient Germanic

**Erodia | Erodya**
**Meaning:** Ode To A Heroine
**Origin Language:** Ancient Greek

**Ersilia | Ercilia**
**Meaning:** Dew
**Origin Language:** Ancient Greek

**Eseld | Esold, Esolt, Esylt, Esyllt**
**Meaning:** Ice Cold Battler
**Origin Language:** Ancient Germanic

**Esha**
**Meaning:** Desire
**Origin Language:** Sanskrit

**Esma**
**Meaning:** Supreme
**Origin Language:** Arabic

**Esme | Esmae, Esmé, Esmee, Esmée**
**Meaning:** Esteemed / Loved
**Origin Language:** Old French

**Esmeralda | Esmaralda, Esmerelda**
**Also:** Esmeraude | Esmeraud
**Meaning:** Emerald
**Origin Language:** Ancient Greek

**Esra**
**Meaning:** Nocturnal Wanderer
**Origin Language:** Arabic

**Essence**
**Meaning:** Essence
**Origin Language:** English

**Essy | Essi, Essie**
**Also:** Esta
**Also:** Estee | Estae, Estay, Estée
**Also:** Estelle | Estel, Estela, Estella
**Meaning:** Star
**Origin Language:** Latin

**Estera | Ester, Esteri, Eszter, Esztera, Eszti**
**Also:** Esther | Esfir
**Meaning:** Lady Of The Heavens / Lady Of The Sky
**Origin Language:** Akkadian

**Esti**
**Meaning:** Sweet / Honey
**Origin Language:** Basque

**Estrella**
**Meaning:** Star
**Origin Language:** Spanish

**Estrid | Estrida**
**Also:** Estrina | Estrena, Estrene, Estrine
**Meaning:** Beautiful And Divine
**Origin Language:** Old Norse

**Eteela | Eteeylah, Eteile, Etelah, Eteleh, Etilah, Etileh, Etylah, Etyleh**
**Meaning:** Unbiased
**Origin Language:** Arabic

**Etel | Etela, Etell, Etella, Etelle**
**Meaning:** Noble
**Origin Language:** Ancient Germanic And Old English (Cognates)

**Eteri | Etery**
**Meaning:** Ether
**Origin Language:** Georgian

Etta | Ettie, Etty
**Meaning:** Ruler Of The Homeland
**Origin Language:** Ancient Germanic

Euadne | Euadni
**Meaning:** Truly Chaste
**Origin Language:** Ancient Greek

Euanthe | Euantha
**Meaning:** Blooming
**Origin Language:** Ancient Greek

Eudocia | Eudokia, Eudokiya
**Meaning:** Good Judgement
**Origin Language:** Ancient Greek

Eudora
**Meaning:** A Genuine Gift
**Origin Language:** Ancient Greek

Eudoxia
**Meaning:** Good Reputation
**Origin Language:** Ancient Greek

Eugenie | Eugeneia, Eugenia, Eugeniya, Eugeny
**Meaning:** Well-Born
**Origin Language:** Ancient Greek

Eula
**Meaning:** Well-Spoken
**Origin Language:** Ancient Greek

Eunice | Eunika, Eunike
**Meaning:** A Happy Victory
**Origin Language:** Ancient Greek

Eunomia
**Meaning:** Is True To The Law
**Origin Language:** Ancient Greek

Euphemia | Eufemia, Eupheme
**Meaning:** Well-Spoken
**Origin Language:** Ancient Greek

Euri | Euria
**Meaning:** Rain
**Origin Language:** Basque

Eustacia
**Meaning:** Grows/Harvests Grain Well
**Origin Language:** Ancient Greek

Evadne
**Meaning:** Truly Chaste
**Origin Language:** Ancient Greek

Evangelia | Evangeliya
**Also:** Evangeline | Evangelina
**Also:** Evangelyn | Evangelin, Evangelynn
**Meaning:** Bringer Of Good News
**Origin Language:** Ancient Greek

Eve | Eva, Evi, Evie, Evy
**Also:** Evelia | Evalia
**Also:** Evelyn | Evalin, Evalina, Evaline, Evalyn, Eveleen, Evelien, Evelin, Evelina, Eveline, Evelyne, Evelynn
**Meaning:** Breathes (Hebrew) / Forever / Eternity (Ancient Germanic)
**Origin Language:** Hebrew And Ancient Germanic

Ever
**Meaning:** Ever
**Origin Language:** English

Everarda | Evra, Evrada, Evrarda
**Also:** Everette | Everata, Everatta, Everett, Everetta, Everita
**Meaning:** Hardy As A Boar
**Origin Language:** Ancient Germanic

Everild | Everhild, Everill
**Meaning:** Boar Battler
**Origin Language:** Old English

Everiss | Everisa, Everise,

Everissa, Everisse, Everris, Everrisa, Everrise
**Meaning:** From Évreux (A Commune In Normandy, France) / Yew Tree / Wields Weapons Made From A Yew Tree
**Origin Language:** Gaulish

Everleigh | Everlea, Everlee, Everley, Everlie, Everly
**Meaning:** From A Meadow Of Boars
**Origin Language:** Old English

Evette | Evetta
**Meaning:** Yew Tree
**Origin Language:** Ancient Germanic

Evita
**Meaning:** Breathes (Hebrew) / Forever / Eternity (Ancient Germanic)
**Origin Language:** Hebrew And Ancient Germanic

Evonne
**Meaning:** Yew Tree
**Origin Language:** Ancient Germanic

Eydis
**Meaning:** Island Goddess
**Origin Language:** Old Norse

Ezelina | Ezelena, Ezzelena, Ezzelin, Ezzelina, Ezzelyn
**Meaning:** Tender Noble
**Origin Language:** Ancient Germanic

# Chapter 32 - Names For Girls Beginning With F

Fabia
**Also:** Fabienne | Fabiana
**Also:** Fabiola
**Meaning:** Shaped Like A Bean
**Origin Language:** Latin

Fabricia | Fabrice, Fabrizia
**Meaning:** Crafter
**Origin Language:** Latin

Faesyle | Faesile, Faisile, Faisyle, Faysile, Faysyle
**Also:** Faina | Faena
**Meaning:** Shining
**Origin Language:** Ancient Greek

Faith | Faithe, Fayth
**Meaning:** Faith
**Origin Language:** English

Famke | Femke
**Meaning:** Little Girl
**Origin Language:** Ancient Germanic

Fantine | Fantena, Fantene, Fantina
**Meaning:** Infant
**Origin Language:** French

Farah | Farrah
**Meaning:** Happy
**Origin Language:** Arabic

Fauna
**Meaning:** Approvable
**Origin Language:** Latin

Faye | Fae, Faie, Fay
**Meaning:** Fairy
**Origin Language:** English

Fedelma | Fedelm, Fidelm, Fidelma
**Meaning:** Lasting
**Origin Language:** Old Irish

Federica | Federika, Fedrica, Fedrika
**Meaning:** Peaceful And Rich
**Origin Language:** Ancient Germanic

Felecia | Felice, Felicia, Felicie, Felicy, Felisa, Felise, Felisha
**Meaning:** Lucky
**Origin Language:** Latin

Felicity | Felicita, Felicite, Felicitia, Felicitie, Felicyta, Felisita, Felizita
**Meaning:** Luck
**Origin Language:** Latin

Felina | Felena
**Meaning:** Of Cats
**Origin Language:** Latin

Felippa | Felipa, Filipa, Filippa
**Meaning:** Lover Of Horses
**Origin Language:** Ancient Greek

Femie | Femi, Femy
**Meaning:** Well-Spoken
**Origin Language:** Ancient Greek

Fenella | Finella
**Meaning:** Blessed Shoulder
**Origin Language:** Old Irish

Fenna
**Meaning:** Strives For Peace
**Origin Language:** Ancient Germanic

Fern | Ferne
**Meaning:** Fern
**Origin Language:** English

Ffion
**Meaning:** Purple Foxglove
**Origin Language:** Welsh

Fia
**Meaning:** Untamed
**Origin Language:** Irish

Fiamma | Fiammetta, Fiammette
**Meaning:** Flame
**Origin Language:** Italian

Fianna
**Meaning:** Band Of Warriors
**Origin Language:** Irish

Fiera
**Meaning:** Proud
**Origin Language:** Esperanto

Fifi
**Meaning:** God Will Add
**Origin Language:** Hebrew

Fina | Feena
**Meaning:** Burning / Glowing / Seraphim
**Origin Language:** Latin

Finola | Fionola
**Meaning:** Blessed Shoulder
**Origin Language:** Old Irish

Fiona
**Meaning:** Blessed / Bright
**Origin Language:** Old Irish

Fiore
**Meaning:** Flower
**Origin Language:** Italian

Fiorella
**Meaning:** Little Flower
**Origin Language:** Italian

Fiorenza
**Meaning:** Flourishing
**Origin Language:** Latin

Flavia | Flavie, Flavy
**Also:** Flavienne | Flaviana, Flavienna
**Meaning:** Has Golden/Yellow Hair
**Origin Language:** Latin

Fleur
**Also:** Fleuretta | Fleurette
**Meaning:** Flower

**Origin Language:** French

Floella | Floelle
**Also:** Flora | Flo, Flor, Flore
**Meaning:** Flower
**Origin Language:** Latin

Florence | Floireans, Florance
**Also:** Florencia
**Also:** Florentina | Florentia, Florentine
**Meaning:** Flourishing
**Origin Language:** Latin

Floretta | Florette
**Also:** Floriana | Floriane, Florianne, Florina, Florine
**Also:** Florica | Florika
**Also:** Florinda | Florinde
**Also:** Floris
**Also:** Florrie | Flor, Flori, Florry
**Meaning:** Flower
**Origin Language:** Latin

Fortuna | Fortune
**Also:** Fortunata
**Meaning:** Fortunate
**Origin Language:** Latin

France
**Also:** Frances | Francis
**Also:** Francesca
**Also:** Francette | Francetta
**Also:** Francine | Francene
**Also:** Francisca
**Meaning:** Of The Franks (The Name Of A Germanic Tribe) (Ancient Germanic) / Javelin-Like (Latin)
**Origin Language:** Ancient Germanic And Latin

Frederica | Frederika, Frederique, Fredrica, Fredrika
**Meaning:** Peaceful And Rich
**Origin Language:** Ancient Germanic

Freya | Frea, Freja, Freyja
**Meaning:** Lady
**Origin Language:** Old Norse

Frida | Freda, Freida, Frieda, Friede
**Meaning:** Peace
**Origin Language:** Old Norse

# Chapter 33 - Names For Girls Beginning With G

Gabi | Gabbie, Gabby, Gaby
**Also:** Gabriella | Gabriela, Gabriele, Gabrielle
**Also:** Gabrysia
**Meaning:** God Is My Strength
**Origin Language:** Hebrew

Gaea | Gaia
**Meaning:** The Earth
**Origin Language:** Ancient Greek

Gaelle
**Meaning:** Speaker Of Gaelic
**Origin Language:** Old Breton

Gaetana | Gaitana, Gayetana
**Meaning:** From Caieta (An Ancient Town On The Coast Of Latium, A District Located In West Central Italy)
**Origin Language:** Latin

Gaiana | Gaiane
**Meaning:** The Earth
**Origin Language:** Ancient Greek

Gail | Gaila, Gale, Gayla, Gayle
**Meaning:** My Father Is Joyful
**Origin Language:** Hebrew

Gal

**Meaning:** An Ocean Wave
**Origin Language:** Hebrew

## Gala | Galla
**Meaning:** Rooster (Latin) / From Gaul (An Ancient Region Of Western Europe) (Ancient Celtic) / An Outlander (Ancient Celtic)
**Origin Language:** Latin And Ancient Celtic

## Galatea | Galateia, Galathe, Galatia
**Meaning:** Milk
**Origin Language:** Ancient Greek

## Galena | Galene, Galina, Galine, Galini, Galya
**Meaning:** Calm
**Origin Language:** Ancient Greek

## Gali
**Meaning:** My Wave In The Ocean
**Origin Language:** Hebrew

## Galia
**Meaning:** An Ocean Wave
**Origin Language:** Hebrew

## Galilea | Galila, Galilee, Galileia, Galilia
**Meaning:** Galilean / From Galilee (A Mountainous Region In Israel)
**Origin Language:** Hebrew

## Garance
**Meaning:** Madder (Genus Rubia) Plant
**Origin Language:** French

## Gardenia
**Meaning:** Gardenia (Flower)
**Origin Language:** English

## Garland
**Meaning:** Garland
**Origin Language:** English

## Garnet | Garnett, Garnette
**Meaning:** Garnet
**Origin Language:** English

## Gaynor | Gaenor
**Meaning:** Blessed Phantom / White Phantom
**Origin Language:** Welsh

## Gemma | Gema
**Meaning:** Precious Stone / Jewel
**Origin Language:** Latin

## Genesis
**Meaning:** Origin / Horoscope
**Origin Language:** Latin

## Genette
**Meaning:** Graced By God
**Origin Language:** Hebrew

## Geneva | Geniva
**Also:** Genevieve | Genevieva, Genovefa, Genoveffa, Genoveva, Genoveve, Genoviva, Genovive
**Meaning:** Family Woman
**Origin Language:** Ancient Germanic

## Genevra | Ginevra
**Meaning:** Blessed Phantom / White Phantom
**Origin Language:** Welsh

## Genna
**Also:** Gennadia | Gennadiya
**Meaning:** Calm
**Origin Language:** Ancient Greek

## Gentiana | Genta
**Meaning:** Gentian (A Flowering Plant)
**Origin Language:** Albanian

## Georgetta | Georgette, Giorgetta, Giorgette
**Also:** Georgia | Georgeah, Georgeia, Giorgeah, Giorgeia, Giorgia

**Also:** Georgina | Georgeanna,
Georgeanne, Georgena, Georgene,
Georgiana, Georgianna, Georgine,
Giorgena, Giorgene, Giorgina,
Giorgine
**Meaning:** Farmer
**Origin Language:** Ancient Greek

Geraldine | Geraldina, Giraldina,
Giraldine
**Meaning:** Powerful Spear
**Origin Language:** Ancient Germanic

Gerarda | Gerrarda
**Meaning:** Spear Of Hardiness
**Origin Language:** Ancient Germanic

Geri | Gerrie, Gerry, Gery
**Meaning:** Powerful Spear
**Origin Language:** Ancient Germanic

Germaine | Germaina, Germana
**Meaning:** Sister
**Origin Language:** Latin

Gervaise
**Meaning:** Strong Spear
**Origin Language:** Ancient Germanic

Gesine | Gesena Gesene, Gesina
**Meaning:** Spear Of Strength
**Origin Language:** Ancient Germanic

Ghislaine | Ghislaina, Ghyslaina,
Ghyslaine
**Meaning:** Pledge
**Origin Language:** Ancient Germanic

Gia
**Also:** Giavanna | Giovanna,
Giovannetta, Giovannette,
Giavannetta, Giavannette
**Meaning:** Graced By God
**Origin Language:** Hebrew

Gigi
**Meaning:** Farmer
**Origin Language:** Ancient Greek

Gillian
**Also:** Gilly | Gill, Gillie
**Meaning:** Downy (Down As In Soft
Fluffy Hairs)
**Origin Language:** Latin

Gina | Geena, Gena, Gine
**Meaning:** Queen
**Origin Language:** Latin

Ginette
**Meaning:** Family Woman
**Origin Language:** Ancient Germanic

Ginger
**Also:** Ginnie | Ginny
**Meaning:** Virgin / Of The Vergiliae
(Vergilae Is The Name The Romans Used
For The Star Constellation That Is Mostly
Know Today As "The Pleiades")
**Origin Language:** Latin

Giselle | Gisela, Gisela, Gisele,
Gisella, Gisila, Gissella, Gisselle,
Gizela, Gizele, Gizella, Gizelle
**Also:** Giza | Gisa, Gizi
**Meaning:** Pledge
**Origin Language:** Ancient Germanic

Gladys | Gladis
**Meaning:** Of The Realm
**Origin Language:** Old Welsh

Glenda
**Also:** Glenna
**Meaning:** From A Valley
**Origin Language:** Welsh

Glenys | Glenice, Glennis
**Meaning:** Pure / Clean
**Origin Language:** Welsh

Glinda | Glynda
**Meaning:** From A Fenced Enclosure
**Origin Language:** Old English

Gloria
**Also:** Gloriana | Glorianne,
Glorina, Glorine
**Also:** Gloriela | Gloriella, Glorielle
**Also:** Glorinda | Glorinde
**Meaning:** Glory
**Origin Language:** Latin

Godiva
**Meaning:** God's Gift
**Origin Language:** Old English

Gordana
**Meaning:** Dignified
**Origin Language:** Common Slavic

Grace | Gracie, Gracy
**Also:** Gracelyn | Gracelin,
Gracelina, Gracelynn
**Also:** Gracia | Gratia, Grazia
**Also:** Graciana | Gratiana, Graziana
**Also:** Graciela | Graciella, Gracielle
**Meaning:** Grace
**Origin Language:** Latin

Granya | Grania
**Meaning:** Hatred
**Origin Language:** Old Irish

Gray | Grey
**Meaning:** Grey/Gray
**Origin Language:** English

Graziella | Grazielle
**Meaning:** Grace
**Origin Language:** Latin

Greer | Grier
**Meaning:** Watchful
**Origin Language:** Ancient Greek

Greta | Grete, Grethe, Gretta
**Also:** Gretchen
**Also:** Gretel | Gretal
**Meaning:** Pearl
**Origin Language:** Latin

Guinevere | Guenevere,
Gwenevere
**Meaning:** Blessed Phantom / White
Phantom
**Origin Language:** Welsh

Gwen | Gwenn
**Meaning:** Blessed / White
**Origin Language:** Old Welsh

Gwenaelle | Gwenaella
**Meaning:** Happy And Generous
**Origin Language:** Old Breton

Gwenda
**Meaning:** Well-Blessed
**Origin Language:** Welsh

Gwendolen | Guendolen,
Guendolena, Guendolin,
Guendolina, Guendoline,
Guendoloena, Guendolyn,
Gwendolena, Gwendolin,
Gwendolina, Gwendoline,
Gwendolyn
**Meaning:** Blessed Ring / White Ring
**Origin Language:** Old Welsh

Gweneth | Gwenith, Gwenneth,
Gwennith, Gwennyth, Gwenyth,
Gwynedd, Gwyneth, Gwynith
**Meaning:** From Gwynedd (Wales) /
From The Woods / From A Band Of
Warriors
**Origin Language:** Welsh

Gwyneira | Gweneira, Gwenira,
Gwynira
**Meaning:** As White As Snow

**Origin Language:** Welsh

# Chapter 34 - Names For Girls Beginning With H

Haddriona | Haddrionne, Haidriona, Haidrionne, Haydriona, Haydrionne
**Meaning:** From Hadria (The Name Of Two Ancient Roman Settlements Which Were Located In What Are Now Northern Italy And Central Italy) / From The Water
**Origin Language:** Latin

Hadiya | Hadia, Hadya
**Meaning:** Leader
**Origin Language:** Arabic

Haizea | Haizia
**Meaning:** Wind
**Origin Language:** Basque

Hala
**Meaning:** Halo Around The Moon
**Origin Language:** Arabic

Halena | Halene, Halina, Haline
**Meaning:** At Peace
**Origin Language:** Ancient Greek

Halienne | Haliena, Halienna
**Meaning:** Torch
**Origin Language:** Ancient Greek

Halle
**Meaning:** Manor Worker / Manor Dweller
**Origin Language:** German

Hallie | Hally
**Meaning:** Home Ruler
**Origin Language:** Ancient Germanic

Hana
**Meaning:** Flower
**Origin Language:** Japanese

Haniyah | Hania, Haniya, Haniyya
**Meaning:** Pleasant
**Origin Language:** Arabic

Hanley | Hanlea, Hanlee, Hanleigh, Hanlie
**Meaning:** From A High Meadow
**Origin Language:** Old English

Hannah | Hanna
**Meaning:** Gracious
**Origin Language:** Hebrew

Harleigh | Harlea, Harlee, Harley, Harlie, Harrlea, Harrlee, Harrleigh, Harrley, Harrlie
**Meaning:** From A Meadow Of Hares
**Origin Language:** Old English

Harleth | Harletha
**Also:** Harlette | Harlet, Harlett, Harletta, Harletty
**Also:** Harleva
**Meaning:** Noble Heritage
**Origin Language:** Ancient Germanic

Harlina | Harlena, Harlene, Harline
**Meaning:** Friendly Warrior
**Origin Language:** Ancient Germanic

Harlotta | Harlotte
**Meaning:** Rascal
**Origin Language:** Old French

Harlowe | Harlow
**Meaning:** From A Rocky Hill
**Origin Language:** Old English

Harluina | Harlewina, Harlewine, Harluine
**Meaning:** Friendly Warrior

**Origin Language:** Ancient Germanic

Harmana
**Also:** Harmanda
**Also:** Harmona
**Meaning:** Army Woman
**Origin Language:** Ancient Germanic

Harmonia
**Also:** Harmony | Harmonee,
Harmoni, Harmonie
**Meaning:** In Harmony
**Origin Language:** Ancient Greek

Harper
**Meaning:** Harp Maker / Harp Player
**Origin Language:** Old English

Harriett | Harriet, Harrietta,
Harriette
**Meaning:** Sovereign Of The Homeland
**Origin Language:** Ancient Germanic

Hartlea | Hartlee, Hartleigh,
Hartley, Hartlie
**Meaning:** From A Meadow Where Deer
Frequent
**Origin Language:** Old English

Harvina
**Also:** Harwina
**Meaning:** Friendly Soldier
**Origin Language:** Ancient Germanic

Hasena | Hasenia, Hasna, Hasnaa,
Hesna, Hesnaa
**Meaning:** Handsome / Virtuous And
Devoted To God
**Origin Language:** Arabic

Hatice
**Meaning:** Premature Child
**Origin Language:** Arabic

Hattie | Hatty
**Meaning:** Ruler Of The Homeland

**Origin Language:** Ancient Germanic

Haven
**Meaning:** Haven
**Origin Language:** English

Haya
**Meaning:** Hurry
**Origin Language:** Arabic

Hayden | Hadyn, Haiden, Haidyn
**Meaning:** From A Valley With Lots Of
Hay
**Origin Language:** Old English

Hazal
**Meaning:** Fallen Leaf
**Origin Language:** Turkish

Hazel
**Also:** Hazie | Hazey, Hazy
**Meaning:** Hazel
**Origin Language:** English

Heather
**Meaning:** Heather
**Origin Language:** English

Heaven
**Meaning:** Heaven
**Origin Language:** English

Hecate | Hekate
**Also:** Hecuba
**Meaning:** Long After / Far Away
**Origin Language:** Ancient Greek

Heidella | Heidel, Heidela, Heidelle
**Also:** Heidi | Heida, Heide, Heidie,
Heidy
**Meaning:** Of The Noble Sort
**Origin Language:** Ancient Germanic

Helda
**Meaning:** Battler
**Origin Language:** Old Norse

Helen | Helin, Hellen, Hellin, Hellyn, Hellynn, Helyn, Helynn
**Also:** Helena | Heleen, Helene, Helenka, Heliena, Helina, Heline
**Meaning:** Torch
**Origin Language:** Ancient Greek

Helga
**Also:** Helgina | Helgena
**Meaning:** Holy
**Origin Language:** Old Norse

Helioda
**Meaning:** Gift Of The Sun
**Origin Language:** Ancient Greek

Hella
**Meaning:** Torch
**Origin Language:** Ancient Greek

Helle
**Meaning:** From Greece
**Origin Language:** Ancient Greek

Helmine | Helmena, Helmene, Helmina
**Meaning:** Desires Protection
**Origin Language:** Ancient Germanic

Heloise | Heloisa, Helouise, Helousia
**Meaning:** Her Holiness Extends Far And Wide
**Origin Language:** Ancient Germanic

Helvia
**Meaning:** Has Hair The Shade Of Honey
**Origin Language:** Latin

Hemera
**Meaning:** Day
**Origin Language:** Ancient Greek

Henley | Henlea, Henlee,

Henleigh, Henlie
**Meaning:** From A High Meadow
**Origin Language:** Old English

Henna | Hennie, Henny
**Also:** Henrietta | Henriett, Henriette
**Also:** Henrika | Henrica, Henrike, Henryka
**Meaning:** Sovereign Of The Homeland
**Origin Language:** Ancient Germanic

Hepsie | Hepsy
**Meaning:** My Delight Is In Her
**Origin Language:** Hebrew

Hera
**Meaning:** Heroine
**Origin Language:** Ancient Greek

Heradia
**Meaning:** Ode To A Heroine
**Origin Language:** Ancient Greek

Herais
**Meaning:** Heroine
**Origin Language:** Ancient Greek

Herlotta | Herlotte
**Meaning:** Rascal
**Origin Language:** Old French

Hermana
**Also:** Hermanda
**Meaning:** Army Woman
**Origin Language:** Ancient Germanic

Hermia
**Also:** Hermina | Hermena
**Also:** Hermione
**Meaning:** Of Hermes (Hermes Is The Name Of The Greek God Of Boundaries, Roads And Travelers, Thieves, Athletes, Shepherds, Commerce, Speed, Cunning, Wit And Sleep, Psychopomp And Divine Messenger)

**Origin Language:** Ancient Greek

Hermona
**Meaning:** Army Woman
**Origin Language:** Ancient Germanic

Herodia
**Meaning:** Ode To A Heroine
**Origin Language:** Ancient Greek

Hersilia | Hercilia
**Meaning:** Raindrops
**Origin Language:** Ancient Greek

Hertha | Hirtha
**Meaning:** Strong
**Origin Language:** Old Norse

Hestia
**Meaning:** Of House And Family
**Origin Language:** Ancient Greek

Heta | Hetta
**Meaning:** Warrior Of Battle
**Origin Language:** Ancient Germanic

Hettie | Hetty
**Meaning:** Ruler Of The Homeland
**Origin Language:** Ancient Germanic

Hilana | Hillana
**Meaning:** Anguish
**Origin Language:** Hebrew

Hilaria | Hillaria
**Meaning:** Light-Hearted / Jovial
**Origin Language:** Ancient Greek

Hilda | Hildi, Hildie, Hildy, Hylda
**Also:** Hildara | Hildora, Hildura
**Also:** Hildina | Hildena, Hildene, Hildine
**Meaning:** Battler
**Origin Language:** Old Norse

Hillary | Hilarie, Hilary, Hillarie

**Meaning:** Light-Hearted / Jovial
**Origin Language:** Ancient Greek

Hilmara | Hilma
**Meaning:** Battle Famous
**Origin Language:** Ancient Germanic

Hira
**Meaning:** Diamond
**Origin Language:** Sanskrit

Holandia | Holandiya
**Also:** Holland | Hollanda, Hollande
**Meaning:** From A Forested Land
**Origin Language:** Old Dutch

Hollis
**Meaning:** Holly Trees
**Origin Language:** Old English

Holly | Hollie
**Meaning:** Holly
**Origin Language:** English

Honey
**Meaning:** Honey
**Origin Language:** English

Honor | Honora, Honoria, Honour, Honoura, Honouria
**Meaning:** Dignity / Esteem
**Origin Language:** Latin

Honorata
**Meaning:** Esteemed
**Origin Language:** Latin

Honorina | Honorena, Honorene, Honorine
**Meaning:** Dignity / Esteem
**Origin Language:** Latin

Hope
**Meaning:** Hope
**Origin Language:** English

Hortensia | Hortense, Hortensie
**Meaning:** Gardener
**Origin Language:** Latin

Hosanna | Hosanne
**Meaning:** Deliver Us
**Origin Language:** Hebrew

Hyacinthe | Hyacintha
**Meaning:** Hyacinth (Flower)
**Origin Language:** Ancient Greek

# Chapter 35 - Names For Girls Beginning With I

Ia | Iya
**Meaning:** Flower
**Origin Language:** Swahili

Iadonia | Iadona
**Meaning:** Shining
**Origin Language:** Ancient Greek

Ianeira
**Meaning:** Ionian (The Name Of An Ancient Greek Tribe)
**Origin Language:** Ancient Greek

Ianthe | Iantha
**Meaning:** Violet
**Origin Language:** Ancient Greek

Iara
**Meaning:** Lady Of The Water
**Origin Language:** Tupi

Ibbie | Ibbi, Ibby
**Meaning:** God Is My Oath
**Origin Language:** Hebrew

Ida | Iida
**Also:** Idalia

**Also:** Idelle | Idella
**Meaning:** Worker
**Origin Language:** Ancient Germanic

Idoia | Idoya
**Meaning:** Pond
**Origin Language:** Basque

Idony | Idonea, Idoni, Idonia, Idonie
**Also:** Idunn | Idun
**Meaning:** Loves Again
**Origin Language:** Old Norse

Iesha | Ieasha, Ieashia, Ieashiah, Ieesha, Ieeshah, Ieeshia, Ieshah, Ieshia, Ihisha
**Meaning:** Alive
**Origin Language:** Arabic

Ieva
**Meaning:** Lives
**Origin Language:** Hebrew

Ignacia | Iga, Ignatia
**Meaning:** Fire
**Origin Language:** Latin

Igona
**Meaning:** Ascension
**Origin Language:** Basque

Igraine | Igraina
**Meaning:** Maiden
**Origin Language:** Welsh

Ilana
**Meaning:** Tree
**Origin Language:** Hebrew

Ilaria | Ilarie, Ilary
**Meaning:** Light-Hearted / Jovial
**Origin Language:** Ancient Greek

Ilda | Ildi, Ildie, Ildy
**Meaning:** Battler

**Origin Language:** Old Norse

Ileana | Ilenia
**Meaning:** Torch
**Origin Language:** Ancient Greek

Ilene | Ilean, Ileen
**Meaning:** Forever / Eternity
**Origin Language:** Ancient Germanic

Iliana | Ilin, Ilina, Iline, Ilinka, Iliyana, Ilyn
**Meaning:** My God Is God
**Origin Language:** Hebrew

Ilithyia | Eileithyia, Elithyia
**Meaning:** The Deliverer (In Regards To Childbirth)
**Origin Language:** Ancient Greek

Ilma | Ilme, Ilmi
**Also:** Ilmata
**Meaning:** Air
**Origin Language:** Finnish

Ilona | Ilonka
**Meaning:** Torch
**Origin Language:** Ancient Greek

Ilsa | Ilsie, Ilsy, Ilza, Ilzie, Ilzy
**Meaning:** My God Is An Oath
**Origin Language:** Hebrew

Ilyana
**Meaning:** Fragile
**Origin Language:** Arabic

Imani
**Meaning:** Faith
**Origin Language:** Swahili

Imelda
**Meaning:** Universal Battler
**Origin Language:** Ancient Germanic

Imogen | Imogene

**Meaning:** Daughter / Maiden
**Origin Language:** Old Irish

Ina
**Meaning:** Illuminate
**Origin Language:** Chamorro

Inana | Inanna
**Meaning:** Lady Of The Heavens
**Origin Language:** Sumerian

Inaya | Inaaya, Inayah
**Meaning:** Concern
**Origin Language:** Arabic

Indah
**Meaning:** Beautiful
**Origin Language:** Indonesian

India | Indie, Indy
**Meaning:** From India (English) / River (Sanskrit)
**Origin Language:** English And Sanskrit

Indiana
**Meaning:** From Indiana (United States)
**Origin Language:** English

Indira
**Meaning:** Beauty
**Origin Language:** Sanskrit

Inessa | Ines, Inesa, Inese, Inez, Ineza, Ineze, Inezza
**Meaning:** Chaste
**Origin Language:** Ancient Greek

Inga | Inge
**Meaning:** Ancestor
**Origin Language:** Old Norse

Ingra
**Also:** Ingrid | Ingerid, Ingred, Ingreda, Ingrida
**Meaning:** Beloved Of Ing/Yngvi (Ing/Yngvi Is Another Name Of The

God Freyr In Norse Mythology)
**Origin Language:** Old Norse

Inina
**Meaning:** Glimmer Of Light
**Origin Language:** Chamorro

Inka
**Meaning:** Ancestor
**Origin Language:** Old Norse

Inna
**Meaning:** Little Girl
**Origin Language:** Ancient Greek

Innis
**Meaning:** Island
**Origin Language:** Scottish Gaelic

Innogen
**Meaning:** Daughter / Maiden
**Origin Language:** Old Irish

Inola
**Meaning:** Black Fox
**Origin Language:** Cherokee

Io
**Meaning:** The Meaning Of This Name Is Lost To Time. Io Was A Princess In Greek Mythology
**Origin Language:** Ancient Greek

Iola | Iole
**Meaning:** Violet
**Origin Language:** Ancient Greek

Iolanda
**Meaning:** Violet
**Origin Language:** Latin

Iona
**Meaning:** Yew Tree
**Origin Language:** Old Irish

Ione
**Meaning:** Violet

**Origin Language:** Ancient Greek

Iradia
**Meaning:** Ode To A Heroine
**Origin Language:** Ancient Greek

Irene | Irena, Irenee, Irenka, Iria, Irina, Irine, Irini, Iryna
**Also:** Iria | Iri, Irie, Irri, Irria, Irrie, Irry, Iry
**Meaning:** Peace
**Origin Language:** Ancient Greek

Irida
**Also:** Iris | Irys
**Meaning:** Rainbow
**Origin Language:** Ancient Greek

Irma
**Meaning:** Universal
**Origin Language:** Ancient Germanic

Irmalinda | Irmalinde, Irmelinda, Irmelinde
**Meaning:** Completely Gentle
**Origin Language:** Ancient Germanic

Irmina | Irmena
**Meaning:** Universal
**Origin Language:** Ancient Germanic

Iroda
**Meaning:** Will
**Origin Language:** Uzbek

Irodia | Irodya
**Meaning:** Ode To A Heroine
**Origin Language:** Ancient Greek

Irune
**Meaning:** Trinity
**Origin Language:** Basque

Isabeau
**Also:** Isabel | Isa, Isabela, Isabella, Isabelle, Isbel, Iseabail, Isebella,

Isebelle, Isobel, Iza, Izabel, Izabel,
Izabela, Izabella, Izabelle, Izbel,
Izeabail, Izebel, Izebella, Izebelle,
Izobel
**Meaning:** God Is My Oath
**Origin Language:** Hebrew

Isadora | Isidora
**Meaning:** Gift Of Isis (Isis Is The Name
Of An Egyptian Goddess (Her Original
Egyptian Name Is Aset, Isis Is The Name
The Ancient Greeks Gave Her) She Was
One Of The Most Important Goddesses
Of Ancient Egypt)
**Origin Language:** Ancient Greek

Isaura | Isaure, Isauria
**Meaning:** From Isauria (An Ancient
Country In Asia Minor)
**Origin Language:** Latin

Iset
**Meaning:** Throne
**Origin Language:** Ancient Egyptian

Iseult | Iseut, Ishild, Isolt, Isotta,
Isyllt
**Meaning:** Ice Cold Battler
**Origin Language:** Ancient Germanic

Isha
**Meaning:** Alive
**Origin Language:** Arabic

Ishani
**Meaning:** Possessing
**Origin Language:** Sanskrit

Ishtar | Ishtara
**Meaning:** Lady Of The Heavens / Lady
Of The Sky
**Origin Language:** Akkadian

Isi
**Meaning:** Deer
**Origin Language:** Choctaw

Isla | Islay, Iyla
**Meaning:** From The Island Of Islay
(Scotland)
**Origin Language:** Scottish Gaelic

Isleen | Islene, Isleyne, Islin, Islinn,
Islyn, Islynn
**Meaning:** Dream
**Origin Language:** Irish

Ismene | Ismena, Ismeni, Ismina,
Ismine, Ismini, Izmena, Izmene,
Izmeni, Izmina, Izmine, Izmini
**Meaning:** Knowledge
**Origin Language:** Ancient Greek

Ismet | Ismat
**Meaning:** Safeguarded
**Origin Language:** Arabic

Isolda | Isolde, Izolda, Izolde
**Meaning:** Ice Cold Battler
**Origin Language:** Ancient Germanic

Isra | Israa
**Meaning:** Nocturnal Wanderer
**Origin Language:** Arabic

Italaia | Itala, Italia
**Meaning:** Young Bull / Calf
**Origin Language:** Oscan

Iva
**Meaning:** Willow Tree
**Origin Language:** South Slavic

Ivanna | Ivana, Ivanka
**Meaning:** God Is Gracious
**Origin Language:** Hebrew

Ivayla
**Meaning:** Wolf
**Origin Language:** Bulgar

Ivette | Ivet, Iveta, Iveta, Ivett,

Ivetta
**Also:** Ivona
**Also:** Ivonette
**Also:** Ivonne
**Meaning:** Yew Tree
**Origin Language:** Ancient Germanic

Ivory | Ivorie
**Meaning:** Ivory
**Origin Language:** English

Ivy | Ivie
**Meaning:** Ivy
**Origin Language:** English

# Chapter 36 - Names For Girls Beginning With J

Jaci
**Meaning:** The Moon
**Origin Language:** Tupi

Jacinda
**Also:** Jacintha | Giacinta, Jacinta, Jacinth, Jacinthe
**Meaning:** Hyacinth (Flower)
**Origin Language:** Ancient Greek

Jacira
**Meaning:** Moon Of Honey
**Origin Language:** Tupi

Jacomina | Giacomina, Giacomine, Jacomine
**Also:** Jacqueline | Jackalin, Jackalina, Jackalyn, Jacklin, Jacklina, Jacklyn, Jaclin, Jaclina, Jaclyn, Jacquelin, Jacquelina, Jacquelyn, Jaquelin, Jaquelina, Jaqueline, Jaquelyn
 **Also:** Jacquette | Jacquetta

**Also:** Jacqui | Jacki, Jackie, Jacky, Jaki, Jakki
**Meaning:** Supplanter (Wrongfully Seizes And Holds The Place Of Another)
**Origin Language:** Hebrew

Jada
**Meaning:** He Knows
**Origin Language:** Hebrew

Jade | Jaede, Jaida, Jayda, Jayde
**Meaning:** Jade
**Origin Language:** French

Jadzia | Jadsia
**Meaning:** Warrior Of Battle
**Origin Language:** Ancient Germanic

Jae | Jai, Jaye
**Meaning:** Supplanter (Wrongfully Seizes And Holds The Place Of Another)
**Origin Language:** Hebrew

Jaelana | Jailana, Jaylana
**Also:** Jailyn | Jaelin, Jaelyn, Jaelynn, Jailin, Jailynn, Jaylin, Jaylyn, Jaylynn
**Meaning:** Healer
**Origin Language:** Ancient Greek

Jaimie | Jaime, Jaimy, Jamey, Jami, Jamie, Jamy, Jayma, Jayme
**Meaning:** Supplanter (Wrongfully Seizes And Holds The Place Of Another)
**Origin Language:** Hebrew

Jalila
**Meaning:** Excellence
**Origin Language:** Arabic

Jaliyah | Jalia, Jaliya
**Meaning:** Downy (Down As In Soft Fluffy Hairs)
**Origin Language:** Latin

Jalmara | Jalma, Jalmari
**Also:** Jalmina | Jalmena

**Meaning:** Protected By The Army
**Origin Language:** Old Norse

**Jamila** | Gamila, Jameela, Jamilah, Jamileh, Jamillah
**Meaning:** Beautiful
**Origin Language:** Arabic

**Jana** | Jaana, Jan, Janna, Jannah, Janne
**Also:** Janae | Janai, Janay, Janaye
**Also:** Jane | Jaina, Jaine, Jaine, Jayna, Jayne, Janey, Janie, Jany, Jaynie, Jayny
**Also:** Janelle | Janela, Janele, Janella
**Also:** Janessa
**Also:** Janet
**Also:** Janeth
**Also:** Janice | Janis, Janys
**Also:** Janika | Janeka, Jannicke, Jannike
**Also:** Janine | Giannina, Giannine, Janene, Janina, Jannine, Jeanine, Jeannine
**Also:** Janiyah | Jania, Janiya
**Also:** Jantine
**Meaning:** Graced By God
**Origin Language:** Hebrew

**Jarmila**
**Meaning:** Dear Fierce One
**Origin Language:** Common Slavic

**Jaromila**
**Meaning:** Adored Of Spring
**Origin Language:** Common Slavic

**Jarona**
**Meaning:** She That Sings Or Shouts
**Origin Language:** Hebrew

**Jaslina** | Jaslena, Jaslene, Jasline, Jazlena, Jazlene, Jazlina, Jazline
**Also:** Jaslyn | Jaslin, Jaslynn, Jazlin,

**Jazlyn, Jazlynn**
**Also:** Jasmine | Jasmin, Jasmina, Jasminka, Jasmyn, Jazmin, Jazmine, Jazmyn
**Meaning:** Jasmine Flower / Gift From God
**Origin Language:** Persian

**Javiera**
**Meaning:** From Etxeberria (Navarre, Spain)
**Origin Language:** Basque

**Jaya** | Jaia
**Meaning:** Victory
**Origin Language:** Sanskrit

**Jayanti** | Jayanthi
**Meaning:** Victorious
**Origin Language:** Sanskrit

**Jaycee** | Jacee, Jacey, Jacie, Jacy, Jaicee, Jaicey, Jaicie, Jaicy, Jaycie
**Meaning:** Healer
**Origin Language:** Ancient Greek

**Jaydyn** | Jadin, Jadyn, Jaedin, Jaedyn, Jaidin, Jaidyn, Jaydin
**Meaning:** Thankful
**Origin Language:** Hebrew

**Jayla** | Jaylah
**Also:** Jaylani | Jaylaani
**Also:** Jaylee
**Also:** Jaylene | Jaelena, Jaelene, Jaelina , Jaeline, Jailena, Jailene, Jailina, Jailine, Jaylena, Jaylina, Jayline
**Meaning:** Healer
**Origin Language:** Ancient Greek

**Jean** | Jeana, Jeane, Jeanie, Jeannie, Jeanny, Jeany
**Also:** Jeanette | Janetta, Janette, Jannette, Jeanetta, Jeannetta,

Jeannette
**Also:** Jehanna
**Meaning:** God Is Gracious
**Origin Language:** Hebrew

Jelena | Jelene, Jelina, Jeline
**Meaning:** Torch
**Origin Language:** Ancient Greek

Jelica | Jelika
**Meaning:** Angel/Messenger
**Origin Language:** Latin

Jemima | Jemimah, Jemiymah
**Meaning:** Dove
**Origin Language:** Hebrew

Jemma
**Meaning:** Precious Stone / Jewel
**Origin Language:** Latin

Jenae | Jenai, Jenay, Jenaye
**Also:** Jenelle | Jenella
**Also:** Jenesis
**Meaning:** Origin / Horoscope
**Origin Language:** Latin

Jenessa
**Also:** Jennica
**Meaning:** Observant Blessed Phantom / Observant White Phantom (A Combination Of Jennifer And Jessica)
**Origin Language:** Hebrew And Welsh (In Combination)

Jennifer | Jenifer
**Also:** Jenny | Jen, Jen, Jena, Jeni, Jenn, Jenn, Jenna, Jenni, Jennie
**Meaning:** Blessed Phantom / White Phantom
**Origin Language:** Welsh

Jera
**Also:** Jeran
**Meaning:** Year
**Origin Language:** Old English

Jerarda | Jerrarda
**Meaning:** Spear Of Hardiness
**Origin Language:** Ancient Germanic

Jeraz
**Meaning:** Year
**Origin Language:** Old English

Jeri | Jerrie, Jerry, Jery
**Meaning:** Powerful Spear
**Origin Language:** Ancient Germanic

Jerlinda | Jerlinde
**Meaning:** Spear Of The Serpent / Spear Of Tenderness
**Origin Language:** Ancient Germanic

Jermaine | Jermaina, Jermana
**Meaning:** Sister
**Origin Language:** Latin

Jescha
**Also:** Jessa | Jess, Jessi, Jessia
**Also:** Jessalina | Jessaline
**Also:** Jessalyn | Jessalin, Jessalynn
**Meaning:** Observant
**Origin Language:** Hebrew

Jessamine | Jessamin, Jessamina, Jessamyn
**Also:** Jessamond
**Meaning:** Jessamine (Flower)
**Origin Language:** English

Jessenia | Jesenia
**Meaning:** Jessenia (Palm Tree)
**Origin Language:** Spanish

Jessica | Gessica, Gessika, Jessika
**Meaning:** Observant
**Origin Language:** Hebrew

Jessie | Jesi, Jess, Jessa, Jessi
**Meaning:** A Gift
**Origin Language:** Hebrew

**Jetta**
**Meaning:** Sovereign Of The Homeland
**Origin Language:** Ancient Germanic

**Jette | Jet, Jett**
**Meaning:** Jet Black / Jet (Aircraft)
**Origin Language:** English

**Jeunesse**
**Meaning:** Youth
**Origin Language:** French

**Jewel | Jewell**
**Meaning:** Jewel
**Origin Language:** English

**Jezebel | Jezabel**
**Meaning:** Unchaste
**Origin Language:** Hebrew

**Jia**
**Meaning:** Beautiful / Family
**Origin Language:** Chinese

**Jianna | Gianna, Jeanna, Jeanne**
**Meaning:** Graced By God
**Origin Language:** Hebrew

**Jillian | Jill, Jillie, Jilly**
**Meaning:** Downy (Down As In Soft Fluffy Hairs)
**Origin Language:** Latin

**Jindra**
**Meaning:** Ruler Of The Homeland
**Origin Language:** Ancient Germanic

**Jinny | Jinnie**
**Meaning:** Virgin / Of The Vergiliae (Vergilae Is The Name The Romans Used For The Star Constellation That Is Mostly Know Today As "The Pleiades")
**Origin Language:** Latin

**Jiraiya | Jiraya**
**Meaning:** Lightning Child
**Origin Language:** Japanese

**Jirina | Jirena, Jirene, Jirine**
**Meaning:** Farmer
**Origin Language:** Ancient Greek

**Jo | Jojo**
**Meaning:** God Will Add
**Origin Language:** Hebrew

**Joan | Joana, Joanie, Joany**
**Meaning:** God Is Gracious
**Origin Language:** Hebrew

**Joandra**
**Meaning:** Brave Warrior Graced By God (A Combination Of Joan And Andra)
**Origin Language:** Ancient Greek And Hebrew (In Combination)

**Joanna | Joann, Joanne**
**Also:** Joasia
**Meaning:** Graced By God
**Origin Language:** Hebrew

**Jobina | Jobena, Jobyna**
**Meaning:** Hated
**Origin Language:** Hebrew

**Jocasta | Jocaste**
**Meaning:** Decorated With Violet Flowers
**Origin Language:** Ancient Greek

**Jocelyn | Jocelin, Jocelina, Joceline, Jocelyne, Joscelina, Josceline, Joscelyn, Joselin, Joselina, Joselyn, Joslin, Joslina, Joslyn, Josselina, Josseline, Josselyn, Josslin, Josslina, Josslyn**
**Meaning:** Of The Goths (The Name Of A Germanic Tribe)
**Origin Language:** Ancient Germanic

**Jocosa**
**Meaning:** Lady

**Origin Language:** Old Breton

Jodene
**Also:** Jodie | Jodee, Jodi, Jody
**Also:** Jodith
**Meaning:** He Will Be Praised
**Origin Language:** Hebrew

Joelle | Joella
**Meaning:** God Is God
**Origin Language:** Hebrew

Joetta | Joette
**Meaning:** God Will Add
**Origin Language:** Hebrew

Johanna | Johana, Johanne
**Meaning:** God Is Gracious
**Origin Language:** Hebrew

Jola
**Also:** Jolana | Jolania
**Also:** Jolanda
**Also:** Jolanta | Jolenta
**Also:** Jolanthe | Jolantha
**Meaning:** Violet
**Origin Language:** Latin

Jolene | Joleen, Jolena, Jolin,
Jolina, Joline, Jolyn, Jolynn
**Also:** Jolie | Jolee, Joli, Joly
**Meaning:** Pretty
**Origin Language:** French

Jonelle
**Also:** Jonette
**Meaning:** Graced By God
**Origin Language:** Hebrew

Jonquil
**Meaning:** Jonquil (Flower)
**Origin Language:** English

Jordan | Jordana, Jordane, Jordyn
**Meaning:** Descending Flow
**Origin Language:** Semitic

Jorie | Jory
**Meaning:** Pearl
**Origin Language:** Latin

Jorja | Jorjeah, Jorjeia, Jorjia
**Also:** Jorjetta | Jorgetta, Jorgette
**Also:** Jorjina | Jorjana, Jorjeanna,
Jorjene, Jorjiana, Jorjine
**Meaning:** Farmer
**Origin Language:** Ancient Greek

Josepha | Josefa, Jozefa
**Also:** Josephine | Josefin, Josefina,
Josefine, Josephina, Jozefina,
Jozefine, Jozephina, Jozephine
**Also:** Josette | Josetta, Jozetta,
Jozette
**Also:** Josiane | Josiana, Josianna,
Josianne, Joziana, Joziane,
Jozianna, Jozianne
**Also:** Josie | Josee, Josey, Josy,
Jozee, Jozey, Jozie, Jozy
**Meaning:** God Will Add
**Origin Language:** Hebrew

Joss
**Meaning:** Of The Goths (The Name Of
A Germanic Tribe)
**Origin Language:** Ancient Germanic

Journee | Journey, Journi
**Meaning:** Journey
**Origin Language:** English

Jovana
**Meaning:** Graced By God
**Origin Language:** Hebrew

Joviala | Jovial
**Also:** Jovie | Jovi, Jovy
**Meaning:** Jovial
**Origin Language:** English

Jovita

**Meaning:** Of Jove (Jove Is An Alternate Name Of Jupiter The Name Of The Roman God of the sky and lightning)
**Origin Language:** Latin

Joy | Joi, Joye
**Meaning:** Joy
**Origin Language:** English

Joyce | Joice, Joise, Joisse, Joyse
**Meaning:** Lady
**Origin Language:** Old Breton

Juanita | Juana
**Meaning:** Graced By God
**Origin Language:** Hebrew

Judene | Judena, Judina, Judine
**Also:** Judita | Giuditta, Judit, Judite, Juditte, Judyta
**Also:** Judith | Judif, Judyth
**Meaning:** He Will Be Praised
**Origin Language:** Hebrew

Judy | Jude, Judi, Judie
**Meaning:** Praised
**Origin Language:** Hebrew

Jules | Jooles, Jools
**Also:** Julianna | Giuliana, Giulianna, Giulianne, Jiuliana, Jiulianna, Jiulianne, Juliana, Juliane, Juliann, Julianne, Julienna, Julienne
**Also:** Julie | Giulia, Jiulia, Julee, Juli, Julia, Juliya
**Also:** Juliet | Giulietta, Giuliette, Jiulietta, Jiuliette, Julieta, Julietta, Juliette
**Also:** Julissa | Julisa, Jusliska
**Also:** Julita
**Meaning:** Downy (Down As In Soft Fluffy Hairs)
**Origin Language:** Latin

Jumanah | Jumana

**Meaning:** Pearl
**Origin Language:** Arabic

June | Juni, Juny
**Meaning:** June
**Origin Language:** English

Junia
**Meaning:** Of Juno (Juno Is The Name Of The Roman Goddess Of Marriage And Childbirth) / June
**Origin Language:** Latin

Juniper | Junipa
**Meaning:** Juniper
**Origin Language:** English

Juno
**Meaning:** Young
**Origin Language:** Latin

Justice
**Meaning:** Justice
**Origin Language:** English

Justine | Giustena, Giustene, Giustina, Giustine, Jiustena, Jiustene, Jiustina, Jiustine, Justena, Justene, Justina
**Meaning:** Just
**Origin Language:** Latin

Juvela
**Meaning:** Jewel
**Origin Language:** Esperanto

# Chapter 37 - Names For Girls Beginning With K

Kadi | Kadee, Kadia, Kadie, Kady, Kaidee, Kaidi, Kaidie, Kaidy
**Meaning:** Pure
**Origin Language:** Ancient Greek

Kaetana | Kaitana, Kayetana
**Meaning:** From Caieta (An Ancient Town On The Coast Of Latium, A District Located In West Central Italy)
**Origin Language:** Latin

Kahina | Kahene, Kahine, Kehena
**Meaning:** The Fortuneteller
**Origin Language:** Arabic

Kaia | Khaia, Kya, Kyea
**Meaning:** Sea
**Origin Language:** Hawaiian

Kaieta | Kaeta
**Meaning:** From Caieta (An Ancient Town On The Coast Of Latium, A District Located In West Central Italy)
**Origin Language:** Latin

Kailani | Kaylani
**Meaning:** Heavenly Seas
**Origin Language:** Hawaiian

Kailyn | Kaelena, Kaelene, Kaelin, Kaelina, Kaelyn, Kailena, Kailene, Kailin, Kailina, Kaylena, Kaylene, Kaylin, Kaylina, Kaylyn
**Meaning:** From Cailly (France)
**Origin Language:** Old French

Kaimana
**Meaning:** Diamond / The Power Of The Ocean
**Origin Language:** Hawaiian

Kairi
**Meaning:** Sea / Nautical Mile
**Origin Language:** Japanese

Kaisley | Kaislea, Kaislee, Kaisleigh, Kaislie, Kaselea, Kaselee, Kaseleigh, Kaseley, Kaselie
**Meaning:** From A Meadow Where Cats Roam

**Origin Language:** Old English

Kaitlyn | Kaetlin, Kaitlin, Katelin, Katelyn, Kattalin, Kattalyn
**Also:** Kaitria | Kaitra, Kaitrie
**Meaning:** Pure
**Origin Language:** Ancient Greek

Kaiya
**Meaning:** Forgiveness
**Origin Language:** Japanese

Kaja
**Meaning:** The Earth
**Origin Language:** Ancient Greek

Kala
**Meaning:** Virtue
**Origin Language:** Sanskrit

Kalandra | Kalandre, Kallandra, Kallandre
**Meaning:** Beauty Of Mankind / Invoker Of Mankind
**Origin Language:** Ancient Greek

Kalani | Kahlani
**Meaning:** Heaven
**Origin Language:** Hawaiian

Kalantha | Kalanthe, Kalanthia
**Meaning:** Beautiful Flower
**Origin Language:** Ancient Greek

Kalea
**Meaning:** Joy / Happiness
**Origin Language:** Hawaiian

Kalei
**Meaning:** The Flowers / The Child
**Origin Language:** Hawaiian

Kali
**Meaning:** The Black One
**Origin Language:** Sanskrit

Kaliandra | Kaliandre, Kalliandra, Kalliandre
**Meaning:** Beauty Of Mankind / Invoker Of Mankind
**Origin Language:** Ancient Greek

Kalina | Kalena, Kalene, Kaline
**Meaning:** Viburnum Tree
**Origin Language:** Bulgarian And Macedonian (Cognates)

Kalisha
**Meaning:** Like A Noble
**Origin Language:** Ancient Germanic

Kaliyah
**Meaning:** Exalted
**Origin Language:** Arabic

Kalla
**Meaning:** Calla (Type Of Lily)
**Origin Language:** English

Kallandria | Kalandria
**Meaning:** Beauty Of Mankind / Invoker Of Mankind
**Origin Language:** Ancient Greek

Kallie | Kaleigh, Kali, Kalleigh, Kalli, Kally
**Also:** Kallina | Kallena, Kallene, Kalline
**Meaning:** From Cailly (France)
**Origin Language:** Old French

Kallista | Kalista, Kaliste, Kalliste, Kallysta, Kalysta
**Meaning:** Beautiful
**Origin Language:** Ancient Greek

Kaltrina | Kaltrine
**Meaning:** Blue
**Origin Language:** Albanian

Kalydon
**Meaning:** From Kalydon/Calydon (A Greek City In Ancient Aetolia)
**Origin Language:** Ancient Greek

Kalyna
**Meaning:** Guelder Rose (Viburnum Opulus) (Flowering Plant)
**Origin Language:** Ukrainian

Kalypso
**Meaning:** She That Conceals Herself
**Origin Language:** Ancient Greek

Kamala
**Meaning:** Lotus / Pale Red
**Origin Language:** Sanskrit

Kamalani
**Meaning:** Heavenly Child / Royal Child
**Origin Language:** Hawaiian

Kamari | Kamaria
**Meaning:** Moon
**Origin Language:** Arabic

Kamelia | Kamellia
**Meaning:** Camellia Flower
**Origin Language:** Latin

Kami | Kamia
**Meaning:** Flower
**Origin Language:** Chamorro

Kamila | Kamilla, Kammila, Kammilla
**Also:** Kamille | Kamylle
**Meaning:** Acolyte
**Origin Language:** Latin

Kamini
**Meaning:** Desirable
**Origin Language:** Sanskrit

Kamiyah | Kamiah
**Also:** Kammy | Kammi, Kammie
**Meaning:** Acolyte
**Origin Language:** Latin

Kamryn | Kam, Kameron, Kamrin
**Meaning:** Crooked Nose
**Origin Language:** Scottish Gaelic

Kanani
**Meaning:** The Beauty
**Origin Language:** Hawaiian

Kandace | Kandase, Kandee, Kandice, Kandis, Kandise, Kandyce, Kandyse
**Also:** Kandy | Kandee, Kandi
**Meaning:** Queen Mother
**Origin Language:** Cushitic

Kanna
**Meaning:** Bookmark / Greens
**Origin Language:** Japanese

Kaori
**Meaning:** Fragrance / Fragrant Weaving
**Origin Language:** Japanese

Kaprice | Kapricia
**Meaning:** Whim
**Origin Language:** Italian

Kara | Karaugh
**Meaning:** Beloved
**Origin Language:** Latin

Karenza | Karensa, Kerensa, Kerenza
**Meaning:** Love
**Origin Language:** Cornish

Karima | Kerima
**Meaning:** Generous
**Origin Language:** Arabic

Karin | Karen, Karyn
**Also:** Karina | Karena, Karene, Karine
**Meaning:** Pure
**Origin Language:** Ancient Greek

Karissa | Kharissa
**Meaning:** Kindness
**Origin Language:** Ancient Greek

Karita | Kharita
**Meaning:** Charity
**Origin Language:** Latin

Karla
**Also:** Karlina | Karleen, Karlena, Karlene, Karline, Kharleen, Kharlena, Kharlene, Kharlina, Kharline
**Also:** Karlotta | Karlota
**Also:** Karly | Karley, Karlie
**Also:** Karlynne | Karlyn, Karlynn, Kharlyn, Kharlynn, Kharlynne
**Meaning:** Has Freedom
**Origin Language:** Ancient Germanic

Karma
**Meaning:** Action / Fate / Deed
**Origin Language:** Sanskrit

Karme
**Meaning:** Shearer Of The Harvest
**Origin Language:** Ancient Greek

Karmel | Karmela, Karmella
**Also:** Karmella | Karmela
**Meaning:** Garden
**Origin Language:** Hebrew

Karmen
**Also:** Karmina | Karmena
**Meaning:** Song
**Origin Language:** Latin

Karol | Karola, Karole, Karrol, Karyl
**Also:** Karoline | Karolena, Karolene, Karolina
**Also:** Karolyn | Karolin, Karolynn
**Also:** Karrie | Carri, Kari, Karry

**Meaning:** Has Freedom
**Origin Language:** Ancient Germanic

Karsyn
**Meaning:** Rock
**Origin Language:** Scottish Gaelic

Kasey | Kacey, Kacie, Kacy, Kaycee
**Meaning:** Vigilant
**Origin Language:** Old Irish

Kasimira | Kasimiera, Kazimiera, Kazimira
**Meaning:** Destroyer Of Peace
**Origin Language:** Slavic

Kasley | Kaslea, Kaslee, Kasleigh, Kaslie
**Meaning:** From A Meadow Where Cats Roam
**Origin Language:** Old English

Kassandra | Kasandra, Kasandre, Kass, Kassandre, Kassie, Kassy
**Meaning:** Surpasses Men
**Origin Language:** Ancient Greek

Kassia | Kassiah
**Meaning:** Cinnamon
**Origin Language:** Ancient Greek

Kassidy | Kass, Kassidie, Kassie, Kassy
**Meaning:** Curly Haired
**Origin Language:** Old Irish

Kassiopeia | Kassiopea, Kassiopia
**Meaning:** Throned
**Origin Language:** Ancient Greek

Kataleya | Kattleya
**Meaning:** Cattleya (A Genus Of Orchids)
**Origin Language:** English

Katalina | Kataleen, Katalena, Katalene, Kataline
**Also:** Katalyn | Katalin, Katalynn
**Also:** Katelina | Kaitlina, Kaitline, Kateline, Kattalina, Kattaline
**Also:** Katherine | Katharina, Katharine, Katherin, Katherina, Katheryn
**Also:** Kathleen | Kathlena, Kathlene, Kathlina, Kathline, Kathlyn
**Also:** Kathlyn | Kathlin, Kathlynn
**Also:** Kathy | Kath, Kathee, Kathie
**Also:** Katica | Katika, Kattica, Kattika
**Meaning:** Pure
**Origin Language:** Ancient Greek

Katida
**Meaning:** Kitten
**Origin Language:** Esperanto

Katie | Kaitie, Kate, Katia, Katy
**Meaning:** Pure
**Origin Language:** Ancient Greek

Katla
**Meaning:** Cauldron
**Origin Language:** Old Norse

Katlea | Katslea, Katslee, Katsleigh, Katsley, Katslie
**Meaning:** From A Cat's Meadow
**Origin Language:** Old English

Katniss
**Meaning:** Katniss (Flower)
**Origin Language:** English

Katrina | Katrena, Katrine, Katrine
**Also:** Katrinel | Katrinella, Katrinelle
**Also:** Katriona | Katreona, Katreone, Katri, Katrione

**Meaning:** Pure
**Origin Language:** Ancient Greek

Katslea | Katlea, Katlee, Katleigh, Katley, Katlie
**Meaning:** From A Cat's Meadow
**Origin Language:** Old English

Kattalin | Kattalyn, Kattalynn
**Also:** Kattaline | Kattalina
**Meaning:** Pure
**Origin Language:** Ancient Greek

Kay
**Meaning:** A Short Form Of Any Of The Numerous Names Beginning With K
**Origin Language:** Various

Kaydence | Kaedence, Kaedense, Kaidence, Kaidense, Kaydense
**Meaning:** Cadence (Rhythm)
**Origin Language:** English

Kayla | Kaela, Kaila, Kailla
**Also:** Kayleigh | Kaeleigh, Kaeley, Kaelie, Kaely, Kaileigh, Kailey, Kaillie, Kailly, Kayley, Kaylie, Kayly
**Meaning:** From Cailly (France)
**Origin Language:** Old French

Kazia
**Meaning:** Destroyer Of Peace
**Origin Language:** Slavic

Keala
**Meaning:** The Path
**Origin Language:** Hawaiian

Kealoha
**Meaning:** The Loved One
**Origin Language:** Hawaiian

Keavy | Keavie, Keeva
**Meaning:** Beloved
**Origin Language:** Old Irish

Keeley | Keelea, Keelee, Keeleigh, Keelie, Keely
**Meaning:** Slender
**Origin Language:** Old Irish

Kei
**Meaning:** Intelligent / Gemstone / Congratulate
**Origin Language:** Japanese

Keighley | Keeley, Keelie, Keighlee, Keighlie, Keylee, Keylie
**Also:** Keila
**Meaning:** From Cailly (France)
**Origin Language:** Old French

Keilani | Kelani
**Meaning:** Heavenly Glory
**Origin Language:** Hawaiian

Keisha | Keysha, Kisha
**Meaning:** Cassia
**Origin Language:** Hebrew

Keithia | Keitha
**Meaning:** From The Woods
**Origin Language:** Scottish Gaelic

Kelda
**Meaning:** Spring (Of Water)
**Origin Language:** Old Norse

Kelia | Kellia, Kellya, Kelya
**Meaning:** Strife / Sociable / Church
**Origin Language:** Old Irish

Kelila
**Meaning:** Crown Of Laurel
**Origin Language:** Hebrew

Kelly | Kelee, Kell, Kellee, Kelleigh, Kelley, Kelli, Kellie
**Meaning:** Strife / Sociable / Church
**Origin Language:** Old Irish

Kelsey | Kelcey, Kelsi, Kelsie, Kelsy
**Meaning:** From Cenel's Island / From A Fierce Island
**Origin Language:** Old English

Kemina | Kemena
**Meaning:** Courage
**Origin Language:** Basque

Kendall | Kendal
**Meaning:** From A Coastal Valley
**Origin Language:** Old English

Kendra
**Meaning:** Keen And Rich
**Origin Language:** Old English

Kenina | Kenena, Kenene, Kenine
**Also:** Kenna
**Meaning:** Beautiful
**Origin Language:** Old Irish

Kennedi | Kennedie, Kennedy
**Meaning:** Ugly
**Origin Language:** Old Irish

Kenslie | Kenslea, Kenslee, Kensleigh, Kensley
**Meaning:** From Cyne's Meadow / From A Royal Meadow
**Origin Language:** Old English

Kenya
**Meaning:** From Kenya (English) / From The White (Snowcapped) Mountain (Kikuyu)
**Origin Language:** English And Kikuyu

Kenzie | Kensey, Kensie, Kenzey
**Meaning:** Beautiful
**Origin Language:** Old Irish

Keren
**Meaning:** Ray Of Light
**Origin Language:** Hebrew

Keres
**Meaning:** Spirits Of Death
**Origin Language:** Ancient Greek

Kerry | Keri, Kerri, Kerrie
**Meaning:** Dark
**Origin Language:** Old Irish

Keshia
**Also:** Kessie | Kesi, Kessy
**Meaning:** Cassia
**Origin Language:** Hebrew

Kestrel
**Meaning:** Kestrel (Bird)
**Origin Language:** English

Ketura | Ketourah, Keturah, Ktura
**Meaning:** Incense
**Origin Language:** Hebrew

Ketzia
**Meaning:** Cassia
**Origin Language:** Hebrew

Keyla | Keighla, Keila
**Meaning:** From Cailly (France)
**Origin Language:** Old French

Keziah | Kezia
**Meaning:** Cassia
**Origin Language:** Hebrew

Khadija | Khadiga, Khadijah
**Meaning:** Premature Child
**Origin Language:** Arabic

Khaleesi
**Meaning:** Female Warlord
**Origin Language:** Dothraki (Fictional Language Devised By George R. R. Martin For Use In His Fantasy Stories, Such As A Game Of Thrones)

Khalilah
**Meaning:** Friend

**Origin Language:** Arabic

Kharis | Kharys
**Meaning:** Kindness
**Origin Language:** Ancient Greek

Kharla
**Also:** Kharlene | Kharleen,
Kharlena, Kharlina, Kharline
**Also:** Kharlynn | Kharlin, Kharlyn
**Meaning:** Has Freedom
**Origin Language:** Ancient Germanic

Khary | Karey, Karie, Kary
**Meaning:** Dark
**Origin Language:** Old Irish

Khava | Chava
**Meaning:** Lives
**Origin Language:** Hebrew

Khiara
**Also:** Khiarine | Khiarina
**Meaning:** Bright And Clear
**Origin Language:** Latin

Khloe | Khloie, Kloe, Kloie
**Meaning:** Yellow-Green Springtime
Grass
**Origin Language:** Ancient Greek

Khloris | Khlorys
**Meaning:** Pale Green
**Origin Language:** Ancient Greek

Khrissy | Khrissie, Khryssie,
Khryssy, Krissie, Krissy, Kryssie,
Kryssy
**Also:** Khristen | Khrysten, Kristen,
Kristyn, Krysten, Krystin
**Meaning:** Christ / The Anointed One /
Messiah
**Origin Language:** Ancient Greek

Khristiana | Khristiane,
Khristianna, Khristianne,

Khristianne, Kristiann, Kristianna,
Kristianne, Krystiana
**Also:** Khristina | Khristine,
Khrystina, Khrystine, Kristina,
Kristine, Krystina, Krystine
**Also:** Khristy | Khrista, Khristi,
Khristie, Khrysta, Khrysti,
Khrystie, Khrysty, Krista, Kristi,
Kristie, Kristy, Krysta, Krysti,
Krystie, Krysty
**Also:** Khrizanne | Khrizanna
**Meaning:** A Christian
**Origin Language:** Latin

Khrysa | Khryssa
**Meaning:** Golden Flower
**Origin Language:** Ancient Greek

Khrysanta
**Meaning:** Chrysanthemum (Flower)
**Origin Language:** English

Khrystel | Khristel, Khristella,
Khristelle, Khrystella, Khrystelle,
Kristel, Kristella, Kristelle, Krystel,
Krystella, Krystelle
**Meaning:** Christ / The Anointed One /
Messiah (Ancient Greek) / Crystal
(English)
**Origin Language:** Ancient Greek And
English

Kia
**Also:** Kianna | Keana, Keanna,
Kiana
**Meaning:** Qiana (A Type Of Material)
**Origin Language:** English

Kiara | Keara, Keira, Kiarra, Kiera,
Kierra
**Meaning:** Dark
**Origin Language:** Old Irish

Kiele
**Meaning:** Gardenia (Flower)

**Origin Language:** Hawaiian

## Kielo
**Meaning:** Lily Of The Valley
**Origin Language:** Finnish

## Kiersten | Kierstin
**Meaning:** Christ / The Anointed One / Messiah
**Origin Language:** Ancient Greek

## Kiki
**Meaning:** Sovereign
**Origin Language:** Ancient Greek

## Kim | Kimmie, Kimmy, Kym
**Also:** Kimber | Kimbra
**Also:** Kimberlin | Kimberlina, Kimberlyn, Kymberlynn
**Also:** Kimberly | Kimberlea, Kimberlee, Kimberleigh, Kimberley, Kimberlie
**Meaning:** From Cynebald's Meadow / From The Meadow By A Royal Fortress
**Origin Language:** Old English

## Kimiko
**Meaning:** Valuable Beautiful Child
**Origin Language:** Japanese

## Kimimela
**Meaning:** Butterfly
**Origin Language:** Sioux

## Kimora | Kimura
**Meaning:** Wooded Village
**Origin Language:** Japanese

## Kinborough | Kynborough
**Meaning:** Royal Fortress
**Origin Language:** Old English

## Kincie | Kincey, Kinsey, Kinsie, Kinzey, Kinzie
**Meaning:** Royal And Victorious
**Origin Language:** Old English

## Kinga
**Meaning:** Warrior Of The Clan
**Origin Language:** Ancient Germanic

## Kinley | Kinlea, Kinlee, Kinleigh, Kinlie, Kinly
**Meaning:** Blessed Warrior / Bright Warrior
**Origin Language:** Scottish Gaelic

## Kinneret | Kineret
**Meaning:** From Near Lake Kinneret/The Sea Of Galilee (A Lake In Northern Israel) / From A Harp Shaped Lake
**Origin Language:** Hebrew

## Kinsey | Kincey, Kincie, Kinsie, Kinzey, Kinzie
**Meaning:** Royal And Victorious
**Origin Language:** Old English

## Kinslee | Kinslea, Kinsleigh, Kinsley, Kinslie, Kynslea, Kynslee, Kynsleigh, Kynsley, Kynslie
**Meaning:** From Cyne's Meadow / From A Royal Meadow
**Origin Language:** Old English

## Kira | Keera
**Meaning:** Dark
**Origin Language:** Old Irish

## Kiri
**Meaning:** The Skin Of A Tree/Fruit
**Origin Language:** Maori

## Kirsten | Kersteen, Kersten, Kerstene, Kerstin, Kirsteen, Kirstene, Kirstin, Kirstine, Kyrsteen, Kyrsten, Kyrstene, Kyrstin
**Also:** Kirsty | Kersti, Kirstie
**Meaning:** Christ / The Anointed One / Messiah

**Origin Language:** Ancient Greek

Kizzie | Kizzy
**Meaning:** Cassia
**Origin Language:** Hebrew

Klaire | Klare
**Also:** Klara
**Also:** Klarette | Klaretta
**Also:** Klarice
**Also:** Klarinda
**Also:** Klarissa | Klarisa, Klarisse
**Also:** Klaritia
**Meaning:** Illustrious / Clear And Gleaming
**Origin Language:** Latin

Klaudette | Klaudetta
**Also:** Klaudia | Klaudie
**Also:** Klaudine | Klaudena, Klaudene, Klaudina
**Meaning:** Limps / Stumbles / Wavers / Hesitates
**Origin Language:** Latin

Klazina | Klasina, Klasine, Klazine
**Meaning:** The People's Victory
**Origin Language:** Ancient Greek

Klelia | Klelie, Klely
**Meaning:** Illustrious
**Origin Language:** Latin

Klemence | Klemencie, Klemency, Klimence, Klimencie, Klimency
**Also:** Klementia | Klimentia
**Meaning:** Clemency
**Origin Language:** Latin

Kleo | Klea, Kleio, Klio, Klio
**Also:** Kleona | Kliona
**Meaning:** Glory
**Origin Language:** Ancient Greek

Kleopatra

**Meaning:** A Father's Glory
**Origin Language:** Ancient Greek

Kloelia
**Meaning:** Illustrious
**Origin Language:** Latin

Koda
**Meaning:** Friend
**Origin Language:** Sioux

Koko
**Meaning:** Night
**Origin Language:** Algonquin

Koleen | Kolene, Kolleen, Kollene, Kollina
**Meaning:** Girl
**Origin Language:** Irish

Kolette
**Meaning:** The People's Victory
**Origin Language:** Ancient Greek

Konny | Konnie
**Also:** Konstance | Konstancia, Konstanta, Konstantena, Konstantia, Konstantina, Konstanza, Konstanze
**Meaning:** Constant (Unchanging)
**Origin Language:** Latin

Kora
**Meaning:** Maiden
**Origin Language:** Ancient Greek

Koralie | Koralia, Koraly
**Also:** Koraline | Koralin, Koralina, Koralyn, Koralynn
**Meaning:** Coral
**Origin Language:** Ancient Greek

Koreen | Korie, Korina, Korine, Korinna, Korinne, Korrie, Korrina, Korrine, Korry, Kory, Korynn

**Also:** Korette | Koretta
**Meaning:** Maiden
**Origin Language:** Ancient Greek

Kornelia | Korneliya
**Meaning:** Horned
**Origin Language:** Latin

Kosima | Kosma, Kosmia
**Also:** Kosmina | Kosmena,
Kosmene, Kosmine
**Meaning:** The Universe / The Cosmos
**Origin Language:** Ancient Greek

Kourtney | Kortney, Kourteney
**Meaning:** Short Nosed
**Origin Language:** Old French

Kressida | Kreseida, Kreseyde,
Krisede, Kriseida, Kriseyde,
Krissida, Kryseida, Kryseide
**Meaning:** Golden
**Origin Language:** Ancient Greek

Kristabelle | Kristabel, Kristabella,
Kristobel, Kristobela, Kristobella,
Kristobelle
**Meaning:** Beautiful Christian
**Origin Language:** Latin

Krysia | Khrisia, Khrysia, Krisia
**Meaning:** Christ / The Anointed One /
Messiah
**Origin Language:** Ancient Greek

Krystal | Khristal, Khrystal,
Kristal, Krystelle, Krystle
**Meaning:** Crystal
**Origin Language:** English

Ksenia | Kseniya
**Also:** Ksyusha
**Meaning:** Friendly To Guests/Strangers
(Hospitable)
**Origin Language:** Ancient Greek

Kyara | Kyarah
**Meaning:** Dark
**Origin Language:** Old Irish

Kyla
**Meaning:** Slender
**Origin Language:** Old Irish

Kylie | Kiley, Kilie, Kily, Kylee,
Kyleigh, Kyly
**Meaning:** Boomerang
**Origin Language:** Nyungar

Kynthia | Kynthaia, Kyntheia
**Meaning:** Woman From Kynthos /
From Mount Cynthus (A Mountain On
The Isle Of Delos, Part Of The Greek
Cyclades)
**Origin Language:** Ancient Greek

Kyra | Kyrah
**Meaning:** Dark
**Origin Language:** Old Irish

Kyrene
**Meaning:** From Cyrene (An Ancient
Greek City) / Sovereign Queen
**Origin Language:** Ancient Greek

Kyrie | Kyrea, Kyria, Kyry
**Meaning:** Sovereign
**Origin Language:** Ancient Greek

Kythera | Kytheraia, Kytherea,
Kythereia, Kytheria
**Meaning:** From Kythira (A Greek
Island)
**Origin Language:** Ancient Greek

# Chapter 38 - Names For Girls Beginning With L

Lacey | Laci, Lacie, Lacy

**Meaning:** From Lassy (Normandy, France)
**Origin Language:** Gaulish

Lachina | Lachyna
**Meaning:** From China
**Origin Language:** English

Ladonna
**Meaning:** Chief/Ruler Of The World
**Origin Language:** Old Irish

Laelia | Lailia, Laylia, Lelia
**Meaning:** Inept
**Origin Language:** Latin

Laetitia | Latisha, Leticia, Letitia, Letizia
**Meaning:** Happiness
**Origin Language:** Latin

Laia
**Meaning:** Well-Spoken
**Origin Language:** Ancient Greek

Laine | Lainey, Lane, Laney, Layne, Leyne
**Meaning:** Wave
**Origin Language:** Estonian

Laith | Leith
**Meaning:** From A Damp Town
**Origin Language:** Scottish Gaelic

Lakeisha | Lakeshia, Lakisha
**Meaning:** Cassia
**Origin Language:** Hebrew

Lala | Lalla
**Meaning:** Tulip
**Origin Language:** Bulgarian

Laleh
**Meaning:** Tulip
**Origin Language:** Turkish

Lalia
**Meaning:** Well-Spoken
**Origin Language:** Ancient Greek

Lalita
**Also:** Lalitha
**Meaning:** Playful
**Origin Language:** Sanskrit

Lallie | Lally
**Meaning:** Babbler
**Origin Language:** Ancient Greek

Lamia
**Meaning:** Voracious
**Origin Language:** Ancient Greek

Lana | Lahna, Larna
**Meaning:** Light / World
**Origin Language:** Slavic

Landrie | Landry
**Meaning:** From A Rich Land
**Origin Language:** Ancient Germanic

Laney | Laine, Lainey, Lane, Layne
**Meaning:** Lives On A Lane
**Origin Language:** English

Lani
**Meaning:** Sky / Heaven
**Origin Language:** Hawaiian

Lara
**Meaning:** From Larissa (A City In Thessaly Greece)
**Origin Language:** Ancient Greek

Laraina | Laraine, Larayna, Larayne
**Meaning:** Famous Soldier
**Origin Language:** Ancient Germanic

Larissa | Larisa, Larysa, Laryssa
**Meaning:** From Larissa (A City In Thessaly Greece)
**Origin Language:** Ancient Greek

Lark
**Meaning:** Lark (Bird)
**Origin Language:** English

Larunda
**Meaning:** Talkative
**Origin Language:** Latin

Lashay | Lashae, Lashaye, Lashea
**Meaning:** Approvable
**Origin Language:** Old Irish

Lashonda | Lashawnda
**Meaning:** Graced By God
**Origin Language:** Hebrew

Lassie | Lassy
**Meaning:** Young Girl
**Origin Language:** English

Latasha
**Meaning:** Birthday Of The Lord / Christmas Day
**Origin Language:** Latin

Latifah | Lateefah, Latifa, Latife
**Meaning:** Kind
**Origin Language:** Arabic

Latona
**Meaning:** Forgotten
**Origin Language:** Ancient Greek

Latoya
**Meaning:** Victory
**Origin Language:** Latin

Laudine
**Meaning:** From Lothian (Scotland)
**Origin Language:** Latin

Laura | Llora, Lora
**Meaning:** Laurel
**Origin Language:** Latin

Lauraine | Lauraina
**Meaning:** From Laurentum (An Ancient Roman City That Was Considered The Capital Of Italy) / Laurel Tree
**Origin Language:** Latin

Laureen | Laurene, Laurine, Loreen, Lorene, Lorine
**Meaning:** Laurel
**Origin Language:** Latin

Laurel
**Meaning:** Laurel Tree
**Origin Language:** English

Lauren | Lauryn, Loren, Lorin, Lorrin, Lorryn, Loryn
**Also:** Laurencia
**Also:** Laurentine | Laurentina
**Meaning:** From Laurentum (An Ancient Roman City That Was Considered The Capital Of Italy) / Laurel Tree
**Origin Language:** Latin

Laurinda | Lorinda
**Also:** Lauris | Laurys
**Also:** Laurissa | Lauressa
**Also:** Laurita
**Also:** Laury | Laure, Lauri, Lori, Lorie, Lorri, Lorrie, Lorry, Lory, Lowri
**Meaning:** Laurel
**Origin Language:** Latin

Lavanya
**Meaning:** Grace
**Origin Language:** Sanskrit

Lavender
**Meaning:** Lavender
**Origin Language:** English

Laverne | Lavern, Laverna
**Meaning:** From Near An Alder Tree
**Origin Language:** Old French

Lavinia | Lavena, Lavene, Lavenia,

Lavina, Lavine
**Meaning:** From Lavinium (An Ancient Town In Latium, West Central Italy)
**Origin Language:** Latin

Lavonne | Lavone
**Meaning:** Yew Tree
**Origin Language:** Ancient Germanic

Lavra
**Meaning:** Laurel
**Origin Language:** Latin

Lawanda
**Meaning:** Of The Vandals (The Name Of A Germanic Tribe)
**Origin Language:** Ancient Germanic

Layana
**Meaning:** Radiant
**Origin Language:** Persian

Leah | Lea, Leia, Leya, Lia, Liya, Liyah, Lya
**Meaning:** Weary
**Origin Language:** Hebrew

Leandra
**Meaning:** Has The Qualities Of A Lion
**Origin Language:** Ancient Greek

Leanna | Leana, Leana, Leane, Leann, Leanne, Leeann, Liane, Lianne
**Meaning:** From A Graced Meadow (A Combination Of Lee And Anna)
**Origin Language:** Hebrew And Old English (In Combination)

Leatrice
**Meaning:** Weary Voyager (A Combination Of Leah And Beatrice)
**Origin Language:** Hebrew And Latin (In Combination)

Leda

**Meaning:** Wife
**Origin Language:** Lycian

Leelo
**Meaning:** Folk Song
**Origin Language:** Estonian

Lei
**Meaning:** Flowers / Child
**Origin Language:** Hawaiian

Leida
**Meaning:** Finder
**Origin Language:** Estonian

Leigh | Lea
**Meaning:** From A Meadow
**Origin Language:** Old English

Leighton | Layton, Leyton
**Meaning:** From A Town Where Leeks Are Grown
**Origin Language:** Old English

Leila | Laila, Layla, Laylah, Leilah, Leyla
**Meaning:** Night
**Origin Language:** Arabic

Leilani | Lailani, Lailany, Leilany
**Meaning:** Heavenly Flowers / Royal Child
**Origin Language:** Hawaiian

Leire | Leyre
**Meaning:** From Leire (A Mountain In Navarre, Spain)
**Origin Language:** Basque

Lela
**Meaning:** Night
**Origin Language:** Arabic

Lelise
**Meaning:** Admirer
**Origin Language:** Oromo

Lena | Lene, Leni, Lenka
**Meaning:** Torch
**Origin Language:** Ancient Greek

Lennon
**Meaning:** Lover / Sweetheart
**Origin Language:** Old Irish

Lennox | Lenox
**Meaning:** From Lennox (Scotland)
**Origin Language:** Scottish Gaelic

Lenore | Lenora
**Meaning:** Noble Of The North
**Origin Language:** Ancient Germanic

Leocadia | Leokadia, Leucadia, Leukadia
**Meaning:** From Leucadia/Leukas (An Ancient Greek Island Now Known As Lefkada)
**Origin Language:** Latin

Leola | Liola, Lyola
**Meaning:** Lion
**Origin Language:** Latin

Leona | Liona
**Meaning:** Lion
**Origin Language:** Ancient Greek

Leonarda
**Meaning:** Hardy Lion
**Origin Language:** Ancient Germanic

Leonce | Lionce
**Also:** Leonella | Leonelle, Lionella, Lionelle
**Also:** Leonie | Leoni, Leonia, Leony, Lioni, Lionia, Lionie, Liony
**Meaning:** Lion
**Origin Language:** Latin

Leonora | Leanora, Leonor, Leonore
**Meaning:** Noble Of The North

**Origin Language:** Ancient Germanic

Leontia | Liontia
**Also:** Leontina | Leontena, Leontene, Leontine, Liontena, Liontene, Liontina, Liontine
**Meaning:** Lion
**Origin Language:** Ancient Greek

Lera
**Meaning:** Strong Enough
**Origin Language:** Latin

Leri
**Meaning:** From Near The River Leri (Wales)
**Origin Language:** Welsh

Lesedi
**Meaning:** Light
**Origin Language:** Tswana

Lesha | Lecia, Licia, Lisha
**Meaning:** Lucky
**Origin Language:** Latin

Lesia | Lesya
**Meaning:** Defender Of Mankind
**Origin Language:** Ancient Greek

Leslie | Lesleigh, Lesly, Lessie
**Also:** Lessie | Lessy
**Meaning:** From A Garden Of Hollies
**Origin Language:** Scottish Gaelic

Lestari
**Meaning:** Eternal
**Origin Language:** Indonesian

Leta
**Meaning:** Glad
**Origin Language:** Latin

Letha
**Meaning:** Truth
**Origin Language:** Ancient Greek

**Leto**
**Meaning:** Forgotten
**Origin Language:** Ancient Greek

**Lettice | Lettie, Letty**
**Meaning:** Happiness
**Origin Language:** Latin

**Levana**
**Meaning:** Lifts Up Others And Comforts Them
**Origin Language:** Latin

**Lewella | Lewelle**
**Meaning:** Famous Battler
**Origin Language:** Ancient Germanic

**Lexi | Lexa, Lexia, Lexie, Lexy**
**Also:** Lexine | Lexena, Lexene, Lexina
**Meaning:** Defender
**Origin Language:** Ancient Greek

**Lian**
**Meaning:** Lotus / Water Lily / Waterfall
**Origin Language:** Chinese

**Liana | Lianah, Liyana, Liyanah**
**Meaning:** Tenderness
**Origin Language:** Arabic

**Libby | Libbie**
**Meaning:** My God Is An Oath
**Origin Language:** Hebrew

**Libena | Libina**
**Meaning:** Love
**Origin Language:** Common Slavic

**Liberty | Liberata, Libertie**
**Meaning:** Liberty
**Origin Language:** English

**Libi**
**Meaning:** My Heart

**Origin Language:** Hebrew

**Libitina | Libitine**
**Meaning:** Undertaker
**Origin Language:** Latin

**Liboria | Liberia**
**Meaning:** Liberated
**Origin Language:** Latin

**Liddie | Liddy, Lydie, Lydy**
**Also:** Lidzia | Lidziya
**Also:** Lieda | Lyda
**Meaning:** Noble One / Beautiful One / From Lydia (An Ancient Kingdom In Western Anatolia)
**Origin Language:** Ancient Greek

**Lila | Leela**
**Meaning:** Amusement
**Origin Language:** Sanskrit

**Lilac**
**Meaning:** Lilac
**Origin Language:** English

**Lilas**
**Meaning:** Lilac
**Origin Language:** French

**Lilibet | Lilibeth**
**Meaning:** God Is My Oath
**Origin Language:** Hebrew

**Lilit**
**Meaning:** Lily
**Origin Language:** Armenian

**Lilita**
**Also:** Lilith
**Meaning:** Demon Of The Night
**Origin Language:** Akkadian

**Lillian | Lilian, Liliana, Liliane, Lilianna, Lilianne, Lilien, Lilliana, Lilyana**

**Also:** Lillias | Lilea, Lilias
**Meaning:** Lily
**Origin Language:** Latin

Lilo
**Meaning:** Generous One
**Origin Language:** Hawaiian

Lilou | Lylou
**Meaning:** Lily
**Origin Language:** Latin

Lilura
**Meaning:** Enchantment
**Origin Language:** Basque

Lily | Lile, Lili, Lilia, Lilie, Liliya, Lilla, Lilli, Lillia, Lillie, Lilly, Lilya
**Meaning:** Lily
**Origin Language:** Latin

Lin
**Meaning:** Forest / Gem
**Origin Language:** Chinese

Lina | Leena
**Meaning:** United
**Origin Language:** Sanskrit

Linda | Lind, Linde, Linde, Lindie, Lindy
**Meaning:** Soft And Tender
**Origin Language:** Ancient Germanic

Lindita
**Meaning:** The Day Is Born
**Origin Language:** Albanian

Lindsay | Lindsey, Lindsie, Lindsy, Lindzay, Lindzey, Lindzie, Lindzy, Linsay, Linsey, Linsi, Linsie, Linzay, Linzey, Linzi, Linzie, Lyndsay, Lyndsea, Lyndsey, Lyndzay, Lyndzea, Lyndzey, Lynsay, Lynsey, Lynzay, Lynzey
**Meaning:** From Lincoln's Island / From

An Island With A Lake Colony
**Origin Language:** Old English

Linnaea | Linnea
**Meaning:** Twinflower
**Origin Language:** Swedish

Linza
**Meaning:** Soft And Tender
**Origin Language:** Ancient Germanic

Lionors | Leonors, Lyonors
**Meaning:** Lion
**Origin Language:** Latin

Lior
**Also:** Liora
**Also:** Liorit
**Meaning:** My Light
**Origin Language:** Hebrew

Liridona
**Meaning:** Desires Freedom
**Origin Language:** Albanian

Liron
**Meaning:** A Song For Me
**Origin Language:** Hebrew

Lisa | Leesa, Leese, Liesa, Liese, Lise
**Also:** Lisabet | Lizabet
**Meaning:** God Is My Oath
**Origin Language:** Hebrew

Lisanne | Lysanne
**Meaning:** God Is My Oath And I Am Gracious (A Combination Of Anna And Lisa)
**Origin Language:** Hebrew

Lisavet | Lizavet
**Also:** Lisbet | Lisbeta, Lizbet, Lizbeta
**Also:** Lisbeth | Lizbeth
**Also:** Lisette | Lizette, Lysette,

**Lyzette**
**Meaning:** God Is My Oath
**Origin Language:** Hebrew

**Lisha | Lecia, Leesha, Leesha, Leisha, Leisha, Lesia, Letia, Lisha**
**Meaning:** Like A Noble
**Origin Language:** Ancient Germanic

**Lissa | Lissah**
**Meaning:** Bee
**Origin Language:** Ancient Greek

**Lisvet | Lisveta, Lizvet, Lizveta**
**Meaning:** God Is My Oath
**Origin Language:** Hebrew

**Lita**
**Meaning:** Glad
**Origin Language:** Latin

**Livia | Liv, Livie, Livvie, Livvy, Livy**
**Meaning:** Olive Tree
**Origin Language:** Latin

**Liviana | Livie, Livy**
**Meaning:** Envious
**Origin Language:** Latin

**Livnah | Livna**
**Also:** Livnath | Livnat
**Meaning:** Transparency
**Origin Language:** Hebrew

**Liza**
**Also:** Lizzy | Liz, Lizzie
**Meaning:** God Is My Oath
**Origin Language:** Hebrew

**Llewella | Llewela**
**Meaning:** Of Lugus And Belenos (Lugus And Belenos Are The Names Of Two Celtic Gods)
**Origin Language:** Ancient Celtic

**Loane**
**Meaning:** Light
**Origin Language:** Old Breton

**Lochana**
**Meaning:** The Eye
**Origin Language:** Sanskrit

**Loes**
**Meaning:** Famous Battler
**Origin Language:** Ancient Germanic

**Logan**
**Meaning:** From A Little Hollow
**Origin Language:** Old English

**Lois**
**Meaning:** Most Desirable
**Origin Language:** Ancient Greek

**Lokelani**
**Meaning:** Little Red Rose
**Origin Language:** Hawaiian

**Lola**
**Also:** Lolicia
**Also:** Lolita
**Meaning:** Sorrows
**Origin Language:** Spanish

**London | Londyn**
**Meaning:** From London (English) / From A Place That Floods (Ancient Celtic)
**Origin Language:** English And Ancient Celtic

**Lordita**
**Meaning:** Laurel
**Origin Language:** Latin

**Lorea | Loria**
**Meaning:** Flower
**Origin Language:** Basque

**Loredana**

**Meaning:** From Loreo (Italy)
**Origin Language:** Latin

Lorelei | Lorelai, Loreley
**Meaning:** Waits By The Rock
**Origin Language:** Ancient Germanic

Lorelle | Laurelle
**Meaning:** Laurel Tree
**Origin Language:** English

Lorena | Lorina
**Also:** Lorenza
**Meaning:** From Laurentum (An Ancient Roman City That Was Considered The Capital Of Italy) / Laurel Tree
**Origin Language:** Latin

Loretta | Lauretta, Laurette, Lorette
**Meaning:** Laurel
**Origin Language:** Latin

Lorna
**Meaning:** From Lorne (Scotland)
**Origin Language:** Scottish Gaelic

Lorraine | Loraina, Loraine, Lorainna, Lorainne, Lorayna, Lorayne, Lorraina
**Meaning:** Famous Soldier
**Origin Language:** Ancient Germanic

Lottie | Lotta, Lotte, Lotti, Lotty
**Meaning:** Has Freedom
**Origin Language:** Ancient Germanic

Lotus
**Meaning:** Lotus
**Origin Language:** English

Lou
**Also:** Louise | Louisa, Louiza, Louize, Luisa, Luise, Luiza
**Also:** Louisette | Louisetta
**Meaning:** Famous Battler

**Origin Language:** Ancient Germanic

Lourdes | Lorda, Lordes
**Meaning:** Laurel
**Origin Language:** Latin

Lova
**Meaning:** Famous Battler
**Origin Language:** Ancient Germanic

Love
**Meaning:** Love
**Origin Language:** English

Lovise | Lovis, Lovisa, Lovys
**Meaning:** Famous Battler
**Origin Language:** Ancient Germanic

Luanne | Louanna, Louanne, Luana, Luann, Luanna
**Meaning:** Graceful Famous Battler (A Combination Of Louise And Anne)
**Origin Language:** Ancient Germanic And Hebrew (In Combination)

Lucasta
**Meaning:** Pure Light
**Origin Language:** Latin

Lucette | Lucetta
**Also:** Luciana | Lucianna, Luciene, Lucienne
**Also:** Lucille | Lucila, Lucile, Lucilia, Lucilla
**Also:** Lucinda | Lucinde
**Also:** Lucine | Louscine, Lousin, Lousina, Lousine, Lousyna, Lousyne, Lucina, Lucyna, Lucyne
**Meaning:** Light
**Origin Language:** Latin

Lucretia | Lucrecia, Lucrezia
**Meaning:** Lucrative
**Origin Language:** Latin

Lucy | Luce, Lucia, Lucie

**Meaning:** Light
**Origin Language:** Latin

Luella | Louella
**Also:** Luigina | Louigia, Louigina, Louigine, Luigia, Luigine
**Also:** Luisella | Louisella, Louiselle, Luiselle
**Also:** Luisine | Louisina, Louisine, Luisina
**Also:** Luisita | Louisita
**Also:** Lula
**Meaning:** Famous Battler
**Origin Language:** Ancient Germanic

Lulu
**Meaning:** Pearls
**Origin Language:** Arabic

Lumi
**Meaning:** Snow
**Origin Language:** Finnish

Luna | Louna, Lunah
**Meaning:** The Moon
**Origin Language:** Latin

Lunette | Lunete, Lunett
**Meaning:** Idol
**Origin Language:** Welsh

Lusine
**Meaning:** The Moon
**Origin Language:** Armenian

Luvenia | Luvinia
**Meaning:** From Lavinium (An Ancient Town In Latium, West Central Italy)
**Origin Language:** Latin

Lux
**Also:** Luzia | Luz
**Meaning:** Light
**Origin Language:** Latin

Lyanna | Lyana, Lyanne

**Meaning:** From A Graced Meadow (A Combination Of Ly (Lea) And Anna)
**Origin Language:** Hebrew And Old English (In Combination)

Lydia | Lidia, Lidiya
**Meaning:** Noble One / Beautiful One / From Lydia (An Ancient Kingdom In Western Anatolia)
**Origin Language:** Ancient Greek

Lyla | Lilah, Lylah
**Meaning:** Night
**Origin Language:** Arabic

Lynette | Linet, Linette, Linnet, Linnette, Lynet, Lynnet, Lynnette
**Meaning:** Idol
**Origin Language:** Welsh

Lynn | Lin, Linn, Linnie, Linny, Lyn
**Also:** Lynna | Linna
**Meaning:** Soft And Tender
**Origin Language:** Ancient Germanic

Lyonora | Leonora, Lionora
**Meaning:** Lion
**Origin Language:** Latin

Lyra
**Meaning:** Lyre
**Origin Language:** Latin

Lyric | Lyrica, Lyrique
**Meaning:** Lyric / Poem
**Origin Language:** Latin

Lysa
**Meaning:** God Is My Oath
**Origin Language:** Hebrew

Lysandra | Lisandra
**Meaning:** Liberator
**Origin Language:** Ancient Greek

Lyssa | Lissa
**Meaning:** Rage
**Origin Language:** Ancient Greek

# Chapter 39 - Names For Girls Beginning With M

Mabel | Mabella, Mabelle, Mable
**Meaning:** Lovable
**Origin Language:** Latin

Macaria
**Meaning:** Blessed
**Origin Language:** Ancient Greek

Mackenzie | Mackenzy, Mckenzie, Mckenzy
**Meaning:** Beautiful
**Origin Language:** Old Irish

Macy | Macey, Maci, Macie
**Meaning:** Unknown Meaning (Latin) / Mace (English)
**Origin Language:** Latin And English

Madara
**Meaning:** Madara (A Type Of Flower Known As Bedstraw In English)
**Origin Language:** Latvian

Maddison | Maddie, Maddy, Madison, Madisyn, Madyson
**Meaning:** Mighty Battler
**Origin Language:** Ancient Germanic

Madeleine | Madalena, Madalin, Madalina, Madalyn, Maddalena, Madelaina, Madelaine, Madelin, Madelina, Madeline, Madelon, Madelyn, Madelynn, Madilin, Madilina, Madilyn, Madilynn, Madlenka, Madlin, Madlina,

Madlyn, Madolin, Madolina, Madoline, Madolyn
**Meaning:** Of Magdala (A Village On The Sea Of Galilee)
**Origin Language:** Ancient Greek

Madina | Madinah, Madine, Medina, Medine
**Meaning:** The City
**Origin Language:** Arabic

Madonna | Madona
**Meaning:** My Lady
**Origin Language:** Italian

Mae | Mai, May
**Meaning:** May (As In The Month)
**Origin Language:** English

Maeleth
**Meaning:** Lyre
**Origin Language:** Hebrew

Maelle | Maela, Maelie, Maella, Maelly, Maely
**Meaning:** Noble
**Origin Language:** Old Breton

Maelys | Mailys, Maylis
**Meaning:** Mother Of The Lily (Occitan) / From Maylis (A Commune In France) (French)
**Origin Language:** Occitan And French

Maeva
**Meaning:** Welcome
**Origin Language:** Tahitian

Maeve | Maev, Mave, Meave
**Also:** Maeveen | Maevena, Maevene, Maevina, Maevine
**Meaning:** Intoxicating
**Origin Language:** Old Irish

Magali | Magalie, Magaly
**Also:** Magda

**Also:** Magdalena | Magdalen, Magdalene, Magdalina, Magdaline, Magdalini
**Also:** Magdalyn | Magdalin, Magdalynn
**Meaning:** Of Magdala (A Village On The Sea Of Galilee)
**Origin Language:** Ancient Greek

Maggie | Maggy
**Meaning:** Pearl
**Origin Language:** Latin

Magnolia
**Meaning:** Magnolia
**Origin Language:** English

Maha
**Meaning:** Oryx (A Variety Of Antelope)
**Origin Language:** Arabic

Mahala | Mahalia
**Meaning:** Sick / Weak
**Origin Language:** Hebrew

Mahine | Mahin, Mahina
**Meaning:** Related To The Moon
**Origin Language:** Persian

Maia | Maya, Mya, Myah
**Meaning:** Lady / Mother
**Origin Language:** Ancient Greek

Maialen
**Meaning:** Of Magdala (A Village On The Sea Of Galilee)
**Origin Language:** Ancient Greek

Maiana
**Meaning:** Flower
**Origin Language:** Chamorro

Maiara
**Meaning:** Great Grandmother
**Origin Language:** Tupi

Maie
**Meaning:** Rebellious
**Origin Language:** Hebrew

Mairead | Maighread
**Meaning:** Pearl
**Origin Language:** Latin

Mairwen
**Meaning:** Blessed Rebellion / White Rebellion (A Combination Of Mary And Gwen)
**Origin Language:** Hebrew And Old Welsh (In Combination)

Maisie | Maisi, Maisy, Maizi, Maizie, Maizy
**Meaning:** Pearl
**Origin Language:** Latin

Maitena
**Meaning:** Darling
**Origin Language:** Basque

Makala
**Meaning:** Myrtle
**Origin Language:** Hawaiian

Makana
**Meaning:** Gift
**Origin Language:** Hawaiian

Makara
**Meaning:** January
**Origin Language:** Khmer

Makayla | Mckayla
**Meaning:** "Who Is Like God?"
**Origin Language:** Hebrew

Makeda
**Meaning:** Greatness
**Origin Language:** Ethiopic

Makena
**Meaning:** Happy One
**Origin Language:** Kikuyu

**Mala**
**Meaning:** Necklace
**Origin Language:** Sanskrit

**Malaia | Malaya, Malayah, Maliya, Maliyah**
**Meaning:** Independent
**Origin Language:** Tagalog

**Malaika**
**Meaning:** Angel
**Origin Language:** Swahili

**Malandra**
**Meaning:** Beauty Of Mankind / Invoker Of Mankind
**Origin Language:** Ancient Greek

**Malani | Malana**
**Meaning:** Buoyant
**Origin Language:** Hawaiian

**Malasintha | Millisintha**
**Meaning:** Strong Worker
**Origin Language:** Ancient Germanic

**Malee**
**Meaning:** Flower
**Origin Language:** Thai

**Malena | Malene, Malin, Malina, Maline, Malyn, Malynn**
**Meaning:** Of Magdala (A Village On The Sea Of Galilee)
**Origin Language:** Ancient Greek

**Malentha | Malantha, Melantha, Melentha**
**Meaning:** Darkness
**Origin Language:** Ancient Greek

**Mali**
**Meaning:** Jasmine Flower
**Origin Language:** Thai

**Malia | Maleah**
**Meaning:** Rebellious
**Origin Language:** Hebrew

**Malila**
**Meaning:** Salmon Swimming Fast Up A Rippling Stream
**Origin Language:** Miwok

**Malina | Maline**
**Meaning:** Raspberry
**Origin Language:** Slavic

**Malinalli**
**Meaning:** Grass
**Origin Language:** Nahuatl

**Malinda**
**Meaning:** Darkness
**Origin Language:** Ancient Greek

**Malini**
**Meaning:** Fragrant
**Origin Language:** Sanskrit

**Mallory | Mallorie**
**Meaning:** Unfortunate
**Origin Language:** Old French

**Malvina | Malvena**
**Meaning:** Has Smooth Brows
**Origin Language:** Scottish Gaelic

**Malvolia**
**Meaning:** Ill-Willed
**Origin Language:** Italian

**Malwina | Malwena**
**Meaning:** Has Smooth Brows
**Origin Language:** Scottish Gaelic

**Malynn | Malin, Malyn**
**Meaning:** Raspberry
**Origin Language:** Slavic

**Manaia**
**Meaning:** The Manaia (A Mythological

Creature In Maori Culture)
**Origin Language:** Maori

Mandica
**Meaning:** Of Magdala (A Village On The Sea Of Galilee)
**Origin Language:** Ancient Greek

Mandy | Manda, Mandee, Mandi, Mandie
**Meaning:** Worthy Of Love
**Origin Language:** Latin

Manuela | Manuella, Manuelle
**Also:** Manuelita
**Meaning:** God Is With Us
**Origin Language:** Hebrew

Mara | Mahra, Marah
**Meaning:** Rebellious
**Origin Language:** Hebrew

Maral
**Meaning:** Deer
**Origin Language:** Mongolian And Armenian And Azerbaijani (Cognates)

Maraline | Maralena, Maralene, Maralina
**Also:** Maralyn | Maralin, Maralynn
**Meaning:** Rebellious
**Origin Language:** Hebrew

Marama
**Meaning:** Moon
**Origin Language:** Maori

Marcela | Marsela
**Also:** Marceline | Marcelena, Marcelene, Marcelina, Marcellena, Marcellene, Marcellina, Marcelline, Marcellyn, Marcelyn
**Also:** Marcellette | Marcelletta
**Also:** Marcia | Marci, Marcie, Marcy, Marsha

**Also:** Marciana | Marciane
**Also:** Maren
**Meaning:** Of Mars (Mars Is The Name Of The Roman God Of War, Guardian Of Agriculture And The Roman People)
**Origin Language:** Latin

Margalita | Margalit
**Meaning:** Pearl
**Origin Language:** Hebrew

Marganita
**Meaning:** Marganita (A Flower Known As The Scarlet Pimpernel In English)
**Origin Language:** Hebrew

Margaret | Margareeta, Margareta, Margarete, Margaretha, Margarethe, Margaretta, Margarit, Margarita, Margherita
**Also:** Margot | Margaux, Margo
**Also:** Margreet | Margit, Margita, Margitta, Margret, Margrete, Margrethe, Margriet, Margrit
**Also:** Marguerite | Marguerita
**Meaning:** Pearl (Latin)
**Origin Language:** Latin

Mari
**Meaning:** Real Logic / Genuine Village
**Origin Language:** Japanese

Mariabella
**Meaning:** Rebellious Beauty (A Combination Of Marie And Bella)
**Origin Language:** Hebrew And Latin (In Combination)

Mariah | Marriah
**Also:** Mariamne | Mariamni
**Meaning:** Rebellious
**Origin Language:** Hebrew

Marian | Marianne
**Meaning:** Rebel Of Grace (A Combination Of Maria And Anne)

**Origin Language:** Hebrew

Marianela | Marianella, Marianelle
**Meaning:** Rebellious
**Origin Language:** Hebrew

Mariangela
**Meaning:** Angel Of Rebellion (A Combination Of Marie And Angela)
**Origin Language:** Hebrew And Latin (In Combination)

Marianita
**Also:** Marianna | Mariana, Mariann, Marianne, Mariyana
**Meaning:** Rebel Of Grace (A Combination Of Maria And Anita/Anna)
**Origin Language:** Hebrew

Marice | Marise, Maryce, Maryse
**Meaning:** Rebellious
**Origin Language:** Hebrew

Maricela | Marisela
**Meaning:** Aimless Battling Rebel (A Combination Of Marie And Celia)
**Origin Language:** Latin And Hebrew (In Combination)

Marie | Mahree, Mahri, Maree, Mari, Maria, Marya, Marye
**Meaning:** Rebellious
**Origin Language:** Hebrew

Mariel
**Meaning:** Bright Sea
**Origin Language:** Old Irish

Marielle | Mariella, Marriel, Marriela
**Also:** Mariette | Mariet, Marieta, Marietta
**Meaning:** Rebellious
**Origin Language:** Hebrew

Marigold

**Meaning:** Golden Rebel (A Combination Of Marie And Gold) (Also Marigold (Flower))
**Origin Language:** English And Hebrew (In Combination)

Marika | Marica, Marike, Mariyka
**Meaning:** Rebellious
**Origin Language:** Hebrew

Marilena
**Meaning:** Torch Of A Rebel (A Combination Of Marie And Helena)
**Origin Language:** Ancient Greek And Hebrew (In Combination)

Marilou | Marilu, Marylou, Marylu
**Meaning:** Famous Battling Rebel (A Combination Of Marie And Louise)
**Origin Language:** Ancient Germanic And Hebrew (In Combination)

Marilyn | Marilin, Marilina, Marilynn, Marylin, Marylina, Marylyn
**Meaning:** Rebellious
**Origin Language:** Hebrew

Marina | Marena, Maryna
**Meaning:** Of Mars (Mars Is The Name Of The Roman God Of War, Guardian Of Agriculture And The Roman People)
**Origin Language:** Latin

Marinda | Marinde
**Meaning:** Admirable
**Origin Language:** Latin

Marinelle | Marinela, Marinella
**Also:** Marinette
**Meaning:** Of Mars (Mars Is The Name Of The Roman God Of War, Guardian Of Agriculture And The Roman People)
**Origin Language:** Latin

Mariona | Marion, Marriona
**Meaning:** Rebellious

**Origin Language:** Hebrew

Maris
**Meaning:** Of The Sea
**Origin Language:** Latin

Mariska | Marisca
**Meaning:** Rebellious
**Origin Language:** Hebrew

Marisol | Mariasol
**Meaning:** Sun Of Maria (A Combination Of Marie And Sol, The Spanish Word For Sun)
**Origin Language:** Hebrew And Spanish (In Combination)

Marissa | Marisa
**Meaning:** Famous Battling Rebel (A Combination Of Marie And Louise)
**Origin Language:** Ancient Germanic And Hebrew (In Combination)

Maristela | Maristella
**Meaning:** Rebellious Star (A Combination Of Marie And Stella)
**Origin Language:** Hebrew And Latin (In Combination)

Marit
**Meaning:** Pearl
**Origin Language:** Latin

Marita | Maritta
**Also:** Maritza | Maritsa
**Meaning:** Rebellious
**Origin Language:** Hebrew

Marjory | Margaerie, Margaery, Margerie, Margery, Marjorie
**Meaning:** Pearl
**Origin Language:** Latin

Marla
**Also:** Marlene | Marleen, Marlen, Marlena, Marlina, Marline

**Meaning:** Rebellious One From Magdala (A Village On The Sea Of Galilee) (A Combination Of Marie And Magdalene)
**Origin Language:** Ancient Greek And Hebrew (In Combination)

Marley | Marlea, Marlee, Marleigh, Marlie, Marly
**Meaning:** From A Pleasant Woodland
**Origin Language:** Old English

Marlina | Marlena, Marlene, Marline
**Meaning:** Citadel On The Sea
**Origin Language:** Welsh

Marlowe | Marlow
**Meaning:** From Near The Remnants Of A Lake
**Origin Language:** Old English

Marni | Marna, Marnie, Marny
**Meaning:** Of Mars (Mars Is The Name Of The Roman God Of War, Guardian Of Agriculture And The Roman People)
**Origin Language:** Latin

Marquita
**Meaning:** Marquis (A Noble Title)
**Origin Language:** English

Marsaili
**Meaning:** Of Mars (Mars Is The Name Of The Roman God Of War, Guardian Of Agriculture And The Roman People)
**Origin Language:** Latin

Marta
**Also:** Martha
**Meaning:** The Lady
**Origin Language:** Old Aramaic

Martina | Martine, Martyna, Martyne
**Meaning:** Of Mars (Mars Is The Name Of The Roman God Of War, Guardian Of Agriculture And The Roman People)

**Origin Language:** Latin

Marwen
**Also:** Marwenna | Marwena
**Meaning:** White Sea (Breton) / Maiden (Old Cornish)
**Origin Language:** Breton And Old Cornish

Mary | Mhairi
**Meaning:** Rebellious
**Origin Language:** Hebrew

Maryanne | Maryana, Maryann
**Meaning:** Rebel Of Grace (A Combination Of Mary And Anne)
**Origin Language:** Hebrew

Maryla
**Meaning:** Rebellious
**Origin Language:** Hebrew

Marzanna
**Meaning:** Rebel Of Grace (A Combination Of Mary And Anna)
**Origin Language:** Hebrew

Marzena
**Meaning:** Pearl
**Origin Language:** Latin

Marzia
**Meaning:** Of Mars (Mars Is The Name Of The Roman God Of War, Guardian Of Agriculture And The Roman People)
**Origin Language:** Latin

Matea | Mattea
**Also:** Mathea | Mathia
**Meaning:** Gift Of God
**Origin Language:** Hebrew

Matilda | Mathilda, Mathilde, Mathildis, Matild, Matilde, Matylda
**Meaning:** Mighty Battler
**Origin Language:** Ancient Germanic

Matleena | Matlena, Matlina
**Meaning:** Of Magdala (A Village On The Sea Of Galilee)
**Origin Language:** Ancient Greek

Matriona | Matryona
**Also:** Matrona
**Meaning:** Matron
**Origin Language:** Latin

Maude | Maud, Maudie, Maudy
**Meaning:** Mighty Battler
**Origin Language:** Ancient Germanic

Maura
**Meaning:** From Mauretania (An Ancient Kingdom On The Coast Of North West Africa)
**Origin Language:** Latin

Maureen | Maurene, Maurine
**Meaning:** Rebellious
**Origin Language:** Hebrew

Mauricette
**Also:** Maurizia
**Meaning:** From Mauretania (An Ancient Kingdom On The Coast Of North West Africa)
**Origin Language:** Latin

Mavis
**Meaning:** Mavis (Bird)
**Origin Language:** English

Maxima | Maxema
**Also:** Maximilienne | Maximiliana, Maximiliane, Maximilienna
**Also:** Maxine | Max, Maxene, Maxi, Maxie
**Meaning:** The Greatest
**Origin Language:** Latin

Maybelle
**Also:** Maybelline | Maybellena, Maybellene, Maybellin, Maybellina,

Maybellyn
**Meaning:** Lovable
**Origin Language:** Latin

Maylea
**Meaning:** Wildflower
**Origin Language:** Hawaiian

Mayra
**Meaning:** Rebellious
**Origin Language:** Hebrew

Maytal | Meital
**Meaning:** Dew Drop
**Origin Language:** Hebrew

Mckenna | Makenna
**Meaning:** Beautiful
**Origin Language:** Old Irish

Medeia | Medea, Media
**Also:** Medora
**Meaning:** Ruler
**Origin Language:** Ancient Greek

Megaera | Megaira
**Meaning:** Envious
**Origin Language:** Ancient Greek

Megan | Maegan, Maeghan,
Meagan, Meaghan, Meg, Megane,
Meggie, Meggy, Meghan, Meghann
**Meaning:** Pearl
**Origin Language:** Latin

Mei
**Meaning:** Beautiful / Chinese Plum
**Origin Language:** Chinese

Meilin
**Meaning:** Plum Jade
**Origin Language:** Chinese

Meira | Meiri
**Meaning:** Light Giver
**Origin Language:** Hebrew

Meiriona | Mairiona, Mariona,
Maryona
**Meaning:** Of Mars (Mars Is The Name
Of The Roman God Of War, Guardian
Of Agriculture And The Roman People)
**Origin Language:** Latin

Meirit
**Meaning:** Light Giver
**Origin Language:** Hebrew

Melaina | Melaena, Melaene,
Melaine
**Also:** Melanie | Melania, Melaniya,
Melany, Mellonie, Mellony
**Meaning:** Darkness
**Origin Language:** Ancient Greek

Melba
**Meaning:** From A Mill Near A Stream
**Origin Language:** Old English

Melcha | Milcah, Milkah
**Meaning:** Queen
**Origin Language:** Hebrew

Melesine | Melesina
**Meaning:** Strong Worker
**Origin Language:** Ancient Germanic

Melete
**Meaning:** Meditator
**Origin Language:** Ancient Greek

Melia
**Meaning:** Honey / Ash Tree
**Origin Language:** Ancient Greek

Melika | Melica
**Meaning:** Bee
**Origin Language:** Ancient Greek

Melina | Melena, Melene, Meline
**Meaning:** Honey
**Origin Language:** Greek

Melinda
**Meaning:** Darkness
**Origin Language:** Ancient Greek

Meliora
**Meaning:** Always Improving
**Origin Language:** Latin

Melisende | Melisande
**Also:** Melisendra | Melisandra,
Melisandre, Melisendre
**Also:** Melisent | Melicent
**Meaning:** Strong Worker
**Origin Language:** Ancient Germanic

Melissa | Melis, Melisa, Meliss,
Melys, Melyss, Melyssa
**Meaning:** Bee
**Origin Language:** Ancient Greek

Melita | Melite, Melitta, Mellita,
Mellite
**Meaning:** Honey / Bee
**Origin Language:** Ancient Greek

Melody | Melodia, Melodie
**Meaning:** To Sing / Melody
**Origin Language:** Ancient Greek

Melusine | Melusina
**Meaning:** Melodious
**Origin Language:** Latin

Melva
**Meaning:** From A Bad Town
**Origin Language:** Old French

Menna
**Meaning:** Grace
**Origin Language:** Arabic

Meral
**Meaning:** Deer
**Origin Language:** Mongolian And
Armenian And Azerbaijani (Cognates)

Meraud | Meraude
**Meaning:** Emerald
**Origin Language:** Ancient Greek

Mercedes
**Meaning:** Mercies
**Origin Language:** Spanish

Mercia
**Also:** Mercy
**Meaning:** Mercy
**Origin Language:** English

Meredith | Meredeth, Merideth,
Meridith
**Meaning:** Great Lady
**Origin Language:** Old Welsh

Merel
**Meaning:** Blackbird
**Origin Language:** Dutch

Merete
**Meaning:** Pearl
**Origin Language:** Latin

Meri
**Meaning:** The Sea
**Origin Language:** Finnish

Merida
**Meaning:** From Mérida (Extremadura,
Spain) / From A Veterans' Colony
**Origin Language:** Latin

Meriel
**Meaning:** Bright Sea
**Origin Language:** Old Irish

Meriem | Meriam
**Meaning:** Rebellious
**Origin Language:** Hebrew

Merika | Merica, Merike
**Meaning:** Little Sea

**Origin Language:** Estonian

Merita
**Meaning:** Worthy
**Origin Language:** Esperanto

Merla
**Also:** Merlette | Merletta
**Meaning:** Blackbird
**Origin Language:** French

Merlina | Merlena, Merlene, Merline
**Meaning:** Citadel On The Sea
**Origin Language:** Welsh

Merrilyn | Merilin, Merilina, Merilyn, Merilynn, Merrilin, Merrilina, Merrilynn
**Also:** Merrion | Merriona
**Meaning:** Rebellious
**Origin Language:** Hebrew

Merryn | Meryn
**Meaning:** White Sea (Breton) / Maiden (Old Cornish)
**Origin Language:** Breton And Old Cornish

Meryl
**Meaning:** Bright Sea
**Origin Language:** Old Irish

Mia | Mie, Miia, Miya, My
**Meaning:** Rebellious
**Origin Language:** Hebrew

Michelangela
**Meaning:** The Angel That Asks "Who Is Like God?" (A Combination Of Michelle And Angela)
**Origin Language:** Hebrew And Latin (In Combination)

Michelle | Michala, Michela, Michele, Michalla, Michella
**Meaning:** "Who Is Like God?"
**Origin Language:** Hebrew

Michi
**Meaning:** Path
**Origin Language:** Japanese

Michlina | Michalena, Michalene, Michalina, Michaline, Michalyn, Michelena, Michelene, Michelina, Micheline, Michelyna, Michelyne
**Meaning:** "Who Is Like God?"
**Origin Language:** Hebrew

Midori
**Meaning:** Green
**Origin Language:** Japanese

Miela
**Meaning:** Sweet / Honey
**Origin Language:** Esperanto

Miguela
**Also:** Mihaila | Mihaela
**Meaning:** "Who Is Like God?"
**Origin Language:** Hebrew

Mika
**Meaning:** Beautiful Fragrance
**Origin Language:** Japanese

Mikaela | Micaela, Michaela, Michayla, Mikaila, Mikayla, Mikhaila, Mykaila, Mykayla, Mykhaila
**Meaning:** "Who Is Like God?"
**Origin Language:** Hebrew

Miki
**Meaning:** Beautiful Chronicle
**Origin Language:** Japanese

Mila | Milla
**Also:** Milada
**Also:** Milana
**Meaning:** Gracious

**Origin Language:** Common Slavic

## Milani
**Meaning:** Darkness
**Origin Language:** Ancient Greek

## Milena
**Meaning:** Torch Of A Rebel (A Combination Of Miriam And Helena)
**Origin Language:** Ancient Greek And Hebrew (In Combination)

## Mileva
**Meaning:** Gracious
**Origin Language:** Common Slavic

## Miley | Mylee, Mylie
**Meaning:** Gracious
**Origin Language:** Ancient Germanic

## Miliani
**Meaning:** Gentle Caress
**Origin Language:** Hawaiian

## Milica
**Also:** Militsa
**Meaning:** Gracious
**Origin Language:** Common Slavic

## Millicent | Mallicent, Milicent, Milisent, Millesant
**Also:** Millie | Milly
**Meaning:** Strong Worker
**Origin Language:** Ancient Germanic

## Milou | Malou
**Meaning:** Famous Battling Rebel (A Combination Of Miriam/Marie And Louise)
**Origin Language:** Ancient Germanic And Hebrew (In Combination)

## Mimi
**Meaning:** Rebellious
**Origin Language:** Hebrew

## Mimmi | Mimmie, Mimmy
**Meaning:** Desires Protection
**Origin Language:** Ancient Germanic

## Mina | Meena, Mena
**Meaning:** Azure
**Origin Language:** Persian

## Mindy | Mindi, Mindie
**Meaning:** Mind / Intellect
**Origin Language:** Latin

## Minea | Minia
**Meaning:** Queen
**Origin Language:** Ancient Greek

## Minerva | Minirva
**Meaning:** Mind / Intellect
**Origin Language:** Latin

## Minnie | Minna, Minni, Minny
**Meaning:** Desires Protection
**Origin Language:** Ancient Germanic

## Minta | Mynta
**Meaning:** Defender
**Origin Language:** Ancient Greek

## Mira | Meera, Mera
**Meaning:** The Ocean
**Origin Language:** Sanskrit

## Mirabelle | Mirabella
**Meaning:** Wonderful
**Origin Language:** Latin

## Miranda | Myranda
**Meaning:** Admirable
**Origin Language:** Latin

## Mireia | Miraya, Mireya, Miria
**Meaning:** Peace
**Origin Language:** Occitan

## Mirele | Mireille, Mirell, Mirelle
**Meaning:** Rebellious
**Origin Language:** Hebrew

Mirella | Mireilla, Mirela
**Meaning:** Peace
**Origin Language:** Occitan

Miri | Mirri
**Also:** Miriam | Mariam, Mariama, Mariami, Mariyam, Maryam, Miriama, Miryam, Myriam, Myriama
**Also:** Miriana | Mirianna, Mirianne
**Meaning:** Rebellious
**Origin Language:** Hebrew

Mirica | Mirika
**Meaning:** Peace
**Origin Language:** Occitan

Mirinda
**Meaning:** Wonderful
**Origin Language:** Esperanto

Mirit
**Meaning:** Rebellious
**Origin Language:** Hebrew

Mirna
**Meaning:** Peaceful
**Origin Language:** Serbian And Croatian (Cognates)

Mirren | Miran, Miren, Mirran
**Meaning:** Rebellious
**Origin Language:** Hebrew

Mirta | Merta, Myrta
**Meaning:** Myrtle
**Origin Language:** Ancient Greek

Misae
**Meaning:** White Sun
**Origin Language:** Osage

Missandei
**Meaning:** This Name Has No Meaning (Missandei Is A Fictional Character Featuring In The TV Series Game Of Thrones)
**Origin Language:** Invented

Missy | Missi, Missie
**Meaning:** Bee
**Origin Language:** Ancient Greek

Mistie | Misti, Misty
**Meaning:** Misty
**Origin Language:** English

Mitra
**Meaning:** Friend
**Origin Language:** Sanskrit

Mitzi | Mitzie, Mitzy
**Meaning:** Rebellious
**Origin Language:** Hebrew

Mneme
**Meaning:** Memory
**Origin Language:** Ancient Greek

Moa
**Meaning:** Mother
**Origin Language:** Swedish

Moana
**Meaning:** Ocean
**Origin Language:** Maori And Hawaiian (Cognates)

Modesta | Modeste
**Also:** Modestine | Modestina
**Meaning:** Modest
**Origin Language:** Latin

Modesty | Modestie
**Meaning:** Modesty
**Origin Language:** English

Modrona | Modron
**Meaning:** Matron
**Origin Language:** Latin

Mohana

**Meaning:** Bewitching
**Origin Language:** Sanskrit

Moira | Moire, Moyra
**Meaning:** Rebellious
**Origin Language:** Hebrew

Molina | Moline, Mollene, Molyna
**Meaning:** From A Mill
**Origin Language:** Old English

Molly | Molle, Mollie
**Meaning:** Rebellious
**Origin Language:** Hebrew

Mona | Monna
**Also:** Monat
**Meaning:** Little Noble One
**Origin Language:** Old Irish

Monet
**Meaning:** He Has Heard
**Origin Language:** Hebrew

Monica | Monika
**Also:** Monique
**Meaning:** Warns Other (Gives Advice)
**Origin Language:** Latin

Monroe | Monro
**Meaning:** From The Mouth Of A River
**Origin Language:** Old Irish

Monserrat | Montserrat
**Meaning:** Jagged Mountain
**Origin Language:** Catalan

Montana
**Meaning:** Mountainous
**Origin Language:** Latin

Mora
**Meaning:** Rebellious
**Origin Language:** Hebrew

Morag

**Meaning:** Great
**Origin Language:** Irish

Morana
**Meaning:** Death / Plague
**Origin Language:** Common Slavic

Moreen
**Meaning:** Great
**Origin Language:** Irish

Morena
**Meaning:** Dark Skinned
**Origin Language:** Spanish

Morgan | Morgaina, Morgaine, Morgana, Morgane, Morgen
**Meaning:** Bright Sea / Together With The Sea
**Origin Language:** Old Welsh

Moriah
**Meaning:** Seen By God
**Origin Language:** Hebrew

Morna
**Meaning:** Festivity
**Origin Language:** Old Irish

Morrigan | Morigan
**Meaning:** Great Queen
**Origin Language:** Old Irish

Morta
**Meaning:** The Lady
**Origin Language:** Old Aramaic

Morven
**Meaning:** From Morven (Scotland)
**Origin Language:** Scottish Gaelic

Morwen
**Also:** Morwenna | Morwena
**Meaning:** White Sea (Breton) / Maiden (Old Cornish)
**Origin Language:** Breton And Old Cornish

Moyna | Moina
**Meaning:** Alone / Monkish (Ancient Greek) / Little Noble One (Old Irish)
**Origin Language:** Ancient Greek And Old Irish

Mozelle | Mozella
**Meaning:** Rescued
**Origin Language:** Hebrew

Muirenn | Mairenn, Muireann
**Meaning:** Blessed Sea / Bright Sea
**Origin Language:** Old Irish

Muna | Mouna
**Meaning:** Wishes
**Origin Language:** Arabic

Murielle | Muireall, Muiriel, Muiriella, Muirielle, Muriel, Muriela, Muriell, Muriella
**Meaning:** Bright Sea
**Origin Language:** Old Irish

Murphie | Murphia, Murphy
**Meaning:** Battler At Sea
**Origin Language:** Old Irish

Myla | Mylah
**Meaning:** Gracious
**Origin Language:** Ancient Germanic

Myra | Myrah
**Meaning:** Myrrh
**Origin Language:** Latin

Myrcella
**Meaning:** This Name Has No Meaning (Myrcella Is A Fictional Character Featuring In The TV Series Game Of Thrones)
**Origin Language:** Invented

Myrina | Myrena
**Meaning:** Swiftly Bounding
**Origin Language:** Ancient Greek

Myrna | Muirna, Muirne, Murna
**Meaning:** Festivity
**Origin Language:** Old Irish

Myrthe | Mertha, Merthe, Mirtha, Mirthe, Myrtha
**Also:** Myrtle | Mertle, Mirtle
**Meaning:** Myrtle
**Origin Language:** Ancient Greek

Mysie | Mysey, Mysi, Mysy
**Meaning:** Pearl
**Origin Language:** Latin

# Chapter 40 - Names For Girls Beginning With N

Nadene | Nadine
**Also:** Nadia | Nadiya, Nadiyya, Nadya
**Meaning:** Hope
**Origin Language:** Common Slavic

Nadie
**Meaning:** Wise
**Origin Language:** Algonquin

Nadira
**Meaning:** Rare
**Origin Language:** Arabic

Naenia | Naenea
**Meaning:** A Mournful Song
**Origin Language:** Latin

Naiara | Nayara
**Meaning:** From Nájera (Spain)
**Origin Language:** Basque

Naida
**Meaning:** Water Nymph
**Origin Language:** Ancient Greek

Naila | Nayla
**Meaning:** Attainer
**Origin Language:** Arabic

Naima
**Meaning:** Tranquil
**Origin Language:** Arabic

Naira
**Meaning:** Eye
**Origin Language:** Aymara

Nala | Nalah
**Meaning:** Stem / Reed / Vine
**Origin Language:** Sanskrit

Nalani
**Meaning:** Calm Skies
**Origin Language:** Hawaiian

Naliaka
**Meaning:** Born During The Weeding
Season
**Origin Language:** Luhya

Nanai | Nanay
**Also:** Nanaya | Nanaea, Nanaia
**Meaning:** Lady Of The Heavens
**Origin Language:** Sumerian

Nancy | Nance, Nancie
**Meaning:** Chaste
**Origin Language:** Ancient Greek

Nanette | Nanetta
**Meaning:** Gracious
**Origin Language:** Hebrew

Naomi | Naomie, Noemi, Noemi,
Noemie, Noemy, Nohemi, Nyomi
**Meaning:** My Pleasantness
**Origin Language:** Hebrew

Narcissa | Narcisa, Narcisse
**Meaning:** Narcissus (Flowering Plant)

**Origin Language:** Ancient Greek

Narelle | Narella
**Meaning:** From Narellan (Australia)
**Origin Language:** Australian

Narine | Nareen, Narene
**Meaning:** Pomegranate
**Origin Language:** Persian

Nastasia | Nastassia, Nastasya,
Nastia, Nastya
**Meaning:** Resurrected
**Origin Language:** Ancient Greek

Natalie | Natalee, Natali, Natalia,
Nataliya, Natallia, Nataly, Natalya,
Natille
**Also:** Natalina | Natalena, Natalene,
Nataline
**Also:** Natalyn | Natalin, Natalynn
**Meaning:** Birthday Of The Lord /
Christmas Day
**Origin Language:** Latin

Natasa | Natassa
**Meaning:** Resurrected
**Origin Language:** Ancient Greek

Natasha | Natacha, Natasza
**Meaning:** Birthday Of The Lord /
Christmas Day
**Origin Language:** Latin

Natela
**Meaning:** Light
**Origin Language:** Georgian

Nathalie | Nathalia, Nathaly
**Meaning:** Birthday Of The Lord /
Christmas Day
**Origin Language:** Latin

Natisha
**Meaning:** Birthday Of The Lord /
Christmas Day

**Origin Language:** Latin

Naya | Naia
**Meaning:** Wave / Sea Foam
**Origin Language:** Basque

Nayeli
**Meaning:** I Love You
**Origin Language:** Zapotec

Nazaria | Nazareia
**Meaning:** From Nazareth (The Childhood Home Of Jesus)
**Origin Language:** Latin

Neda
**Also:** Nedelya
**Meaning:** Sunday
**Origin Language:** Bulgarian

Neela | Nila
**Meaning:** Dark Blue
**Origin Language:** Sanskrit

Neema
**Meaning:** Divine Grace
**Origin Language:** Swahili

Neilina | Nealena, Nealene, Nealina, Nealine, Neilena, Neilene, Neilin, Neiline, Neilyn
**Meaning:** Champion
**Origin Language:** Old Irish

Neith
**Meaning:** Terrible One
**Origin Language:** Ancient Egyptian

Nekesa
**Meaning:** Born During The Harvest
**Origin Language:** Luhya

Nektaria
**Meaning:** Nectar
**Origin Language:** Ancient Greek

Nelda
**Meaning:** Noble Of The North
**Origin Language:** Ancient Germanic

Nella | Nela
**Also:** Nellie | Neli, Nell, Nelle, Nelli, Nelly
**Meaning:** Horned
**Origin Language:** Latin

Nellinore | Nellinora
**Meaning:** Noble Of The North
**Origin Language:** Ancient Germanic

Nena
**Meaning:** Fire
**Origin Language:** Quechua And Aymara (Cognates)

Nephele | Nefeli
**Meaning:** Cloud
**Origin Language:** Ancient Greek

Nerea | Nere, Neri, Neria
**Meaning:** Mine
**Origin Language:** Basque

Nereida | Nerida
**Meaning:** Sea Sprite
**Origin Language:** Ancient Greek

Nerezza | Nereza
**Meaning:** Darkness
**Origin Language:** Italian

Nerina | Nerena, Nerene, Nerine
**Also:** Nerissa | Neryssa
**Meaning:** Sea Sprite
**Origin Language:** Ancient Greek

Nerys
**Meaning:** Heroine
**Origin Language:** Welsh

Nessa | Neas, Neasa, Neassa, Ness
**Meaning:** Miracle

**Origin Language:** Hebrew

Netta | Neta, Nettie, Netty
**Meaning:** Shrub
**Origin Language:** Hebrew

Neva | Niva
**Meaning:** Family Woman
**Origin Language:** Ancient Germanic

Nevada
**Meaning:** Snowcapped
**Origin Language:** Spanish

Nevaeh
**Meaning:** Heaven (Backwards)
**Origin Language:** English

Neve
**Meaning:** Bright
**Origin Language:** Old Irish

Nevena
**Meaning:** Marigold
**Origin Language:** South Slavic

Nia | Nyah
**Meaning:** Purpose
**Origin Language:** Swahili

Nicky | Nickie, Nika, Niki, Nikki
**Also:** Nicola | Nichola, Nikola
**Also:** Nicole | Nichole, Nicolle, Nikkole, Nikole
**Also:** Nicolette | Nicolet, Nicoleta, Nicoletta, Nikoleta, Nikolett, Nikoletta
**Also:** Nicolina | Nicolin, Nicoline, Nicolyn, Nikolin, Nikolina, Nikoline, Nikolyn
**Meaning:** Victory Of The People
**Origin Language:** Ancient Greek

Nida
**Meaning:** Proclaim
**Origin Language:** Arabic

Nieve | Neves, Nieves, Nives
**Meaning:** Snow
**Origin Language:** Spanish

Nigella | Nigela
**Meaning:** Champion
**Origin Language:** Old Irish

Nikeisha | Nikeesha, Nikeysha, Nikisha
**Meaning:** Cassia
**Origin Language:** Hebrew

Nikita | Niketa, Nikitha
**Meaning:** House
**Origin Language:** Sanskrit

Nilda
**Meaning:** Protected Battler
**Origin Language:** Ancient Germanic And Old Norse (Cognates)

Nima
**Meaning:** Blessing
**Origin Language:** Arabic

Nimue | Nimuë, Nymue
**Meaning:** Lady Of The Lake
**Origin Language:** Old French

Ninette
**Meaning:** Of Ani (Ani Is The Name Of An Etruscan God, Thought To Be Equivalent To The Roman God Janus, The God Of Beginnings, Gates, Transitions, Time, Duality, Doorways, Passages, And Endings)
**Origin Language:** Latin

Ninona | Nynona
**Meaning:** Gracious
**Origin Language:** Hebrew

Niobe
**Meaning:** Snowy
**Origin Language:** Ancient Greek

Nisha | Neesha
**Meaning:** Night
**Origin Language:** Sanskrit

Nissa | Nisa
**Meaning:** Sign
**Origin Language:** Hebrew

Nnenna
**Meaning:** Father's Mother (This Name Is Sometimes Given To A Child When It Is Believed That She Is A Reincarnation Of Her Paternal Grandmother)
**Origin Language:** Igbo

Nnenne
**Meaning:** Mother's Mother
**Origin Language:** Igbo

Noelani
**Meaning:** Heavenly Mist
**Origin Language:** Hawaiian

Noelene | Noelena, Noelina, Noeline
**Also:** Noelle | Noela, Noelia, Noella, Noellia
**Meaning:** Christmas
**Origin Language:** Old French

Noemina | Noemin, Noemine, Noemyn
**Meaning:** My Pleasantness
**Origin Language:** Hebrew

Nola | Nolia
**Also:** Nolene | Nolena, Nolenia
**Meaning:** Magnolia
**Origin Language:** English

Nona | Noni
**Meaning:** Ninth
**Origin Language:** Latin

Nonie | Nony

**Meaning:** Violet
**Origin Language:** Ancient Greek

Nora | Norah
**Meaning:** Noble Of The North
**Origin Language:** Ancient Germanic

Noreen | Norena, Norene, Norina, Norine
**Meaning:** Dignity / Esteem
**Origin Language:** Latin

Noriko
**Meaning:** Child Of Rule / Child Of The Ceremony
**Origin Language:** Japanese

Norma
**Also:** Normina | Normena, Normene, Normine
**Meaning:** Viking
**Origin Language:** Ancient Germanic

Nousha
**Meaning:** Sweet
**Origin Language:** Persian

Nova | Novah
**Also:** Novalee
**Meaning:** New
**Origin Language:** Latin

Nox
**Meaning:** Night
**Origin Language:** Ancient Greek

Nuala
**Meaning:** Blessed Shoulder
**Origin Language:** Old Irish

Nydia | Nidia
**Meaning:** Nest
**Origin Language:** Latin

Nyla | Nylah
**Meaning:** Surpasses All Rivals

**Origin Language:** Old Irish

Nymeria | Nimeria
**Meaning:** This Name Has No Meaning
(Nymeria Is A Fictional Character
Featuring In The TV Series Game Of
Thrones)
**Origin Language:** Invented

Nyneve | Nenyve, Nineve, Ninyve
**Meaning:** Lady Of The Lake
**Origin Language:** Old French

Nyra | Nyree
**Meaning:** From Ngaere (New Zealand)
**Origin Language:** Maori

Nyx | Nix
**Meaning:** Night
**Origin Language:** Ancient Greek

# Chapter 41 - Names For Girls Beginning With O

Oakleigh | Oaklea, Oaklee, Oakley
**Also:** Oaklynn | Oaklin, Oaklina,
Oaklyn
**Meaning:** From An Oak Tree Meadow
**Origin Language:** Old English

Oana | Oanna
**Meaning:** Graced By God
**Origin Language:** Hebrew

Obara
**Meaning:** Small Plain
**Origin Language:** Japanese

Ocean
**Meaning:** Ocean
**Origin Language:** English

Octavia | Octavie, Oktave,

Oktavia, Oktavie
**Meaning:** Eighth
**Origin Language:** Latin

Odalys | Oda, Odalis
**Meaning:** Wealthy
**Origin Language:** Ancient Germanic
And Old English And Old Norse
(Cognates)

Odelia
**Meaning:** I Will Thank God
**Origin Language:** Hebrew

Odessa | Odesa, Odesse
**Meaning:** Hateful
**Origin Language:** Ancient Greek

Odette | Odeta, Odetta
**Also:** Odilia | Odila, Odile, Odilie,
Odily
**Meaning:** Wealthy
**Origin Language:** Ancient Germanic
And Old English And Old Norse
(Cognates)

Odina | Odena
**Meaning:** The Mad One
**Origin Language:** Old English And Old
Norse (Cognates)

Ofira
**Meaning:** From Ophir (The Name Of A
Port Mentioned In The Bible Of
Unknown Location)
**Origin Language:** Hebrew

Ofra
**Meaning:** Fawn
**Origin Language:** Hebrew

Ohndrea | Ohndraia, Ohndreea,
Ohndreia, Ohndria
**Meaning:** Brave Warrior
**Origin Language:** Ancient Greek

Okelani
**Meaning:** From Heaven
**Origin Language:** Hawaiian

Oksana | Oxana
**Meaning:** Friendly To Guests/Strangers (Hospitable)
**Origin Language:** Ancient Greek

Ola
**Meaning:** Remainder Of The Ancestors
**Origin Language:** Old Norse

Olalia | Olalla
**Meaning:** Well-Spoken
**Origin Language:** Ancient Greek

Olanda
**Meaning:** From A Forested Land
**Origin Language:** Old Dutch

Olaya | Olaia
**Meaning:** Well-Spoken
**Origin Language:** Ancient Greek

Oleksandra | Oleksandria, Oleksandrina, Oleksandrine, Olexandra, Olexandria, Olexandrina, Olexandrine
**Meaning:** Mankind's Defender
**Origin Language:** Ancient Greek

Olena | Olene, Olenna
**Meaning:** Torch
**Origin Language:** Ancient Greek

Olesya | Olesia
**Meaning:** Mankind's Defender
**Origin Language:** Ancient Greek

Olga
**Meaning:** Holy
**Origin Language:** Old Norse

Olina | Oleena, Olene, Oline
**Also:** Olive | Oliveira, Olivera

**Also:** Oliveira | Oliva, Olive
**Also:** Olivera
**Also:** Olivette | Olivetta
**Also:** Olivia | Olivie, Olivy, Olyvia, Olyvie, Olyvy
**Meaning:** Olive Tree
**Origin Language:** Latin

Olrica | Olrika, Olrike
**Meaning:** Rich Heritage
**Origin Language:** Ancient Germanic

Olwen | Olwin, Olwyn
**Meaning:** Blessed Footprint / White Footprint
**Origin Language:** Welsh

Olympia | Olimpia
**Meaning:** From Olympos (Olympos Is The Name Of The Home Of The Greek Gods And The Tallest Mountain In Greece) / From A Mountain
**Origin Language:** Ancient Greek

Ona
**Meaning:** Gracious
**Origin Language:** Hebrew

Ondria | Ondra, Ondrea, Ondreea, Ondreia, Onndrea, Onndreia, Onndria
**Meaning:** Brave Warrior
**Origin Language:** Ancient Greek

Oneida
**Meaning:** Standing Stone
**Origin Language:** Tuscarora

Oona | Oonagh
**Meaning:** Lamb
**Origin Language:** Irish

Opal
**Also:** Opalina | Opaline
**Meaning:** Opal
**Origin Language:** English

Ophelia | Ofelia, Ofeliya, Ophelie
**Meaning:** She That Brings Aid
**Origin Language:** Ancient Greek

Oprah
**Meaning:** Stubborn
**Origin Language:** Hebrew

Ora | Orah
**Meaning:** Praying (Latin) / Light (Hebrew)
**Origin Language:** Latin And Hebrew

Orabella | Orabel, Orabela, Orabelle
**Meaning:** Entreated
**Origin Language:** Latin

Oralee | Oralie, Oraly
**Meaning:** Made Of Gold
**Origin Language:** Latin

Orenda
**Meaning:** Mystical Powers
**Origin Language:** Iroquois

Oria
**Also:** Oriana | Oriane, Orianna, Orianne
**Also:** Orietta | Oriette
**Meaning:** Golden
**Origin Language:** Latin

Orinda
**Meaning:** Gold
**Origin Language:** Spanish

Orinthia
**Meaning:** Golden Goddess (A Combination Of Orinda And Thia)
**Origin Language:** Ancient Greek And Spanish (In Combination)

Oriola | Oreola
**Meaning:** Made Of Gold

**Origin Language:** Latin

Orla | Orlagh
**Meaning:** Golden Princess
**Origin Language:** Old Irish

Orlanda
**Meaning:** Famous Throughout The Land
**Origin Language:** Ancient Germanic

Orlie | Orli, Orly
**Meaning:** The Light For Me
**Origin Language:** Hebrew

Orna
**Meaning:** Little Grayish-Brown One
**Origin Language:** Old Irish

Ornella
**Meaning:** Flowering Ash Tree
**Origin Language:** Italian

Orpha | Oprha, Orpa, Orpah
**Meaning:** Stubborn
**Origin Language:** Hebrew

Osha
**Meaning:** Shining
**Origin Language:** Sanskrit

Orsina | Orsena, Orsene, Orsine
**Also:** Orsola | Orsolya
**Meaning:** Bear
**Origin Language:** Latin

Orwella | Orewela, Orewella, Orwela
**Meaning:** From Near The Branch Of A River
**Origin Language:** Old English

Osanna | Osana, Osanne, Ozana, Ozanna, Ozanne
**Meaning:** Deliver Us
**Origin Language:** Hebrew

Ossia
**Meaning:** Little Deer
**Origin Language:** Old Irish

Ostara | Ostra
**Meaning:** Easter
**Origin Language:** Ancient Germanic And Old English (Cognates)

Othilda | Othild, Othilde
**Also:** Otilda | Otild, Otilde
**Meaning:** Wealthy Battler
**Origin Language:** Ancient Germanic And Old Norse (Cognates)

Otillia | Otilia, Otilie, Otily, Ottilia, Ottilie, Ottily, Ottylia, Otylia
**Meaning:** Wealthy
**Origin Language:** Ancient Germanic And Old English And Old Norse (Cognates)

Ottavia | Ottavie
**Also:** Ottaviana
**Meaning:** Eighth
**Origin Language:** Latin

Ottoline | Ottolina
**Meaning:** Wealthy
**Origin Language:** Ancient Germanic And Old English And Old Norse (Cognates)

Ourana | Ourania, Ouranie, Ourena, Ourenia, Ourenie
**Meaning:** Heavenly
**Origin Language:** Ancient Greek

Ovidia
**Meaning:** Shepherdess
**Origin Language:** Latin

Owena
**Meaning:** Well-Born
**Origin Language:** Ancient Greek

# Chapter 42 - Names For Girls Beginning With P

Pacey | Pacie
**Meaning:** Peace
**Origin Language:** Old English

Paige | Page, Payge
**Meaning:** Young Attendant (To An Important Person)
**Origin Language:** Old French

Paisley | Paislea, Paislee, Paisleigh, Paislie, Paisly
**Meaning:** From Pæssa's Meadow / From A Clearing In The Woods
**Origin Language:** Old English

Paityn | Paetyn
**Meaning:** From Pæga's Town / From A Rural Town
**Origin Language:** Old English

Palaima | Palaema
**Meaning:** Wrestler
**Origin Language:** Ancient Greek

Palesa
**Meaning:** Flower
**Origin Language:** Sotho

Palina | Palena, Palene, Paline
**Meaning:** Small / Humble
**Origin Language:** Latin

Palmira | Palmera
**Meaning:** Pilgrim / Palm Tree
**Origin Language:** Italian

Paloma | Palloma
**Meaning:** Dove
**Origin Language:** Spanish

Pamela | Pam, Pamelia, Pamella, Pamila
**Meaning:** All Sweet
**Origin Language:** Ancient Greek

Pandora
**Meaning:** All Of The Gifts
**Origin Language:** Ancient Greek

Pansy | Pansie, Panzie, Panzy
**Meaning:** Pansy
**Origin Language:** English

Paola
**Meaning:** Small
**Origin Language:** Latin

Paridis | Paridys
**Also:** Paris | Parisse, Parris, Parriss, Parys
**Meaning:** Combative
**Origin Language:** Ancient Greek

Parisa | Pari
**Meaning:** Like A Fairy
**Origin Language:** Persian

Parker
**Meaning:** Park Keeper
**Origin Language:** Old English

Parnella
**Meaning:** Mountainous
**Origin Language:** Latin

Patience
**Meaning:** Patience
**Origin Language:** English

Patrice | Patrece, Patrese
**Also:** Patricia | Patrizia
**Also:** Patritsia | Patritsiya, Patritzia, Patritziya
**Also:** Patsy | Patsie, Patzie, Patzy
**Also:** Patty | Pat, Patti, Pattie

**Meaning:** Patrician / Aristocrat
**Origin Language:** Latin

Paula
**Also:** Paulina | Pauleen, Paulena, Paulene, Pauline
**Also:** Pavica | Pavika
**Also:** Pavla | Pavlia
**Also:** Pavlina | Pavlena, Pavlene, Pavline, Pavlyn, Pavlynn
**Meaning:** Humble
**Origin Language:** Latin

Pax
**Meaning:** Peace
**Origin Language:** Latin

Peace
**Meaning:** Peace
**Origin Language:** English

Pearl | Pearle, Pearlee, Pearlie, Pearly, Perla, Perle, Perlee, Perlie, Perly
**Meaning:** Pearl
**Origin Language:** English

Peggy | Peg, Peggie
**Meaning:** Pearl
**Origin Language:** Latin

Penelope | Penelopi, Pinelope, Pinelopi
**Meaning:** Has An Eye For Weaving
**Origin Language:** Ancient Greek

Penina | Peninah, Peninna, Peninnah
**Meaning:** Coral / Pearl
**Origin Language:** Hebrew

Penny | Pennie
**Meaning:** Has An Eye For Weaving
**Origin Language:** Ancient Greek

Peony | Peonie
**Meaning:** Peony
**Origin Language:** English

Perdita
**Meaning:** Lost
**Origin Language:** Latin

Perlita
**Meaning:** Pearl
**Origin Language:** Spanish And Italian
(Cognates)

Permelia | Permela, Permella,
Permila
**Meaning:** All Sweet
**Origin Language:** Ancient Greek

Pernilla | Pernella
**Also:** Peronelle | Peronella
**Meaning:** Mountainous
**Origin Language:** Latin

Perrine | Perrena, Perrene, Perrina
**Meaning:** Stone
**Origin Language:** Ancient Greek

Petal
**Meaning:** Petal
**Origin Language:** English

Petra
**Also:** Petrina | Petrana, Petrena,
Petrene, Petrine
**Meaning:** Stone
**Origin Language:** Ancient Greek

Petrona | Petronia
**Meaning:** Mountainous
**Origin Language:** Latin

Petroula | Petroulla, Petrula,
Petrulla
**Meaning:** Stone
**Origin Language:** Ancient Greek

Petula
**Meaning:** Petunia (Flower)
**Origin Language:** English

Phaedra | Phaidra, Phaydra
**Meaning:** Luminous
**Origin Language:** Ancient Greek

Phaenna | Phainna, Phaynna
**Also:** Phaesyle | Phaesile, Phaysile,
Phaysyle, Phesile, Phesyle
**Meaning:** Shining
**Origin Language:** Ancient Greek

Pharah | Pharrah
**Meaning:** Happy
**Origin Language:** Arabic

Phemie | Phemy
**Meaning:** Well-Spoken
**Origin Language:** Ancient Greek

Pherenike
**Meaning:** Bringer Of Victory
**Origin Language:** Ancient Greek

Phillipa | Philipa, Philippa
**Meaning:** Lover Of Horses
**Origin Language:** Ancient Greek

Philomela | Philomel, Philomele
**Meaning:** Lover Of Song
**Origin Language:** Ancient Greek

Philomena | Philoumene
**Meaning:** Loved / Lover Of The Mind
**Origin Language:** Ancient Greek

Philyra | Philyre
**Meaning:** Linden Tree
**Origin Language:** Ancient Greek

Phoebe | Phebe, Pheobe, Phoibe
**Meaning:** Radiant
**Origin Language:** Ancient Greek

Phoenix | Phoinix
**Meaning:** Phoenix
**Origin Language:** English

Photina | Photena, Photene, Photine
**Meaning:** Light
**Origin Language:** Ancient Greek

Phyllida | Phillida
**Also:** Phyllis | Philis, Phillis, Phyliss
**Meaning:** Foliage
**Origin Language:** Ancient Greek

Piera
**Also:** Pierina | Pierena, Pierene, Pierine
**Also:** Pierrette | Pierretta
**Also:** Pietra
**Also:** Pietrine | Pietrina
**Meaning:** Stone
**Origin Language:** Ancient Greek

Piety | Pietie
**Meaning:** Piety
**Origin Language:** English

Piper
**Meaning:** Flute Player
**Origin Language:** Old English

Pippa | Pip, Pipa
**Meaning:** Lover Of Horses
**Origin Language:** Ancient Greek

Pipra
**Meaning:** Pepper
**Origin Language:** Esperanto

Pixie | Pixi, Pixy
**Meaning:** Pixie
**Origin Language:** English

Polina | Pola, Polena, Polene, Poline
**Meaning:** Of Apollo (Apollo Is The Name Of The Greek God Of Oracles, Healing, Archery, Music And Arts, Sunlight, Knowledge, Herds And Flocks, And Protection Of The Young)
**Origin Language:** Ancient Greek

Polissena | Polissenia
**Meaning:** Very Hospitable
**Origin Language:** Ancient Greek

Polly | Pollie
**Meaning:** Rebellious
**Origin Language:** Hebrew

Pollyanna | Pollyanne
**Meaning:** Rebel Of Grace (A Combination Of Polly And Anna)
**Origin Language:** Hebrew

Pololena
**Meaning:** Flourishing
**Origin Language:** Latin

Poloma
**Meaning:** Bow
**Origin Language:** Choctaw

Polona
**Meaning:** Of Apollo (Apollo Is The Name Of The Greek God Of Oracles, Healing, Archery, Music And Arts, Sunlight, Knowledge, Herds And Flocks, And Protection Of The Young)
**Origin Language:** Ancient Greek

Pomona
**Meaning:** Fruit Tree
**Origin Language:** Latin

Poppy | Poppie
**Meaning:** Poppy
**Origin Language:** English

Portia | Porcia
**Meaning:** Pig
**Origin Language:** Latin

**Posie | Poesie, Poesy, Posey, Posy**
**Meaning:** A Bunch Of Flowers
**Origin Language:** English

**Prairie | Praerey, Praerie, Praery, Prairey, Prairy**
**Meaning:** Meadow
**Origin Language:** Old French

**Preslie | Preslea, Preslee, Presleigh, Presley, Presly**
**Meaning:** From A Priest's Meadow
**Origin Language:** Old English

**Pria | Priya**
**Meaning:** Beloved
**Origin Language:** Sanskrit

**Pridwen | Prydwen**
**Meaning:** Fair Faced
**Origin Language:** Old Welsh

**Priscilla | Pris, Prisca, Priscila, Priscille, Priska, Priskilla, Prissie, Prissy**
**Meaning:** Ancient
**Origin Language:** Latin

**Pru | Prue**
**Meaning:** Prudent
**Origin Language:** Latin

# Chapter 43 - Names For Girls Beginning With Q

**Qeren | Querena**
**Meaning:** Horn Of An Animal
**Origin Language:** Hebrew

**Qiana | Quiana, Quianna**
**Meaning:** Qiana (A Type Of Material)
**Origin Language:** English

**Quella | Quellia, Quelle**
**Meaning:** Slayer
**Origin Language:** Old English

**Quennelle | Quennell, Quennella, Quenelle**
**Meaning:** Woman Of Battle
**Origin Language:** Old English

**Quinn | Quin**
**Meaning:** The Head (The Most Important Person)
**Origin Language:** Old Irish

**Quinnelle | Quinnell, Quinnella, Quinelle**
**Meaning:** Woman Of Battle
**Origin Language:** Old English

**Quinnette | Quinnetta**
**Meaning:** Supplanter (Wrongfully Seizes And Holds The Place Of Another)
**Origin Language:** Hebrew

**Quintella | Quintelle**
**Meaning:** Fifth
**Origin Language:** Latin

**Quirina | Quirena, Quirene, Quirine**
**Meaning:** Armed With A Spear
**Origin Language:** Latin

# Chapter 44 - Names For Girls Beginning With R

**Rachel | Rachael, Racheal, Rachele, Rachelle, Rachyl, Rhachel**
**Meaning:** Ewe
**Origin Language:** Hebrew

**Raegan | Rae, Reagan, Regan**
**Meaning:** Little Royal

**Origin Language:** Old Irish

Raelina | Rae, Raelena, Raelene, Raelin, Raeline, Raelyn, Raelynn, Raylena, Raylene, Raylina, Rayline, Raylyn, Raylynn
**Meaning:** Ewe
**Origin Language:** Hebrew

Raimonda | Raimunda, Raymonda, Raymunda
**Meaning:** Protecting Governor
**Origin Language:** Ancient Germanic

Raine | Raen, Raene, Rain, Raina, Rayn, Rayna, Rayne, Reina, Reine, Reyna, Reyne
**Meaning:** Rain (English) / Queen (Latin)
**Origin Language:** English And Latin

Ramira
**Meaning:** Famous Regulator
**Origin Language:** Ancient Germanic

Ramona
**Meaning:** Protecting Governor
**Origin Language:** Ancient Germanic

Raphaella | Rafaela, Rafaella, Raffaela, Raffaella, Raphaela, Raphaela, Raphaele, Raphaelle
**Meaning:** Healed By God
**Origin Language:** Hebrew

Raquel | Racquel, Rakel
**Also:** Raschelle | Raschel
**Meaning:** Ewe
**Origin Language:** Hebrew

Raven | Raeven, Raiven, Rayven
**Also:** Ravenna | Ravenne
**Meaning:** Raven
**Origin Language:** English

Raya | Rae, Rai, Rey, Reya

**Meaning:** Ray Of Light
**Origin Language:** English

Rayan | Rayaan, Rayyan
**Meaning:** Luxuriant
**Origin Language:** Arabic

Rayen
**Meaning:** Flower
**Origin Language:** Mapuche

Rayhana | Reyhana
**Meaning:** Basil
**Origin Language:** Arabic

Raziela | Raziella
**Meaning:** God Is My Secret
**Origin Language:** Hebrew

Reanna | Rheanna, Rhianna, Rianna
**Meaning:** Divine Queen
**Origin Language:** Ancient Celtic

Reba | Reeba
**Also:** Rebecca | Rebeca, Rebeccah, Rebecka, Rebeckah, Rebeka, Rebekah, Rebekka, Rhebekka
**Meaning:** Shackled By Her Own Beauty
**Origin Language:** Hebrew

Reena | Rena, Rina
**Meaning:** Song
**Origin Language:** Hebrew

Reenie | Reene, Reeny, Rene, Renie, Reny
**Meaning:** Reborn
**Origin Language:** Latin

Reese | Reece
**Meaning:** Ardent
**Origin Language:** Old Welsh

Reeta | Reta, Rita
**Meaning:** Pearl

**Origin Language:** Latin

Reeva | Reva, Riva
**Meaning:** Moves
**Origin Language:** Sanskrit

Regana
**Also:** Regina | Regena, Regine
**Meaning:** Queen
**Origin Language:** Latin

Rei
**Meaning:** Bell / Beautiful / Lovely / The Tinkling Of Jade
**Origin Language:** Japanese

Reign
**Meaning:** Reign
**Origin Language:** English

Reilly | Reillie
**Meaning:** Of The Social People / Of The Warring People / Of The Church People
**Origin Language:** Old Irish

Remi | Remie, Remy
**Meaning:** Rower
**Origin Language:** Latin

Renae | Renay, Renee
**Also:** Renata
**Also:** Renita
**Meaning:** Reborn
**Origin Language:** Latin

Renlea | Renleigh, Renley
**Meaning:** From A Meadow Of Wrens
**Origin Language:** Old English

Reverie | Revery
**Meaning:** Reverie (Daydream)
**Origin Language:** English

Rexana | Rexanna, Rexanne
**Meaning:** Monarch

**Origin Language:** Latin

Rhaenyra
**Meaning:** This Name Has No Meaning (Rhaenyra Is A Fictional Character Featuring In The TV Series House Of The Dragon)
**Origin Language:** Invented

Rhea | Rheia, Rheie, Rhia
**Meaning:** Flowing
**Origin Language:** Ancient Greek

Rhetta | Rheta
**Meaning:** Gives Advice
**Origin Language:** Dutch

Rhian
**Meaning:** Maiden
**Origin Language:** Welsh

Rhiannon | Reannon, Reanon, Rhianon, Riannon, Rianon
**Meaning:** Divine Queen
**Origin Language:** Ancient Celtic

Rhoda | Rhode
**Meaning:** Rose
**Origin Language:** Ancient Greek

Rhona
**Meaning:** From One Of The Two Islands Of Rona (Scotland)
**Origin Language:** Scottish Gaelic

Rhonda | Ronda
**Meaning:** From The Rhondda Valley (Wales)
**Origin Language:** Welsh

Rhonwen
**Meaning:** Famous and Happy
**Origin Language:** Ancient Germanic

Rhosyn | Rhosin
**Meaning:** Rose
**Origin Language:** Welsh

Ria | Rea, Riya
**Meaning:** Singer
**Origin Language:** Sanskrit

Rianne
**Meaning:** Rebel Of Grace (A Combination Of Ria (Maria) And Anne)
**Origin Language:** Hebrew

Ricarda | Riccarda, Rickarda, Rikarda
**Meaning:** Rich And Hardy
**Origin Language:** Ancient Germanic

Richa
**Meaning:** Sacred Text / Praise
**Origin Language:** Sanskrit

Richelle | Richella
**Meaning:** Ewe
**Origin Language:** Hebrew

Ricki | Rikki
**Meaning:** Rich And Hardy
**Origin Language:** Ancient Germanic

Ridleigh | Ridlea, Ridley, Ridlie
**Meaning:** From A Meadow With Reeds
**Origin Language:** Old English

Rihanna | Rihana
**Meaning:** Basil
**Origin Language:** Arabic

Rilinda
**Meaning:** Reincarnation
**Origin Language:** Albanian

Ripleigh | Riplea, Ripley, Riplie
**Meaning:** From A Divided Meadow
**Origin Language:** Old English

Riva | Reva
**Meaning:** Shackled By Her Own Beauty
**Origin Language:** Hebrew

Roberta
**Also:** Robin | Robyn
**Meaning:** Famous And Bright
**Origin Language:** Ancient Germanic

Rochelle | Rochele, Rochell
**Meaning:** Little Rock
**Origin Language:** Old French

Rodia | Rodya
**Meaning:** Ode To A Heroine
**Origin Language:** Ancient Greek

Rodina | Rodena, Rodene, Rodine
**Meaning:** From Hroda's Island / From A Famous Island
**Origin Language:** Old English

Roesia | Roesa, Roese
**Also:** Rohais | Rohaisa
**Also:** Rohese | Rohesia
**Meaning:** Of The Famous Sort
**Origin Language:** Ancient Germanic

Roksana
**Meaning:** Dawn / Light
**Origin Language:** Persian

Roma
**Also:** Romaine | Romaina, Romane, Romayna, Romayne
**Also:** Romana
**Meaning:** From Rome
**Origin Language:** Latin

Romilda | Romilde
**Meaning:** Famous Battler
**Origin Language:** Ancient Germanic

Romilly | Romillie
**Also:** Romina | Romena, Romene, Romine
**Also:** Romola
**Meaning:** From Rome
**Origin Language:** Latin

Romy | Romey, Romi, Romie
**Meaning:** My Exaltation
**Origin Language:** Hebrew

Ros | Roz
**Also:** Rosa | Rose, Rosie, Rosy,
Roza, Roze, Rozie, Rozy
**Meaning:** Of The Famous Sort (Ancient
Germanic) / Rose (Latin)
**Origin Language:** Ancient Germanic
And Latin

Rosalba
**Meaning:** Rose Of Dawn
**Origin Language:** Latin

Rosalie | Rosalee, Rosaleigh,
Rosalia, Rosaly, Rozalee, Rozaleigh,
Rozalia, Rozalie, Rozaly
**Meaning:** Of The Famous Sort (Ancient
Germanic) / Rose (Latin)
**Origin Language:** Ancient Germanic
And Latin

Rosalinda | Rosalind, Rosalinde,
Roselind, Roselinda, Roselinde,
Rozalind, Rozalinda, Rozalinde,
Rozelind, Rozelinda, Rozelinde
**Meaning:** Tender Towards Horses /
Gentle Serpent
**Origin Language:** Ancient Germanic

Rosalva
**Meaning:** Rose Of Dawn
**Origin Language:** Latin

Rosana | Rossana, Rozana
**Meaning:** Dawn / Light
**Origin Language:** Persian

Rosaria | Rozaria
**Meaning:** Rosary
**Origin Language:** Spanish

Rosasharn | Rozasharn
**Meaning:** Rose Of Sharon

**Origin Language:** English

Rose | Rosa, Rosie, Rosy, Roza,
Roze, Rozie, Rozy
**Meaning:** Of The Famous Sort (Ancient
Germanic) / Rose (Latin)
**Origin Language:** Ancient Germanic
And Latin

Roseangela | Rosangela
**Meaning:** Angelic Rose (A Combination
Of Rose And Angela)
**Origin Language:** Latin

Roseanne | Rosanna, Rosannah,
Rosanne, Roseann, Rozanna,
Rozannah, Rozanne, Rozeann,
Rozeanne
**Meaning:** Graced Rose (A Combination
Of Rose And Anne)
**Origin Language:** Hebrew And Latin
(In Combination)

Roselle | Rosella, Rozella, Rozelle
**Meaning:** Of The Famous Sort (Ancient
Germanic) / Rose (Latin)
**Origin Language:** Ancient Germanic
And Latin

Roselyn | Rosaleen, Rosalena,
Rosalene, Rosalin, Rosalina,
Rosaline, Rosalyn, Rosalynn,
Roselena, Roselene, Roselin,
Roselina, Roseline, Rozaleen,
Rozalena, Rozalene, Rozalin,
Rozalina, Rozaline, Rozalyn,
Rozalynn, Rozelena, Rozelene,
Rozelin, Rozelina, Rozeline,
Rozelyn
**Meaning:** Tender Towards Horses /
Gentle Serpent
**Origin Language:** Ancient Germanic

Rosemary | Rosemarie, Rosmarie,
Rosmary

**Meaning:** Rebellious Rose (Flower) (A Combination Of Rose And Mary)
**Origin Language:** Hebrew And Latin (In Combination)

Rosette | Rosetta, Rozetta, Rozette
**Also:** Rosheen | Roshene, Roshine
**Also:** Rosica | Rosika, Rozica, Rozika
**Also:** Rosie | Rosi, Rosy, Rozi, Rozie, Rozy
**Also:** Rosina | Rosena, Rosene, Rosine, Rozena, Rozene, Rozina, Rozine
**Also:** Rosita | Rozita
**Meaning:** Of The Famous Sort (Ancient Germanic) / Rose (Latin)
**Origin Language:** Ancient Germanic And Latin

Roslina | Roslin, Rosline, Roslyn, Rozlin, Rozlina, Rozline, Rozlyn
**Also:** Roslindis | Roslindys, Rozlindis, Rozlindys
**Meaning:** Tender Towards Horses / Gentle Serpent
**Origin Language:** Ancient Germanic

Rossella | Rosselle
**Meaning:** Red
**Origin Language:** Italian

Rowan | Rowanna, Rowanne
**Meaning:** Little One With Red Hair
**Origin Language:** Old Irish

Rowena | Rowina, Rowine
**Meaning:** Famous and Joyful
**Origin Language:** Ancient Germanic

Roxanna | Rhoxane, Roxana, Roxane, Roxanne
**Meaning:** Dawn / Light
**Origin Language:** Persian

Roxelana | Roksolana
**Meaning:** From Ruthenia (An Ancient Region)
**Origin Language:** Turkish

Roxie | Roxi, Roxy
**Meaning:** Dawn / Light
**Origin Language:** Persian

Ru
**Meaning:** Scholar
**Origin Language:** Chinese

Rubena
**Meaning:** Red / Ruby
**Origin Language:** Esperanto

Rubina | Rubena, Rubene, Rubine
**Meaning:** Red / Ruby
**Origin Language:** Italian

Ruby | Rubie, Rubye
**Meaning:** Red / Ruby
**Origin Language:** English

Rue
**Meaning:** Friend
**Origin Language:** Hebrew

Runa
**Meaning:** Rune / Mystery / Secret
**Origin Language:** Old Norse

Ruperta
**Meaning:** Famous And Bright
**Origin Language:** Ancient Germanic

Ruth | Rhouth, Ruthi, Ruthie, Ruthy
**Meaning:** Friend
**Origin Language:** Hebrew

Ruxandra
**Meaning:** Dawn / Light
**Origin Language:** Persian

Ryann | Ryan, Ryana, Ryanna, Ryanne
**Meaning:** Little Royal
**Origin Language:** Old Irish

Rylee | Riley, Ryleigh, Ryley, Rylie, Ryly
**Meaning:** From A Meadow Of Rye
**Origin Language:** Old English

# Chapter 45 - Names For Girls Beginning With S

Sabana
**Meaning:** Grass Covered Mountain
**Origin Language:** Chamorro

Sabeen
**Meaning:** Follower Of Another Religion
**Origin Language:** Arabic

Sabella | Sabela
**Meaning:** God Is My Oath
**Origin Language:** Hebrew

Sabia
**Meaning:** Sweet
**Origin Language:** Old Irish

Sabine | Sabena, Sabene, Sabina
**Meaning:** Of The Sabines (An Ancient Italic Peoples)
**Origin Language:** Latin

Sable
**Meaning:** Sable (Black)
**Origin Language:** English

Sabrina | Sabrena, Sabrene, Sabrine
**Meaning:** From Near The River Severn (United Kingdom)
**Origin Language:** Latin

Sachie | Sachy
**Meaning:** Branch Of Happiness / Branch Of Good Luck
**Origin Language:** Japanese

Sadie | Sady
**Meaning:** Princess
**Origin Language:** Hebrew

Saffron
**Meaning:** Saffron
**Origin Language:** English

Safia | Safa, Safiya, Safiyah
**Meaning:** Pure
**Origin Language:** Arabic

Safira
**Meaning:** Sapphire
**Origin Language:** Esperanto

Sage | Saige, Sayge
**Meaning:** Sage
**Origin Language:** English

Saira
**Meaning:** Explorer
**Origin Language:** Arabic

Sakina | Sakena, Sakene, Sakine
**Meaning:** Calmness
**Origin Language:** Arabic

Sakura
**Meaning:** Virtuous Cherry Blossom / Good Blossom
**Origin Language:** Japanese

Salem
**Also:** Salima
**Meaning:** Safe
**Origin Language:** Arabic

Salina | Salena, Salene, Salin, Saline, Salyn
**Meaning:** The Moon

**Origin Language:** Ancient Greek

Salka
**Also:** Sally | Salli, Sallie
**Meaning:** Princess
**Origin Language:** Hebrew

Salma
**Meaning:** Safe
**Origin Language:** Arabic

Salome | Solome
**Also:** Salomea | Saloma, Salome, Solomia, Solomiya
**Meaning:** Peace
**Origin Language:** Hebrew

Samanta
**Also:** Samantha
**Meaning:** His Name Is "El" (His Name Is God)
**Origin Language:** Hebrew

Samara | Samaria
**Meaning:** Elm Seed
**Origin Language:** Latin

Samia | Samiya, Samiyah
**Meaning:** Elevated
**Origin Language:** Arabic

Samira | Sameera, Samirah
**Meaning:** Evening Conversation Companion
**Origin Language:** Arabic

Sammie | Sammi, Sammy
**Also:** Samuela | Samuella
**Meaning:** His Name Is "El" (His Name Is God)
**Origin Language:** Hebrew

Sancha
**Meaning:** Saintly
**Origin Language:** Latin

Sandra
**Also:** Sandrine | Sandrena, Sandrene, Sandrina
**Also:** Sandy | Sandi, Sandie
**Meaning:** Mankind's Defender
**Origin Language:** Ancient Greek

Sanea | Saneya, Sania, Saniya, Sanya
**Meaning:** Brilliant
**Origin Language:** Arabic

Sanela | Sanella
**Meaning:** In Good Health
**Origin Language:** Latin

Sanna | Sanne
**Meaning:** Lily / Rose
**Origin Language:** Hebrew

Sansa
**Meaning:** Olive Pomace
**Origin Language:** Latin

Santina | Santena, Santene, Santine
**Meaning:** Saint
**Origin Language:** Latin

Saphira | Safeira, Safeire, Saffeira, Saffeire, Saffira, Safira, Sappheira, Sappheire, Sapphira
**Meaning:** Sapphire
**Origin Language:** Ancient Greek

Sapphire
**Meaning:** Sapphire
**Origin Language:** English

Saqui
**Meaning:** Popular
**Origin Language:** Mapuche

Sara | Saara, Sarra, Sarrha
**Also:** Sarah | Saira, Sairah, Sairra, Sairrah, Saraa
**Meaning:** Princess

**Origin Language:** Hebrew

Sarai | Saray
**Meaning:** My Princess
**Origin Language:** Hebrew

Sarala
**Meaning:** Straight
**Origin Language:** Sanskrit

Saranna
**Meaning:** Princess Of Grace
**Origin Language:** Hebrew

Sariah | Sariya
**Meaning:** Princess
**Origin Language:** Hebrew

Sarine | Sarena, Sarene, Sarina
**Meaning:** Serene
**Origin Language:** Latin

Sarita
**Meaning:** Flowing
**Origin Language:** Sanskrit

Sariyah | Saraiah, Sarayah
**Meaning:** God Rules
**Origin Language:** Hebrew

Sasha | Sacha, Sascha, Sashka
**Meaning:** Mankind's Defender
**Origin Language:** Ancient Greek

Saskia | Saskya
**Meaning:** Of The Saxons (The Name Of A Germanic Tribe)
**Origin Language:** Ancient Germanic

Saundra
**Meaning:** Mankind's Defender
**Origin Language:** Ancient Greek

Savannah | Savanna
**Meaning:** Savannah
**Origin Language:** English

Saveria
**Meaning:** From Etxeberria (Navarre, Spain)
**Origin Language:** Basque

Savina | Savena, Savene, Savine
**Meaning:** Of The Sabines (An Ancient Italic Peoples)
**Origin Language:** Latin

Sawsana | Sawsan
**Meaning:** Lily / Rose
**Origin Language:** Hebrew

Saxa | Saxxa
**Meaning:** Of The Saxons (The Name Of A Germanic Tribe)
**Origin Language:** Ancient Germanic

Sayen
**Meaning:** Sweet
**Origin Language:** Mapuche

Saylor
**Meaning:** Acrobat
**Origin Language:** Old French

Scarlet | Scarlett, Scarletta, Scarlette
**Meaning:** Scarlet Red
**Origin Language:** English

Scout
**Meaning:** Scout
**Origin Language:** English

Sebastiana | Sebastianna, Sebastienne
**Meaning:** From Sebaste (An Ancient City In Asia Minor) / Venerable
**Origin Language:** Latin

Sela
**Meaning:** Rock
**Origin Language:** Hebrew

**Selah**
**Meaning:** A Musical Interlude In A Psalm
**Origin Language:** Hebrew

**Selbie | Selby**
**Meaning:** From A Farmstead With Willow Trees
**Origin Language:** Old Norse

**Selene | Selena, Selina, Seline, Selini**
**Meaning:** The Moon
**Origin Language:** Ancient Greek

**Selima**
**Also:** Selma
**Meaning:** Safe
**Origin Language:** Arabic

**Selisa | Selise, Selysa, Selyse**
**Meaning:** Of The Noble Sort
**Origin Language:** Ancient Germanic

**Selynn | Selin, Selyn**
**Meaning:** The Moon
**Origin Language:** Ancient Greek

**Semele**
**Meaning:** Earth Mother
**Origin Language:** Ancient Greek

**Seneia | Seneea**
**Meaning:** Brilliant
**Origin Language:** Arabic

**Senna**
**Meaning:** Senna (Plant)
**Origin Language:** Arabic

**Seona**
**Meaning:** God Is Gracious
**Origin Language:** Hebrew

**Sephora | Seffora, Sefora, Sepphora**

**Meaning:** Bird
**Origin Language:** Hebrew

**Sequoia**
**Meaning:** Sequoia (Tree)
**Origin Language:** English

**Sera | Serah**
**Also:** Seraphina | Serafima, Serafina, Serafine, Seraphema, Seraphine
**Meaning:** Burning / Glowing / Seraphim
**Origin Language:** Latin

**Serayah | Seraiah, Seriyah**
**Meaning:** God Rules
**Origin Language:** Hebrew

**Seren**
**Meaning:** Star
**Origin Language:** Welsh

**Serena | Serene, Serina, Serine, Serrena**
**Also:** Serenata
**Meaning:** Serene
**Origin Language:** Latin

**Sevan**
**Meaning:** Lake
**Origin Language:** Armenian

**Sevara**
**Meaning:** Love
**Origin Language:** Uzbek

**Shadia | Shadiya, Shadya**
**Meaning:** Singer
**Origin Language:** Arabic

**Shaelyn | Shaelin, Shaelina, Shaylin, Shaylina, Shaylyn**
**Meaning:** Approvable
**Origin Language:** Old Irish

Shai
**Meaning:** Gift
**Origin Language:** Hebrew

Shaima | Shaimaa, Shayma
**Meaning:** Has Beauty Marks
**Origin Language:** Arabic

Shaina | Shainie, Shana, Shayna,
Shaynah, Shaynie, Sheina, Sheinie
**Meaning:** Beautiful
**Origin Language:** Yiddish

Shakira
**Meaning:** Thankful
**Origin Language:** Arabic

Shanae | Shanay
**Meaning:** God Is Gracious
**Origin Language:** Hebrew

Shanelle | Shanel
**Meaning:** From Near A Channel Of
Water
**Origin Language:** Old French

Shanene | Shanena, Shanina,
Shanine
**Meaning:** God Is Gracious
**Origin Language:** Hebrew

Shani
**Meaning:** Scarlet Red
**Origin Language:** Hebrew

Shania | Shaniya
**Meaning:** On My Way
**Origin Language:** Ojibwe

Shaniqua | Shanequa
**Meaning:** God Is Gracious
**Origin Language:** Hebrew

Shanna | Shannah
**Also:** Shannon | Shanen, Shannen,
Shanon

**Meaning:** Ancient
**Origin Language:** Old Irish

Shantae | Shantay, Shante
**Meaning:** Sung
**Origin Language:** French

Shantelle | Shantal, Shantalle,
Shantel
**Meaning:** Stony / Song
**Origin Language:** French

Shanti | Shanthi
**Meaning:** Peace / Tranquility
**Origin Language:** Sanskrit

Shaquila | Shakila
**Meaning:** Handsome
**Origin Language:** Arabic

Shari
**Meaning:** Plain (Of Land)
**Origin Language:** Hebrew

Sharice | Sharise, Sharisse
**Meaning:** The Shade Of A Cherry
**Origin Language:** Anglo-Norman
French

Sharilina | Sharilena, Sharilene,
Shariline
**Also:** Sharilyn | Sharilin, Sharilynn
**Meaning:** Darling
**Origin Language:** French

Sharlene | Sharla, Sharleen,
Sharlena, Sharlina, Sharline
**Meaning:** Has Freedom
**Origin Language:** Ancient Germanic

Sharmaine | Sharmain, Sharmaina,
Sharmion
**Meaning:** Delight
**Origin Language:** Ancient Greek

Sharmila

**Meaning:** Protection
**Origin Language:** Sanskrit

Sharn
**Also:** Sharnette
**Also:** Sharon | Sharona, Sharown, Sharron, Sharyn
**Meaning:** Plain (Of Land)
**Origin Language:** Hebrew

Sharyl | Sharryl
**Meaning:** Darling
**Origin Language:** French

Shavonne | Shavon, Shevaun, Shevon
**Also:** Shawna | Seanna, Shauna
**Meaning:** God Is Gracious
**Origin Language:** Hebrew

Shawnee
**Meaning:** Of The Southern People
**Origin Language:** Algonquin

Shay | Shae, Shaye, Shea
**Meaning:** Approvable
**Origin Language:** Old Irish

Shayla
**Meaning:** Aimless / Without Sight
**Origin Language:** Latin

Sheena | Sheenagh, Shena
**Meaning:** Graced By God
**Origin Language:** Hebrew

Sheila | Sheela, Sheelagh, Shelagh, Shelia
**Meaning:** Aimless / Without Sight
**Origin Language:** Latin

Shelbie | Shelby
**Meaning:** From A Farmstead With Willow Trees
**Origin Language:** Old Norse

Shelena | Shelina
**Meaning:** The Moon
**Origin Language:** Ancient Greek

Shell
**Meaning:** Shell
**Origin Language:** English

Shelley | Shellie, Shelly
**Meaning:** From A Meadow On A Bank
**Origin Language:** Old English

Sheona | Shiona
**Meaning:** God Is Gracious
**Origin Language:** Hebrew

Sher
**Meaning:** Darling
**Origin Language:** French

Sherah
**Meaning:** Kinswoman
**Origin Language:** Hebrew

Sherette | Sheretta
**Meaning:** Darling
**Origin Language:** French

Sheri | Sherie, Sherri, Sherrie, Sherry, Shery
**Meaning:** Sherry
**Origin Language:** English

Sherice | Sherise, Sherisse
**Meaning:** The Shade Of A Cherry
**Origin Language:** Anglo-Norman French

Sheridan
**Meaning:** Seeker
**Origin Language:** Old Irish

Sherie | Sheree
**Also:** Sherilina | Sherilena, Sherilene, Sheriline
**Also:** Sherilyn | Sherilin, Sherilynn

**Also:** Sheryl | Sherryl
**Meaning:** Darling
**Origin Language:** French

Shi
**Meaning:** Era / Season / Honest / Stone
**Origin Language:** Chinese

Shiloh
**Meaning:** Tranquil
**Origin Language:** Hebrew

Shiori
**Meaning:** Weave / Bookmark / Lithe / Bending
**Origin Language:** Japanese

Shira
**Meaning:** Lion
**Origin Language:** Persian

Shireen | Shereen, Sherin, Sheryn, Shirin, Shiryn
**Meaning:** Sweet
**Origin Language:** Persian

Shiri
**Meaning:** My Song
**Origin Language:** Hebrew

Shirley | Sherley, Shirlee
**Also:** Shirlina | Sherlin, Sherlina, Sherlyn, Shirlin, Shirlyn
**Meaning:** From A Bright Meadow
**Origin Language:** Old English

Shona
**Also:** Shonda | Shawnda
**Meaning:** Graced By God
**Origin Language:** Hebrew

Shoshana | Shoshan, Shoshanah, Shoshannah, Shoushan
**Meaning:** Lily / Rose
**Origin Language:** Hebrew

Shura
**Meaning:** Mankind's Defender
**Origin Language:** Ancient Greek

Shyama
**Meaning:** Dark Blue
**Origin Language:** Sanskrit

Shyla
**Meaning:** Aimless / Without Sight
**Origin Language:** Latin

Sian | Siana, Siani
**Meaning:** Graced By God
**Origin Language:** Hebrew

Sidonia | Sidonie, Sidony
**Meaning:** From Sidon (An Ancient Phoenician Port City)
**Origin Language:** Latin

Sienna | Siena
**Meaning:** Sienna
**Origin Language:** English

Sierra | Siera
**Meaning:** Mountain Range
**Origin Language:** Spanish

Silvestra
**Meaning:** Of The Forest
**Origin Language:** Latin

Simone | Simona
**Meaning:** He Has Heard
**Origin Language:** Hebrew

Sinaida | Senaida, Senaide, Sinaide
**Meaning:** Of Zeus (Zeus Is The Name Of The Roman God Of The Sky, Lightning, Thunder, Law, Order, And Justice)
**Origin Language:** Ancient Greek

Sindra
**Meaning:** Sparkling One

**Origin Language:** Old Norse

Sindy | Sindee, Sindi
**Meaning:** Woman From Kynthos / From Mount Cynthus (A Mountain On The Isle Of Delos, Part Of The Greek Cyclades)
**Origin Language:** Ancient Greek

Sinead | Sinéad
**Meaning:** God Is Gracious
**Origin Language:** Hebrew

Sini
**Meaning:** Blue
**Origin Language:** Finnish

Siran
**Meaning:** Lovely
**Origin Language:** Armenian

Sireen | Sirena, Sirene, Sirina, Sirine
**Meaning:** Serene
**Origin Language:** Latin

Siri
**Meaning:** Beautiful And Victorious
**Origin Language:** Old Norse

Sita | Seeta
**Meaning:** Furrow
**Origin Language:** Sanskrit

Siwan
**Meaning:** Graced By God
**Origin Language:** Hebrew

Skye | Skie, Sky
**Meaning:** Sky
**Origin Language:** English

Skylar | Skyla, Skyler
**Meaning:** Student
**Origin Language:** German

Sloane | Sloan

**Meaning:** Little Raider
**Origin Language:** Old Irish

Solange
**Meaning:** Solemnity
**Origin Language:** Latin

Soleil
**Meaning:** The Sun
**Origin Language:** French

Solina | Soline
**Also:** Sollemnia
**Meaning:** Solemnity
**Origin Language:** Latin

Solomia | Salomea, Salomia, Solomea, Solomiya
**Meaning:** Peace
**Origin Language:** Hebrew

Sona
**Meaning:** Gold
**Origin Language:** Hindi

Sondra
**Meaning:** Defender Of Mankind
**Origin Language:** Ancient Greek

Sonora
**Meaning:** Resounding
**Origin Language:** Latin

Sonya | Sonia
**Also:** Sophie | Sofee, Sofia, Sofie, Sofiya, Sofy, Sofya, Sophi, Sophia, Sophy
**Meaning:** Wisdom
**Origin Language:** Ancient Greek

Sophronia | Sofronia
**Meaning:** Of Sound Mind
**Origin Language:** Ancient Greek

Sora
**Meaning:** Sky

**Origin Language:** Japanese

Soraya | Soraia
**Meaning:** The Pleiades (A Group Of Stars In The Constellation Taurus) / Brilliant Gem
**Origin Language:** Arabic

Sorcha
**Meaning:** Radiant
**Origin Language:** Irish

Sorina | Sorena, Sorene, Sorine
**Meaning:** The Sun
**Origin Language:** Romanian

Sorrel
**Meaning:** Has Chestnut Hair
**Origin Language:** Old French

Sovanna | Sovann, Sovanne, Sovenne
**Meaning:** Gold
**Origin Language:** Khmer

Stacy | Stace, Stacee, Stacey, Staci, Stacia, Stacie
**Meaning:** Grows/Harvests Grain Well
**Origin Language:** Ancient Greek

Starla
**Meaning:** Star
**Origin Language:** English

Stasia | Stasya
**Meaning:** Resurrected
**Origin Language:** Ancient Greek

Stelara
**Meaning:** Star Constellation
**Origin Language:** Esperanto

Stella | Stela
**Meaning:** Star
**Origin Language:** Latin

Stephanie | Stefana, Stefani, Stefania, Stefanie, Stefaniya, Stefany, Steffi, Steffie, Steffy, Steph, Stephani, Stephania, Stephany
**Meaning:** Wears The Conqueror's Crown
**Origin Language:** Ancient Greek

Steren | Steryn
**Meaning:** Star
**Origin Language:** Latin

Stevie
**Meaning:** Wears The Conqueror's Crown
**Origin Language:** Ancient Greek

Sue
**Meaning:** Lily / Rose
**Origin Language:** Hebrew

Suellen
**Meaning:** Light Of The Lily/Rose (A Combination Of Sue And Ellen)
**Origin Language:** Ancient Greek And Hebrew (In Combination)

Suette
**Meaning:** Good Fortune
**Origin Language:** Chamorro

Suky | Suki, Sukie
**Meaning:** Lily / Rose
**Origin Language:** Hebrew

Summer | Sommer
**Meaning:** Summer
**Origin Language:** English

Suna
**Meaning:** Gold
**Origin Language:** Hindi

Sunita | Sunitha
**Meaning:** Well-Conducted

281

**Origin Language:** Sanskrit

Sunniva | Sunnifa
**Meaning:** Gift Of The Sun
**Origin Language:** Old English

Suraya | Surayya
**Meaning:** The Pleiades (A Group Of Stars In The Constellation Taurus) / Brilliant Gem
**Origin Language:** Arabic

Suri
**Meaning:** Princess
**Origin Language:** Hebrew

Susan | Suzan
**Also:** Susanita
**Also:** Susanna | Sousanna, Susann, Susannah, Susanne, Suzana, Suzanna, Suzanne, Syuzanna, Syuzanne
**Also:** Susette | Susetta, Suzetta, Susetta
**Also:** Susie | Suse, Susi, Susy, Suz, Suze, Suzi, Suzie, Suzy
**Meaning:** Lily / Rose
**Origin Language:** Hebrew

Suvi
**Meaning:** Summer
**Origin Language:** Finnish

Svana
**Meaning:** Swanlike
**Origin Language:** Old Norse

Sybil | Sibella, Sibelle, Sibil, Sibill, Sibilla, Sibille, Sibyl, Sibylla, Sibylle, Sybella, Sybelle, Sybill, Sybilla, Sybille, Sybyl, Sybylla, Sybylle
**Meaning:** Prophetess / Oracle
**Origin Language:** Latin

Sydney | Sidne, Sidnee, Sidney,

Sidni, Sidnie, Sidny, Sydne, Sydnee, Sydni, Sydnie, Sydny
**Meaning:** From A Wide Island
**Origin Language:** Old English

Sylvana | Silvaina, Silvaine, Silvana, Silviane, Silvianne, Silvianne, Sylvaina, Sylvaine, Sylviane, Sylvianne
**Also:** Sylvia | Silva, Silvia, Silvie, Silviya, Silvy, Sylva, Sylvi, Sylvie, Sylvy
**Meaning:** Forest / Of The Forest
**Origin Language:** Latin

# Chapter 46 - Names For Girls Beginning With T

Tabitha | Tabatha, Tabbea, Tabbia, Tabbie, Tabby, Tabea, Tabia, Tabita
**Meaning:** Gazelle
**Origin Language:** Ancient Greek

Tacey
**Also:** Tacita
**Meaning:** Silent
**Origin Language:** Latin

Tahira
**Meaning:** Virtuous
**Origin Language:** Arabic

Tai
**Meaning:** Extreme
**Origin Language:** Chinese

Taika
**Meaning:** Magic
**Origin Language:** Finnish

Taimi

**Meaning:** Plant
**Origin Language:** Estonian

Taina
**Meaning:** Reputable
**Origin Language:** Latin

Taisia | Taisiya
**Meaning:** Bandage
**Origin Language:** Ancient Greek

Takara
**Meaning:** Treasure / Jewel
**Origin Language:** Japanese

Tali
**Meaning:** My Dew
**Origin Language:** Hebrew

Talia | Tahlia, Talya
**Meaning:** God's Dew
**Origin Language:** Hebrew

Talina | Taleen, Talene, Taline
**Meaning:** From Talin (A Town In Armenia)
**Origin Language:** Armenian

Talisa | Talesa
**Also:** Talisha | Taleisha
**Meaning:** Of The Noble Sort
**Origin Language:** Ancient Germanic

Talitha
**Meaning:** Maiden
**Origin Language:** Ancient Greek

Tallulah | Tallula, Talulla, Talullah
**Meaning:** Leaping Waters
**Origin Language:** Choctaw

Talyn | Talin, Talynn
**Meaning:** From Talin (A Town In Armenia)
**Origin Language:** Armenian

Tam

**Meaning:** Innocent
**Origin Language:** Hebrew

Tamanna
**Meaning:** Wish / Desire
**Origin Language:** Bengali

Tamara | Tamarah, Tamari, Tamera, Tamira, Tammara, Tammera, Tammira
**Meaning:** Date Palm
**Origin Language:** Hebrew

Tamaya
**Meaning:** Centered
**Origin Language:** Quechua

Tamela
**Meaning:** All Sweet / Date Palm (A Combination Of Tamara And Pamela)
**Origin Language:** Ancient Greek And Hebrew (In Combination)

Tamila
**Meaning:** Torture
**Origin Language:** Common Slavic

Tammy | Tami, Tamia, Tammi, Tammie
**Also:** Tamra
**Meaning:** Date Palm
**Origin Language:** Hebrew

Tamsin | Tamsen, Tamson, Tamsyn, Tamsyn, Tamzen, Tamzin, Tamzon, Tamzyn
**Meaning:** Twin
**Origin Language:** Old Aramaic

Tanisha | Tanesha
**Meaning:** Confusing
**Origin Language:** Swahili

Tanith | Tanyth
**Meaning:** The Meaning Of This Name Is Unknown (Tanith is the name of an

ancient Carthaginian Lunar Goddess)
**Origin Language:** Semitic

Tansy | Tansi, Tansie, Tanzi, Tanzie, Tanzy
**Meaning:** Tansy (Flower)
**Origin Language:** English

Tanvi
**Meaning:** Slender Woman
**Origin Language:** Sanskrit

Tanya | Tania
**Meaning:** Reputable
**Origin Language:** Latin

Tara | Tarah
**Meaning:** Star
**Origin Language:** Sanskrit

Tarana
**Meaning:** Music
**Origin Language:** Azerbaijani

Taria | Tarya
**Meaning:** Possesses Goodness
**Origin Language:** Old Persian

Tarina | Tarena, Tarene, Tarine
**Meaning:** Star
**Origin Language:** Sanskrit

Taryn | Tarin
**Meaning:** Born Of The Yew Tree
**Origin Language:** Old Irish

Tasha | Tacha
**Meaning:** Birthday Of The Lord / Christmas Day
**Origin Language:** Latin

Tasia
**Meaning:** Resurrected
**Origin Language:** Ancient Greek

Tatiana | Tatianna, Tatienna,

Tatienne, Tatyana, Tatyanna
**Meaning:** Reputable
**Origin Language:** Latin

Tatum | Taytum
**Meaning:** From Tata's Homestead (The Meaning Of The Old English Personal Name Tata Is Unknown)
**Origin Language:** Old English

Tawnee | Tahnee, Tawnie, Tawny
**Also:** Tawnya | Tawnia
**Meaning:** Tawny
**Origin Language:** English

Taylor | Tailor, Tayla, Tayler
**Meaning:** Tailor
**Origin Language:** English

Teagan | Taegan, Tegan
**Meaning:** Fair (Complexion) / Jewel
**Origin Language:** Welsh

Tempest
**Meaning:** Tempest
**Origin Language:** English

Tenzin
**Meaning:** Upholder Of Teachings
**Origin Language:** Tibetan

Teona
**Meaning:** God
**Origin Language:** Ancient Greek

Teresa | Terese, Teresia, Tereza, Terezia, Terezie, Terezy, Therasia, Theresa, Therese, Theresia
**Meaning:** Summer / Harvester
**Origin Language:** Ancient Greek

Terra | Tera
**Meaning:** Star
**Origin Language:** Sanskrit

Terri | Tere, Teri, Terrie, Terry

**Meaning:** Summer / Harvester
**Origin Language:** Ancient Greek

Terrwen | Terrwyn, Terwen,
Terwyn, Terwynne, Terwynne
**Meaning:** Blessed Brave One / Bright
Brave One
**Origin Language:** Old Welsh

Tessa | Tess, Tessie, Tessy
**Meaning:** Summer / Harvester
**Origin Language:** Ancient Greek

Tethys | Tethis
**Meaning:** Grandmother
**Origin Language:** Ancient Greek

Tetiana | Tetianna, Tetianne,
Tetienna, Tetienne, Tetyana
**Meaning:** Reputable
**Origin Language:** Latin

Thais | Thaisa
**Meaning:** Bandage
**Origin Language:** Ancient Greek

Thalassa
**Meaning:** Sea
**Origin Language:** Ancient Greek

Thalia | Thaleia
**Meaning:** Blossoms
**Origin Language:** Ancient Greek

Thana
**Meaning:** Praise
**Origin Language:** Arabic

Thandeka
**Meaning:** Loved
**Origin Language:** Ndebele And Zulu
(Cognates)

Thandi | Thandiwe
**Meaning:** Loving One
**Origin Language:** Ndebele And Zulu
And Xhosa (Cognates)

Thea | Theia, Thia
**Meaning:** Goddess
**Origin Language:** Ancient Greek

Theda | Thida
**Meaning:** Gift Of God
**Origin Language:** Ancient Greek

Thekla | Thecla
**Meaning:** The Glory Of God
**Origin Language:** Ancient Greek

Thelma | Telma
**Meaning:** Will / Desire
**Origin Language:** Ancient Greek

Thema
**Meaning:** Queen
**Origin Language:** Akan

Themis | Themys
**Meaning:** The Law
**Origin Language:** Ancient Greek

Theodora | Thiodora
**Meaning:** God's Gift
**Origin Language:** Ancient Greek

Thera
**Also:** Therine | Therena, Therene,
Therina
**Meaning:** Summer / Harvester
**Origin Language:** Ancient Greek

Thersa | Thirza
**Meaning:** Delightsomeness
**Origin Language:** Hebrew

Thisbe
**Meaning:** From Thisbe (An Ancient
Town On The Coast Of Boeotia Greece)
**Origin Language:** Ancient Greek

Thora
**Meaning:** Thunder

**Origin Language:** Old Norse

Tia | Tea, Teah, Tiah
**Meaning:** Aunt
**Origin Language:** Spanish And Portuguese (Cognates)

Tiana | Tianna
**Meaning:** A Christian
**Origin Language:** Latin

Tiara
**Meaning:** Tiara
**Origin Language:** English

Tibby | Tibbie
**Meaning:** Gazelle
**Origin Language:** Ancient Greek

Tierra
**Meaning:** Earth
**Origin Language:** Spanish

Tiffany | Tiffani, Tiffanie, Tiffinie, Tiffiny, Tiphani, Tiphanie, Tiphany
**Meaning:** Manifester Of God
**Origin Language:** Ancient Greek

Tilda | Til, Tilde, Tildi, Tildie, Tildy
**Also:** Tilly | Til, Tillie
**Meaning:** Mighty Battler
**Origin Language:** Ancient Germanic

Timothea | Timothia
**Meaning:** Respects God
**Origin Language:** Ancient Greek

Tina | Teena
**Meaning:** A Short Form Of Any Of The Numerous Names Ending In Tina
**Origin Language:** Various

Tindra
**Meaning:** Twinkle
**Origin Language:** Swedish

Tinlea | Tinleigh, Tinley
**Also:** Tinslie | Tinsely, Tinsey, Tinslea, Tinsleigh, Tinsley
**Also:** Tinsy | Tinsi, Tinsie, Tinzi, Tinzie, Tinzy
**Meaning:** From Tynni's Meadow (It Is Unknown What The Meaning Of The Old English Personal Name Tynni Is)
**Origin Language:** Old English

Tiphaine | Tiphaina
**Meaning:** Manifester Of God
**Origin Language:** Ancient Greek

Tisha | Tischa, Tish
**Meaning:** Happiness
**Origin Language:** Latin

Tiziana
**Meaning:** Titled
**Origin Language:** Latin

Toinette | Toinetta
**Meaning:** Of Ani (Ani Is The Name Of An Etruscan God, Thought To Be Equivalent To The Roman God Janus, The God Of Beginnings, Gates, Transitions, Time, Duality, Doorways, Passages, And Endings)
**Origin Language:** Latin

Tomila
**Meaning:** Torture
**Origin Language:** Common Slavic

Tomina | Tomena, Tomene, Tomine
**Meaning:** Twin
**Origin Language:** Old Aramaic

Tonalli
**Meaning:** Warmth Of The Sun
**Origin Language:** Nahuatl

Tondra

**Meaning:** Thunderous
**Origin Language:** Esperanto

Toni | Tonia, Tonie, Tonii, Tony
**Also:** Tonina | Tonena, Tonene, Tonine
**Also:** Tonya | Tonia
**Meaning:** Of Ani (Ani Is The Name Of An Etruscan God, Thought To Be Equivalent To The Roman God Janus, The God Of Beginnings, Gates, Transitions, Time, Duality, Doorways, Passages, And Endings)
**Origin Language:** Latin

Tora
**Meaning:** Thunder
**Origin Language:** Old Norse

Tori | Toria, Torie, Tory
**Meaning:** Victory
**Origin Language:** Latin

Torvi
**Meaning:** Thor's Priestess / Priestess Of Thunder (Thor Is The Name Of The Norse God Of Thunder And Lightning)
**Origin Language:** Old Norse

Tova | Tovah
**Meaning:** Good
**Origin Language:** Hebrew

Tovia
**Meaning:** God Is Good
**Origin Language:** Hebrew

Toya | Toia
**Meaning:** Victory
**Origin Language:** Latin

Toyin
**Meaning:** Praise Worthy
**Origin Language:** Yoruba

Tracey | Tracee, Traci, Tracie,

Tracy
**Meaning:** Of The Thracian People (An Ancient People Who Once Inhabited Eastern And Southeastern Europe)
**Origin Language:** Latin

Treasa | Treesa
**Meaning:** Summer / Harvester
**Origin Language:** Ancient Greek

Trena
**Meaning:** Eglantine / Sweetbrier
**Origin Language:** Macedonian

Tria
**Meaning:** Of Demeter (Demeter Is The Name Of The Greek Goddess Of The Harvest, Agriculture, Fertility, And Sacred Law)
**Origin Language:** Ancient Greek

Trinity | Trinitie
**Meaning:** Trinity
**Origin Language:** English

Trisha | Trecia, Tresha, Tricia, Trish
**Meaning:** Patrician / Aristocrat
**Origin Language:** Latin

Trista | Tristia
**Also:** Tristina | Tristena
**Meaning:** Tumultuous
**Origin Language:** Ancient Celtic

Trixie | Trix, Trixi, Trixy
**Meaning:** Female Voyager
**Origin Language:** Latin

Tru | True
**Meaning:** True
**Origin Language:** English

Trudie | Trude, Trudey, Trudi, Trudy
**Meaning:** Strength Of The Spear

**Origin Language:** Ancient Germanic

**Tsila | Tsillah, Tzila, Tzillah**
**Meaning:** Shade
**Origin Language:** Hebrew

**Tula | Toula**
**Also:** Tulisa | Toulisa
**Meaning:** Light
**Origin Language:** Ancient Greek

**Tulla | Tullia**
**Meaning:** Waterfall
**Origin Language:** Latin

**Tuula | Tuule, Tuuli**
**Meaning:** Wind
**Origin Language:** Finnish And Estonian (Cognates)

**Twila | Twyla**
**Meaning:** Twilight
**Origin Language:** English

**Tyene | Tyine**
**Meaning:** This Name Has No Meaning (Tyene Is A Fictional Character Featuring In The TV Series Game Of Thrones)
**Origin Language:** Invented

**Tyla**
**Meaning:** Roof Tiler
**Origin Language:** Old English

**Tyra**
**Meaning:** Thor's Priestess / Priestess Of Thunder (Thor Is The Name Of The Norse God Of Thunder And Lightning)
**Origin Language:** Old Norse

**Tzara**
**Meaning:** Anguish
**Origin Language:** Hebrew

**Tziporah | Tsipporah, Tzipora, Tzipporah**
**Meaning:** Bird

**Origin Language:** Hebrew

**Tzofi | Tzofia, Tzofie, Tzofiya**
**Meaning:** Guard / Scout
**Origin Language:** Hebrew

# Chapter 47 - Names For Girls Beginning With U

**Udara**
**Meaning:** Summer
**Origin Language:** Basque

**Ula**
**Meaning:** Bear
**Origin Language:** Latin

**Ulrica | Ulrika, Ulrike**
**Meaning:** Rich Heritage
**Origin Language:** Ancient Germanic

**Ulyssa | Ulysa**
**Meaning:** Hateful
**Origin Language:** Ancient Greek

**Uma**
**Meaning:** Flax
**Origin Language:** Sanskrit

**Unice | Unise**
**Meaning:** A Happy Victory
**Origin Language:** Ancient Greek

**Unity | Unitie**
**Meaning:** Unity
**Origin Language:** English

**Uriela | Uriella**
**Meaning:** God Is My Flame
**Origin Language:** Hebrew

**Ursina | Ursena, Ursene, Ursine**
**Also:** Ursula | Ursa, Ursala, Ursel,

Ursella, Ursule, Urszula
**Meaning:** Bear
**Origin Language:** Latin

# Chapter 48 - Names For Girls Beginning With V

Vada
**Meaning:** Knowledge
**Origin Language:** Sanskrit

Valda
**Meaning:** Ruler Of The Army
**Origin Language:** Ancient Germanic

Valencia
**Also:** Valentina | Valentena, Valentene, Valentine, Valentyna, Valentyne
**Meaning:** Strong / Healthy
**Origin Language:** Latin

Valeriana | Valeriane, Valerianna, Valerianne, Valeriena, Valeriene, Valerienna, Valerienne
**Also:** Valerie | Valarie, Valary, Valeria, Valery, Valeryia, Valorie, Valory
**Meaning:** Strong Enough
**Origin Language:** Latin

Valora | Valoria
**Meaning:** Valuable
**Origin Language:** Esperanto

Vana
**Meaning:** Graced By God
**Origin Language:** Hebrew

Vanda
**Meaning:** Of The Vandals (The Name Of A Germanic Tribe)

**Origin Language:** Ancient Germanic

Vanessa | Vanesa, Vannesa, Vannessa
**Meaning:** Vanessa (A Genus Of Butterfly)
**Origin Language:** English

Vanna
**Meaning:** Vivid / Hued
**Origin Language:** Khmer

Varda | Vardah
**Meaning:** Rose
**Origin Language:** Hebrew

Varinia
**Meaning:** Varied
**Origin Language:** Latin

Varya | Varia
**Also:** Varvara
**Meaning:** Foreign
**Origin Language:** Latin

Vasa | Vasia
**Also:** Vasilisa
**Meaning:** Queen
**Origin Language:** Ancient Greek

Veda
**Meaning:** Knowledge
**Origin Language:** Sanskrit

Velda
**Meaning:** Ruler
**Origin Language:** Ancient Germanic

Velia
**Meaning:** Concealed
**Origin Language:** Latin

Vellama
**Meaning:** Surges
**Origin Language:** Finnish

## Velma
**Meaning:** Desires Protection
**Origin Language:** Ancient Germanic

## Velta
**Meaning:** A Tribute
**Origin Language:** Latvian

## Vena | Veena, Vina
**Meaning:** Noble Friend
**Origin Language:** Ancient Germanic And Old English (Cognates)

## Vendela | Vendella, Vendelle
**Meaning:** Of The Vandals (The Name Of A Germanic Tribe)
**Origin Language:** Ancient Germanic

## Venera | Vanira
**Meaning:** Beauty / Charm
**Origin Language:** Latin

## Venetia
**Meaning:** From Venice (Italy)
**Origin Language:** Latin

## Vera | Veera, Viera, Vira
**Meaning:** Faith
**Origin Language:** Russian

## Verena
**Meaning:** Sincere
**Origin Language:** Latin

## Verica
**Meaning:** Faith
**Origin Language:** Serbian And Croatian (Cognates)

## Verity | Veritie
**Meaning:** Verity (Truth)
**Origin Language:** English

## Verna
**Meaning:** Alder Tree
**Origin Language:** Gaulish

## Veronica | Veronika, Veronique
**Meaning:** True Image
**Origin Language:** Latin

## Vespera
**Meaning:** Of The Evening
**Origin Language:** Latin

## Veva | Viva
**Meaning:** Family Woman
**Origin Language:** Ancient Germanic

## Vianne | Vianna
**Meaning:** Alive
**Origin Language:** Latin

## Viara | Vyara
**Meaning:** Faith
**Origin Language:** Russian

## Viatrix
**Meaning:** Female Voyager
**Origin Language:** Latin

## Vicky | Vicci, Vicki, Vickie, Vikki
**Also:** Victoria | Viktoria, Viktorie, Viktoriya, Viktory, Viktoryia
**Meaning:** Victory
**Origin Language:** Latin

## Vida
**Meaning:** Of The Forest
**Origin Language:** Ancient Germanic

## Viena
**Meaning:** Gentle
**Origin Language:** Finnish

## Vienna | Vienne
**Meaning:** Forest Stream
**Origin Language:** Ancient Celtic

## Vilda | Vilde
**Meaning:** Elven Battler
**Origin Language:** Old Norse

Vilhelmina | Vilhelma, Vilhelmine
**Also:** Vilma
**Meaning:** Desires Protection
**Origin Language:** Ancient Germanic

Vimala
**Meaning:** Clean
**Origin Language:** Sanskrit

Viola
**Meaning:** Violet
**Origin Language:** Latin

Violet | Vi, Violeta, Violetta, Violette
**Meaning:** Violet
**Origin Language:** Latin

Viona
**Meaning:** Blessed / Bright
**Origin Language:** Old Irish

Viorela
**Meaning:** Sweet Violet Flower
**Origin Language:** Romanian

Viorica | Vioricca, Viorika, Viorikka
**Meaning:** Sweet Violet Flower
**Origin Language:** Romanian

Virginia | Vergenia, Vergenie, Vergeny, Verginia, Verginie, Verginy, Virginie, Virginy
**Meaning:** Virgin / Of The Vergiliae (Vergilae Is The Name The Romans Used For The Star Constellation That Is Mostly Know Today As "The Pleiades")
**Origin Language:** Latin

Vita
**Meaning:** Life
**Origin Language:** Latin

Vitalia | Vitaliya
**Meaning:** Vital

**Origin Language:** Latin

Viveka | Viveca
**Meaning:** Battler
**Origin Language:** Ancient Germanic

Vivienne | Vivi, Vivian, Viviana, Viviane, Vivianne, Vivyan
**Also:** Viviette | Vivietta
**Meaning:** Alive
**Origin Language:** Latin

Vonda
**Meaning:** Of The Vandals (The Name Of A Germanic Tribe)
**Origin Language:** Ancient Germanic

Vonna | Vonnia
**Meaning:** Yew Tree
**Origin Language:** Ancient Germanic

# Chapter 49 - Names For Girls Beginning With W

Wanda
**Meaning:** Of The Vandals (The Name Of A Germanic Tribe)
**Origin Language:** Ancient Germanic

Waverly | Waverlea, Waverlee, Waverleigh, Waverlie
**Meaning:** From A Meadow Filled With Waving Trees (Trees That Are Being Blown By The Wind)
**Origin Language:** Old English

Wendy | Wenda, Wendi, Wendie
**Meaning:** From An Island With A Bend
**Origin Language:** Old English

Whitley | Whitlea, Whitlee, Whitleigh
**Meaning:** From The White Woods

**Origin Language:** Old English

Whitney | Whitnee, Whitnie, Whitny
**Meaning:** From A White Island
**Origin Language:** Old English

Wilfreda
**Meaning:** Desires Peace
**Origin Language:** Old English

Wilhelmina | Wilhelmine, Willemina, Willemine
**Also:** Willa
**Meaning:** Desires Protection
**Origin Language:** Ancient Germanic

Willow | Willo, Willoe, Willough
**Meaning:** Willow Tree
**Origin Language:** English

Wilma
**Meaning:** Desires Protection
**Origin Language:** Ancient Germanic

Wina | Wena, Wyna, Wynna
**Meaning:** Friendly
**Origin Language:** Ancient Germanic And Old English (Cognates)

Winifred | Winifreda, Winnifred, Winnifreda
**Meaning:** Friendly And Peaceful
**Origin Language:** Old English

Winnie | Winni, Winny
**Meaning:** Friendly
**Origin Language:** Ancient Germanic And Old English (Cognates)

Winona | Wenona, Wenonah, Wenonna, Wenonnah, Winonna, Winonnah, Wynona, Wynonna, Wynonnah
**Meaning:** First Born Daughter
**Origin Language:** Sioux

Winter | Wynter
**Meaning:** Winter
**Origin Language:** English

Wren
**Meaning:** Wren
**Origin Language:** English

Wrenley | Wrenlea, Wrenleigh
**Meaning:** From A Meadow Of Wrens
**Origin Language:** Old English

# Chapter 50 - Names For Girls Beginning With X

Xandra | Xandria, Xandrina, Xandrine
**Meaning:** Mankind's Defender
**Origin Language:** Ancient Greek

Xanthe | Xantha, Xanthi, Xanthia
**Meaning:** Yellow/Golden Haired
**Origin Language:** Ancient Greek

Xara
**Meaning:** Shining / Blooming / Flower
**Origin Language:** Arabic

Xaviera | Xavia
**Meaning:** From Etxeberria (Navarre, Spain)
**Origin Language:** Basque

Xena | Xene, Xeni, Xenia, Xenie, Xeny
**Meaning:** Friendly To Guests/Strangers (Hospitable)
**Origin Language:** Ancient Greek

Xia
**Meaning:** Summer
**Origin Language:** Old Chinese

Ximena
**Meaning:** He Has Heard
**Origin Language:** Hebrew

Xiomara
**Meaning:** Famous Warrior
**Origin Language:** Ancient Germanic

Xylia | Xylina
**Meaning:** Wooden
**Origin Language:** Ancient Greek

# Chapter 51 - Names For Girls Beginning With Y

Yael
**Meaning:** Mountain Goat
**Origin Language:** Hebrew

Yaliyah | Yaaliya, Yaaliyah
**Meaning:** Exalted
**Origin Language:** Arabic

Yamila | Yamilla
**Also:** Yamileth | Yamilet
**Meaning:** Beautiful
**Origin Language:** Arabic

Yanine | Yanena, Yanene, Yanina
**Meaning:** Graced By God
**Origin Language:** Hebrew

Yanira
**Meaning:** Ionian (The Name Of An Ancient Greek Tribe)
**Origin Language:** Ancient Greek

Yanna | Yana
**Meaning:** God Is Gracious
**Origin Language:** Hebrew

Yara

**Meaning:** Friend
**Origin Language:** Persian

Yardena | Yardene, Yardina, Yardine
**Meaning:** Descending Flow
**Origin Language:** Semitic

Yareli | Yarelli, Yarreli, Yarrelli, Yarrelly, Yereli, Yerelli, Yerrelly, Yireli, Yirelli, Yirrelly
**Meaning:** From A Hill With A Muddy Spring
**Origin Language:** Old English

Yarlet | Yarleta, Yarleth, Yarletha
**Meaning:** From Near A Gravelly Slope
**Origin Language:** Old English

Yarona
**Meaning:** She That Sings Or Shouts
**Origin Language:** Hebrew

Yasmine | Yasamin, Yasamine, Yasemin, Yasmeen, Yasmin, Yasmina, Yazmeen, Yazmin, Yazmina, Yazmine, Yazmyn
**Meaning:** Jasmine Flower / Gift From God
**Origin Language:** Persian

Yelena | Yelene, Yelina, Yeline, Ylena, Ylene, Ylenia, Ylina, Yline
**Meaning:** Torch
**Origin Language:** Ancient Greek

Yemima | Yemimah, Yemiymah
**Meaning:** Dove
**Origin Language:** Hebrew

Yennifer | Yenifer, Yennie, Yenny
**Meaning:** Blessed Phantom / White Phantom
**Origin Language:** Welsh

Yessenia | Yesenia, Yeseniya

**Meaning:** Jessenia (Palm Tree)
**Origin Language:** Spanish

Ygritte | Ygritt
**Meaning:** This Name Has No Meaning (Ygritte Is A Fictional Character Featuring In The TV Series Game Of Thrones)
**Origin Language:** Invented

Yianna
**Meaning:** Graced By God
**Origin Language:** Hebrew

Ylva | Ylfa
**Meaning:** Wolf
**Origin Language:** Old Norse

Yoana
**Meaning:** God Is Gracious
**Origin Language:** Hebrew

Yoko | Youko
**Meaning:** Child Of Light / Child Of The Sun / Child Of The Ocean
**Origin Language:** Japanese

Yolanda | Yolande
**Also:** Yolonda
**Meaning:** Violet
**Origin Language:** Latin

Yona | Yonah
**Also:** Yonina | Yonena
**Meaning:** Dove
**Origin Language:** Hebrew

Yordana | Yordanka
**Meaning:** Descending Flow
**Origin Language:** Semitic

Yoselin | Yocelin, Yocelina, Yoceline, Yocelyn, Yocelyne, Yoscelina, Yosceline, Yoscelyn, Yoselina, Yoselyn, Yoslin, Yoslina, Yoslyn, Yosselina, Yosseline,

Yosselyn, Yosslin, Yosslina, Yosslyn
**Meaning:** Of The Goths (The Name Of A Germanic Tribe)
**Origin Language:** Ancient Germanic

Ysabeau
**Also:** Ysabel | Ysa, Ysabela, Ysabella, Ysabelle, Ysbel, Yseabail, Ysebella, Ysebelle, Ysobel, Yza, Yzabel, Yzabel, Yzabela, Yzabella, Yzabelle, Yzbel, Yzeabail, Yzebel, Yzebella, Yzebelle, Yzobel
**Meaning:** God Is My Oath
**Origin Language:** Hebrew

Yseult | Ysolt, Ysyllt
**Meaning:** Ice Cold Battler
**Origin Language:** Ancient Germanic

Yue
**Meaning:** Moon
**Origin Language:** Chinese

Yuki
**Meaning:** Valuable Happiness / Valuable Snow / Valuable Cause
**Origin Language:** Japanese

Yulia | Yuliya
**Also:** Yuliana | Yuliane, Yuliann, Yulianna, Yulianne, Yulienna, Yulienne
**Meaning:** Downy (Down As In Soft Fluffy Hairs)
**Origin Language:** Latin

Yumi
**Meaning:** Beautiful Archery Bow / Beautiful Reason / Beautiful Cause / Beautiful Friend
**Origin Language:** Japanese

Yuna | Yuuna
**Meaning:** Excellence / Superiority / Gentleness / Grapefruit / Pomelo /

Citrus Fruit / Greens
**Origin Language:** Japanese

Yvette | Yveta, Yvett, Yvetta
**Also:** Yvonne | Yvona, Yvonna
**Meaning:** Yew Tree
**Origin Language:** Ancient Germanic

# Chapter 52 - Names For Girls Beginning With Z

Zahara
**Meaning:** Radiance
**Origin Language:** Hebrew

Zaharina | Zaharine, Zaharinka
**Meaning:** God Remembers
**Origin Language:** Hebrew

Zahia
**Meaning:** Beautiful
**Origin Language:** Arabic

Zahira | Zaahira
**Meaning:** Shining / Blooming
**Origin Language:** Arabic

Zahra | Zahrah, Zara
**Meaning:** Shining / Blooming / Flower
**Origin Language:** Arabic

Zaida
**Meaning:** Increasing
**Origin Language:** Arabic

Zaina | Zaine, Zayna
**Meaning:** Grace / Beauty
**Origin Language:** Arabic

Zaira
**Meaning:** Shining / Blooming / Flower
**Origin Language:** Arabic

Zaire | Zyair, Zyaire
**Meaning:** A River That Swallows Other Rivers
**Origin Language:** Kikongo

Zakia | Zakiah, Zakiya, Zakiyya
**Meaning:** Pure
**Origin Language:** Arabic

Zala
**Meaning:** Albino
**Origin Language:** Persian

Zamira
**Meaning:** Good Voice
**Origin Language:** Arabic

Zandra | Zandria, Zandrina, Zandrine
**Meaning:** Mankind's Defender
**Origin Language:** Ancient Greek

Zaniah | Zaniya
**Meaning:** Corner (Also An Alternate Name Of Eta Virginis, A Triple Star System In The Virgo Constellation)
**Origin Language:** Arabic

Zanna
**Meaning:** Lily / Rose
**Origin Language:** Hebrew

Zareen | Zarina, Zarine, Zerina, Zerine
**Meaning:** Golden
**Origin Language:** Persian

Zaria | Zariah, Zariyah, Zarya
**Meaning:** Shining / Blooming / Flower
**Origin Language:** Arabic

Zarita
**Meaning:** Princess
**Origin Language:** Hebrew

Zavia

**Meaning:** From Etxeberria (Navarre, Spain)
**Origin Language:** Basque

Zaya
**Meaning:** Fate / Destiny
**Origin Language:** Mongolian

Zayla | Zaila
**Also:** Zaylee | Zailee, Zailie, Zaylie
**Meaning:** Princess
**Origin Language:** Hebrew

Zehra | Zehrah, Zera
**Meaning:** Shining / Blooming / Flower
**Origin Language:** Arabic

Zelda | Zelde
**Meaning:** Blessed
**Origin Language:** Yiddish

Zelia | Zellia
**Meaning:** Small Land
**Origin Language:** Latin

Zelie | Zellie, Zelly, Zely
**Meaning:** Of The Noble Sort
**Origin Language:** Ancient Germanic

Zelina | Zelena, Zelene, Zeline
**Meaning:** Small Land
**Origin Language:** Latin

Zella | Zela
**Meaning:** Of Mars (Mars Is The Name Of The Roman God Of War, Guardian Of Agriculture And The Roman People)
**Origin Language:** Latin

Zelma
**Meaning:** Divine Protector
**Origin Language:** Ancient Germanic

Zelpha
**Meaning:** Frailty
**Origin Language:** Hebrew

Zena | Zina
**Also:** Zenaide | Zenaida, Zinaida, Zinaide
**Also:** Zenais | Zinais
**Meaning:** Of Zeus (Zeus Is The Name Of The Roman God Of The Sky, Lightning, Thunder, Law, Order, And Justice)
**Origin Language:** Ancient Greek

Zendaya | Zendaia
**Meaning:** Be Thankful
**Origin Language:** Shona

Zenia
**Meaning:** Friendly To Guests/Strangers (Hospitable)
**Origin Language:** Ancient Greek

Zenobia | Zinobia
**Also:** Zenovia | Zinovia
**Meaning:** Life Of Zeus (Zeus Is The Name Of The Roman God Of The Sky, Lightning, Thunder, Law, Order, And Justice)
**Origin Language:** Ancient Greek

Zephyra | Zephyria
**Also:** Zephyrina | Zephyrine
**Meaning:** West Wind
**Origin Language:** Ancient Greek

Zhanna
**Also:** Zhannochka
**Meaning:** God Is Gracious
**Origin Language:** Hebrew

Zhenya
**Meaning:** Well-Born
**Origin Language:** Ancient Greek

Ziggy | Ziggi
**Meaning:** A New Victory
**Origin Language:** Old Norse

Zilla | Zillah

**Meaning:** Shade
**Origin Language:** Hebrew

Zinnia
**Meaning:** Zinnia (Flower)
**Origin Language:** English

Zipporah | Zipora, Ziporah, Zippora
**Meaning:** Bird
**Origin Language:** Hebrew

Zita | Zeta, Zyta
**Meaning:** Luck
**Origin Language:** Latin

Ziva | Ziv
**Meaning:** Glowing
**Origin Language:** Hebrew

Zoe | Zoë, Zoey, Zoi, Zoie, Zowie, Zowy
**Meaning:** Life
**Origin Language:** Ancient Greek

Zofia | Zofie
**Meaning:** Wisdom
**Origin Language:** Ancient Greek

Zola | Zolah
**Meaning:** Calm
**Origin Language:** Xhosa

Zora
**Meaning:** Dawn
**Origin Language:** Slavic

Zoraida
**Meaning:** Enchanting
**Origin Language:** Arabic

Zorana
**Also:** Zoria | Zorica, Zorika
**Meaning:** Aurora
**Origin Language:** Slavic

Zosia
**Meaning:** Wisdom
**Origin Language:** Ancient Greek

Zoya | Zoia
**Meaning:** Life
**Origin Language:** Ancient Greek

Zsanett | Zsaneta, Zsanetta, Zsanette
**Meaning:** God Is Gracious
**Origin Language:** Hebrew

Zsazsa | Zaza, Zsuzsa, Zuza
**Also:** Zsuzsanna | Zuzana, Zuzanna
**Also:** Zsuzsi | Zuzsi
**Meaning:** Lily / Rose
**Origin Language:** Hebrew

Zuleika | Zulaykha, Zuleica, Zulekha
**Meaning:** Brilliant Beauty
**Origin Language:** Persian

Zuri | Zurie, Zury
**Also:** Zurina | Zurena, Zurene, Zurine
**Meaning:** Beautiful
**Origin Language:** Swahili

Zyanya
**Meaning:** Forever
**Origin Language:** Zapotec

Printed in Great Britain
by Amazon

29336251R00171